# SHAM

## Great Was Second Best

A Brave Bay's Rivalry with the Legendary Secretariat

### Phil Dandrea

**ACANTHUS PUBLISHING**

www.AcanthusPublishing.com

Copyright ©2010, Phillip Dandrea
All rights reserved.

Printed in the United States of America
ISBN: 978-0-9842173-3-551795

All rights reserved. No part of this book may be reproduced or transmitted in any form or by any means, electronic or mechanical, including photocopying, recording, or by any information storage and retrieval system, without written permission of the author, except for the inclusion of brief quotations in a review.

Published by Acanthus Publishing, Boston, Massachusetts.

Publisher's Cataloging-In-Publication Data
(Prepared by The Donohue Group, Inc.)

Dandrea, Phil.
  Sham : great was second best : a brave bay's rivalry with the legendary Secretariat / Phil Dandrea.

  p. : ill. ; cm.

  Includes bibliographical references.
  ISBN: 978-0-9842173-3-551795

  1. Sham (Race horse) 2. Secretariat (Race horse) 3. Race horses. I. Title.

SF355.S43 D36 2010
636.12

For Sham, who proved you don't have to finish first to be a winner.

# Acknowledgements

I offer my sincere thanks to Frank "Pancho" Martin for allowing me to stop by Barn 15 at Belmont Park and for taking time to share his vast knowledge of horses and his recollections of Sham. Not only did the trainer make this book possible, but the jockeys did too. I want to express my gratitude to Jorge Velasquez (now that I can no longer properly pronounce the name Jorge and automatically say "Georgie" whenever I see it in print) and to Walter Blum for talking with me about his Kentucky Derby experience and the horses he rode. He warned me if he got started he could talk all day about the old horses. I assured him I could listen all day. And to Sham's first jockey, Heliodoro "Gus" Gustines, I express my thanks not only for his time, but for his patience in allowing me to follow up with multiple interviews at Aqueduct, Belmont Park, and Saratoga. Gus is a true gentleman of the sport.

I also want to thank Butch Simpson of Walmac Farm for talking with me near Sham's old stall and for sharing his memories of "Bandit." Thank you to Viola Sommer who spoke to me during the races at Aqueduct about her time in thoroughbred racing and about her husband, Sigmund Sommer, as well as about Sham and Knightly Dawn. I can't thank enough Bill Mochon, an excellent source of information, a great photographer, and an even better friend. The book would have suffered without his knowledge of Santa Anita Park and without his archival photos of the track, the people, and the horses of Sham's day.

Cathy Schenck and Phyllis Rogers at the Keeneland Association Library in Lexington, Kentucky provided immeasurable help with sources and fact-checking. At the National Museum of Racing and Hall of Fame in Saratoga Springs, New York, Tom Gilcoyne shared his experiences in attending races at Saratoga since he was a boy in the 1920s and provided an historical perspective of Belmont Park. Allan Carter was a great help in locating sources. Jim Melia allowed me to look through his old scrapbook and memorabilia from the 1973 Kentucky Derby, which he attended, and told me about his memories of Sham. Thank you all for your help. I also cannot overlook the editorial assistance of Susannah Bruck, and I thank her for her keen eye for detail and for her patience with my many revisions made in the final furlong.

With love, I offer my utmost thanks to my wife, Michele, who spent countless hours helping me to collect stacks of research documents and made numerous photocopies of which I read and annotated throughout the rest of the year—only to repeat the process the following year. I also thank her for her interest and encouragement throughout the process and for understanding all the time and work involved wasn't really for me but was for Sham, who deserved to have his story told.

# Contents

| | | |
|---|---|---|
| Copyrights | | iv |
| Acknowledgements | | vii |
| Prologue | | 4 |
| 1. | Nearly Decked at the Derby | 10 |
| 2. | Best of the Lot | 21 |
| 3. | First Time on the Oval | 30 |
| 4. | Early Days on the Farm | 37 |
| 5. | Trainer Tries Again | 61 |
| 6. | A Change of Order | 69 |
| 7. | Last Chance for the Two-Year-Old | 79 |
| 8. | Sham's New Stable | 85 |
| 9. | Go West, Young Horse | 96 |
| 10. | A Derby Winner in this Field? | 104 |
| 11. | Best Ever Three-Year-Old | 116 |
| 12. | Pincay Chooses | 122 |
| 13. | Rival in the East, Challenge in the West | 131 |
| 14. | The Field Takes Shape | 144 |
| 15. | High Pressure Before the Storm | 151 |

| 16. | Rivals Finally Meet | 162 |
| 17. | Other Contenders | 174 |
| 18. | Prep for the Roses | 185 |
| 19. | It's Official | 190 |
| 20. | The Day Arrives | 201 |
| 21. | The Derby Dust Settles | 214 |
| 22. | Round Two in Baltimore | 220 |
| 23. | Facing the Phantom of Pimlico | 229 |
| 24. | Daisies on Old Hilltop | 238 |
| 25. | Broken Record and Broken Clock? | 251 |
| 26. | The Test of Champions | 261 |
| 27. | Sham Refuses to Yield the Crown | 271 |
| 28. | Battling a Tremendous Machine | 283 |
| 29. | All Over but the Shouting | 297 |
| 30 | Sham's Biggest Challenge | 304 |
| 31. | Adding to the Princequillo Legacy | 314 |
| Bibliography | | 325 |
| Endnotes | | 361 |
| About the Author | | 415 |

# Prologue

In a sprint to the wire along the home stretch at Del Mar, a dark bay named Pretense captured the 1968 Bing Crosby Handicap in a time equaling the track record. Blessed with speed and stamina, Pretense had built himself a reputation winning multiple stakes races from 1966 to 1968 while burdened with heavy weight assignments from racetrack officials attempting to even the playing field. Pretense carried the weight and continued to win.

Rather than challenge more records in more races, the Bing Crosby would be his last. The five-year-old Pretense entered stud in 1969 with the hope he'd pass his traits onto the next generation. His first crop produced a foal at Claiborne Farm in Paris, Kentucky on April 9, 1970. A bay like his father, the colt was named Sham. Considering the paternal side of Sham's pedigree, with a father named Pretense, a grandmother named Imitation, and a great-grandmother named Flattery, the name fit.

The name was by no means an indication of Sham's ability nor of his heart. It would prove ironic, however, regarding his fate, a race career in which great wasn't good enough. Sham was among the best ever to contest thoroughbred racing's Triple Crown (comprising the Kentucky Derby, the Preakness Stakes, and the Belmont Stakes), yet his name is virtually unknown today. In the prime of his career as a three-year-old, Sham was pitted against a legend in the making. Simply put, 1973 was the wrong year.

Sham capped off his campaign as a two-year-old in New York with an easy six-length victory at Aqueduct in Jamaica, New York. By New Year's Day of 1973, he was winning in California. After just two races at Santa Anita Park, Pat Rogerson described in the pages of the *Daily Racing Form* the excitement surrounding Sham: "He has seasoned horsemen comparing him favorably to the best three-year-olds ever campaigned in the West."

A dark brown colt with dark black legs, "graced with a beautifully muscled and streamlined conformation," writer, photographer Raymond G. Woolfe Jr. wrote, "he looked fast when he was just standing still." In an isolated still shot, Sham looked as gentle as a rocking horse, but at full speed he'd go after any competitor who tried to keep him from the lead. When Sham meant business in mounting a long-striding charge, he resembled the smooth design of a jet. His green and gold hood with blinkers added to the image, like a flier's hood. His long tail fluttered like a kite when he ran. Throughout a rainy California winter, many a colt watched that kite fly past, powerless to catch it.

The stage was set for Sham-mania to sweep the nation at a time when the country needed a hero. With rising inflation, the Vietnam conflict, and Watergate dominating current events, people were ready to cheer for someone, for something. But by early June of 1973 a new hero had conquered the imagination of the American public. That hero was Secretariat. The chestnut colt known affectionately as "Big Red," running under the white and blue silks of Meadow Stable, was the embodiment of the American flag. He was America's horse.

Billed by the media as a "Superhorse," Secretariat graced the covers of *Newsweek*, *Time*, and *Sports Illustrated* all within the span of a week that June of 1973. Superlatives followed the horse from all arenas. Don Clippinger of *The Thoroughbred Record* wrote, "He captured the imagination, filling it with conquests of Arthurian immensity." Jack Krumpe, president of the New York Racing Association, said, "He was a power that transcended racing. You didn't have to know *anything* about racing to appreciate that great mass of power, that beauty." Long-time trainer Syl Veitch said, "I don't believe you could find a better looking Thoroughbred—or have one molded any better, mentally, physically, everyway." Edward L. Bowen of *The Blood-Horse* labeled Secretariat "*equinus maximus*," while veteran turf writer Charles Hatton called him an "equine Adonis." Secretariat biographer Timothy T. Capps wrote, "He had it all—looks, style, and charisma." Arnold Kirkpatrick pulled no punches in declaring in *The Thoroughbred Record*, "There's absolutely no doubt in my mind that he is the finest athlete of any race, color, family, genus or species ever to have lived." Chick Lang, general manager of Pimlico Race Course proclaimed, "It is as if God decided to create the perfect horse." Even *Vogue* magazine got in on the act, stating Secretariat represented "power, money, and total male beauty: a triple-win sex symbol."

With Secretariat hype in full bloom, the William Morris Agency booked the star's appearances and handled merchandising. Secretariat joined the firm's stable of clients that included Elvis Presley, Sophia Loren, and Bill Cosby. Chicago Mayor Richard Daley proclaimed June 30, 1973 Secretariat Day. The horse was awarded a key to the city.

Secretariat was a merchandiser's dream. Ads bearing his name flooded the media. Inspired artists and profit seekers created items such as sculptures in solid walnut, sold in various sizes as budget allowed, and a commemorative one-ounce ingot collection in solid bronze, 0.999 pure silver, or 24K gold on silver. A record album featuring the calls of all of Secretariat's races hit the market, along with a Secretariat watch, which came in the standard model or the deluxe 17-jewel version. Kentucky jewelers Merkley Kendrick produced a sterling silver Secretariat julep cup for more discerning tastes. Lithographs by artist Richard Stone Reeves, noted for his paintings of racehorses, appeared, while *Sports Illustrated* offered a more affordable image of the four-legged athlete on a poster. In keeping with the stature of a Superhorse, the full color, oversized two-by-three-foot poster caught Secretariat charging at the camera with jockey Ron Turcotte tucked behind, nearly obscured by the hero's enormity.

True to the tradition of athletes and their footwear deals,

Secretariat had his own shoe endorsement. In their *Daily Racing Form* ad, the Victory Racing Plate Company made it clear Secretariat wore their horseshoes.

So confident were bettors of a Secretariat victory, at times he ran at ridiculously low odds such as 1 to 10 and 1 to 20 (where a $2 wager would pay to the winner $2.10, a net profit of only a dime). Secretariat drew comparisons to Man o' War, the original Big Red from 50 years earlier, as the 20$^{th}$ century's greatest thoroughbred. Hall of Fame trainer Hollie Hughes, who had himself saddled a Kentucky Derby winner in 1916 and personally saw Man o' War run, declared of Secretariat, "He's the greatest horse that has yet developed in this century."

As Secretariat challenged the near mythical status of Man o' War, Sham challenged the status of Secretariat. Both Sham and Secretariat stood approximately 16 hands 2 inches in height, Secretariat with an imposing, powerful build, Sham, sturdy and sleek. When necessary, Secretariat used his size and strength to barrel to the lead, splitting between horses in his way. Secretariat's jockey Ron Turcotte once commented, "He takes off like a derailed roller-coaster." Sports writer Bill Nack described Secretariat's commanding looks and musculature: "His neck and quarters lined in packs of muscle over which his coat seemed drawn too tight—perhaps a half size too small, as if he were outgrowing it."

"Sham is an eye-filling specimen," Barry H. Irwin wrote in *Thoroughbred of California*. "He is everything a horseman would want. His stride is as reaching as a shopper's arm for 39-cents-a-pound sirloin, as forceful when it meets the ground as a high-powered riveter." Sham's trainer, Frank "Pancho" Martin, called his colt the perfect thoroughbred. "He is made like a good horse," Martin said, "like a classic horse who can run all day."

Despite impressive victories and heroic, record-breaking performances, Sham's popularity paled in comparison with that of the Superhorse, swallowed by Secretariat's growing fame. If Secretariat were America's horse, Sham might well have been everyman's horse, a working-class hero who couldn't get the recognition he deserved. It would prove ironic that Sham, in colors representing the Sigmund Sommer stable, wore a hood with the letter S embossed over his forehead—ironic, in that Secretariat was the one compared to the superhero who boldly wore the same letter across his chest.

The rivalry hailed the end of horse racing's glory days. Waning were the times when the likes of Bing Crosby (who founded Del Mar), Fred Astaire, the Kennedys, Bouviers, and Vanderbilts regularly attended. Though an era was ending, track veterans who could still recall past greats like Man o' War, Seabiscuit, and Citation saw it off with the thrill and the glory delivered by the run for the 1973 Triple Crown. Sham and Secretariat battled four times during their careers. The clashes produced the best performances of their lives.

# Chapter 1

## Nearly Decked at the Derby

*Until you go to Kentucky and with your own eyes behold a Derby, you ain't been nowhere and you ain't seen nothing.*
—Irvin S. Cobb, Kentucky-born humorist

A crowd ten bodies deep packed the main gate of Churchill Downs waiting to storm the Louisville landmark. The city's finest, along with the Kentucky State Police and Army National Guard, stood for order, but the overwhelming number surrounding Central Avenue and South 9th Street, those taking up Racine and Longfield Avenues could have easily threatened with riot if the mob turned unruly.

They'd been gathering since early Saturday morning, 7 AM, when the gates still weren't scheduled to open for another hour. Many had spent the night in their cars or in tents pitched on a strip of grass along the roadside. Double lines of vehicles crammed both sides of the street pointing to the Ch[...] since filled to its limit. The 1973 Kentucky D[erby,...] card race, was nearly half a day away, set for 5:3[...] great length, the lines nor the wait, deterred fans [...] see an historic duel: Secretariat, the East Coast Sup[er...] Sham, his challenger from the West.

Few options remained for those without a Derby D[...] Most would be sent to the infield. Grandstand seats we[re...] gone; advance ticket sales had been the greatest in the track'[s his]tory. Even some 1,400 Churchill Downs stockholders had be[en] shut out and put on a waiting list.

The boxes near the finish line, Section F and Section G, belonged to the wealthy and powerful. Businessmen, horse breeders, and racing people took Section F, with Section G reserved for politicians like the Kentucky Governor Wendell Ford and Louisville mayor Frank Burke. Along "Millionaire's Row," the Skye Terrace in the observatory above the clubhouse, the aristocrats of the sport watched from private tables with waitstaff at their call, assuming a caterer hadn't been hired for the occasion.

After the gates opened, thousands began to fill the infield. Despite the increase in the centerfield admission price, nearly double that of the year before, they kept coming. Pedestrians poured through the tunnel leading to the infield, many feeling the need to yelp and holler on their way through, bouncing echoes above, below, and side to side.

Several thousand gate-crashers also made it onto the Downs. An adventurous trespasser climbed a ladder over a locked gate and was soon followed by others. When a forced lock opened

it through. The infield
 Churchill Downs tally
 crowd to see a horse
 racetrack seated only
 left to fill the cracks
 to the track's center

 their own, turning the
 ival. The six-foot-nine
 n Celtics was spotted among
 ors hawking their products filled the
 own signs too, displayed at various times
 day.

 much activity in too little space wasn't exclusive to the
 field. Whether the destination was the concession stands for a
buck-and-a-half julep topped with a limp mint sprig that looked
like a weed the groundskeeper had pulled, the souvenir tables for
anything commemorating the day, or the betting lines that seemed
to run longer than the one-and-a-quarter-mile main event, no effort to part with one's money was made easy.

Under blue skies amid 70-degree temperatures, the bugle call welcomed the horses onto the track for the Kentucky Derby post parade. They marched along the front stretch identified by the digit on their saddlecloth and the colors of their jockey's silks. Bronze capped spires atop the main building, a green turf track within the main chocolate-colored oval, and blooming geraniums and marigolds filled the eye. Swallows circled calmly above the tension building below.

The University of Louisville Marching Band played the melody to Stephen Foster's "My Old Kentucky Home" while thousands of voices accompanied the tune. Even for those who knew the long tradition, knew the song was sure to come, it could be hard to fight a stir of sentiment. It took an exercise in concentration not to raise a lump in the throat and choke up on the lyrics when joining in.

"The sun shines bright in the old Kentucky home...." It was like a scene from a movie seen a dozen times, but the effect could still be touching, if not overpowering. Thirteen horses on the track turned at the clubhouse and headed down the front stretch toward the starting gate. One would soon be an important part of racing history, his name added to those who could call themselves his peer. The names of 98 past victors hung above a garden of red and yellow tulips and circled the Churchill Downs paddock.

All hype and excitement aside, no one likely predicted the 99th running of the Kentucky Derby would be a battle more worthy a heavyweight contender than a thoroughbred. To begin, Restless Jet, Angle Light, and Warbucks entered the starting gate smoothly, like the tried stakes contenders they were. Next was Sham at the fourth post-position, followed by Navajo at the five. When it came to Twice a Prince, an inexperienced colt with only six career starts to his name, he grew agitated as assistant starters took hold to lead him in.

It might have been the buzzing magnitude of the record-breaking attendance that set him off. Boisterous adulation came from all corners, including those packed in box seats, spread along balconies, and squeezed into standing room. It came from the infield throng who spread themselves over the grass, dirt, and mud and crammed along the restraining fence that ran the perimeter of the track.

Twice a Prince refused to enter his stall. He reared and rose to his hind legs for a stand-up fight, rattling the starting gate. His jockey, Angel Santiago, fell backward and hung from the stirrups, dangling upside down by his feet for several seconds. An alert assistant starter caught the jockey and helped to free him. Shaken, Santiago was escorted from the gate while Twice a Prince continued the scrap. Another assistant starter to the right of the colt grabbed at the bridle to contain him. Still free and still on his hind legs, Twice a Prince stood in retaliation, throwing vicious hooves at the man. It looked as if the two were trading punches as the man swiped at the bridle trying to take hold in between the colt's jabs. Twice a Prince also banged about his adjacent competitors with wildly flailing hooves. He clanged Navajo's stall to his left, then Our Native's on his right. As he became more belligerent, the fit-pitching colt entangled himself in Our Native's saddle.

Don Brumfield, who witnessed the attack on his mount, Our Native, later described it: "First, Twice a Prince got his feet in Navajo's stall, then in my stall. He kicked my horse once, and his hoof made a mark on my saddle."

As Twice a Prince concentrated his battery to the man on his right, a second assistant starter was able to grab the reins to the colt's left. Twice a Prince froze, finally accepting a truce. Brumfield and Weston Soirez on Navajo were forced to dismount. To untangle the unruly Twice a Prince, handlers opened the gate in front of Our Native and took him from his stall. He was brought to the rear of the starting gate and reloaded.

"He was bad all right," starter Jim Thomson later said about Twice a Prince. "He gave us enough trouble for all of the rest put together."

Assistant starters walked Twice a Prince in a circle in an attempt to calm him down. Santiago climbed back aboard and the two re-entered the gate. The delay cost nearly five full minutes. Jockey Ron Turcotte, who had the number ten post-position, watched while waiting on the track. He had wisely led Secretariat from the gate during the scuffle, away from the assistant starter who had attempted to take the bridle and lead him in.

"We weren't in the gate yet," Turcotte said afterward, "so the delay didn't hurt us. But it sure didn't help the horses who had to stand in there all that time."

It didn't help Sham, who was left alone in his stall with no assistant starter.

"When I went into the gate," Sham's jockey, Laffit Pincay, said after the race, "I asked the man to help keep Sham's head straight. But for some reason nobody showed up. He was alone in the gate. When we broke, he went sharply to the outside and hit the door-bars hard."

As the starting gate doors burst open, Sham banged his head on a support strut, cutting deep gashes along his jaw line and loosening two teeth. It was like taking a shot from Muhammad Ali wearing brass knuckles. The blow knocked Sham off balance. He stumbled, brushing the gate, then collided with the rushing Navajo. Somewhere along the way, Sham suffered a cut to his left front leg.

The brave bay continued. Sham had no time to coddle his wounds. The battered colt dashed the entire length of the stretch to avoid being boxed in by the mass of charging horseflesh swarming the clubhouse turn.

All the cheers, applause, and uproar from along the rails up to the highest luxury box walled the course in from both sides. Thousands crammed in place, shoulder to shoulder, with barely enough room to shift their weight. Waving programs and flashing cameras added to the mass enthusiasm, all of it spent as the horses had only begun their route. For their second pass around, in the final stretch, the intensity would multiply with the shouts of agony for the losers and elation for the winner, of which there could be only one. Beyond and above it all, a glimpse of the twin spires peeked from the rooftop, two accent marks over what was to come. But the jockeys out on the track had no time to admire the view.

As practically every horseman in Louisville had called, the speedy Shecky Greene took the early lead and set the pace. Jockey Larry Adams steered the leader all the way from his number eleven post-position to the rail. To get there, he had cut off ten thundering competitors, quality horses who had run big races, like Forego, a giant at 17 hands who had finished second in the Florida Derby; Royal and Regal, winner of the Florida Derby and the Bahamas Stakes; Our Native, winner of the Flamingo Stakes and second in the Blue Grass Stakes; Navajo, second in the Louisiana Derby; Warbucks, third in both the Arkansas Derby and Blue Grass Stakes and one of the favorites in the traditional Derby Eve preliminary betting; Angle Light, winner of the Wood Memorial; and Restless Jet, winner of the Everglades Stakes, second in the Stepping Stone Purse, and third in the Florida Derby.

From further out at post-position thirteen, Gold Bag followed a similar route to fall in behind the leader. Royal and Regal took third alongside Gold Bag, with Angle Light fourth. Sham ran fifth. Secretariat ran last in the field, all of twelve horses in front of him, causing no lack of concern for his trainer, Lucien Laurin, who watched nervously from his box near the finish line. Earlier in the season Laurin had seen his horse take on Sham with spectacularly disappointing results. Sham had beaten Secretariat soundly by four lengths. As the entire Kentucky Derby field ran ahead of his horse, Laurin exclaimed, "God Almighty, don't tell me it's gonna be another one of them!"

Laffit Pincay's strategy was to stick close to the pace-setter. Sham concurred, passing rivals with no urging from Pincay. He took Angle Light first, while heading to the turn. By the quarter-mile mark, Sham moved over Royal and Regal and ran within a head of Gold Bag. Gold Bag chased three lengths behind the leader. Shecky Greene, a sprinter, would be dangerous if allowed to build too great a lead.

Shecky Greene carried the lead to the backstretch, while Sham edged past Gold Bag by a length. Now, only one horse ran before Sham, and the leader's stamina was spreading thin.

"The only way Shecky can win at the Derby distance," *Sports Illustrated*'s Whitney Tower had sarcastically predicted, "is to open up 10 lengths and hope that the opposition runs through or over the stable gap on the backstretch." His words, to some degree, were proving true, and other horses in the field had something to say about it.

Running sixth near the half-mile pole roughly 15 feet out, Forego veered from another horse and slammed the rail halfway through the turn. "You should have seen the whitewash dust fly when he hit," jockey Pete Anderson commented later. "I hit the fence so hard when he changed leads, I don't know how I stayed on him," he said. "I don't know how we both didn't wind up in the infield." Forego recovered to continue, sporting a white strip of paint along his side as a mark of the altercation.

Pincay wanted to sit in the second position a little while longer to save as much horse as he could for the final stretch. His plans changed when Shecky Greene veered out sharply, perhaps startled by the shadows cast upon the rail. He nearly bumped Sham. To avoid the danger of a collision, or possibly having to yank the reins to check Sham's speed, Pincay set Sham after the leader rounding the far turn.

Working from the outside, Sham nudged ahead of Shecky Greene. Entering the final stretch, Sham ran in the clear and in front. But Pincay still kept Sham under a hold to prevent him from moving too fast too soon. The long Churchill Downs stretch stared them both in the face.

Royal and Regal battled for the third position, and jockey Walter Blum had not yet asked his horse for a closing move. About a month earlier in the Florida Derby, Blum had gotten Royal and Regal in the clear at the top of the stretch without yet asking him to run. Royal and Regal had come through for him then. Blum couldn't help but think he was setting up the Kentucky Derby for a replay. While he entertained the idea of charging strongly to the wire for victory, the hope was dashed when a muscular red colt in a white and blue hood of checker-board design blew past him—Secretariat. Royal and Regal could only watch.

"Secretariat came by us and took a little bit of heart out of him, *and* me," Blum recalled later. "I thought I had a good chance. Thought I had a chance until this chestnut freak came on the outside of all of us." As Sham and Shecky Greene battled on the front lines for position, Secretariat had assaulted the flank, gradually building momentum. "I felt this big whoosh of air go by and that was all there was to it," Blum remarked.

Aboard Shecky Greene, Larry Adams saw Secretariat gaining on the outside. "I glanced back and saw him coming and thought, if I get in his way, I'll get killed!" Adams said after the race.

Sham refused to give up anything. Pincay put him along the rail to save ground. Ron Turcotte took Secretariat to the outside, then swatted him with the whip. Pincay didn't need the whip to keep Sham to task, not yet. Sham knew what to do.

To complement Secretariat's stride with his momentum, Turcotte forced his body forward, driving his weight and strength as the colt thrust forward, then pulling back to repeat the drive. Turcotte stood only 5 feet 1 inch but possessed a muscular frame he had built as a lumberjack cutting New Brunswick timber.

Trusting his colt's courage, Pincay let Sham drift as close to the action as possible hoping to coax a greater reaction. When Sham saw Secretariat, he responded, running in a game effort.

In the upper stretch, Pincay cocked the whip to prepare for the final drive. Secretariat gained ground. The remaining field faded from contention in the dust behind the furious pace. It was now a two-horse race.

Secretariat drew eye-to-eye with Sham. Pincay's and Turcotte's silks bellowed with the rush of air, Pincay's green with gold diamond hoop, Turcotte's blue and white blocks. Sham and Secretariat seemed stuck side by side, neither one able to put away the other.

Writhing for position, spectators in the grandstands stood on seats and benches for a better look. Beneath the low grandstand ceiling, onlookers braced themselves from a fall by pressing a hand above and shifting their feet below. From the infield, they crammed together in various styles of dress and undress. Unless they had stationed themselves in prime real estate for viewing along the fence or had climbed atop a step or stand of some creation, they unlikely saw anything in the way of a horse. Even those along the fence saw little more than the area of track directly in front of them. But they knew when the charging Sham and Secretariat approached. The crowd's roar followed them around the final turn to the top of the stretch. Collective voices of the record-breaking crowd built like a tidal wave, cresting and curling as if to crash over the horses to sweep them down the final furlong. Sham and Secretariat continued neck-and-neck through the flood of cheers.

Sham's dark, black legs traded even strides with the one red and three white of Secretariat. Pincay and Turcotte worked the whip, Pincay delivering quick lashes with his left hand. Tearing down the final stretch, swallowing his own blood, Sham fought the gutsiest battle of his life.

## Chapter 2

## Best of the Lot

On a mild spring morning in 1972, a year before Sham's historic duel with a legend, Heliodoro Gustines pulled himself out of bed at 5 AM, as he did every day. The sun had not risen over New York City by the time he sat down for a cup of coffee, nothing more. He couldn't afford it. The man who had earned over $600,000 in purse money the previous year, $7 million overall in his career, limited himself to one meal a day. He ate in the evening.

It had been a long road to New York, beginning in his native Panama, through Mexico, Florida, Louisiana, Ohio, with stints stretching from California to Canada. Gustines wouldn't jeopardize his success with indulgence, having learned the hard way in Mexico City where he had put on extra pounds, weight unacceptable to the jockey.

Gustines' experience with horses had begun in the mid-1940s, at an age and stature when he could no more than look the animal in the legs. Born to a racing family in Panama, he shared a connection with horses for as long as he could remember. He had grown up on the racetrack and had spent much of his youth at the barn of his grandfather, Isaac Gustines, a blacksmith turned horse trainer with a stable of some forty horses.

Gustines spent his childhood days alternating between school and work at the barn. He wasn't formally schooled in the art of riding, however. His father, Oscar Gustines, a former jockey himself, didn't give his son any professional instruction. Perhaps it worked to his son's advantage. Gustines once noted of his father's riding career, "He wasn't that good."

On the job, around the track, the young Gustines spent his time observing, patiently gleaning the skills he would need to make riding his profession. By the age of 15, he rode his first race as an apprentice jockey at the Juan Franco track in Panama City. By then he was hooked—the excitement had claimed him.

"I loved it. I always loved it," he said in looking back on his early years riding. "When you're young, 15 or 16 years old, grown people are cheering you. It's not so much the money. It's an ego thing. To be a winner. The winning is the whole thing, even if it's a dollar."

Though the Juan Franco track would eventually close, Gustines continued riding at the newly opened Hipodromo President Remon outside Panama City. At 16, Gustines turned professional, but earning a living wasn't easy. Racing was limited to weekends and holidays at President Remon. Gustines succeeded nonetheless. At a time when the average Panamanian worker was earning $200 a month, Gustines was bringing home $200 to $300 a week.

At 17, Gustines was off for a stint in Mexico at the Hipodromo de las Americas in Lomas de Sotelo, then returned home to Panama nine months later.

Gustines later visited Miami with a friend from Panama who had attended college in the United States. Gustines could spare the time away from the track since he was serving a suspension in Panama for what was termed "rough riding" (or as Gustines later explained it, "Doing things you're not supposed to do.").

Specifically, he had bumped a closing horse as it tried to pass. Gustines had considered rough riding a necessity when racing dates were so few. "That's the way it used to be down there," Gustines recalled, referring to the challenge of earning a living. "You gotta do that. You race only two nights a week."

After a month's stay in the United States, the friend returned home. Gustines stayed. Following a brief stop at Tropical Park in Coral Gables, Florida in 1960, the 19-year-old Gustines turned to America's "Grand Dame" of racing, Hialeah Park in Hialeah, Florida, which featured royal palms and coconut trees that surrounded an infield lake famous for its flock of pink flamingos imported from Cuba.

By March of 1961, Gustines was off to New York, where he continued to ride and to win. He managed more than $500,000 a year in purse money eight times since arriving in the United States in 1960 and would again in 1972. In 1972, the average income per year in the United States was $11,800. This was in an era before athletes were paid offensively bloated salaries. The average major league baseball player earned $34,527 with the minimum salary set at $13,500. Standouts like two-time Most Valuable Player and baseball Triple Crown winner Frank Robinson earned $147,000; Cy Young winner Gaylord Perry earned $75,000; strikeout ace Nolan Ryan earned $27,000. All three would one day be enshrined in baseball's Hall of Fame. Gustines, in his worst year (his first in the United States), still managed to win nearly $250,000 in purses.

But even after finding success on the New York racing circuit, Gustines was not one impressed by money or a flashy lifestyle. An acquaintance once bragged to him of earning $500 a week. "Big deal," Gustines thought, managing to hold his tongue, "I make that in two minutes."

In recognition of his leadership, Gustines was elected director of the eastern section of the Jockey's Guild in 1970 to represent his fellow jockeys in addressing their concerns and hearing their disputes with racing officials. He was re-elected in 1972.

After his morning coffee, Gustines left his Queens apartment to lend a hand at the nearby stables, where he galloped horses for various trainers. At that listless hour, little traffic hindered the eastbound flow; the westbound route suffered the heavier city congestion. Between AM radio pop music and commercials, the day's headlines filled the airwaves. Gustines switched stations, alternating the country music of Eddie Arnold and Johnny Cash with standards by Frank Sinatra. But references to President Nixon, Vietnam, Soviet détente, and Senator George McGovern's growing grass-roots support in the upcoming presidential election were as unavoidable as 30-second radio ads.

The early morning workforce along the way showed their '70s style with double-knit polyester, flared legs, white belts, and prairie skirts. The look included wide-cuffed and wide-sleeved shirts, busy patterns, suede and rawhide accessories. Gustines reached western Long Island after a short twelve-minute commute.

He drove his Pontiac Grand Prix through the finial-topped iron gates that separated the stables from the comings and goings of Hempstead Avenue. Among gas stations, restaurants, and small businesses was not a common location to look for horses, but along the edge of Elmont, New York was Belmont Park.

Gustines was a regular rider for trainer Woody Stephens. Stephens had opened a public stable along the track's backstretch after a long career as a private trainer. He kept a simple office in a cottage decorated by scenery no more glamorous than the surrounding barns. Horses were walked, bathed, or allowed simply to graze in a yard through the back door. No name was painted on the barns, only numbers. If horse owners wanted Stephens, they knew where to find him.

Woody Stephens claimed, in an evident Kentucky drawl, to be "without no education," but there were those who believed he could communicate with horses as if he possessed a sixth sense. He had grown up on the backs of the mules pulling plows against the backdrop of the Allegheny Mountains on his father's farm in Stanton, Kentucky. In 1929 Stephens had dropped out of high school halfway through his freshman year to begin a career as a horseman. He had held various positions from hot walker (walking horses after workouts or races to cool them out), groom, jockey, exercise boy, stable foreman, and trainer while earning a reputation for being able to read a horse and pick up the smallest details regarding the animal.

That morning Gustines, or "Gus" as friends called him, met

Stephens at Barn 3. They looked over a crop of two-year-olds from breeder Bull Hancock's Claiborne Farm. For generations Claiborne Farm in Paris, Kentucky had been among the top breeders in the country and in the world. Hancock was once described by the trade publication *The Blood-Horse* as "the biggest, the most successful, the single most important man in the Thoroughbred industry." He had made the trip from Kentucky eager to hear the trainer's assessment. Stephens was eager to hear his jockey's opinion.

Gustines knew Hancock's reputation and he himself considered Hancock to be "very sharp." But Gustines wasn't overly impressed by the Hancock lot. Only two in the group of eight or nine stood out. He was frank in mentioning the animals by name, telling Stephens and Hancock, "The only two horses that are any good are Sham and Breakfast Bell." Stephens agreed. Though taken aback, Bull Hancock accepted the assessment without protest.

Gustines fixed his attention on Sham, a solid-looking, well built bay colt. His dark coat, practically black, ran from thigh to croup and up over his shoulder, neck, and withers. It lightened to walnut brown along his abdomen, head, and snout. Wide-set eyes gave him an intelligent expression.

"This horse was the best horse of all of them," Gustines reflected years later. "Sometimes you get nasty ones. But he was good," he said of the well-behaved colt. Gustines knew the nasty representatives of the species to bite, kick, or pin their ears back "like a grouchy person," as he put it. Gustines considered personality types for horses as he did for people, and Sham had one he liked. "He was a nice horse to be around."

Gustines had ridden Sham in workouts and had felt his power.

A month earlier, Gustines had walked along the Belmont stalls, some empty, some occupied by horses waiting to be worked. He had met Sham and had given him a quick look over.

The colt possessed a sound conformation and didn't fuss when Gustines climbed up and took him to the track as some young horses do when unaccustomed to a rider. Sham responded well to his jockey's cues.

With the workout underway, Gustines locked his legs around the colt for balance. Breaking into a gallop, Gustines focused on the straight and turn directly ahead as he asked Sham for more speed. Gustines heard nothing but the rush of wind past his ears along with the graceful, striding hooves below. He prepared to shift his weight with each jolt from the track, but Sham's agility made the adjustments unnecessary.

"You can feel a nice horse," Gustines recalled years after the experience, likening a trip aboard Sham to driving a Lincoln Continental or a Mercedes-Benz. "Nice and smooth." He compared his experience on lesser horses to "riding a road with potholes."

Breakfast Bell, a chestnut filly, would win just four races in her career but later produced well as a broodmare. Sham's success on the track would be tested for the first time late in the summer of 1972.

Sham spent August in Saratoga Springs, society's playground once known as the "Queen of Spas." Horse racing had been part of the landscape since its first meet in August of 1863.

The Saratoga Race Course grandstand, remodeled in 1902, maintained the architectural integrity of the era. It featured steeples topped by gilded finials, dormer windows, and Queen Anne turrets on opposite sides of a two-story porch by the finish line. The training facility across the avenue called "Horse Haven" was noted as "a summer hotel for blooded horses."

The main racetrack of the modern facility ran one and one-eighth miles, encircling a one-mile turf course. Tucked inside the turf was a second inner turf and steeplechase course. From within an infield surrounded by tightly trimmed shrubs of varying heights and shades of green, a fountain sprayed streams of water and spewed mist from a central body of water representing a country lake. Surrounding the immaculately kept acres, Gilded Age Victorian houses ran the length of Union Avenue until the affluence met a public garden at the end of the street.

Sham, however, was not in Saratoga to relax at a country retreat. Nor was he there to race. He'd have no opportunity to enjoy a leisurely stroll along the paddock past trees numbered with the day's post-positions, where jockeys took a moment to shake hands with fashionable owners in tailored jackets and silk ties or greet ladies in the latest summer dresses and elaborate hats. There'd be no post parade for him among the red- and white-striped awnings that circled the grandstands. Sham was at Saratoga to work.

When he walked to the track, it was along dirt roads and among waves of dust that enveloped the everyday workings of the true horsemen. He was stabled behind the fanfare and luxury, fed among countless horses in endless rows of barns with heavy doors layered with years of old paint. Inside the barns, stable hands of various backgrounds, with ages ranging from boy to old man, mucked out stalls and did menial chores for the lowest of wages. A sweet whiff of horse feed accompanied the smell of manure.

A groom came by and secured Sham by his halter to a shed before hosing him down. The cool water provided a break from the August heat. Dousing from a bucket of sudsy water followed aside pattern-worn grass and white leg wraps that hung from clotheslines after being laundered. A bundle of hay was suspended just outside Sham's stable door for him to nibble on or to play with to help pass the time until his name would finally appear in a race day program.

His workouts came along nicely. The age and sex of a horse, as well as track condition, were contributing factors, but generally, a decent time for a furlong work would be 12 seconds. A fast furlong would be run between 11 and 12 seconds. Eleven seconds would be very fast, particularly as the distance increased—a horse would not be expected to run multiple furlongs at top speed. Sustaining a pace of 12 seconds per furlong beyond a mile would be very difficult. Sham ran three furlongs in :35 on August 14, four furlongs in :48⅕ on August 17, and five furlongs in 1:00⅕ on August 21.

Woody Stephens had reason to be encouraged by his colt's works, but soon the racing world would see if Sham was ready to face more than a clock. His first race was scheduled for August 28, 1972, opening day of the new season at Belmont Park. Heliodoro Gustines would get the mount.

## Chapter 3

## First Time on the Oval

Heliodoro Gustines found the orange silks the Belmont Park valet had left for him in the jockeys' room. Along with white riding pants and black polished boots, Gustines put on the color representing Claiborne Farm, which looked more yellow-gold than the orange under which Claiborne was officially listed. He gathered his riding crop and left to meet the rest of his team, Woody Stephens and Sham.

Sham left the stables along a walking path that stretched beside the expanse of the Belmont parking lot. He and ten other horses made the trip to the paddock for the third race on the August 28 card. The paddock stalls sat behind an English walking circle lined with benches and trees, including a giant, spreading white pine, some 150 years old. Across the circle, fans and amateur handicappers stood on tiered steps to view the horses below.

Sham entered with the number four saddle-cloth across his back, indicating the post-position he'd drawn for the race. He strolled past with the other numbered competitors while onlookers muttered comments and verified their remarks against figures in their programs or tout sheets.

Sham was one of only two entries who hadn't run a race before this day. His debut was a six-furlong maiden race for two-year-old colts and geldings. Maiden races were for horses (male or female) who had never won a race.

Despite his immaturity, pre-race jitters weren't evident in Sham. Inexperienced horses sometimes fought, bucked, or otherwise acted up in the paddock or out on the track. Walkers could be knocked down and dragged while trying to lead a horse to the stable for saddling. At times, jockeys were thrown immediately after mounting an irascible animal. At the starting gate, one nervous horse could set off the others, leaving assistant starters with a half-dozen spooked animals to contend with. "He wasn't that way," Gustines said, recalling the race years later. Sham, always the gentleman, kept his cool. "He was a nice, quiet horse."

Woody Stephens gave his jockey few instructions before the race. Gustines didn't need them. "I ride a horse once or twice beforehand," Gustines said, "I get to know the horse the second it pulls up." He knew Sham.

Saddled with Gustines up, Sham joined the procession of horses and riders who marched past the tall arched windows of the main building, with its garden blooming white, green, and yellow below. Through a tunnel to the grandstands, the post parade came out on the track by the winner's circle.

Two balconies provided an aerial view of the longest track in the country at one and a half miles. Its turns and long straights encircled a vast infield too big for scattered shrubbery and a chain of miniature lakes to fill. Heavier foliage grew near the red-, white-, and blue-striped pole at the finish line where the eye was naturally drawn. A tight, precise hedge followed the turns and down the stretch of the inner turf course to separate it from the infield. Facing the track, an enormous tote board flashed yellow odds against a black backdrop, tallying amounts bet to win, place, and show. The numbers told the story: the crowd made a colt named Angle Light the favorite, sent off at even money, odds of 1 to 1.

Angle Light was coming in off a strong five-furlong workout in :58⅗ nine days earlier and an impressive :47 four-furlong performance under sloppy track conditions on August 24. The combination of Angle Light's workout times and confidence in trainer Lucien Laurin and jockey Ron Turcotte made the colt the popular choice with bettors. Laurin was an ex-jockey from the Quebec and Ontario racing circuits during the 1930s and 1940s who trained Riva Ridge, winner of the 1972 Kentucky Derby and Belmont Stakes run just a few months earlier. Turcotte had ridden Riva Ridge to those victories. Like Sham, Angle Light had never run a race before this day, but the two would meet several times during their careers in big races. Lucien Laurin and Ron Turcotte would also prove to be Sham's long-time adversaries. This was just their first clash.

The second choice at 4 to 1 was Delta's Moneytree, who had finished third in his only other career start. Delta's Moneytree also had an experienced jockey aboard in Laffit Pincay. Pincay led all jockeys with races won in 1971 and was the leading money-winning jockey for the year, one of only four riders ever to win as much as $3 million in a single season.

Master Achiever, a colt trained by New York trainer Frank "Pancho" Martin, was sent off at odds of 6 to 1 and had demonstrated some success in earlier races. Master Achiever had earned two second-place finishes, one third, and one fourth-place finish in five prior races. Other entries in the field of 11 included Timeless Moment, another popular choice, at odds of 5 to 1, while Sham was shown little interest at long odds of 29 to 1.

The line of competitors idled behind the starting gate, moving closer with each minute nearing post-time. Outriders on horseback brought each entry forward. Belmont Park's official starter stood like a sentry watching over a line of waiting thoroughbreds. Snouts and pointed ears peeked from behind metal bars while jockeys staggered and danced on their mounts for balance. A chorus of "No! No! No!" rang from the riders until they found the right step. Balance was essential, and each jockey wanted his mount facing forward, not looking at his neighbor, which might put the horse on a path veering toward a rival.

No sooner was the last horse loaded when the bell sounded to the simultaneous slam of metal on metal as the starting gate doors burst open. The field exploded forward in a blur. With surging, half-ton animals charging onward, no hooves slapped the earth with thundering claps like those heard in Western movies. Instead there was a silent grinding of earth. Horses and riders to the rear endured a shower of dirt while the group blew past.

Sham preferred to be near the leader, one or two back, in a

running style known as a pace stalker. Gustines wouldn't mess with it to suit his own preference. When asked, his approach to riding his horse was, "Leave him alone because sometimes if you try to change their style they get all confused." But Sham broke next to last in tenth position, just behind Laffit Pincay and Delta's Moneytree.

By the quarter mile Angle Light moved strongly to take the lead by five lengths. Sumthin Else Again, a bay gelding piloted by jockey Jorge Velasquez, ran second by a head over Timeless Moment. Sham, lacking early speed, was still far back in ninth, roughly 14 lengths off the pace.

Angle Light sprinted clear of the competition and settled into a comfortable stride. By the half mile Timeless Moment raced to the second position and closed the gap behind the leader to four lengths. Sham still struggled at ninth, and there was only a quarter mile to go in the race.

Angle Light continued to cruise with a four-length lead at the stretch. Though Timeless Moment was unable to gain on the leader, he did double his lead over the third place horse, who was now Tell It Like It Is, whose past performances indicated he could be a strong closer. Pancho Martin's Master Achiever had been creeping forward in the pack, starting at eighth, working his way to sixth, fifth, then fourth place. Sham gained ground too, moving up to fifth, only a head behind Master Achiever.

Gustines had the difficult task of acting quickly yet maintaining his patience in making a move. If there was no room, no lane to pass, he couldn't force one. Trying to fit two horses where there was room for only one might lead to a disqualification or suspension or worse. The pushing and bumping he got away with in Panama wouldn't fly with New York racing officials. If a flash of daylight revealed an opening, quick action required Gustines' full attention before the slightest hole slammed shut.

"It's a split of a second," Gustines commented about an opportunity's longevity during a race. "You don't got all day to think about it. You make a quick decision. It's very important, your timing and reflex. Gotta be sharp."

Many race fans were unable to see the skirmishes that arose while jockeys guided their mounts for position, steering them through potential gaps between crushing hooves with a margin of error on either side measured only in inches. The clang of metal stirrups between horses sometimes told just how tight a fit was made. Too close a pass, and a clipping of hooves—the clap of one horse's foot to the foot of another horse—could foretell a disastrous spill of horse and rider.

All the while, Gustines perilously balanced his weight on the small metal peg of the stirrup. "You can lose your balance very easy," Gustines said. "Gotta have good balance." A pitch fore or aft could throw him to the silt, sand, and clay below to be trampled by trailing also-rans.

Gustines worked the whip to let Sham know it was time to get serious. "Some of them respond, some don't," he said. Gustines knew various strategies if one should fail, including talking to the horse and chirping into the horse's ear. "Some people sing at them," he said.

Sham knew it was time to move. "He was back," Gustines said, remembering Sham's closing bid. "He was fifth, something like that. He came at the end." Sham tore down the stretch to pick off Master Achiever and Tell It Like It Is, settling into third.

But rather than take the remaining field, the inexperienced Sham ran into trouble. "He didn't make the turn the right way," Gustines said. "He was drifting out." Sham fanned wide, nearing the middle of the track. "Five, six wide," Gustines recalled Sham's position. "I don't know what was bugging him. Something was bothering him." In losing ground along an outside path, Sham lost the opportunity to challenge the leaders.

Angle Light held for the win, giving Ron Turcotte all he needed for victory with little difficulty. Timeless Moment closed the gap behind the winner to three-quarters of a length for second place. Sham ran well enough to take third, though still a fair seven lengths behind second-place Timeless Moment, and one length ahead of Master Achiever in fourth. Tell It Like It Is dropped to fifth, ahead of Delta's Moneytree in sixth.

The race was an ironic prelude to coming events. Pancho Martin's Master Achiever finished closely behind Sham, giving the trainer an opportunity to take notice of the bay colt. In finishing roughly four and a half lengths behind Sham on Delta's Moneytree, Laffit Pincay got a close view of Sham's move down the stretch. Jorge Velasquez, finishing back in tenth place on Sumthin Else Again, also witnessed Sham's run. Martin, Pincay, and Velasquez would all play important roles in Sham's future, not to mention the subsequent meetings with trainer Lucien Laurin, jockey Ron Turcotte, and rival colt Angle Light.

## Chapter 4
## Early Days on the Farm

When friends of Arthur Boyd Hancock Jr., or "Bull" as he was known, came to visit Claiborne Farm, he took them to see Sham first. "My great horse," he called him, and Bull was the authority. He had seen many great horses on which to base the call.

Bull's father, Arthur Boyd Hancock Sr., had begun operation of Claiborne in 1915. The farm had been named after a Hancock ancestor, Sir William Claiborne, one of the first treasurers of Virginia. Guests lucky enough for a full tour where Sham grew up might see Bull enter a field of grazing mares and coax a close-up visit by removing his hat and pretending it was full of oats, prompting a curious one to wander past and poke her nose across the brim for a look.

Black stained fence, 156 miles of it, surrounded the farm, situated among the grazing land of Paris, Kentucky in country south of the Ohio River. In early June, the thick, green plains bloomed in blue, giving credibility to the name The Bluegrass State. Narrow roads rolled between hilly pastures. Heavier traffic was kept to the distant, larger roadways.

A quiet stream flowed to divide Claiborne Farm, clear water among the colorful pink and white dogwood, yellow forsythia, and fuchsia azalea. Maples, oaks, and sycamores, covered the land where stallions roamed during off hours, tempting one former champion colt, Buckpasser, to run past and pull twigs between his teeth before tossing them over his shoulder.

The gates and trim bordering the farm's black barns were painted orange to represent the color of the Claiborne racing silks. A crushed stone driveway ran between moss- and ivy-covered stone pillars with the name "Claiborne Farm" carved on the side, leading to a Georgian-style brick structure. Painted white, the two stories of the house's central body were fronted by fluted cylindrical columns and square pillars supporting a triangular pediment and veranda above the main entrance.

From pegs in the walnut-paneled walls of the Claiborne Farm office building, halters of celebrated horses hung displaying each name on a brass tag riveted to the leather strapping. Along a path behind the office and a tall hedge, headstones marked the plots of past stars who represented Claiborne, winners like Sham's grandfather, Princequillo.

Among the tributes to the thoroughbreds before him, Sham was led by a halter from barn to paddock to pasture when he was a foal. At first, he was led behind his mother, a mare named Sequoia. Later, he could be led by himself.

As a safety measure according to farm policy, Sham, like other males, was separated from the other Claiborne colts for time alone in a private paddock when he was several months old. The boys began to get rough with each other at this age. It wasn't necessary to separate the fillies; the girls were better behaved. Sham watched them run together in groups.

As a youngster himself, 12-year-old Arthur Jr. was paid 50 cents a day by his father to sweep out the yearling barns. The following year, in 1923, Arthur Jr. left for Saint Mark's Academy in Southborough, Massachusetts. He later complained to his father, "They don't have a *Racing Form* within 100 miles of Southborough Mass." Arthur Jr. transferred to Woodberry Forest in Virginia where he picked up the nickname "Bull." The name would prove appropriate. He grew to be a big, heavyset man, 6-foot-2, with a deep voice.

During his summers, he worked various jobs with broodmares, yearlings, stud horses, learning the thoroughbred industry. "I never wanted to be anything but a horseman," Bull realized. "I just never thought of anything else."

Bull Hancock attended Princeton University, where he studied eugenics, genetics, and French. He lettered in baseball and football. Following graduation in 1933, he returned home to be his father's assistant. In 1937, Bull was put in charge of Ellerslie, the family's Virginia estate named for the home of Scottish hero William Wallace.

Under Arthur Sr.'s direction, Celt, a leading sire (which generally meant a stallion whose offspring earned the most money in races for the year) had stood at Ellerslie. At Claiborne Farm, the elder Hancock had foaled and raised Triple Crown winners Gallant Fox (1930 winner) and his son Omaha (1935 winner), the only father and son each to win a Triple Crown. Gallant Fox was the first American horse recognized as leading money-earner of the world. A Claiborne sire, Blenheim II, and former Claiborne mare, Dustwhirl, produced the 1941 Triple Crown winner, Whirlaway.

Claiborne's Sir Gallahad III led the sire list four times. Arthur Sr. bred the 1939 Kentucky Derby and Belmont Stakes winner Johnstown. Triple Crown winner Count Fleet, who won the final jewel of the crown, the 1943 Belmont Stakes, by a staggering 25 lengths, was by Reigh Count, a sire standing at Claiborne. Arthur Sr. also bred the 1947 Kentucky Derby winner, Jet Pilot.

Over the course of the 1930s and 1940s, Ellerslie and Claiborne combined led all American breeders in races won nine times and money won five times. Horse of the Year honors earned by horses born or bred at Claiborne were Granville (1936 winner) and the legendary Seabiscuit (1938 winner). Seabiscuit was also recognized as the leading money-earner of the world.

In merely equaling his father's accomplishments, Bull Hancock faced a nearly impossible task. In a wall bookcase of neatly aligned rows, Arthur Sr. had kept an antique edition of the first English stud book listing thoroughbred family trees back to 1704. He had made marks and notations among its worn pages for reference. He could trace the pedigrees of most of his Claiborne stock to the 17th century. But Bull knew he needed to look forward, not just to the past. Bringing in new bloodstock was important in breeding quality thoroughbreds.

"We had gone for 12 years without replacing stock," Bull said. "When I took over he [Arthur Sr.] had about 75 mares and I didn't like any of them, except two." Bull began replenishing his stock. "An old Hereford breeder one time told me that a good bull was half the herd and a bad bull was all of it," he said. "That has made a lot of sense."

According to *The Thoroughbred Record*, Bull Hancock was an "intense student of international bloodlines." To research pedigrees, he relied on the *Family Tables of Racehorses*, compiled by Captain Kazimierz Bobinski. With detailed, comprehensive information regarding thoroughbred pedigrees, the reference volume was so huge it required its own carrying case.

"I look around and try to see what male lines are doing well in other countries, that we don't have here," Bull said.

Bull felt the male line of a stallion took care of itself, research-wise. "You very seldom get a good stallion by a bad stallion," he said. The stallion's female line required his tighter scrutiny. "I take a good, hard look at the female line," he said.

Bull looked for stallions with a demonstrated ability to stay the American classic distance, one and a quarter miles. He also looked beyond the horse's record, giving consideration to a good performance in a losing race. "What I look for is a good burst of speed at some part of the race," he said. "I like a horse which shows a tremendous burst."

Bull Hancock served with the Army Air Corps prior to his discharge in 1945 with the rank of Captain. Starting the first year of Bull's return, Claiborne Farm would go on to lead America's general sire list for 15 consecutive years thanks to the stallions Bull selected to stand at stud. Bull assumed full management of Claiborne when his father suffered a stroke in 1947. Claiborne was in good hands. Bull continued to acquire new bloodstock.

"Selecting a stallion is at once the most difficult and most important of factors for success in the horse business," the pages of *The Blood-Horse* declared. "Bull Hancock was better at it than any man who came before him."

Bull was the student of a breeding philosophy known as international outcrossing. The practice supported the combination of unrelated or distantly related bloodlines from widely differing environments, and that such an outcross would contribute to a thoroughbred's adaptability and efficiency. Bull's acquisition of the best available bloodstock from varying sources fit the criteria. Of the 27 stallions standing at Claiborne in 1970, representatives included Ambiorix and Herbager from France, Forli and Pronto from Argentina, Pago Pago and Sky High from Australia, Hawaii from South Africa, and Tulyar from Ireland. Bull also believed an individual horse's influence on its offspring was negligible beyond three generations.

"It is the infusion of different blood which invigorates the thoroughbred," was Bull's assertion. Bull Hancock brought new blood to the American thoroughbred, revitalizing the racing stock, not only of Claiborne, but of the nation. His success was praised by Kentucky breeder Charlie Kenney: "When I was young, a long time ago, we used to believe that we had to go to

Great Britain and the European mainland from time to time to bolster 'plebeian' American blood. You just had to do it. Then Americans, in large measure through Hancock's sagacity pretty nearly cornered the winners' market by purchases of bloodstock, not only from Europe but from any quarter of the globe where they raise decent horses.

"America now has the best horses in the world. The world knows it, and now comes to us."

Of the secret to his success at Claiborne, Bull Hancock modestly replied, "We just try to do the usual, unusually well." In 1960, he was the Honored Guest at the testimonial dinner of the Thoroughbred Club of America for his contributions to racing and breeding, following his father who was recognized in 1944—the only father and son to be so honored. Gallant Fox and Omaha were in good company.

In Claiborne's 15 consecutive years leading the American sire list, Nasrullah led the list five times: 1955, 1956, 1959, 1960, and 1962. Nasrullah's run at the top was interrupted by Princequillo for two years, 1957 and 1958, and Ambiorix led for one year in 1961. Then Nasrullah's son, Bold Ruler, joined the competition, leading for seven consecutive years, 1963 to 1969. After the 15-year run had ended, Claiborne stallions still found their way to the top of the sire list. Princequillo's son, Round Table, was the leading sire in 1972, and even after his death, Bold Ruler was again atop the sire list in 1973. Bold Ruler's eight times as leading sire was the most for any horse since a stallion named Lexington began a reign back in 1861.

Of those 15 consecutive years at the top, not only did Claiborne stallions lead the sire list, but for six of those years, also held the second position. In 1960, Claiborne stallions dominated the top three spots. To put the accomplishment in perspective, consider approximately 6,000 different sires in North America each year were vying for the top spot, represented by approximately 50,000 offspring.

To have two champion horses is the envy of any breeder. Hancock had two champion horses born *the same day*. On April 6, 1954, the day Bold Ruler was born, Round Table also entered the world. Round Table earned Horse of the Year honors in 1958, the year after Bold Ruler had earned it in 1957. Another Claiborne Horse of the Year was Dedicate (in 1957—chosen on a separate ballot from Bold Ruler).

But Bull Hancock was not through. Again Claiborne-foaled horses earned Horse of the Year honors: Kelso, an amazing and unequaled five times from 1960 to 1964; Moccasin in 1965, the only two-year-old filly to earn the honor; and Buckpasser in 1966. And like Gallant Fox and Seabiscuit before them, Nashua and Round Table were recognized as leading money earners of the world.

Though the aforementioned list of Claiborne successes may seem exhaustive, it includes, for the most part, only members of an exclusive club, winners of a Horse of the Year award, winners of a Triple Crown race, and leading sires. It doesn't include the names of many stakes-winning horses. From 1952, Bull Hancock bred more than 80 stakes winners.

Under Bull Hancock's tenure, horses owned and raced by Claiborne earned approximately $4.5 million. Reportedly, Bull could recognize any mare at Claiborne on sight, knew what she was worth and to which horse she had been bred. The offspring of the approximately 50 mares he owned earned more than $19 million. Adding horses bred in partnership, the sum soared to nearly $23 million.

Bull increased Claiborne's real estate acreage by adding Raceland Farm, Clay Farm, Stone Farm, and Marchmont Farm. Also, 1,700 acres of Xalapa Farm were leased, including a one-mile training track and 31-stall training barn for yearlings.

Bull recalled the early days, when his father and the superintendent from Ellerslie arrived at Claiborne from Virginia to build three barns that would house approximately 60 horses. "When they finished my father said, 'Well, that's all the barns we'll ever need here.' I can remember him saying that." Bull eventually expanded the empire to 5,700 acres with an estimated 800 stalls. New clients brought their mares, increasing the mare population to 350, complementing Claiborne's own 27 stallions.

Though Bull had all but rebuilt Claiborne, he claimed no monopoly on choosing the names for its stock. "We have a competition around here for horses' names," Bull said. "I pay $10 for every one that's accepted. My wife, our children, the secretaries—everybody can try." The most consistent winner in the naming contest, however, was Bull himself. "I'm the judge, too," he said with a laugh.

Claiborne held a commanding position in the international stallion market due to Bull's ability to pull together the powerful financial resources of wealthy American owner-breeders. He would arrange syndications in which investors could buy a share in a stallion for breeding rights. The pooled resources gave him nearly limitless funding for such transactions.

Inside Claiborne House, paintings of equine greats hung like plaques honoring Hall-of-Fame athletes. Works by important English artists such as John Frederick Herring, Harry Hall, and Samuel Carter depicted Sham's 19th-century ancestors from Ireland and Great Britain, including Bay Middleton, Faugh-a-Ballagh, Flying Dutchman, Voltigeur, and Macaroni.

Sham's lineage, however, could be traced much further back than the 19th century. One of his earliest known ancestors was the Fairfax Morocco Barb. Francis Manners, Sixth Earl of Rutland, was one of the earliest recorded breeders of racehorses in England. Among his properties, the Earl kept breeding stock at his Helmsley Castle. While the Mayflower was delivering Pilgrims to settle the New World in 1620, back in England, the Earl's daughter Lady Katherine Manners married George Villiers, Master of the Horse to King James the First. Villiers was granted the title Duke of Buckingham three years later.

With ships at his disposal as Lord High Admiral of the Navy, the Duke imported horses in his position as Master of the Horse. Eventually Helmsley Castle was granted to Thomas Fairfax in 1651, which likely included the castle's existing horse stock. The Fairfax Morocco Barb was foaled in 1655. Since no record existed of the horse having been imported, he might have been the progeny of the original Helmsley stock crossed with imports of the Duke of Buckingham.

Another of Sham's earliest recorded ancestors was a stallion known as the Lister Turk, foaled in 1683. The horse was reportedly confiscated from the Turks during the siege on Buda during the reign of King James the Second in 1686 and brought to England by the Duke of Berwick. The horse became the property of Matthew Lister in Lincolnshire, England.

Sham's heritage contained figures of historical significance as well as the stuff of legend, like Cade, foaled in 1734, of whom it was said was raised on cow's milk after being orphaned at 10 days of age. Cade was England's champion sire five times.

Potooooooo, foaled in 1773, acquired what appears to be a most unusual name as the result of a prank by his groom, who wrote the name Potatoes in this manner. The horse's owner, Willoughby Bertie—the Fourth Earl of Abingdon, was apparently amused enough to adopt the name as such, though it was later shortened to Pot8os.

Pot8os greatness was not overshadowed by the gimmick of his name, however. He was considered the best horse of his day and possessed power and endurance. During a long career, Pot8os won the Jockey Club Purse three times and the Craven Stakes. He continued to race until the age of ten before he was retired, after winning the Two Hundred Guineas at Newmarket and the Whip, also at Newmarket.

Not to be outdone by his father, Pot8os' son Waxy, foaled in 1790, earned a reputation for his toughness and willingness to compete. Waxy was a handsome bay with one white stocking on his hind leg. A rabbit was kept in his paddock to help keep him calm, but the trick might not have been completely successful, as his exercise rider wrote of him in the *Old Sporting Magazine* in

1828, "Waxy was one of the finest formed, perfect in symmetry, beautiful in colour, admirable in all his paces, and of the finest temper, when in work; but, in the winter, after being weather-bound from frost and snow for some days, on getting out again, it was a case of 'Look out, my boys,' with a vengeance. Oft has he kicked the lappets of my coat over my head."

Waxy won the Epsom Derby in 1793. He was champion sire in 1810 and an important contributor to the thoroughbred as a breed. He was called "the modern ace of trumps in the stud book" by the 19th-century writer The Druid.

Waxy sired Whalebone, foaled in 1807. A small horse, just above 15 hands, Whalebone was mottled brown in color with short legs, and was known for stamina over speed. His groom described him as "the lowest and longest, and most double jointed horse, with the best legs and worst feet I ever saw in my life."

Perhaps inheriting a recalcitrant nature from his sire, Whalebone was described by The Druid, who wrote, "The Earl of Egremont tried to train him after he bought him... but he never ran after he came into the Earl's possession. When in training his chief occupation was to rear and knock his hoofs together like a pair of castanettes."

Whalebone did manage to win 14 career races, 20 if the six forfeits he collected are included as part of his record. In 1810 he won the Epsom Derby after taking an early lead he never relinquished. He was champion sire in 1826 and 1827.

West Australian, foaled in 1850, earned the distinction of winning England's Triple Crown (comprising the Epsom Derby, the Two Thousand Guineas Stakes, and the St. Leger Stakes) in

1853, the first horse ever to do it. He was defeated only once in his career. Other Triple Crown winners in Sham's line included Ormonde in 1886—an undefeated winner of 16 races, Isinglass in 1893, Gay Crusader in 1917, and Gainsborough in 1918.

West Australian, Gay Crusader, and Gainsborough all also won the Gold Cup at Ascot. Isinglass was the only horse ever to win the Triple Crown, the Gold Cup at Ascot, and the Eclipse Stakes. Despite a penchant for laziness, speed and seemingly endless stamina allowed him to win races while expending no more energy than was necessary. It was said of Isinglass, "He often left his jockey rather more tired than he at the end of a race." His winnings of £57,455 remained a record unbroken for 60 years.

Sham's pedigree also included tough luck competitors. Pocahontas, foaled in 1837, was acquired at a dispersal sale of the Royal Stud of King William IV. Standing a diminutive 14.3 hands, Pocahontas was the victim of tough fields of competition. As a two-year-old, she finished third in the Criterion Stakes to an unbeaten and highly acclaimed filly, Crucifix. At age three, Pocahontas again lost to Crucifix in the Epsom Oaks, finishing fourth, but close behind the second and third place finishers. She held the lead after a mile in the Goodwood Cup before being overtaken. Despite a fifth-place finish, Pocahontas was only a length and a neck behind the winner. In her final three races, she finished second in each—seemingly a perennial bridesmaid.

It was in the thoroughbred stud book, however, where Pocahontas made her mark. One of her best offspring, and also part of Sham's pedigree, was Stockwell. Stockwell won two-thirds of the Triple Crown, the Two Thousand Guineas Stakes and the

St. Leger Stakes in 1852 and might have won the Epsom Derby had he not been ill before the race and suffered interference during the running of it. Known as the "Emperor of Stallions," Stockwell was champion sire seven times and second four times.

Voltigeur, foaled in 1847, was described with "fine, sloping shoulders with a good depth of girth, powerful quarters, good knees and hocks with plenty of bone." He was a docile animal, enjoying the company of a cat. In 1850, he won two thirds of the English Triple Crown with the Epsom Derby and St. Leger Stakes. The St. Leger required a run-off following a dead-heat with Russborough. Two days later Voltigeur went on to win the Doncaster Cup, beating The Flying Dutchman (who reportedly was carrying a drunken jockey). At the Cleveland Horse and Hound Show in 1860, Voltigeur was judged most likely to "improve and perpetuate" in the production of horses.

Macaroni, a powerfully built horse with a short, strong back, a head "full of character," and mechanics described as "exceedingly fine and free," also won two-thirds of the Triple Crown, taking the Two Thousand Guineas and Epsom Derby in 1863. Macaroni retired to a successful stud career.

If heroic performers could be manufactured, Hermit might well be the foundation from which to start. His line traced to Whalebone. Foaled in 1864, Hermit, a dark chestnut with a white blaze over his face, was acquired at auction as a yearling by Henry Chaplin (later Lord Chaplin) over the under bidder Harry Plantagenet, Marquis of Hastings.

Hastings had little knowledge of or respect for horses and joked indifferently while stock was auctioned before him at the yearling sale in Eltham. He bid foolishly, disregarding price with no serious interest in the proceedings until Hermit was presented. A suddenly inspired Hastings then entered into a battle of bids with Chaplin. In the aftermath of Chaplin's winning bid, Hastings shrugged and turned away. But it was as if Hastings had been transformed into an aristocratic Ahab. Chaplin became his arch rival, Hermit his white whale.

Hastings, a compulsive gambler known for keeping company with unsavory characters, wagered against Hermit all winter prior to the 1867 Epsom Derby. He openly criticized Hermit, obsessed he should not win the Derby.

In preparation for the Derby, Hermit was worked ten days prior to the race in a one-and-a-half-mile run. After running a mile, Hermit let go with a vicious cough. With a broken blood vessel in his nose, blood streamed out over his chest and covered his jockey. Hermit nearly collapsed in-stride.

After a subsequent workout, it was decided to run Hermit in the Epsom Derby. Chaplin's problems, however, were far from over. He had no jockey and was forced to hire an inexperienced rider, 20-year-old John Daley, the son of a trainer. As incentive, Chaplin offered Daley such a deal, the young jockey would be financially set for life were he somehow to win. But the untried Daley had come to Epsom having been hired for only one other ride. Hermit was just his second.

On a gray, cold, snowy Derby Day, the terrible weather seemed to affect most of the Epsom Derby entries, particularly Hermit. He was described as "a picture of misery." Bold spectators braved the elements, huddled under umbrellas. An anonymous spectator commented the listless Hermit wouldn't fetch £15 at a fair. The remaining crowd, not encouraged by Hermit's chances, bet him down to long odds somewhere between 66 to 1 and 100 to 1. Hastings bet all he could raise on Hermit to lose. As if there weren't enough stacked against poor Hermit, there was the huge field with which he would have to contend, 30 horses in total. Before the race began, Hermit hung his head as if he had already been humiliated, yet obstacles still continued. To make the situation more unbearable, ten false starts caused the race to be delayed nearly an hour. Finally, with the eleventh attempt, the race was underway.

In contrast to an aggressive approach employed by Hermit's former jockey, Daley's gentle touch was perhaps the encouragement a sensitive horse like Hermit needed to give him the spirit and willingness to run. Daley took Hermit to the outside for a sustained run, and when Daley made his move, he needed no whip to motivate his mount. Hermit overtook the race's favorite, Vauban (who had won that year's Two Thousand Guineas Stakes), "as if the latter had been pulling a plough."

With Hermit now moving on the leader, Marksman, the two fought gamely to the wire. Marksman continued to hang on to the lead. But in the final strides, Hermit's weakened body somehow managed a final surge of effort. He took the victory by a neck.

The smug Hastings had taken on Hermit and lost in the neighborhood of £120,000, a fortune in those days. Of his losses, £20,000 of it was to Chaplin himself. Hastings was ruined. Defeated, he could only offer Chaplin his congratulations and a clap to the victor's neck. "A great horse," he said. "A truly great horse."

Hastings' fortune continued to decline as his profligate spending and reckless gambling continued. He fell into debt, squandered his fortune, and drank heavily. Hastings, the fourth and last Marquis of Hastings, died in 1868, just 26 years old. "Hermit broke my heart, but I did not show it, did I?" were reportedly his final words.

Hermit continued his racing career, winning the Biennial Stakes and St. James Palace Stakes at Ascot, racing until age five. After retirement, Hermit was champion sire seven years in succession, from 1880 to 1886, and was second in 1887. He lived into his senior years, and when he finally died in 1890, it was at the same age as the man he had broken. Hermit was 26 years old.

One of Hermit's most famous sons was Tristan, foaled in 1878. In 53 career starts, he finished unplaced only six times (five if the disqualification of his jockey for failing to weigh-in is discarded), while winning 29, some under unthinkable weights greater than 150 pounds.

Unlike the gentle Hermit (reputedly so sweet-natured, Lord Chaplin allowed his small children to ride on the horse's back), Tristan was high-strung with a bad temper, tough, and durable. Tristan was described as having something of a wild animal about him: "When walking in the paddock, he would often stop and look round like a lion, in a way that did not show a kindly temper." What Hermit and Tristan shared in common was stamina and courage.

Among his victories, Tristan won the Hardwicke Stakes three times, July Cup three times, Grand Prix de Deauville three times, Champion Stakes three times—the only horse ever to do it, Epsom Gold Cup twice, Ascot Gold Vase, and Royal Plate at Epsom.

Several of Sham's ancestors had been the property of the 17th Earl of Derby. In 1908, upon the death of his father (the 16th Earl of Derby), Edward George Villiers succeeded to the title. He was known to friends as Eddie Derby. The Derby family had upheld a long tradition of thoroughbred racing. It was the 12th Earl of Derby for whom the Epsom Derby was named. He was the race's sponsor, first run in 1780, and reportedly won a coin toss with Sir Charles Bunburry to decide the name of the race. Had the coin settled on its opposite side, each year Englishmen might eagerly await the running of the Epsom Bunburry, while in the States, the first Saturday in May would celebrate the running of the Kentucky Bunburry (since it was the Epsom Derby that inspired the Kentucky Derby).

Eddie Derby was the leading owner in Britain six times and led the list of winning breeders nine times. His Hyperion was the leading sire six times and Swynford was leading sire once. Both horses were among the branches of Sham's family tree.

Swynford was born in 1907 and grew into a big yearling but was slow in developing. His gallops demonstrated great speed, but he was a disappointment in races during his two-year-old season and the first half of his three-year-old season. After maturing in the latter half of his third year, Swynford won the Hardwicke Stakes, the Liverpool Summer Cup, and the St. Leger in 1910. His success continued on into his fourth year, when he won the Princess of Wales Stakes and the Eclipse Stakes.

When forcing the pace, Swynford was practically unbeatable. But during a half-speed gallop in September of 1911, he smashed a fetlock joint of the lower leg. The accident nearly ended his life at age four. Veterinarians were able to save his life, but his racing days were over. Swynford was retired to stud.

Hyperion, a chestnut colt with four white feet, was foaled in 1930. Hyperion was small, never standing more than 15.1 hands. In his early days there was serious discussion about having him put down on the grounds he would never have the strength to make a racehorse. It didn't take him long to disprove that misguided thinking. Hyperion won his second race as a two-year-old and won the New Stakes at Ascot, besting 21 rivals. For his diminutive size, Hyperion, the little horse that could, became a fan favorite.

In 1933, Hyperion won the Epsom Derby in record time. To celebrate the victory, owner Eddie Derby, who was the vice president of the Berkshire public school Wellington College, granted his students an extra week of summer vacation.

Hyperion was also a favorite to win the St. Leger the same year. Derby invited breeder Jim Joel to watch the race with him. Sitting in his box with eyes tightly shut, too nervous to watch while he shuddered with excitement, Derby asked Joel to call the race for him. Hyperion took the lead at one-half mile, and with two furlongs to go, with Hyperion still in front and on his way to victory, Joel told Derby, "It's all right. You can open your eyes now."

Hyperion became one of breeding's most important influences on top-class thoroughbreds all over the world and was a champion sire six times. He was a *chef-de-race* (chief of the breed) in a system of pedigree analysis that categorized him as a dominant sire regarding the hereditary trait he passed to offspring.

Hyperion's line could be traced to one of the greatest sires in thoroughbred history, the undefeated St. Simon. St. Simon was a leading sire in England nine times and a *chef-de-race*. The St. Simon male line was famous for producing great horses.

The first important stallion Bull Hancock brought to Claiborne Farm, via Ellerslie, was Princequillo. With the dramatics of a Hollywood war movie, the Princequillo saga began with Prince Rose. Prince Rose was a leading sire who was possibly the greatest horse to run in Belgium and whose roots could also be traced to St. Simon. While on a three-year lease, Prince Rose was brought to France in 1938 for stud duty. In the spring of 1939, he was bred to the mare Cosquilla. As war threatened Europe, the in-foal Cosquilla was sent to England to give birth. The colt, Princequillo, was reared in Ireland before being put on a ship and sent across the German U-boat-infested Atlantic. The trip was anything but first-class. Princequillo made the voyage in steerage, a refugee from war. He landed in New York, emerging as a skinny runt.

In 1942, as a two-year-old, he was unclaimed for the low price of $1,500. As a three-year-old, the little bay Princequillo defeated Bolingbroke, an acclaimed and more mature distance runner, in the one-and-five-eighths-mile Old Rosebud Handicap. In the Saratoga Handicap, Princequillo took the victory by five lengths in a time equaling the stakes record, defeating not only Bolingbroke, but also the 1942 Kentucky Derby winner,

Shut Out, who finished third. Princequillo also won the Saratoga Gold Cup and set a record time doing it. He won the Jockey Club Gold Cup at two miles. Princequillo earned recognition as the best distance runner in America. At age four he won the Questionnaire Handicap, equaling the track record. Also at age four, he won the Merchants' and Citizens' Handicap.

Princequillo had won over a distance of six furlongs the same year he won the Saratoga Cup over one and three-quarter miles, demonstrating speed along with his stamina. During his career, Princequillo won 12 races, finished second five times, and finished third seven times to finish in the money 24 times in 33 starts.

"I wanted to buy Princequillo when I was in the Army in 1944," Bull Hancock said, "but then racing was stopped and nothing came of the deal."

After the Saratoga Cup victory, Bull went to New York to make arrangements to bring the horse to Ellerslie. Princequillo was the property of a Russian Prince, Dimitri Djordjadze, and the Prince's wife, heiress Audrey Emery, before being acquired by Bull. The stallion proved less than popular with breeders, however, even at the modest fee of $250. His reputation for stamina didn't impress American horsemen. Nor did his reputation for late maturity and the unfamiliarity of his sire to American breeders help him get mares. With the fashionable list of other Claiborne stallions to choose from, Princequillo was the odd man out. But that would change. Ellerslie was sold in 1946, and Princequillo was sent to Claiborne.

As America's leading sire in 1957, Princequillo's offspring set a world record, winning $1,698,427. The following year, his offspring nearly equaled the mark, winning $1,394,540. In addition to his two-year stint as leading sire, the *chef-de-race* Princequillo developed a reputation as a champion broodmare sire. He led the list five consecutive seasons, 1966 through 1970, and finished second in 1971 before winning his sixth broodmare sire championship in 1972. Racers produced by his daughters that year earned a record $2,722,783 in purses. The record wouldn't hold for long. Princequillo won his seventh broodmare sire championship in 1973 with a record $3,071,322 in purses.

Princequillo was bred with The Squaw II, a French mare foaled in 1939 whose war-time exploits were similar to those of Princequillo. But rather than escaping across the Atlantic, The Squaw II was captured by the Nazis and sent to Germany where she won two races as a three-year-old before being imported to America in 1946. The Squaw II produced several foals with Princequillo, including Sham's mother, Sequoia, foaled in 1955.

Sequoia's best racing days were as a two-year-old, when she won four of eight starts, including the 1957 Spinaway Stakes. The Claiborne-bred Sequoia was leased to Claiborne Farm by her owner, Audrey Emery.

Sham's father, Pretense, was by the Argentine-bred Endeavour II, a top stakes winner in Argentina who won 11 of 18 races in his native country. He stood an imposing 17.1 hands, but possessed an easy-going, gentle disposition. Many of his offspring resembled their sire in temperament and conformation. Pretense's dam, the British-bred Imitation, was by Hyperion. Imitation's line traced to Solario, a St. Leger winner in 1925, and

Fifinella, winner of the English Oaks in 1916 and the Epsom Derby that same year, a race in which the filly defeated rival colts. The bad-tempered Fifinella was the last filly to win both the Derby and Oaks.

Foaled in 1963, Pretense was one of the better handicap performers of the 1960s. In handicap races, different weights are assigned to horses, the idea being to give all entries an equal chance of winning. Often, Pretense ran under high weight assignments. During his career, Pretense won 13 of his 31 races, finished second five times, and finished third six times, finishing in the money 24 times. Among his victories were the Sheridan Handicap, Palos Verdes Handicap, Santa Anita Handicap, Gulfstream Park Handicap (carrying the top weight), San Antonio Handicap, American Handicap (carrying the top weight), Inglewood Handicap (a turf race where he set an American record while carrying the top weight), San Pasqual Handicap, and Bing Crosby Handicap (equaling the track record). Pretense had good speed and stamina and could perform under differing track conditions.

Pretense entered stud in 1969 young and unproven as a sire. One of Bull Hancock's requirements for a potential stallion was that he must have matured reasonably quickly—he must have been a better than average two-year-old. Pretense didn't quite fit the bill. He was a bit slow in developing as a racehorse and didn't race as a two-year-old.

Sham was born at Claiborne Farm on April 9, 1970 from Pretense's first crop of foals. Sham's pedigree demonstrated a strong presence of stamina, suggesting he could be a tough competitor inside the final half furlong of a race at the classic American distance of one and a quarter miles. He should be able to stay the distance, like Princequillo. Sham would be his sire's first stakes winner. "The Pretenses are popular," a Claiborne ad for his services would later declare in *The Thoroughbred Record*.

"He was a lot of nice breeding," Heliodoro Gustines once said of Sham. "There was a lot of nice horses by that horse, Pretense."

Of course, pedigree isn't everything. A prestigious bloodline is no guarantee of success on the racetrack. "I've known plenty of horses that failed although they were bred from winners and stakes-placed parents," Woody Stephens once declared. "And there have been plenty of others that succeeded with nothing much in the way of sire or dam."

## Chapter 5

# Trainer Tries Again

*A man may well bring a horse to the water,
But he cannot make him drinke without he will.*
—John Heywood

Woody Stephens put Sham through early September works at Belmont following his first race. Sham ran a lackluster five furlongs, though under sloppy track conditions, in 1:01 on September 3. He improved four days later, covering six furlongs in 1:12⅗. By the 11th of the month, Sham ran a nice four furlongs in :47. He was coming into his second start off two good workouts.

Sham's second race, scheduled for September 13, was a seven-furlong maiden race at Belmont Park for two-year-old colts and geldings. Heliodoro Gustines was in the saddle again, this time with Sham the favorite, off at 2 to 1 odds. Bettors made Broadway Playboy the second choice at 5 to 2. The chestnut colt was sired by Stage Door Johnny, who Heliodoro Gustines had ridden to victory in the 1968 Belmont Stakes. Laffit Pincay had the ride on Broadway Playboy.

Sham stood at the first post-position in a large field of 13. At the start, he was one of the last out of the gate, breaking eleventh. He rallied for ground and moved up into second place by the quarter mile. He trailed only a head behind leader Broadway Playboy and Laffit Pincay.

Sham and Broadway Playboy dueled for the lead. Pincay and Gustines maneuvered slim margins, alternating the first and second positions. By the half mile Sham fought his way to the front by a half length.

Broadway Playboy continued to keep the battle tight at the stretch. He retook the lead by a head over Sham. Dick's Boots ran third, trailing Sham by three lengths.

Sham pressured the leader. His tightly shorn coat traced his hindquarters, revealing the muscular breadth that rippled and flowed as he ran. Heliodoro Gustines filled the role of both accomplished artist and master technician. As if part of the same machine, the jockey appeared connected to his mount. He kept a rhythm with Sham as the colt charged, bobbing his head in exertion with each stride. Gustines' arms flowed in time with Sham's neck as he urged his colt onward. The horse and rider working together resembled a locomotive, Sham representing the lead wheel, Gustines the second. Arms and reins represented the side rods between them, turning the wheels in unison.

But their effort wasn't enough. Again Sham lost ground by

drifting wide. "He was just drifting out," Gustines recalled. "I think he got a little tired."

Sham eventually weakened in the stretch. Broadway Playboy extended his lead and drew away. This time Gustines watched Pincay finish in front. Broadway Playboy took the win by two and a half lengths. Sham held for second, though he lost ground to Dick's Boots who moved within a half length while finishing third.

Though Sham was still a maiden after two races, it was not Woody Stephens' practice to lose patience and to push a horse too hard to win. He believed a horse had to be studied in order to understand his ways. He felt abusive treatment could so damage a horse's disposition he'd remember it for the rest of his life. Gentle handling from the start could save "a carload of trouble" later, as he put it.

"It's a whole lot easier to ruin a good horse than to train him to bring out his best," was Stephens' argument. "I'd never switched from believing that to do any good as a trainer you had to have affection and respect for the animals in your barn."

Stephens felt every horse should be regarded as a potential winner at some level. "There's no gain in treating a champion like a champion and a loser like a loser," he was known to say.

He had learned the lesson long ago. In 1951, Stephens worked with Blue Man, a two-year-old colt who had been losing claiming races at lower and lower values. In claiming races, a licensed owner or agent is allowed to purchase at a set price any horse entered, regardless of whether the owner wants to part with the animal or not. Since there was a risk of losing the horse, claiming races discouraged a trainer from entering a top horse against lesser competition, thus keeping the playing field even. An owner wouldn't enter a highly regarded animal in a claiming race if he didn't want to risk losing it. This was not a concern regarding Blue Man. He had finished back in tenth place in a $12,500 claimer, went on to lose a $10,000 claimer, and was headed for the low-level $7,500 claimers.

"I found he was washy and awful nervous," Stephens said. "If you tried to take hold of him, he'd fight the bit, throw up his head, and it was over for the day. But I thought he might be a pretty good horse if he was treated right."

Stephens did treat him right. Blue Man had a "skittery streak in his nature," according to Stephens, so he worked with the colt, calming him and transforming the horse from a spooked animal to one eager to win. In 1952, Blue Man won the Flamingo Stakes and finished third in the Kentucky Derby. Two weeks after the Derby, Stephens' kindness was repaid with Blue Man's victory in the Preakness Stakes. "That's the first real classic I ever won," he said. "That was the beginning of me."

Woody Stephens' affection for horses had come about long before he was introduced to Blue Man. When Stephens was a boy, his father drove the family to church on Sunday mornings in a buggy and hitched the horse near the other rigs of the congregation. Woody was allowed to stay outside with the horses where he'd reach up to pat their heads or give their tails a tug. When Woody was six years old, his grandfather gave him a pony named Bill. Woody rode the pony three miles to school each morning. When Woody was near the age of ten, Woody's father let him take a team of horses and a wagon to town to load with lumber or feed.

"I concluded that I liked horses an awful lot," Stephens said. "My daddy told me I was a born horseman. I'd rather heard that than I was a born field hand."

The Stephens family moved to Midway, Kentucky where Woody went to work after school and on weekends for J.M. Parrish, who owned a stable of thoroughbreds. "I'd reached the point where I was eager to ride anything with a mane and a tail," Stephens said. "I started waking up ahead of the roosters," he recalled, "with my heart set on being a jockey."

Stephens helped break yearlings, working horses in a vast field of wheat. While the horses were schooled among the grain, he too learned. He rode his first thoroughbreds for Parrish and, according to Stephens, loved every minute he spent on their backs.

In February 1929, the 15-year-old Stephens, with his father's permission, agreed to a five-year contract with trainer John S. Ward of Everglade Stables. In 1930, wearing the Everglade silks of red stars on white, Stephens rode his first mount, Dodgson. His first winner came the following winter aboard a filly named Directly in the sixth race on opening day at Hialeah Park, January 15, 1931. "The filly carried 100 pounds and I probably didn't weigh 90," Stephens recalled.

A week later Stephens rode her again but lost the lead around the eighth pole, finishing second. The horse was willing to run, so the blame fell to Stephens. The official chart caller was critical of the young jockey in his write up: "Directly… was under restraint to the stretch, but her rider was of little help to her at the finish."

It would soon be clear Stephens was not a highly regarded

jockey. After Stephens finished second on a horse called Brandon Dare, the horse's trainer, Frank Bray, was asked if he wanted to switch riders the next time. "Put him back on the horse," Bray said. "I want to see if he can ride him that bad again."

Stephens became a groom, then assistant trainer for the Wards. He went out on his own as a trainer in 1937, saddling his first winner on opening day at Keeneland in Lexington, Kentucky on April 16, 1940 with Bronze Bugle. Married by then, Stephens asked his wife, Lucille, how much money she had. When she told him $61, he told her to bet $60 on the horse. When she asked him what would happen if the horse lost, Stephens said, "We eat a hot dog and go home." The win was good for over $800.

In 1944, down to his last $400, Stephens went to work in New York for Jule Fink's Marlet Stable.

"When I went with Jule there were some of the fine things I needed to know," Stephens said. "What makes 'em win and what makes 'em lose? He taught me how to claim horses, how to place horses, how to pace horses. He taught me how to stretch out a horse's speed. Jule was the best handicapper around, without question."

Stephens' first stakes winner came for Jule Fink with Saguaro, who won the 1945 Excelsior Handicap. "Woody had his antennae out all the time, very receptive," Fink said. "He had a great eye for a horse and a great touch. A physical touch with a horse. He'd kneel next to a horse and touch and feel around and immediately know where the problem was. He knew when to back off and go on."

Stephens trained for aviator Captain Harry F. Guggenheim

from 1956 to 1965 and made the captain's Cain Hoy Stable the top money winner in 1959, while Stephens himself was the second leading trainer in money won that same year and again in 1960.

Stephens trained champion horses Bald Eagle, Champion Handicap Horse in 1960 and Never Bend, Champion Two-Year-Old Colt in 1962. For his work with Bald Eagle, Stephens was honored by the National Turf Writers Association for the "Outstanding Training Achievement of the Year" in 1961. He saddled winning fillies in the Kentucky Oaks with Hidden Talent in 1959, Make Sail in 1960, and Sally Ship in 1963. After leaving Cain Hoy Stable, Stephens went on to train Bold Bidder, Champion Handicap Horse in 1966.

Stephens and Guggenheim parted ways when Stephens asked to lease barn space from Guggenheim to train some horses owned by Stephens' wife. "I've got a policy," the Captain told him. "Nobody but me puts his horses in my stable." Guggenheim later confided to fellow airman Jimmy Doolittle, "My one mistake in racing was letting Woody get away."

Other than racehorses and jockeys, the affable Kentucky farmboy enjoyed the company of athletes like baseball's Joe DiMaggio and Billy Martin, football's Joe Namath, as well as celebrities like actor Pat O'Brien, musicians Cab Calloway and Harry James, "who played the horses as well as the trumpet," Stephens said, and James' wife, Hollywood's Betty Grable.

"The track is one of the very few places left where a man without the price of a fresh shirt on his back can get to talk on level terms with a millionaire," Stephens said. "It's only the horses that bring them together."

As horses made fellows of unlikely sorts, the workload of a horseman might have just as easily divided them. Woody Stephens' day began well before 6 AM when he'd arrive at the track with a newspaper and thermos of coffee. "Five o'clock sharp, rain or shine, is the time I'm usually getting myself out of bed seven days a week, twelve months of the year, and I don't allow three minutes either side of that," he said. "It isn't hard to do when it's as natural as breathing and a habit that comes from working with horses."

Stephens admitted while good horses made his reputation, he, in turn, made some good horses. His easy-going nature was reflective of his accepting the ups and downs of racing. "When you lose, you go home, and when you win, you go home, and there isn't much more to it than that."

Even with his success as a trainer, Stephens never forgot his love of riding: "I remembered hunching up well forward over the withers of horses long since dead, head down low to cut down resistance, holding still so I didn't disturb the pace, feeling the wind blowing in my face and the ripple of the mount's muscles under my knees, listening to him pull air into his lungs and the drumming of his feet on the track, maybe saying a word or two to encourage him. I'll never forget being a jock even though I didn't make it."

## Chapter 6
## A Change of Order

Tragedy would shape Sham's future. In August of 1972, Bull Hancock was in Saratoga. Soon after, he left for Scotland to hunt grouse and for Ireland to watch some racing. He had planned to watch a Claiborne horse run in France but became ill and returned home. He was hospitalized at Vanderbilt Medical Center in Nashville, Tennessee where he underwent surgery for what *The Blood-Horse* reported was described as an "internal infection." The operation revealed lung cancer. Bull Hancock died shortly thereafter, on September 14, 1972.

When Arthur Hancock Sr. died in 1957, Bull had been forced to sell a majority interest in the promising three-year-old Round Table to pay estate taxes. Round Table earned more than $1.5 million for new owner Travis Kerr, while Bull got only $175,000 for the sale. Now Bull Hancock's sons, Arthur Boyd

III, age 29, and Seth Hancock, age 23, would be forced to do likewise with Claiborne stock.

Eleven days after Bull's death, Sham was scheduled to run his third maiden race at Belmont Park. The winless Sham would be asked to test his stamina in a mile race on September 23. The field was limited to two-year-old colts and geldings. Sham's pre-race workout on September 18 was an excellent five-furlong breeze in 1:00⅘, considering his rider did not push him for speed.

Sham's last race gave bettors enough confidence to make him the second choice at 8 to 3 odds behind the favored Pleasant Brook at 5 to 3. It promised to be an interesting match-up. None in the field of eight had ever run a race as long as a mile. Sham would face two colts he had run against in his second race, Dick's Boots and one named Bid to Win. In finishing third to Sham's second, Dick's Boots had closed the gap between them in the final stretch, reducing Sham's three-length lead to a half length. Bid to Win was right behind in fourth, two and a half lengths behind Dick's Boots. Fortunes could change with the added furlong in distance.

Dick's Boots was being ridden by Braulio Baeza, a childhood friend of Heliodoro Gustines who had played marbles with him at the Gustines barn in Panama. Later, as young jockeys, they had continued the competition on the Panamanian racetrack. "Braulio Baeza, me and him we won all the races," Gustines recalled in later years.

Baeza had made a name for himself when he won the 1961 Belmont Stakes aboard Sherluck, at the time the greatest longshot ever to win the event at 65 to 1. Baeza had been the leading rider in money won in the United States for four consecutive years, from 1965 through 1968.

At the start a bay colt named King Rolf, who was offered no regal deference by bettors at long odds of 34 to 1, jumped out to a lead. Braulio Baeza and Dick's Boots took second. Sham ran fourth.

By the quarter mile Dick's Boots overthrew King Rolf for the lead by a length. Dick's Boots established the pace while still being restrained by Baeza.

Dick's Boots still held the lead by the half mile while Pleasant Brook took the second position and cut the leader's margin to a half length. Sham gained ground for third with only a head separating him from Pleasant Brook. The field ran in a tight formation. Sham led a chestnut colt named Leesnik by one and a half lengths, who led by the same margin over Drollery, a bay gelding.

By the three-quarter-mile mark Sham took both Dick's Boots and Pleasant Brook for the lead. The gap could hardly be narrower, a half length over Pleasant Brook and another head back to Dick's Boots who dropped to third. By the stretch Sham extended his lead to a full length. But now Dick's Boots ran second, having battled back to overtake Pleasant Brook.

Sham fought to protect his lead against the field's final effort. Drollery hadn't given up. He stormed to fourth place and continued to fight. Bid to Win, also in the thick of contention, chased only a length behind in fifth place. The top five horses chased the wire separated by a combined total of only six lengths. It shaped up to be, mixed metaphors aside, a real dogfight.

Braulio Baeza and Dick's Boots worked the inside to save

ground. Heliodoro Gustines tore Sham over an outside path as the two drove to the wire. Sham and Dick's Boots, they would decide who the winner would be. Sham's habit of drifting to the outside, however, again cost him valuable ground.

"All three times he was drifting out," Gustines later reflected upon his races on Sham. "That's the only thing [problem] he had, drifting out. I don't know why. Because he was sound. When a horse does that, it's because something is bothering him."

The real estate Dick's Boots saved in taking the inside route paid off. He poked over the wire just ahead of Sham, winning by a head.

Despite Sham's drifting, Gustines didn't pin the blame for the day's loss on his horse. "I think I got up to the front too early," he said. "And he only got beat a head. I probably lost the race, not the horse."

Sham inched closer to victory with each race, but fell just short again. After three races, he was still a maiden. Horses can be easily distracted by shadows, the movement of the jockey, and other horses. Heliodoro Gustines thought Sham's problem of drifting outside might be solved with blinkers, which attach to a horse's hood to limit his vision. Sham did wear blinkers for his three races, but perhaps a change of equipment was in order.

Gustines otherwise showed little concern over the colt's progress, certain the two-year-old would improve as he got older. "He's like us, you know," Gustines said in a later interview. "Some people are just serious at an early age, others, they're 40 years old and still don't get serious. He wasn't serious. He was immature. He was like a little baby."

Sham's initial losses were no great surprise to Seth Hancock, who recalled years later similarities between son and sire. "He looked a lot like Pretense. That's where he got his looks. Pretense was a big colt that was a little slow to come to hand and so was Sham, but both of them were nice horses."

Since Sham's first race, Seth Hancock liked what he saw. "We were just really trying to get a race in him to educate him, and he took to everything real well," Hancock said. "We were very pleased with him." Hancock hadn't given up on Sham. He was a horse who liked to run, one Hancock called "a good work horse."

"You see, Woody was going easy on him," Heliodoro Gustines said of Sham's development. "Because he wasn't thinking of that year. He was thinking about the next year, the three-year-old. The two-year-old, you give them a chance. They're not mature yet." Woody Stephens' training regimen for Sham in 1973, however, would prove moot.

Bull Hancock's will named Douglas Parrish, Sam Clay, and the First Security National Bank and Trust Company of Lexington as trustees and executors. An advisory committee consisting of three men—breeder Ogden Phipps; William Haggin Perry, a former partner of Bull Hancock's in purchasing a half interest in Claiborne-bred foals; and Charlie Kenney—was named to assist in the operation of thoroughbred matters. The will did not direct, but recommended, the produce of Claiborne mares be sold rather than raced.

Before Bull died, Seth had told him about Sham. "That's a Derby horse," he had said. Seth had spent a lot of time with Sham and had had good reason to recognize him. "He stepped on my foot when I took him to get weighed one morning," he said.

Now, the executors were ordering the sale of all racing stock from the estate. Seth asked to be allowed to keep Sham. Provisions of the will and the reality of inheritance taxes, however, denied his request. Sham had to go.

Claiborne yearlings were shipped from Kentucky for holding at the Michael Phipps estate at Old Westbury, Long Island, New York. Horses of racing age were sent to Woody Stephen's barn at Belmont Park. The first public sale of Claiborne Farm stock (yearlings and horses of racing age), which the *Lexington Herald* called "the lifework of three generations of Hancocks, spanning more than a century of devotion to the thoroughbred," was held on November 20, 1972.

In a yellow and white tent pitched along the training track at Belmont Park, the Fasig-Tipton Company arranged the dispersal sale of stock from the estate of Bull Hancock, as well as the jointly owned stock of Hancock and William Haggin Perry. In a three-day event, the bidding started at 9:30 on Monday morning. Top names in racing were in attendance, Thomas Mellon Evans of Buckland Farm; Penny Tweedy of Meadow Stable, owner of Secretariat and Riva Ridge; Zenya Yoshida, the leading breeder of thoroughbreds in Japan and owner of Fountainebleau Farm in Kentucky; Alfred G. Vanderbilt, chairman of the New York Racing Association (NYRA) and former president of Pimlico Race Course who had arranged the Seabiscuit-War Admiral match race in 1938; television producer and horse owner Quinn Martin; construction magnate and sportsman Sigmund Sommer, to name only a few.

Tad Legere, for many years an assistant to King Ranch trainer Max Hirsch and friend to Sigmund Sommer and his wife, Viola, accompanied Mr. Sommer to the auction. Viola Sommer recalled the event and the advice Tad Legere provided. "She had a marvelous eye for horse conformation," she said.

Sigmund Sommer's trainer, Pancho Martin, also had a say in matters pertaining to the Sommer stable. He had seen Sham run his first race in August when Sommer's Master Achiever finished fourth, a length behind Sham. Martin and Sommer discussed the horses offered for sale, coming to an agreement on the bay colt.

"He liked him," Martin recalled. "I liked him too." Martin looked to the upcoming racing season and told Sommer, "It's our only chance if we want a good 3-year-old."

When Sham's time at the auction block came, Sigmund Sommer engaged in bidding along with Mrs. Cloyce (Liz) Tippett of Llangollen Farm, Ocala, Florida. She was the breeder of Sham's sire, Pretense. Fasig-Tipton president John Finney commented to her, "If anyone should get this colt it should be you."

Liz Tippet's breeding stock included 46 mares (including six Princequillo mares) and several stallions. She had purchased Pretense's sire, the Argentinean Endeavour II, as a stallion. Pretense himself was syndicated for breeding and stood at stud at Claiborne Farm. She kept several shares and sent seven mares to him in 1972. She also had at one time by Pretense two yearlings, four two-year-olds, and three three-year-old fillies.

Her bid reached $195,000. Sommer came in at $200,000. "I desperately wanted Sham," Liz Tippett said. "I tried to persuade a friend to join me and keep on bidding, but he wouldn't—and I didn't have sufficient available cash to carry on alone."

Sommer was firm in his own goal. "I wanted a filly and this colt," he said. "The filly got away, but I was determined to get the colt." Sommer was at the event for only 10 minutes—long enough to make his winning bid. He left immediately after bidding on Sham.

"I'm sure he would have gone higher than the $200,000 if he had to," Pancho Martin said. "He bought a good horse."

Sham had yet to win a race after three attempts and was quickly approaching the end of his two-year-old season. Considering the hefty price tag, Sommer was showing tremendous faith in the colt.

Though Sham didn't earn the event's highest price, he came in an impressive second. The top price paid for a single horse was by Jonathan Irwin of the British Bloodstock Agency, Ireland for a yearling colt out of one of Claiborne's leading sires, Round Table. Irwin was acting as an agent for an undisclosed buyer. Irwin's bid, coming from the last row in the jammed arena, closed the proceedings at $240,000. It was the highest yearling price paid at auction in America that year.

After the dispersal sale, Arthur Boyd Hancock III and Seth Hancock shared supervision of Claiborne Farm with the guidance of the advisory committee appointed by Bull Hancock's will. Arthur was in charge of yearlings, weanlings, and sales operations, while Seth managed bookings for their twenty-five stallions and took charge of the broodmares. By February of 1973, Arthur announced his withdrawal from Claiborne Farm's management to pursue his interest in Stone Farm, a nearby nursery leased from Claiborne.

"Just as my grandfather had sent my father to run our Ellerslie Farm in Virginia when he was 27 years old," he said, "my father wanted me to run Stone Farm." Though Arthur would remain on the Claiborne board of directors, management of the farm would be left to his younger brother, Seth and the advisory committee.

Seth Hancock had been working for his father, learning the breeding business, as Bull had learned it from his own father. Seth, however, was much younger than his father had been, at nearly forty, when he assumed full management of Claiborne.

Seth Hancock had attended the University of the South in Tennessee and the University of Kentucky, graduating with a degree in agriculture in 1971. He learned some of Claiborne's operation during summers off from school and went to work there permanently in 1972. The plan was to focus on various aspects of the farm over a gradual period of time. He had just spent six months learning about broodmares when his father died.

Further education came courtesy of Woody Stephens. "It was Woody who taught me about a horse's form, legs and the inner workings of a racing stable," Seth Hancock said. Of Stephens' affection for his animals, Hancock said horses "knew he loved them, and they ran their hearts out for him."

Though Seth Hancock had seen Stephens around Claiborne Farm, Seth met him formally for the first time in the paddock at Churchill Downs in 1963, just after Stephens had saddled Captain Guggenheim's Never Bend for the Kentucky Derby. Never

Bend ran a good race and finished second. During their meeting Seth wished good luck to the man who would become a second father to him.

# Chapter 7
# Last Chance for the Two-Year-Old

New ownership meant a new trainer. Sham was transferred from Woody Stephens' Barn 3 at Belmont Park to Pancho Martin's Barn 52.

"He had a lot to learn when we bought him," Martin said. "Woody Stephens was the first to tell me so. He said that Mr. Arthur B. Hancock had been ill and they had left instructions to go easy with the good colts until he was back in good health. … Sham's schooling, in the meantime, had been neglected, which perhaps was a blessing in disguise. Most of our young horses in America are ruined before they have a chance. In most cases their knees are not properly grown together and they are out there breaking watches and running in stakes. This didn't happen to Sham."

Martin described Sham as a "kind" horse, which in racing

language usually means easy to train, though in Sham's case, he was good-natured too. "When Mr. Sommer bought him he was very green and really did not know much about running. But he took to his lessons like a genius." Martin admired his new colt's demeanor and work ethic. "He loved to run. When he went to exercise, he didn't do nothing to [show] that he was wild or something. He was a quiet horse. Quiet all the way. In the stall, very easy to [handle]."

During workouts, Martin noticed Sham's propensity for drifting wide. "He had a bad habit of getting out," as the trainer put it. Martin, like Heliodoro Gustines, thought the problem might be solved with a change of blinkers. He switched Sham to a closed right blinker, the type his father, Pretense, had worn in his races. Liz Tippett mentioned Pretense's blinkers had holes cut in the back.

"Sham's don't have any holes in the back," Martin said. "He doesn't care what's going on behind. He's just interested in what's up front."

Martin also fitted Sham with a severe runout bit which would give his jockey better control over the colt's veering path. Time was running out if Sham was to earn his first victory as a two-year-old and avoid a winless juvenile season. Regardless of the actual date of their birth, all thoroughbreds share the same birthday; they are considered a year older on January 1. Sham's fourth attempt to break his maiden, his first under Sigmund Sommer ownership, was December 9, 1972.

For the early December contest, Sham faced another change of scenery. Instead of Belmont Park, the site of his three previous races, Aqueduct in Jamaica, New York would host. The one-mile race was limited to maidens, two-year-old colts and geldings.

Sham's assignment to Pancho Martin also brought with it a new jockey. Jorge Velasquez was now in the irons. Friends and acquaintances called Velasquez "Georgie," instead of using the Spanish pronunciation of Jorge. "People don't pronounce it right," Velasquez explained, "so I tell them to call me George or Georgie."

By either name, Velasquez was one of the top riders in America, having led all jockeys in victories in 1967 with 438, one of only five riders in racing history to have won as many as 400 races in a year. He was the second leading money-winning jockey in 1966, the leader in 1969, and third in 1970 and 1971. In 1972, Velasquez led all New York riders with 190 wins there, 228 overall for the year.

Like Heliodoro Gustines, Velasquez had gotten his start in Panama, where as a youth he had worked in a bakery earning his pay in loaves of bread for his family. Velasquez had begun riding in 1963 and had even ridden for Gustines' uncles Abraham Gustines and Isaac Gustines Jr., who ran horses along with Gus' grandfather Isaac Sr. As an apprentice, Velasquez had broken riding records set by Braulio Baeza before coming to the United States.

Two familiar faces greeted Sham from opposing stalls. Heliodoro Gustines and Woody Stephens were there. Stephens trained a bay colt, Dr. Penny, and Gustines was on another bay colt, Pleasant Brook, who had been the favorite when he had squared off against Sham on September 23, running a good race before tiring and losing ground to finish fifth.

Though disappointed to be off Sham, Gustines understood the nature of the racing business. Horses were bought and sold; trainers were hired and fired; jockeys were given rides and taken off. Regrettably, he wouldn't have the opportunity to share in the success he predicted for Sham. "I thought we were going to have a nice party with him," Gustines later said. "I would be the main guy. But things happen."

In a field of 13, Sham faced only five other horses who had raced the one-mile distance before. Sham's pedigree stressed stamina, and a longer race would give him the opportunity to wear an opponent down. In his previous one-mile contest, Sham had been edged out by only a head. The distance, combined with his recent change of equipment, might give Sham the opportunity to make up that margin.

The crowd made Sham the favorite at odds of 9 to 5, followed by Water Wheel at roughly 4 to 1, and Radnor near 6 to 1. Water Wheel was the son of one of Claiborne Farm's successful sires, Bold Ruler, which likely affected wagering. Having the same sire as Secretariat, Water Wheel was his half-brother. Like Sham, Water Wheel was another horse of racing age acquired at the Hancock dispersal sale, bought by Buckland Farm for $100,000.

Radnor, a bay gelding, had been knocking at victory's door in his previous three starts, finishing second each time. Those second-place finishes had come in one-mile races, so the distance was nothing new to him.

Saddling his colt in the paddock, Pancho Martin had no special instructions to relay to Velasquez regarding Sham's new equipment or his habit of running wide. Over a muddy track, from the number six post-position, Sham broke to a fourth place start. By the quarter mile he raced to the lead by four lengths over Radnor.

At the half mile Sham still held his lead, but Radnor reduced it by a length; Sham led by only three. Woody Stephens' Dr. Penny moved into third, a length over Water Wheel in fourth. The muddy race conditions left jockeys looking battle-worn, covered in the track's surface. The only patch free of mud was beneath the outline of their goggles. The same was true of the horses and their hoods. Mud caked at the point of the snout, across the forehead, up to the tip of the ear—in the other direction, it followed along the neck, chest, and down the leg.

Sham maintained his three lengths at three-quarter miles. Radnor meanwhile increased his lead to three lengths over the third place horse, now Water Wheel. Heliodoro Gustines had worked Pleasant Brook throughout the race from eighth, seventh, sixth, and was now running fourth.

Radnor moved inside Sham along the rail, but Sham increased his lead. He ran four lengths in front in the stretch.

Sham began to ease his effort with a half furlong to go, but Jorge Velasquez allowed no laziness, alternating the whip between his left and right hand. Sham increased his lead to six lengths when Velasquez allowed the colt to relax over the final 70 yards to the wire. "He won…," Pancho Martin struggled for the right word to describe the victory, "easy."

Water Wheel rallied to take second place, while Pleasant Brook with Heliodoro Gustines had taken the stretch wide and faded to finish seventh. Woody Stephens' Dr. Penny, after showing early speed near the rail, was through after a half mile and dropped to last place.

Though Sham kept well off the rail throughout the race, the change of equipment might have prevented further drifting. Jorge Velasquez later commented on Sham's former, errant running style, saying, "He was straightened out when I rode him."

The muddy track surface might not have been ideal, but Sham was up to the task, handling the terrain to earn his first victory in four attempts.

## Chapter 8
# Sham's New Stable

*An expert in caring for bad-legged animals,
an adroit wheeler-dealer with claiming horses.*
—Andrew Beyer, *Daily Racing Form* on Pancho Martin

A self-described "school dropout at the age of 14," Sigmund Sommer left Manhattan Beach High School in Brooklyn to work for the construction company his father, Jacob, had founded in 1885. By the late 1930s, Sigmund Sommer was building small apartment houses in Brooklyn. Along with his brother Abraham, Sommer built approximately 15,000 single-family homes in New Jersey and Maryland. He also developed commercial and residential properties in Manhattan and Long Island.

A successful business didn't keep Sommer from his other long-time interest, however. He once admitted that in his early days in construction he kept one eye on blueprints and contracts and the other on post-time for the first race at the old track in Jamaica, New York.

"I really can't remember when I wasn't a horse player," he said. "I always hoped that some day I could have a few horses of my own. There was work to be done, though," he noted, "many problems, depressions, highs and lows, and other factors." Sommer admitted, "It took a while because the money had to be made first."

A kind, soft-spoken man, stoutly built, with more than a passing resemblance to film director Alfred Hitchcock, Sommer was known to treat a track associate short on his funds to a steak after a visit to his box or to his table in the dining room. For years, he and a roundtable of friends, including Woody Stephens, would meet at the track where, as the *Daily Racing Form*'s Herb Goldstein described, "All facets of racing were discussed and debated, agreement never being reached on any subject."

Sommer acquired his first horse in 1964, the inappropriately named Really Swift, about whom Joe Trimble reported in the *Daily News*, "Couldn't run a lick." Sommer's first winner was at Aqueduct with Dodgertown.

Sommer also acquired the services of Frank "Pancho" Martin in 1964. What interested Sommer in the trainer was something that tends to make a horse owner angry. Martin claimed a horse named Traffic Whirl from Sommer and won several races with him at a higher class. After Martin took possession, "the horse didn't do anything but win," Sommer reported. "He either doubled or tripled his claiming value… making a big profit for his owner," Sommer said. "I decided he was my kind of man and my kind of operation."

A true fan of the sport, Sigmund Sommer wasn't concerned only in winning stakes races for big money. He also maintained a stable of claimers. He welcomed challenges from other owners and wasn't averse to stirring things up at the track. He told Martin to claim any horse he thought would help the Sommer stable, regardless of its owner or trainer. Sommer believed a claiming duel with another owner, a battle of taking and re-taking horses between them, would build interest among race fans.

Sommer's strength was claiming horses. About his *modus operandi* of claiming rather than breeding, he commented, "I have the best breeding establishments: Aqueduct, Saratoga and Belmont Park. It's like dealing in a supermarket." Sommer did, however, recognize the contributions made by the sport's prominent breeders. "The Phippses, Bradys, Mellons—they really make all this possible," he said. "There'd be no racing if it weren't for the big old families. They keep the bloodlines going with glamour horses so that every once in a while a fellow like me can come in with a fluke."

Sommer was a sportsman first, uninterested in making money from horse racing. "My husband was in it for the fun," Viola Sommer said in later years. "He liked to see them run, that's why we had so many horses. He always said that [horse racing] was not his business."

Pancho Martin told a similar story. "He didn't wanna be in building and horse training. He don't believe in that," Martin said. "This is one owner he don't interfere. He let you do what you think was right."

Francisco Martin grew up in Marianao, Cuba, a suburb of Havana, two blocks from the city's famous Oriental Park. "My mother wouldn't let me ride or go around the track," he recalled. But since he was nine years old, the policeman's son had been sneaking out of the house to the racetrack grounds to watch the morning workouts and stay for the races. "I jumped over the fence and a Pinkerton would grab me by the ear and throw me out," he said. "A few minutes later, I jump over the fence again." By age ten, Martin was an Oriental Park regular.

"When I was growing up... young fellows looking ahead to the future could do only two things," Pancho Martin said. "They could play baseball or go to work at Oriental Park. I was a lousy ball player so I wound up with the horses."

He started work at the stables, cleaning up and, as he put it, "getting smart." He had aspired to be a jockey, a goal his weight denied. By age 19, Martin had become a trainer. It was a considerable step up for the boy who was paid to jump on the barns' tin roofs in order to shake the scorpions from their hiding places.

Martin ventured to the American Midwest, beginning with the small Ohio racing circuit in 1947. He started at Ascot Park as an owner and trainer but wouldn't win his first race until later that year at Randall Park. In 1950 and 1951, Martin was among the leading trainers in New England. He spent time at Suffolk Downs in Massachusetts and Lincoln Downs in Rhode Island. With growing success, Martin headed to New York in 1951. He began with a modest stable of low-priced horses.

"I took horses that other trainers didn't want," Martin said. Of their transformation, he explained, "You have to study them, find out what's wrong, and make them over into winners."

Martin's break came in 1958, when he picked up Manassa Mauler for $12,500 with owner Emil Dolce. He got the colt, named after ex-heavyweight boxing champion Jack Dempsey, in a claiming race. Manassa Mauler earned over $300,000 in his career, with victories that included the Wood Memorial at Aqueduct in 1959 against the incredibly long odds of 64 to 1.

Content to watch the races at Aqueduct from a bar in the clubhouse, Martin avoided the fashionable box seats and the company of other notable New York trainers. Considered something of a loner, Martin remained respectful of his fellow New York trainers, whom he called "the best."

He explained the reasoning behind his isolation: "When you live by the sword you've got to be prepared to die by it. You see, basically we have developed our stable through claiming.

"And when you claim a trainer's horse you can't expect him to be too happy or friendly. Their horses are their bread and butter, and when they lose them, many of their owners won't allow them to claim back or replace them."

The nickname "Pancho" came from the Mexican revolutionary Pancho Villa. Pancho Martin employed a loyal, predominantly Spanish-speaking crew. Along with a solid build and gruff voice, he possessed a fiery reputation. He could be moody, impulsive, defiant, or cocky, if his confidence in a runner justified it. Trainer George Handy once said of Martin, "Pancho can be just talking to you, and you think he's shouting. I heard him the other day in the barn, and it sounded like he must be beating up his help, but he was just talking."

When asked of his racing philosophy, Martin once replied, "My philosophy? Mind my own business. This is my first philosophy."

He did offer a philosophy, of sorts, perhaps combined with strategy. "If I had to give a reason why some of my horses win," he said, "I'd point out two things. I try to give them the best care possible and I make sure not to place them over their heads."

He could also be courteous and accessible to racing fans, taking a moment to answer a question or to talk about racing. Though his interest might seemingly wander during discourse, he was keeping one eye on his visitor, the other on a horse being led by one of his men. He didn't lose sight of his first responsibility, suddenly barking an order in Spanish to his man before returning to the topic of conversation.

At times Martin betrayed his tough demeanor while giving a rub on the nose or a pat on the neck to one of his horses. "I have feelings for all my horses," he said. "They don't have to be champions."

Viola Sommer described Pancho Martin as a man not afraid to trust his judgment. "A very fine horseman, who actually identified the horses' ailments," she said. "He felt very close to them. … There were times when he was not satisfied with a vet's diagnosis and would have two or three vets do the same horse. … He was very well informed with horse ailments and physical attributes."

"I tell the veterinarians what's wrong with my horses," Martin was known to say.

Recalling the humble beginnings of his partnership with Sigmund Sommer, Pancho Martin said, "We didn't have much in the way of stock." But that wouldn't always be the case. "I've been very lucky in claiming horses that have developed into stakes winners," Martin said. But in considering a prospect's potential, he explained, "I have to get a 'feeling' about a horse before I even look at his record."

At a Saratoga yearling sale, Sommer once paid the top price for a horse without consulting his trainer. Shortly after, Sommer anticipated Martin's reaction.

"Pancho will scream curses at me in Spanish that I don't understand and tell me he never looked at the horse."

Martin and Sommer won their first stakes races together in 1967 with Darlin Phyllis in the Southern Belles Handicap and with El Bonito in the Tropical Park Handicap. Martin became one of America's winningest trainers after joining Sommer. He saddled 131 winners in 1971, with earnings of over $1 million. In 1972, Martin won 100 races, with earnings again over $1 million.

"Our relationship is as good as anybody can have it," Martin said of his employer. "We discuss all matters pertaining to the stable, the claiming and buying of horses, in fine detail."

"We are a great combination," Sommer said, demonstrating a mutual respect. "I never criticize him. Pancho took over my stable when all I had was four cripples, and he has made us champions."

But Sommer and Martin's horse luck wasn't always good. In December of 1971, Sommer's stakes-winning horse Never Bow was being shipped from New York's John F. Kennedy Airport to Ireland for stud duty. The horse became frightened while being raised on a platform next to the cargo plane on which he was to be loaded. He bolted and fell, shattering his left shoulder. Never Bow died as a result of his injuries, having to be euthanized in what Tad Legere recalled as "the most distressing, accidental death of the fine horse."

Success came with Sommer's purchase of Autobiography in 1971. The horse was injury prone and considered by some to be a cripple. Pancho Martin got him healthy enough to win his first stakes race that same year, the Discovery Handicap.

"I doubt that Autobiography has spent a day of being completely sound since he was foaled," Martin once said. Refusing to take all the credit, Martin added, "A compensating factor is that he is all courage and heart. He sometimes gives magnificent performances when he should be in bed."

Autobiography added four more stakes victories in 1972, including the Jockey Club Gold Cup and was voted the year's Champion Handicap horse. But on February 19, 1973 came the disastrous San Luis Obispo Handicap at Santa Anita. The race had been moved from the turf to the dirt track due to heavy rains. Running third, with approximately a half mile to go, Autobiography broke down and threw his jockey, Eddie Belmonte, to the track, knocking him unconscious. Further up the track, another horse, Tuqui II crashed to the dirt after tossing jockey, Alvaro Pineda. Yvetot, close behind him, staggered, throwing jockey Frank Olivares.

Autobiography sprinted off wildly, likely causing more damage to the initial injury. Yvetot avoided serious injury, but Autobiography and Tuqui II both broke a left foreleg and had to be euthanized. Belmonte fractured a right cheek bone, in addition to other minor injuries, and was unable to ride for 18 days.

The Sommers learned of Autobiography's death like any other race fan, by reading the morning newspaper. The night before they had heard only the name of the first three finishers and that Autobiography had finished out of the money.

"The next morning, I picked up the paper and was stunned," Viola Sommer said. "Frank was so shaken that he didn't have the heart to call us late that preceding evening."

Tad Legere described the Sommers' misfortune in attempting to breed horses. "They had entered the breeding end of racing and, I might say, with some reluctance, mainly for the sake of a horse who had won stakes for them, a horse named El Bonito," she said. "It was purely a sentimental gesture with no ideas of monetary reward.

"Well, [in 1970] El Bonito's first crop… included a colt named Dust the Plate. … The colt had won his first two races and Sig and Viola were elated. It seemed that they were about to become the breeders of a stakes winner, a colt with a future. The colt finished second the next time, but against better company than those he beat in his first two.

"Then, in mid-July [of 1972], Dust the Plate, it seemed was about ready to beat the best… and he was on his way to victory in a race when I saw him bobble. His leg snapped and they had to haul him away. Humanely, they put the colt to sleep."

The misfortune continued. In October of 1972, the German-bred, stakes-winning horse Hitchcock, who had been voted German Horse of the Year in 1969 and had a promising future at stud, suffered a ruptured coronary blood vessel and died while training at Belmont Park.

Up to the challenge of racing fortunes, Sommer declared, "I guess this game… yes, I will call it a game… is perhaps the greatest testing lab of 'em all."

As a full partner to her husband in the racing stable, Viola Sommer took more than a passing interest in the game. Acknowledged by Mr. Sommer as a perceptive student of breeding with an understanding of quality horses in the United States and abroad, Viola Sommer stood in the foreground regarding the operation and decision-making at the Sommer stable. With a fond smile she could recall a horse she had owned years earlier and describe its traits and qualities.

"Viola loves her horses with a passion," Tad Legere said.

Viola Sommer kept a photograph of Sham taken at the Hancock auction at Belmont Park. Standing in the picture with Sham is Tad Legere. Mrs. Sommer said her husband felt it was a "chance of a lifetime" to get a horse of his caliber. She praised his breeding, possessing a "million years of skill" from Bull Hancock.

The Sommers went to the stables at least once a week to visit Sham, usually on Sunday mornings. Mrs. Sommer described him as a gentle horse with no mean characteristics.

"[He] took a nap every day after lunch," she recalled years later. "He would lie down," she said, illustrating the position of his legs with her arms stuck out in front of her. "Most horses don't lie down. They sort of snooze standing up. But he used to lie down and snore."

Unlike some of his long-ago relatives who shared a stable

with a cat or rabbit, Sham needed no pets to help calm him. "Frank Martin never really liked a horse to have a companion unless it was absolutely necessary to keep him quiet," Mrs. Sommer explained. "But he was such a nice, quiet horse he didn't really need any company, I don't think."

Pancho Martin concurred, noting the lack of aggression in Sham's personality and calling him the most relaxed colt he'd ever been around. "He rarely misses his siesta after he has eaten and things begin to settle down under the shedrow," Martin said.

Sham's two-year-old season had come to an end with his first win on December 9. Pancho Martin sent him to California for the winter. Some Martin horses were sent back East for stakes races, but Sham remained in California for a while. Jorge Velasquez did not accompany Sham to California. Instead, he went to ride out the winter in Florida.

"I know he was a nice horse, you know," Jorge Velasquez reflected years later, "potential for the Triple Crown races. But let's face it, I didn't know how nice he was gonna be."

## Chapter 9

## Go West, Young Horse

*For most men (till by losing rendered sager)*
*Will back their own opinions by a wager.*
—Lord Byron

For the opening of the 1973 season, Sham made his residence at the barns of Santa Anita Park with its spectacular view of the San Gabriel Mountains peeking through dangling palm leaves. Tucked in the residential neighborhood of Arcadia, Santa Anita provided the relaxed atmosphere of a Mediterranean villa 14 miles northeast of downtown Los Angeles. A life-sized bronze statue of Seabiscuit graced the grounds, standing regally between the palms and box hedges. Art deco architecture, perennial blooms, and ornamental gardens all contributed to an overall scene that surrounded the racetrack in a Southern California paradise. The

El Camino Real grass course, designed in incomparable European style, descended a hill at the base of the mountains.

Santa Anita Park had opened on Christmas Day, 1934, a gift to the sport of horse racing. A long-time favorite of the Hollywood set, the track was featured in the Marx Brothers' *A Day at the Races* and Shirley Temple's *The Story of Seabiscuit*. As head shots for stars of the screen were common in Hollywood, the same was true for Santa Anita horses. In 1935, the track was the first to use the photo-finish.

Back in its early days, local horse owners included a who's who of the entertainment industry. Bing Crosby, George Raft, Spencer Tracy, Errol Flynn, Al Jolson, Louis B. Mayer, Harry M. Warner, and Darryl F. Zanuck all owned horses. It wasn't unusual to see race fans such as Frank Capra, Fred Astaire, Jack Benny, Walt Disney, or Cecil B. de Mille in their private boxes.

The 1973 calendar was still on its first page when Sham was made ready for his close-up with California race fans. He ran in a New Year's Day contest at Santa Anita. In a mile-and-one-sixteenth race, Sham would be asked to stretch his stamina an extra half furlong. His longest previous race had been one mile. The 1 to 2 odds made him the favorite; his smart six-furlong work in 1:12 on December 27 over the Santa Anita surface no doubt influenced the betting.

Sham, with jockey Laffit Pincay aboard, broke from the gate last in the seven-horse field. Sham moved along the rail early and by the quarter mile worked his way to fifth place. By the half mile Sham still ran fifth, but the distance between the field of horses tightened. The first five horses crowded together, separated by less than two lengths. By the time they cleared three-quarter miles, Sham moved to fourth, however, he trailed the leader by only a little over a length. From the first to fourth positions, the field could scarcely close a tighter grip.

Rallying wide into the stretch, Sham shot to the front with gigantic strides, a whopping eight lengths ahead of a chestnut colt named Quantum Jump, in second place.

If there were any doubt of Sham's ability to go the extra half furlong it was stoutly refuted as he pulled away from the field with a remarkable win of 15 lengths. He completed the mile and one-sixteenth in 1:42, the fastest time at that distance for the season. Martin Kivel wrote in the *Pasadena Star News*, "Sham overcame trouble in the early stages of the mile and one-sixteenth to breeze to the front on the far turn and then draw away as if much the best." Kivel also noted Sham's $200,000 price tag, stating, "The son of Pretense… appeared to be worth every cent."

Sham welcomed the new year in the same manner he had sent off the previous, with a convincing victory. The January 1 contest hadn't resulted in auld acquaintance Jorge Velasquez being forgotten, but Sham had indeed made a convincing mark in his first race with new acquaintance Laffit Pincay.

Pincay continued Sham's streak of jockeys hailing from Panama. Laffit Pincay was born in the San Felipe barrio of Panama City, near the shores of the Gulf of Panama. He was the son of a prominent jockey. Originally, Pincay had wanted to be a baseball player, specifically, an infielder, but his size worked against him. Instead, he turned to the racetrack. Pincay's career in racing began at age 15 when he worked as an unpaid hot walker at the Hipodromo Presidente Remon. At age 17, he worked as a groom.

Pincay attended a local race riding school of former jockey Bolivar Moreno. Early lessons had Pincay sitting on a barrel and using cord stirrups and reins.

"The first thing I had to do was not be afraid of horses," Pincay said. "They are wild over there; very difficult."

By the age of 18, Pincay was Panama's top apprentice rider. In the waning light of the final race at the Hipodromo Presidente Remon, Pincay earned his first win as a professional on May 19, 1964 aboard a longshot named Huelen. Pincay recalled the horse didn't look like he had much of a chance, and "it was getting very, very dark."

Pincay had no helmet and had to borrow one from another rider. "It was kind of big for me," he recalled, "but I need a helmet, so I wore it." The helmet kept slipping down, covering his eyes during the race. Unable to see, Pincay tossed the helmet and found the winner's circle aboard only his second career mount.

"I was so excited," he recalled, "I didn't sleep the whole night."

On his first ride in the U.S., Pincay rode Teacher's Art to victory at Arlington Park on July 1, 1966. The racing scene was different from that of Panama, where aggressive riding and tough tactics were his style. Such tactics earned suspensions on American racetracks. After success in Chicago, Pincay moved on to California.

Pincay's athletic muscularity gave him the look of a gymnast or a boxer more so than a jockey. With thick forearms leading to powerful hands, Pincay established himself as a strong jockey, one able to control unruly horses. He could, however, relax skittish mounts as well, with ever-important gentle hands. He knew when fighting a horse would prove counter-productive.

Pincay had other tools necessary to be a great jockey. He had good balance, was adept with the whip right- or left-handed, and kept a good rhythm with his horse. He was a superb rider who possessed a keen ability to determine pace—whether it was too slow or too fast. In the heat of battle he knew the right move to make and when to make it.

In the saddle, Pincay was his own harshest critic. "Sometimes, they just don't have it and it's very disappointing," he said of his losing mounts. "You feel like you failed." But there was also the excitement of a horse full of run entering the final stretch. "Sometimes," he said, "you get here and you have so much horse left. You get cocky. You feel so good. You start to play. What a feeling."

Success followed Laffit Pincay. He won the George Woolf Memorial Jockey Award, for the jockey who best served as a credit to his profession, in 1970; the Eclipse Award as outstanding jockey in 1971; was the leading jockey in races won in 1971 with 380; second in races won in 1972 with 289; and the leading money-winning jockey in 1970, 1971 (a record high of $3,784,377), and 1972.

Within weeks of Sham's 15-length romp, Sigmund and Viola Sommer were honored at the annual Eclipse Award dinner as owners of the Champion Handicap Horse of 1972, Autobiography. NYRA chairman Alfred G. Vanderbilt presented the award to a smiling Mrs. Sommer. Sadly, less than a month later, Autobiography would be lost at the San Luis Obispo. But for the evening of January 26, 1973, accomplishments in thoroughbred racing for 1972 were celebrated at the black-tie event.

More than 1,200 attended the event, held in the Los Angeles Ballroom of the Century Plaza Hotel in Century City near Beverly Hills. Though it was a black-tie affair, women attired in gaudy patterned dresses, young men with unruly haircuts, and polyester fashion ruled the evening. It was, after all, the 70s.

Braulio Baeza, who had traveled to England to win the 1972 Epsom Derby aboard Roberto and defeated international competitors to take the Washington D.C. International aboard Droll Role, earned the award for the year's Outstanding Jockey. Laffit Pincay, Outstanding Jockey of 1971, presented the award to Baeza with a handshake from ruffled shirtsleeve cuffs in the contemporary style that overflowed the sleeves of his tuxedo.

Seventeen Eclipse Awards were presented that Friday evening, including one for the late Bull Hancock, recognized for his outstanding achievement at Claiborne Farm. Actress Greer Garson was on hand, along with her husband, E.E. "Buddy" Fogelson. The Fogelsons were winners of the Eclipse Award for top owners of 1971. Their horse Ack Ack was voted 1971's Horse of the Year and took honors as the year's Champion Handicap Horse and Champion Sprinter.

Secretariat was voted 1972's Champion Two-Year-Old as well as Horse of the Year. He had won seven of nine races, finishing out of the money only once. With slightly better luck,

Secretariat could have easily gone undefeated for the year.

Secretariat's first race, on July 4, 1972, had nearly been a disaster. He had been mauled only a few steps out of the starting gate. A rival horse, Quebec, had cut in front of one opponent and slammed practically head-on into Secretariat's shoulder, as if he had been trying to make an open-field tackle. Secretariat in turn, knocked off course and staggering, had crashed into Big Burn to his left. A horse less powerful than Secretariat might have fallen. But he had fought, pinned between Quebec and Big Burn who each had leaned into him, to regain his stride.

Later in the race, Secretariat had not only drifted and bumped a horse named Rove, but had also found himself in traffic trouble. Paul Feliciano, Secretariat's jockey, twice had had to check Secretariat's speed to avoid running into the backsides of opponents. With all that went wrong, Secretariat had still managed to come home fourth, only one and a quarter lengths behind the winner.

The only other race Secretariat didn't win as a two-year-old was one in which he actually finished first. In the Champagne Stakes at Belmont Park on October 14, 1972, Secretariat had broken the wire first, two lengths ahead of Stop the Music. But near the final three-sixteenths, four horses, Secretariat, Stop the Music, Linda's Chief, and Puntilla, had raced side by side. Shortly thereafter, in making a move, Secretariat had bumped Stop the Music, who was forced into Linda's Chief. As a result, Secretariat was disqualified by the racing stewards and placed second.

At the Eclipse Award dinner, Secretariat's trainer Lucien

Laurin, and owner and breeder the late Christopher Chenery, were also honored. Penny (Chenery) Tweedy, Secretariat's current owner, accepted on behalf of her father in a trifecta of Meadow Stable personnel.

"Dad set the standards, how the game was to be played," Penny Tweedy said upon accepting the award. "I hope we can live up to them."

## Chapter 10

## A Derby Winner in this Field?

At roughly 8 AM the track at Santa Anita was cleared for daily upkeep and watering. As they waited for the tractors and harrows to leave, trainers and exercise riders looking for work gathered near the top of the stretch where a gap in the outer rail opened up to the stables. Horses to be worked headed toward the half-mile pole along the backside. Some ran along with a stable pony, others made the trip solo. Track personnel at the gap phoned the clockers in a booth below the press box, alerting them to the horse and the distance to be run.

With the busy traffic of a working racetrack, riders waited for an open route. Horses running a light workout kept to the middle of the track, their riders standing erect or high in the stirrups with a tight grip on the reins to keep speed in check. Horses asked for speed took the inner rail with riders tucked tightly along the animal's neck and shoulders. When a clear path appeared, the horse was off, flashing from the half-mile pole around the final turn and down the home stretch to the finish line. Those who completed their work pulled off by the clubhouse turn and headed back across the grandstand toward the stable area on the outside rail. Curious riders asked, "What I do?" Clockers responded by yelling out their time.

Horses returning after a workout passed within five to ten feet of photographer Bill Mochon, who worked for the publication *Thoroughbred of California* photographing horses, track personalities, and behind the scenes for stories featured in the magazine. Mochon had seen many a thoroughbred in his time behind the lens.

Sham took the track for his workout with Laffit Pincay up. Along with Sham, other horses set to run waited to be given the cue to go. When Sham was called, he started out among a mass of horses. His ears were pinned flat against his head as he concentrated on what lay before him. Soon he was clear in front of the pack.

"He blew past the other horses on the track like an express train," Mochon said. "He went past the wire, the finish line, Laffit's feet just went forward in the stirrups instead of being straight down. He went forward like he was putting on the breaks. And the horse was really starting to gain momentum at that point." Mochon added, "When the horse pulled up, Laffit had to really apply all of his energy and strength to slow him down, and this horse was ready to go another mile."

When Pincay had at last reeled in the colt, they returned by the clubhouse turn, with Sham, hot and sweaty, blasting snorting breaths. Steam rose and vaporized off his hindquarters and from his nose.

"Sham was a standout because there was a presence about him," Mochon said. "Some horses command attention. Sham caught everyone's eye when he was on the track."

Sham trained nicely after his last win. On January 12, he worked five furlongs in :59, on January 21, he worked another five furlongs in 1:00, and a week later on January 28, he increased the workload to six furlongs, running in 1:12⅗.

February 2, 1973 was his next test, the mile and one-sixteenth Fleet Nasrullah Purse at Santa Anita. When the entries for the race were drawn, trainer Laz Barrera asked aloud in reference to the upcoming Santa Anita Derby, "Is the Derby winner in this field?"

Sham's talent was no secret to the Arcadia crowd who put enough on him to win to reduce his odds to 1 to 3 for the Fleet Nasrullah. He went off as the heavy favorite. Liz Tippet stood among the crowd.

As a winner of two races, Sham faced tougher competition. In a field of six, Table Run was the second favorite at 7 to 2. Though he had run only three times, each at a mile and one-sixteenth, he had finished third in his first race and won the next two by convincing margins of five and four lengths, respectively. He had run a brisk five furlongs in :58 in a workout at Hollywood Park on January 5.

Black Moss, a decidedly chestnut rather than black colt, was the third choice at 5 to 1. He had won his last three races while finishing second in the fourth, which he lost by only a neck.

Sham had his work cut out for him.

Untangle, who had faced Sham in his last race, Indefatigable, and Sassoon completed the field. Untangle had finished fourth against Sham in their New Year's Day match-up, but he had won a mile-and-one-sixteenth race over the same track nine days later. Indefatigable had won two of eight career starts, but hadn't won since October of 1972. Sassoon, a gray gelding, had beaten Table Run in a previous match-up, the only time Table Run had failed to win in his thus far brief career. Sassoon had also won two of his last three races.

Sham broke well at the start, in the first position, followed by Sassoon and Table Run. Black Moss often went to the front of the pack and either set the pace, or ran just off it. If he failed to do so, he usually finished poorly. He broke fourth, creating an obstacle for himself from the beginning.

Table Run took the lead soon after the break and led by a half length by the quarter mile. Indefatigable held second, one and a half lengths over Black Moss, whose troubles didn't end at the gate. Into the first turn, he was blocked along the rail and his jockey, Jorge Tejeira, was forced to pull him up sharply. Also at the turn, Laffit Pincay steadied Sham's momentum to avoid traffic trouble. He trailed two lengths behind Black Moss and four lengths behind the leader.

Sham settled on the backstretch. By the half mile he still ran fourth, though he lost a little ground and trailed the leader by four and a half lengths. He seemed relaxed, however, and appeared to be in no rush to leave the backstretch.

By the three-quarter-mile mark Sham overtook Black Moss

at third. Table Run and Indefatigable still held their positions at first and second, respectively. Pincay signaled through his hands for Sham to move.

As horse and rider near the finish, the jockey will work the reins as if using a throttle. He eases his grip to give his mount just the right amount of slack, slightly releasing the tension to shift his horse to a higher gear. For a skilled jockey, the key is gentle hands—it's in his touch. There's an unspoken communication between a jockey and his horse. The slightest signal can speak volumes, regardless of who sends the message. The sudden movement of the horse's ear, for example, might foretell the approach of a closing rival. And a skilled jockey can feel how much horse he has left beneath him. He can determine if his horse is strong enough and willing enough to make a final charge when asked. He rates the horse's speed, whether that horse be a pacesetter, a pace stalker who prefers to tuck in behind the leader, or a closer who finishes with a strong move. There's much more to winning than going to the whip.

"There's no sense in whipping a tired horse," Hall of Fame jockey Eddie Arcaro once said, "because he'll quit on you. More horses are whipped out of the money than into it."

In the stretch, Pincay tapped Sham lightly with the whip just once. Sham needed no more urging and responded gamely to Pincay's signal. Table Run was unable to respond to the challenge by the new leader, who rallied along the outside to wear him down. Sham led by a half length. Indefatigable had forced the early pace, but by the stretch he was, contrary to his name, tired. He dropped to third. Untangle had a little spark left and wasn't through yet. He moved to fourth and was improving his position further with a good effort.

Sham increased his lead on his way to the wire. He won going away, with a six-length gap between himself and second-place Table Run, with another six lengths back to third-place Untangle. Sham won easily, accelerating, in the words of the *Daily Racing Form*, "like a Rolls Royce."

He bettered his own mark for the season's best at a mile and one-sixteenth by finishing in 1:41⅖. *The Blood-Horse* answered Laz Barrera's earlier rhetorical question, stating, "Virtually everyone who saw the Fleet Nasrullah had to feel that the eventual winner of the Santa Anita Derby *was*, indeed, in the field, and that his name is Sham."

The morning following the Fleet Nasrullah, Pancho Martin confirmed his colt was ready to run his first stakes race, the Santa Catalina Stakes to be run on February 12. The Santa Catalina had been won two years earlier by Unconscious, who had set a record for the race, running the mile and one-sixteenth in 1:41⅘. Sham's performance in the Fleet Nasrullah beat that time by two-fifths of a second.

While Sham was impressing handicappers, trainers, and turf writers on the West Coast, the colt expected to dominate the East hadn't yet raced in 1973. Secretariat was training in Florida where owner Penny (Chenery) Tweedy ran her horses for the winter, but he hadn't competed since earning the Horse of the Year award for 1972.

Pancho Martin had seen Secretariat as a two-year-old, and

had commented, "I've never seen a more perfectly balanced colt, so large and with such a perfect way of going. He could become one of the truly great ones."

Secretariat had a habit of scaring off opponents and reducing fields, which Martin knew first-hand. Before the Belmont Futurity on September 16, 1972, the field was immediately reduced from ten horses to six following a Secretariat five-furlong workout in :58. Martin scratched his colt, Master Achiever, from the race, commenting, "I took my horse out. I was afraid he might get in Secretariat's way when he starts that move."

Though Secretariat hadn't raced in the new year, he trained at Hialeah Park, which included fine works at five furlongs in :58⅗ on February 7 and six furlongs in 1:11⅖ on February 12. It was neither lack of conditioning nor injury that kept the big red colt from competing, but financial considerations regarding Penny Tweedy's Meadow Farm.

Problems with settling the estate of her late father (Christopher Chenery), and taxes, put Penny Tweedy in a dire situation. For those unwilling to suspend the disbelief of a B-movie script, a horse really can "save the farm." Riva Ridge was the horse who literally did just that with earnings from his Kentucky Derby and Belmont Stakes victories in 1972. But the following year, assets had to be liquidated. Options included selling off racing stock (as Arthur and Seth Hancock were forced to do at Claiborne Farm), selling the Meadow Farm broodmares, or selling part, if not all, of the farm itself. The sale of Riva Ridge and Secretariat was another possibility, albeit a last resort.

John Finney of the Fasig-Tipton auction house was hired as

a consultant. Fasig-Tipton had handled the arrangements of the Bull Hancock dispersal sale. Finney suggested syndicating Secretariat for breeding as a two-year-old, before his three-year-old season, in order to take advantage of his pedigree and Horse of the Year status. Acting sooner rather than later also made sense to avoid the potential risk of Secretariat failing to win as a three-year-old, thus dropping his value. Penny Tweedy contacted Seth Hancock for the job.

The Hancock family had long been involved in syndicating top stallion prospects. When cost made acquiring a horse impractical, Arthur Boyd Hancock Sr. had the idea to ask friends to share in the cost and formed the predecessor of the modern syndicate.

Both Mrs. Tweedy and Seth Hancock agreed Secretariat would not race until the syndication deal was completed. Hancock put together a deal that sold all shares, with a price tag of $190,000 each, within four days. The original price per share had been $200,000, but Mrs. Tweedy wanted to race Secretariat as a three-year-old. "So the bargain-basement price of $190,000 was predicated on letting us race him at three," she said. In 1973, the average cost of a new house was $32,500.

The record total of $6,080,000 was raised by the sale of 32 shares. A share entitled a shareholder to send one mare a year to Secretariat for the duration of his stud career. At roughly $325 an ounce, the 1,154-pound Secretariat was worth more than three times his weight in gold, which sold for a mere $90 an ounce. The completion of the syndication deal was announced on February 26, 1973.

Secretariat was the living embodiment of hybrid vigor championed by Bull Hancock. He was one of the most outcrossed representatives of his generation. No name in his pedigree was repeated within his first five generations, a pedigree that included 22 *chefs-de-race* going back to 1900. Secretariat's breeding was a balance of speed and stamina. He was also a Nearco colt.

Nearco was an undefeated champion two- and three-year-old in Italy who was famous throughout Europe. He was a Grand Prix de Paris and Derby Italiano winner and the leading sire in England in 1947, 1948, and 1949.

Nearco was from the Dormello-Olgiata Stud of the colorful Italian breeder Federico Tesio. Tesio claimed to have picked up his talent with horses while in Patagonia, where he learned about "listening to the stars and speaking to the horse." As a boy, Tesio was interested in astronomy, with a later interest in the occult, giving his breeding formulas a mystical air. He left those interested in his policies with the impression he was "up to his ears in genetic theories," according to the German publication *Der Spiegel*. He believed in a sort of "'blood alchemy'—an intuitive selection of blood lines, which was more witchcraft than science," according to W. Georg Isaak in *The Thoroughbred Record*.

Tesio sought lung capacity, soundness of heart, and courage in a horse. "A horse gallops on lung, sustains its speed on heart, but wins on character," he said.

According to Tesio, the superior runner possessed the two basic qualities of speed and control (the ability to conserve speed for the required distance). Theoretically, this would leave a horse with resources in reserve for the finish of a race and an ability to produce an instantaneous acceleration when needed. This quality seemed in agreement with the "good burst of speed" Bull Hancock sought in a horse. "Timely utilization of speed means control, while absolute speed is never a guarantee of control," Tesio explained.

Considered by some an intuitive genius in the breeding of thoroughbreds, Tesio was also skilled in architecture and furniture making, an expert on Chinese ceramics, and a gifted painter. Many of his horses were named for sculptors and painters: Botticelli, Toulouse Lautrec, Tenerani, Bellini, Donatello, Rosalba Carriera, were only a few of his horses so named. But Nearco was Tesio's masterpiece. As if the horse himself were a work of art in bronze or marble, Tesio described Nearco as "*proportionatissimo*," meaning perfectly proportioned.

Nearco had been a small foal, but soon he demonstrated his character and strength in dominating other colts in the paddocks. He had shown blinding speed in training and had won all seven of his races as a two-year-old. Nearco ran seven more races the following year, again winning them all, including the Gran Premio di Milano. In winning the Grand Prix de Paris, he defeated two Derby-winning horses, Bois Roussel, winner of the Epsom Derby, and Cillas, winner of the French Derby.

"What I wanted," Bull Hancock once confessed, "was a Nearco stallion." By 1951, Bull got one. He acquired the Irish horse Nasrullah, one of Nearco's offspring, to stand at stud. Nasrullah had been a champion two-year-old in England and winner of the Champion Stakes and Coventry Stakes. He had been a leading sire in the British Isles.

Nasrullah had been an accomplished middle-distance racer

who might have been even better had the restrictions on racing during the Second World War not limited his training and racing to Newmarket, England. Newmarket, situated on the Suffolk side of the Cambridgeshire border, had been the headquarters of British racing since the days of Charles II in the 1660s, but that was apparently of little interest to Nasrullah. The boredom resulting from his confinement tested his volatile nature. He was a stubborn racer, with a reputation for refusing to gallop if the mood didn't strike him. He usually cooperated, however, when an umbrella was opened behind him. The odd routine, as writer Mary Jane Gallaher described it, "would send the big bay off as if the devil were on his heels."

During the stallion's stud career, Bull Hancock had been forced to confront Nasrullah's ornery spirit. An unruly stallion can cause a farm employee or a broodmare serious injury or worse. On an occasion when Nasrullah had gotten out of control in the breeding shed, Bull had grabbed a nearby broom to set him straight with a beating. After the incident, Nasrullah would lay his ears back like an angry tomcat whenever he saw Bull, but the horse no longer caused any serious trouble.

Nasrullah had sired 1955 Horse of the Year Nashua, who had narrowly missed winning the 1955 Triple Crown by finishing second in the Kentucky Derby. Nasrullah had also sired 1957 Horse of the Year Bold Ruler—Secretariat's sire.

There was a belief among breeders that certain bloodlines worked particularly well in combination with others. It was desirable to cross certain sires with broodmares sired by another particular stallion when repeated success was demonstrated.

Such a cross was known as a "nick." The Nasrullah-Princequillo nick was found in winning pedigrees in America and Europe. Princequillo's broodmares complemented the bloodline of Nasrullah and his sons. Princequillo contributed stamina, durability, and even temperament, while the Nasrullahs were usually speedy but lacked soundness and could possess difficult attitudes. Secretariat was a product of the Nasrullah-Princequillo nick.

In 1951, Christopher Chenery had sent his mare Imperatice to be bred with Princequillo. She gave birth to a filly foal in 1952. The filly, Somethingroyal, would be one of only two foals ever produced by Imperatice to finish unplaced over the course of a career, though Somethingroyal ran only one race before being retired. Despite the inauspicious credential, Somethingroyal would be Imperatice's most influential offspring. At age 17, Somethingroyal was bred with Bold Ruler. At age 18, she gave birth to Secretariat on March 29, 1970.

Secretariat had a cousin who also possessed a fine pedigree. Their dams were half sisters by the same sire. Secretariat was out of Somethingroyal (by Princequillo), and his cousin was out of Sequoia (by Princequillo). Secretariat's cousin was Sham.

Secretariat, if he were to make his mark in the East, would have only one season to prove himself before retiring to stud duty. In working seven furlongs in 1:23⅖ on February 28 and finishing a mile in a gallop in 1:35⅘, Secretariat prompted trainer Lucien Laurin to say, "I knew right then he was one of the greatest horses I ever saw."

## Chapter 11

## Best Ever Three-Year-Old

The 1973 season at Santa Anita had begun as a wet one. Halfway through the season, 20 of 37 racing days had been run under less than favorable conditions and over what had been considered "off" tracks. Nearly 20 inches of rain had fallen. Three-quarters of the way through the meet, rainfall was three times the normal amount for Southern California.

Three-year-olds were already being asked to stretch themselves and increase their running distances as they matured. Wet, heavy track conditions wouldn't help their performances. Feature races were being run in cold rains and slop. The 75-day meet would prove to be Santa Anita Park's most rain-filled season ever. Sham had been lucky thus far in that both of his races had been on dry, fast tracks.

Sham and 11 other horses were nominated for the Santa

Catalina Stakes, a mile-and-one-sixteenth event. Four of the nominees, Double Variety, Indefatigable, Master Achiever, and Table Run had faced Sham before. He had defeated them all in different races with little trouble. Double Variety had finished 15 lengths behind Sham in their previous meeting. Indefatigable had watched from 12½ lengths behind, and Table Run finished six lengths behind. Master Achiever had come the closest, losing out by one length, and he was a Sigmund Sommer-owned, Pancho Martin-trained colt who had faced Sham when he was still with Claiborne Farm. The *Daily Racing Form* predicted Sham's presence would limit the number of challengers for the Santa Catalina. On February 12, only five of the original 12 nominees showed up. Perhaps to the disappointment of rival owners and trainers, Sham was one of the five.

Presidents' Day of 1973 marked the 35th running of the Santa Catalina Stakes. Muddy track conditions produced after weeklong showers didn't concern Pancho Martin. His colt had won in the mud at Aqueduct. "He can handle any kind of footing," Martin assured. Sham had worked a sharp four furlongs in :47⅖ on February 9 on a sloppy track.

Liz Tippet made it out for the race under cloudy Arcadia skies. She endured the damp, cold elements in a white wrap and a scarf in the light purple that represented her Llangollen Farm. In the paddock, Martin prepared Sham while she looked on. She nodded approvingly as groom Secundino Gato marched Sham in a turn of the saddling area before Gato led him through the mud to the walking ring.

"He has the same size as Pretense had as a three-year-old,"

Mrs. Tippett determined. Bull Hancock had insisted she come to Saratoga to see Sham the previous summer. "Bull loved this colt," she said.

Mrs. Tippet wasn't Sham's only admirer present. An onlooker asked Pancho Martin if Sham was the best three-year-old he had ever trained.

"At the moment, yes," he answered. "But let him tie into some race horses before we say too much about him."

Laffit Pincay met with Pancho Martin, and they exchanged a few words in Spanish. No great details were discussed. The crowd made Sham the favorite, off at ridiculously low odds of 1 to 10. A quick look around the stalls and saddling area revealed none of Sham's previous challengers, Double Variety, Indefatigable, Table Run, or Master Achiever, were entered. Those willing to give it a go against Sham included Out of the East, a California-bred bay colt. Out of the East had a propensity to stalk the pace and close with a strong finish. He was the crowd's second choice, off at odds near 7 to 1. Portentous, a dark bay/brown colt, was another challenger. He was off to a good three-year-old campaign. In three starts, he had won twice and finished second. All three races were at a mile and one-sixteenth. He was also off at odds of 7 to 1.

After only two races at Santa Anita, Pat Rogerson of the *Daily Racing Form* called Sham "one of the most exciting three-year-olds to perform here this season." An inspired Rogerson also wrote, "If Sham does not win the Santa Catalina it will be viewed as an upset of major proportions."

But Rogerson couldn't have foreseen the trouble ahead.

When he made his prediction, he could have no way of knowing Laffit Pincay would be thrown from an earlier mount after the third race while returning to the unsaddling area. The horse, Rebel Promise, after hanging wide in the stretch for a third-place finish, had reared up and dumped Pincay to the mud. Pincay had lain on the ground for a few moments, stunned, before getting up under his own power. Rogerson also didn't know what Sham would face in his opening strides out of the gate.

At the start of the Santa Catalina a gelding named River Lad took an outward bearing path, knocking Sham off-stride and causing him to bobble. Sham was bounced back and forth between River Lad and Portentous for the first 50 yards before getting clear. Leon Rasmussen of *The Thoroughbred Record* later wrote, "Sham broke like the world's unluckiest man had bet on him."

"I tried to hustle Sham away to avoid chances of being cut down in close quarters," Pincay later said, and the jockey kept his colt to task. Sham recovered by the first turn to get close to the leaders while clear off the rail.

By the quarter mile River Lad took the lead by a head over a chestnut colt named Scantling. Sham moved to third, two lengths behind. By the half mile Scantling overtook River Lad for the lead. Sham still ran third.

While Sham trailed Scantling and River Lad, Out of the East moved up alongside and trapped Sham in a pocket. Sham got blocked between horses and pinched back by an immovable barrier. At three-quarters of a mile Scantling still held the lead, but Out of the East was making a move running wide, having escaped early traffic. He took River Lad for second. River Lad ran third over Portentous in fourth place. Sham dropped to last. An "upset of major proportions" appeared to be in the making.

"Around the turn, I had nowhere to go," Pincay said later, "but felt that if I could find racing room I'd have plenty enough horse to win."

Into the stretch Pincay finally saw an opportunity and moved Sham inside to exploit an opening. Sham responded to the jockey's whip. "I hit him five times—two right-handed and three left-handed," Pincay said. "When he got clear he just took off."

Sham moved back into third place, two lengths off the pace with Scantling still holding with a narrow gap of a half length over Out of the East in second.

Out of the East continued to fight into the final stretch and took Scantling for the lead. Scantling dropped to third as Out of the East and Sham rallied for the lead. Sham slashed through the mud along the rail while Out of the East took advantage of the firmer footing near the middle of the track. But he couldn't keep up with a driving Sham as he pulled away in the clear. Sham broke the wire a winner by two and a half lengths.

Ron Cooper wrote of Sham in the *Thoroughbred of California*, "The biggest surprise was not that he won the Santa Catalina (at 1-10), but that he came out with four legs and torso intact."

"If Sham had been beaten he would have had enough excuses," Laffit Pincay said.

Martin Kivel wrote Sham overcame "all sorts of trouble to win" in a "heart-throbbing contest," while the *Lexington Herald-Leader* reported, "Sham demonstrated his class and courage" during the performance.

The win was hardly a surprise to those who had visited the pari-mutuel windows with no portent of trouble and made Sham the overwhelming favorite. Two-dollar winning tickets paid a mere $2.20, a net profit of 20 cents. The payoff equaled the lowest in Santa Anita history.

Having won his first stakes race, Sham was pointed to another holiday match-up, the San Felipe Handicap on St. Patrick's Day, March 17. Secretariat flew out of Miami on March 10 headed for New York and the Bay Shore Stakes at Aqueduct, also to be run on March 17. It would be Secretariat's first race as a three-year-old.

## Chapter 12

## Pincay Chooses

*I was the underbidder at $195,000, and I own the stallion and have six Princequillo mares. Yes, you could say I felt he was worth the money Mr. Sommer gave for him.*

—Mrs. Cloyce (Liz) Tippett on Sham

On March 14, three days before Secretariat's debut as a three-year-old, the colt worked out at Belmont Park. He clocked a phenomenal :32⅗ over three furlongs, going :44⅘ for four furlongs. That turf writers expressed growing interest in thoroughbred racing's latest celebrity was no surprise, but sports commentators who hadn't previously given two hoots about the sport were now paying close attention to his workouts and reporting his racing schedule.

While Secretariat was embraced, Sham was practically ignored outside of California. Eastern turf writers, trainers, and jockeys lauded Secretariat's muscular physique, his ability to barrel through any opposition to victory. Some female admirers practically swooned as if he were the leading man in a Hollywood romance. *Vogue* magazine billed him the "Clark Gable of horses." His good looks and personality had won them over. Tall, red, and handsome, he was the complete package, "not merely," according to *Vogue* magazine's Charlotte Curtis, "the most beautiful horse in the world."

Sham fit the role of character actor. Though he stood the same height, roughly 16.2 to 16.3 hands, his sleek musculature presented a speedy appearance over brute strength. Crowds gathered around Secretariat as if every race day were an opening night. Sham, though making his residence in California, didn't attract an entourage. He was, however, respected. Kent Cochran of the *Daily Racing Form* reported Sham had been winning West Coast races with such authority, "trainers of rival horses… are beginning to shun him." Cochran quoted the sentiment of one rival horseman: "We don't want any part of Sham."

Though Secretariat was adored by the public, few if any trainers were looking to face him either. Bill Resseguet Jr., trainer of Our Native, made his position clear after his horse won the Flamingo Stakes. Resseguet indicated his plans to point the horse toward the Blue Grass Stakes and Kentucky Derby, which put him on a probable collision course with the big red colt. "No, of course I'm not looking forward to running against Secretariat," he said. "Nobody is."

Speculation arose over the future plans of rivals who had yet to meet. Sham and Secretariat would both race on Presidents' Day, but on opposite ends of the country. Sigmund Sommer announced Sham would follow the San Felipe Handicap with the Santa Anita Derby two weeks later. Then Sham was expected to go to Kentucky, where he might compete in the Blue Grass Stakes at Keeneland in Lexington on April 26 before making his appearance in Louisville for the Kentucky Derby on May 5.

After the Bay Shore Stakes, trainer Lucien Laurin planned to run Secretariat in the Gotham Stakes at Aqueduct on April 7, then the Wood Memorial, also at Aqueduct, on April 21. Laurin kept open the possibility of substituting the Wood Memorial with the Blue Grass Stakes. Either way, the Kentucky Derby followed. It looked as though Kentucky would be the battleground where Sham and Secretariat would meet, whether it was Lexington or Louisville.

The nine-horse field of the San Felipe Handicap included the toughest competition Sham faced to date. Among the competitors was Out of the East, who had rallied from early traffic to a hard-fought stretch run with Sham to finish a strong second in the Santa Catalina Stakes. Out of the East had followed with another second-place finish in his next race on February 21 at Santa Anita, then added a win at Golden Gate Fields over a sloppy track on March 3.

Another entry, Groshawk, had been a highly regarded two-year-old who claimed Man o' War in his pedigree. The copper chestnut colt had been acquired at the Widener Dispersal at Hialeah Park in March of 1972 for $120,000 by Hollywood producer Quinn Martin. During his two-year-old campaign, Groshawk had finished in the money in five of six races by winning three and finishing second in two others. The San Felipe was only his second start as a three-year-old, having finished fifth in a six-and-a-half furlong sprint at Santa Anita on February 1.

Sham would also contend with a colt named Gold Bag. He had been bred by Mrs. Lucien Laurin and sold by her husband to a new owner just months earlier in January. Gold Bag had galloped as a youngster with Secretariat. A speedy, aggressive runner, Gold Bag had often stubbornly tried to run away with his exercise riders and had on more than one occasion beaten Secretariat in workout drills. Gold Bag had won his last race, on March 10, and had finished second in his race prior to that on February 24.

A California-bred gelding named Ancient Title was another with a highly successful two-year-old season behind him. He had won five of eight starts, finishing in the money seven times. In the Sunnyslope Stakes during the Oak Tree meet at Santa Anita he had run the fastest seven furlongs in juvenile history in 1:20⅘. As a three-year-old, he had been in the money in all three of his starts with a win and two second-place finishes. The only horse to have beaten him as a three-year-old was a dark bay/brown colt named Linda's Chief.

Ancient Title had set a record time for the San Vicente Stakes with his victory and was just ⅖ of a second off the track record for seven furlongs. "He was so strong after the race that I had to yell to the outrider for help in pulling him up," jockey Fernando Toro said.

Bill Mochon called Ancient Title "a gutsy little campaigner." He was trained by Keith Stucki, who had once been an exercise rider for Seabiscuit.

Sham's biggest challenge, however, would likely come from Linda's Chief. He was owned by Albany, New York hotel and movie theater owner Neil Hellman, who had named the horse for his granddaughter. Linda's Chief was not an imposing figure while standing idle, 15 hands 3 inches with a build somewhat on the thin side, but he brought to his game what Barry H. Irwin reported in the pages of *The Thoroughbred of California* as the capability of a "cat-like burst of speed," inspiring Irwin to call him "an extraordinary racing machine."

Linda's Chief had won six of nine starts as a two-year-old, with a second- and third-place thrown in to finish in the money eight of nine times. As a three-year-old, he had won three of four starts, finishing second the only time he hadn't won. The only horse to have defeated him as a three-year-old had been Ancient Title. In Linda's Chief's last two races, he had won by comfortable margins of four and five lengths.

In the San Jacinto Stakes on March 1, Linda's Chief had run to a five-length victory, setting a track record during the one-mile event in 1:33⅘. The record-setting victory made him the second choice in the Nevada future books to win the Kentucky Derby, behind Secretariat.

In anticipation of the year's Kentucky Derby, Secretariat might have garnered more pats on the back from enamored turf writers, but Western campaigners were beginning to demand attention.

"Up until a week or two ago, horsemen and handicappers were ready to award the mint juleps to Secretariat without even running the race," Gordon Jones wrote in the *Los Angeles Herald-Examiner*. "All of a sudden, though, the notion is circulating out west that

Secretariat may not have a walkover after all come May."

While the praise was welcomed by the locals, it was somehow tempered for one hopeful by an unfortunate typographical error. Jones continued by saying, "It happens that Santa Anita Park is housing three of the swiftest and toughest young colts in memory this winter in the person of Ancient Title, Linda's Chief and Shaw." Poor Shaw.

Laffit Pincay had been Linda's Chief's regular rider in the late summer and fall of 1972, as well as in the winter months of early 1973. Later, for the Santa Anita meet, Pincay was forced to make a difficult choice between mounts for subsequent match-ups, either Linda's Chief or Sham. In the early months of 1973, Linda's Chief was running sprints, while Sham was being pointed to longer races over a mile. Questions remained regarding Linda's Chief's ability to run longer races, particularly the classic distance of a mile and a quarter. When the time came to choose, Pincay and his agent, Vince DeGregory, went with Sham.

"Vince felt Sham would be the better [Kentucky] Derby prospect," Pincay said, "and I went along with him."

"Linda's Chief is super," DeGregory, said, "but the first time we rode Sham we knew he was our Derby horse."

With Pincay's decision to ride Sham, Linda's Chief would be piloted by Braulio Baeza in the San Felipe Handicap. With Pincay absent, Baeza was definitely more than a consolation prize for Linda's Chief. Baeza had ridden him in his first five career starts, winning four, finishing second in the other.

Sham suffered mediocre workouts in March, six furlongs in 1:14 on March 1 and one mile in 1:40⅗ on March 9, before blowing out four furlongs on March 14 in a fantastic :45 ⅕ under the close watch of Pancho Martin. Sham was made the second favorite at 6 to 5 in the San Felipe Handicap, just behind Linda's Chief at even money.

When the starting gate opened, Ancient Title, with mane and tail elaborately braided in purple pom-poms, broke alertly to the lead. The dangerous Linda's Chief was fourth. Sham ran in the seventh position.

At the quarter mile Ancient Title led by a length over Mug Punter with Linda's Chief third. Along the rail into the first turn Sham got in too close to the pack. Lacking room, Pincay drew up Sham to avoid the heels of another horse. Sham ran sixth.

By the half mile Ancient Title seemed to be cruising in the lead with little urging by jockey Fernando Toro. Linda's Chief moved into second place two lengths behind the leader with Gold Bag in third. Sham held his sixth-place position, but even that was in jeopardy as Groshawk moved to within a head of Sham.

Linda's Chief prompted the pace set by Ancient Title while stalking the leader. At the three-quarter-mile mark, Linda's Chief closed the gap between himself and Ancient Title to a length. Gold Bag was still third, only a half length behind Linda's Chief. Groshawk now ran fourth. Sham lingered in the sixth position.

By the stretch the stalking game was over, and Linda's Chief made a move that put him in the lead. He ran a half length ahead of Ancient Title. Groshawk continued to rally and took third, while Out of the East was just beginning to be reckoned with, moving into fourth place heading into the stretch. Sham was making little progress, but began to make a move into the stretch. He got caught in traffic though, into the far turn. Pincay steered him to the inside.

Midway down the stretch Sham faced a barrier of horses. Groshawk came in and a colt named Aljamin drifted out, leaving Sham no room to move. Pincay was forced to check Sham sharply, leaving him unable to threaten the leaders.

Ancient Title couldn't keep up with Linda's Chief, who needed little urging other than a hand ride by Braulio Baeza down the final stretch. Baeza's smooth piloting guided him to draw out to victory by three lengths. "When I asked him for his run, he had it," Baeza said.

Ancient Title was second, while Out of the East finished strongly, charging wide after gaining his full stride, to take third place. Sham battled his obstacles well enough to finish fourth, but the result was still a disappointment.

While Sham was unsaddled and marched back to the barns, Neil Hellman accepted the gold cup presented to the winning owner. His Linda's Chief had finished in 1:41 ⅘, the second fastest running of the San Felipe Handicap. Despite all the obstacles Sham had faced, Laffit Pincay didn't think they changed the outcome of the race, only the margin.

"We had some trouble, but I don't think we were going to beat the winner," he said. "We might have been a lot closer with a better trip. He dropped farther back on the backside than I thought he would."

Pincay admitted he might have taken the wrong approach during the race. "I think I should have taken a hold of him at the start, let him settle and then go about our business," he said. "We might have avoided a lot of trouble that way."

Sham was no longer undefeated as a three-year-old. Though he had proven his mettle in overcoming the problems he had encountered in the Santa Catalina Stakes, critics who questioned his make-up could point out the competition in that field had been limited to horses with career purse earnings under $12,500. Would Laffit Pincay come to regret his choice?

## Chapter 13
# Rival in the East, Challenge in the West

Heavy rains earlier in the day made sloppy track conditions for Secretariat's three-year-old debut. The sight of earlier races had been lost in fog along the backstretch, but the sun came back out for the seventh race, the Bay Shore Stakes.

Since his last race in November of 1972, Secretariat had grown and filled out considerably with a massive, powerful girth, height, and muscularity. Along the saddling enclosure, onlookers stood four deep and cheered for their hero. A crowd of nearly 33,000 bet Secretariat down to odds of 1 to 5. The Bay Shore Stakes offered five challengers to Secretariat in a six-horse field.

When the race was off, a colt named Torsion broke badly from the gate. He slammed into Secretariat with such force, jockey Ron Turcotte feared his horse might fall to the mud.

Secretariat regained his stride and set to rally, working his way from fifth place at the half mile. With a challenge from a roan colt named Champagne Charlie, Secretariat battled that rival, bad footing along the rail, and being boxed in by three horses near the head of the stretch. When a breach between horses briefly appeared, Secretariat barreled through like a gritty running back fighting for a first-down. He survived further contact, a brush with a colt named Impecunious in the stretch, to win by four and a half lengths. Turcotte never needed to apply the whip.

Media hype and the "Superhorse" label followed Secretariat during his workouts prior to his next race, the Gotham Stakes, to be run on April 7. Trainer Lucien Laurin and jockey Ron Turcotte planned to send Secretariat to the front, to set the pace for the race. Secretariat had been strictly a closer, a come-from-behind runner with a strong finish. The test of strategy would see if Secretariat was capable of winning with a different tactic, adding another weapon to his already full arsenal.

Sham worked out over the Santa Anita surface on March 25. He was asked for speed, and he gave it in a swift six furlongs in 1:10⅗. His next race would be the Santa Anita Derby on March 31.

After Sham's disappointing performance in the San Felipe Handicap, skeptics pointed to Linda's Chief as the new force to be reckoned with and considered him the horse to beat in the Santa Anita Derby. Sham supporters pointed out he never really had the opportunity to run in the San Felipe. Skeptics could counter with the Santa Catalina, where Sham was bumped, battered, and blocked between horses, yet still managed to win. Maybe it was the level of competition, not the obstacles, he couldn't handle.

The San Felipe was considered the most important prep race for the Santa Anita Derby. Before the race, Linda's Chief's trainer, the Brooklyn-born Bobby Frankel, had stated, "If Sham doesn't beat me in this one he'll be in real trouble in the Derby."

Sham would face Linda's Chief, Ancient Title, Groshawk, and Out of the East again in the Santa Anita Derby. Linda's Chief and Ancient Title had been considered top-notch sprinters. At a mile and one-eighth, the Santa Anita Derby was a half furlong longer than the San Felipe. The belief surrounding Groshawk was that as the distance increased, the better he'd like it. With further conditioning and extra distance added to the course, Groshawk might arise as an additional threat. Out of the East also could not be ignored, having finished with good speed and closing from as far back as eighth in the San Felipe to take third place. Considering the strong finish, perhaps the added distance would benefit him as well, giving him more room to move.

Linda's Chief had had distance limitations as a sprinter before Bobby Frankel trained the colt to cover middle-distance course races. Frankel's approach to handling his stable differed from that of Pancho Martin or Woody Stephens. Frankel, oft referred to in turf publications as "Mod" Bobby Frankel, wasted little sentiment on horses that weren't doing the job for him.

"I'll get tired of looking at a horse in my barn pretty quick if it doesn't win," he said.

Luckily for Linda's Chief, he did win.

"I've heard those stories about how the owner comes to the barn with sugar," Frankel said. "The horse lets out a whoop and the owner is thrilled because the horse recognizes him. I don't carry sugar." Frankel explained, "Thoroughbreds are trained just to run. They're not that friendly. I don't know if horses recognize people."

Frankel did admit he liked horses, though he said he didn't talk to them. "Thoroughbreds do what they're taught about running," he said of his business-like approach. "You can't teach them to say hello. They don't count, like Trigger."

Frankel confided, "I wouldn't run a horse if I knew it was going to break a leg. I don't run them to kill them. But if it comes down to running a horse that's hurting and you're going to lose him, then I'll run him. That's business."

Neither the Mod Bobby Frankel nor the Cuban expatriate Pancho Martin lacked confidence in their colts. Neither was shy about expressing it. As the race day neared, Pancho Martin warned racing fans not to go overboard for Linda's Chief.

"He had bad racing luck the last time out and will do better," Martin said about Sham. "He's a large, long-striding colt," he said, "and when he gets into traps it's sometimes difficult to get him out of them. He needs to be in the clear." Of the San Felipe result, Martin declared, "Throw it out."

"I'm not afraid of anything in the Derby," Bobby Frankel said. "I'm just hoping for a clean trip," he added, perhaps considering Sham's previous misfortunes and offering a qualifying remark.

"If we have a place to run Saturday," Martin predicted, "this colt will run by Linda's Chief."

With both Martin and Frankel enjoying past success on the New York racing circuit, their brewing rivalry wasn't calmed any by Martin's history of having claimed horses from Frankel's barn. Martin apparently felt "that's business."

Though Pat Rogerson was not one who abandoned Sham, he hardly seemed the ideal cheerleader when he began his March 31 *Daily Racing Form* column with the announcement, "For the student of performance there is no serious way to make Sham beat Linda's Chief Saturday." He went on to remind readers of the San Felipe, when Linda's Chief "left the Shamer eight lengths up the track and bloodied," before professing his partisanship for "the Shamer," whose hindquarters he said were like the archetype of a Derby horse. Copy editors might have pointed to another unfortunate typo. Was "Shamer" a nickname applied by Rogerson, with the intent being "Shammer"? Or did Rogerson mean to imply Sham had brought shame on himself by his performance? Maybe he meant to leave it to the reader.

Sigmund Sommer and Neil Hellman flew in from New York for the Santa Anita Derby. They played gin rummy together on the flight, and if the game was to be any indication of the outcome of the upcoming race, the two broke even. Sommer commented it was too bad Sham would have to beat Linda's Chief because Hellman was such a good guy.

"Sure he's a good guy," Pancho Martin said, though the sentiment didn't seem to carry over to Bobby Frankel. "But his trainer's got too big a mouth. The only way I'm gonna get him to shut it up is to beat him."

The 36th running of the Santa Anita Derby was held over a fast track beneath a blanket of clouds. Laffit Pincay entered the race with two previous victories in the event, in 1968 on Alley Fighter and in 1972 on Solar Salute. If the wins were to instill any confidence in Pincay, it was countered by the frustration of a five-day suspension levied for careless riding announced by racing stewards earlier that day. The infraction had occurred the day before, on Friday in the fifth race, but the suspension would not begin until April 4. Pincay, Santa Anita's leading rider, would be allowed to ride Sham in the Santa Anita Derby.

Bill Mochon was on duty for the featured event. In the paddock, he waited to photograph the horses led from the barn to the saddling area. He felt the tension, the confusion, the effect of nearly fifty thousand people who came to see the event. When Sham walked out, somehow, something about the colt made Mochon take notice.

"When he came out you could hear all the cameras," Mochon recalled. "You had the wire services, newspapers, magazines, and you had other photographers who were not necessarily into racing that would come out and cover this. And when they saw Sham the cameras just went going. Everybody started shooting up a lot of film."

Clicking cameras, rustling programs and racing forms, predictions and conversations among friends, shouting fans, the busy press, the impatient excitement all contributed an energy that built and took hold of the place as it did during major events. Mochon took quick shots in the paddock and headed through the tunnel onto the track. People crammed along the narrow gap on both sides at the end of the path from the tunnel to the track trying to get just a glimpse of the horses and jockeys. Security personnel ran ropes along the path to keep spectators away so the horses could pass. "And they would have a hell of a time with that because people were trying to get as close as they could to see the horse," Mochon said. "They were literally climbing on top of each other. Dads would put kids on their shoulders and women would squeeze through to the front. And that place was just packed."

Linda's Chief, as many had predicted, was the favorite. He went off at odds of 3 to 5, with Sham the second choice at 2 to 1. Bettors made Groshawk the third choice at 7 to 1. To Groshawk's advantage, the legendary Bill Shoemaker, the all-time leading jockey in wins and money won (finishing the 1972 season with 6,439 career wins and lifetime earnings of $49,250,470), was in the irons bringing his 25 years of experience.

After making his way through the tunnel, Mochon headed to the middle of the track and turned to see the post parade. Sham led the line of horses. The disheartening results of the San Felipe Handicap, the tough field of competitors in the Santa Anita Derby, the predictions from rival trainers, and all the numbers and tidbits of trivia that concerned turf writers and handicappers, none of it mattered to Sham. He marched grandly in front. It was then that Mochon defined that "something" Sham had, that air of confidence great athletes have.

"It was something about Sham that when he came out that, okay, this is his day, it's his track, and you knew it. You called it. There was something there about him. The head was up high, the ears were straight, and it made a great photo. The horse was beautiful to photograph."

Out of the East, Sham, Groshawk, Ancient Title, and Linda's Chief entered the gate according to their post-positions. In the sixth position was another bay colt from Sigmund Sommer's stable, Knightly Dawn.

A $57,000 purchase at the 1971 Saratoga yearling sale, Knightly Dawn was not considered a colt of the same caliber as Sham. Viola Sommer, however, felt the horse was "beautifully bred." His pedigree boasted both Nearco and Princequillo on the sire's side (Sir Gaylord) and British Triple Crown winner Gay Crusader on the dam's side (Breath o' Morn).

"He always tries for you," Pancho Martin said of Knightly Dawn. "And that makes you like him."

Knightly Dawn had just come from a win in a six-and-a-half-furlong sprint on March 20 with Laffit Pincay up. But for the year, Knightly Dawn had won only two of six starts, with one third-place finish. As a two-year-old, he had twice faced Secretariat and had fared poorly each time. A tenth-place and a fifth-place finish were the best he could muster in those two match-ups, though he was moved to fourth place in their second meeting when a horse was disqualified for bumping him.

In the Santa Anita Derby, Knightly Dawn was expected to go to the front to challenge the pace. He would be the center of attention before the day was over.

At the start of the race Knightly Dawn took to his task. He led Ancient Title in second and Linda's Chief in third. Sham followed in fourth. Just after the break, however, Ancient Title from gate number four broke outwardly, swerving to his right, to come at Linda's Chief from gate number five. From gate number six, Knightly Dawn also initially broke to his right. Jockey Milo Valenzuela cocked a right-handed whip and laid it to Knightly Dawn to straighten his course. Startled, Knightly

Dawn overreacted and ducked in, veering inward toward Linda's Chief as if he were preparing for a joust. Linda's Chief was expected to go to the front and prompt the pace but was blocked off. Braulio Baeza was forced to gather in the reins and ease his colt back a few strides, losing his momentum and preventing his best chance to get out front.

At the quarter mile Knightly Dawn led by a length. Ancient Title held second by two lengths over Sham, who was one and a half lengths better than Linda's Chief.

When Pincay rounded the first turn, his confidence in Sham grew. He held a good position without having yet asked his colt for an effort. "I knew then he'd be tough," Pincay later said.

He recalled his ride in the San Felipe, the trip in which Pincay said he had ridden Sham the wrong way. "Last time I hustled him going to the front turn because I wanted to be close to Linda's Chief when we hit the stretch. But I think it confused him because he's a big, long-striding horse who doesn't want to be rushed."

This time Pincay didn't hustle Sham and let him go at his own pace.

Knightly Dawn held the lead to the backstretch. But by the half mile Ancient Title had eked past him by a head. Knightly Dawn led by three lengths over his stablemate, Sham, who led Linda's Chief by two lengths.

Sham moved into second place by the three-quarter mark, one and a half lengths behind leader Ancient Title. Linda's Chief also moved up, making a bid in taking third, two and a half lengths back of Sham. Linda's Chief's hold on third was also slim, only a half-length over the rallying Groshawk. Knightly Dawn had done his job and set the early pace, but he was spent and fading.

Pincay sent Sham to the outside after Ancient Title at nearly the same instant when Baeza and Linda's Chief encountered a pocket along the inside. Sham found the better lane. With each stride he closed the gap between himself and the leader. On the far turn Sham wore down Ancient Title to take the lead.

By the stretch Knightly Dawn's brisk early pace had taken its toll on Ancient Title, who now fell to third. It would be a showdown between Sham and the second-place Linda's Chief. Linda's Chief made a move, coming out wider for racing room as Sham moved closer to the rail. Sham led by two lengths.

When Sham took the lead, he began to react to the noise of the crowd and the call of the track announcer. He pricked his ears and pulled himself up. "If he hadn't done that, he would have run even faster," Pincay said later. "I had to dig him a little then."

Pincay prompted Sham to keep his mind on business, and the colt responded. Pincay drove Sham to the wire. Braulio Baeza and Linda's Chief chased in pursuit. Despite the effort, Linda's Chief couldn't make up the difference. Sham kept a safe distance between the two and crossed the wire two and a half lengths ahead for the win.

A visibly cross Bobby Frankel stormed through the box section vowing justice. He met Braulio Baeza trackside after the horses returned to be unsaddled. Frankel was angry over Knightly Dawn's veering in toward Linda's Chief at the start, causing Baeza to check his horse. It hadn't been the first time the two horses had clashed. They had met on a sloppy Santa Anita track on January 18 in the San Miguel Stakes. Linda's Chief, ridden by Laffit

Pincay at the time, had won the race, but had raced wide on the turn after being bumped by Knightly Dawn. Frankel suspected Knightly Dawn had set a pick for Sham this time.

Baeza kept his cool while Frankel steamed, though Baeza commented, "The incident at the start probably cost me several lengths and made me ride differently."

Frankel relayed the story from Baeza. He reported Baeza had had to steady Linda's Chief after being knocked off stride. Baeza then had let him get settled before asking for a late run.

"We wanted to be laying right off Ancient Title," Frankel said, "but after that incident at the start we were way back of him."

Frankel and Baeza claimed a foul against Knightly Dawn. In front of the jockeys' quarters, Frankel slammed his fist to his hand for the benefit of head steward Harold Morrison to demonstrate what had happened to his horse.

"It was intentional. They hit my horse," Frankel said angrily. "Milo [Valenzuela] broke and then he reached down and rapped his horse right into me with his right-hand whip. Braulio Baeza said he lost all chance right then when he had to take back."

Pancho Martin hadn't seen the incident in question. "I had my glasses on Sham," he said. "I didn't see what happened to those other horses on the outside but I can tell you there was plenty of contact against my horses at the start of this meet without anything happening."

Coincidentally, the race was his first in California in which Sham didn't encounter some kind of trouble. "Sham had his best start ever this time," Martin said.

Martin refused to hear anything of the controversy being

intentional. He said Milo Valenzuela was there only to assure a realistic pace. "I told Milo to get him to the lead and then ride his own race," he said, explaining his strategy. "I thought Baeza would take back with Linda's Chief when he saw my other horse going out after Ancient Title and I told Pincay to go ahead of him with Sham."

After reviewing the race films, the stewards ruled Ancient Title had broken outward, and while Knightly Dawn had contributed to Linda's Chief being closed off, it wasn't enough to accept the foul claim. Knightly Dawn had quickly straightened his course while heading for the lead. Ancient Title had instigated most of the problem encountered by Linda's Chief.

"Braulio rode a great race," Frankel said. "If what happened to my horse had happened to Sham, I think we would have been an easy winner. I don't want to take anything away from Sham—he's a good horse—but I think my horse should have won."

Any incident that might have occurred was not caused by Sham. The winner was not penalized, and Sham's victory was official. Robert Hebert noted in the pages of *The Blood-Horse*, "There is the temptation to report that Sham made a shambles of his field in the Santa Anita Derby. The phrase is accurate, descriptive, and has the added virtue of being right to the point."

Writers were later given the opportunity to view the race on tape. Nearly obscured by the initial controversy was that Linda's Chief hadn't broken well from the gate. The ground had given way beneath him, costing him at least some of the distance Braulio Baeza had claimed he'd lost with the alleged infraction.

Sham's time of 1:47 equaled the Santa Anita Derby record set by Lucky Debonair in 1965. Sham was keeping good company. Lucky Debonair went on to win the 1965 Kentucky Derby.

Sham redeemed himself, and perhaps, silenced some critics. For the Santa Anita Derby, neither Sham nor his stablemate Knightly Dawn would have to watch the winner's cup be handed over to any owner but their own. Sigmund Sommer accepted the award from the winner's circle. Liz Tippett joined him for the ceremony.

"Sham is a beautiful colt," she said. "He's just like his daddy."

If Bobby Frankel felt the race wasn't won fairly and there was still something to be settled, Pancho Martin publicly offered him a rematch in a match race, which could be run a week later on the closing day of the Santa Anita season.

"If they think they can beat us, they can meet us in a match race a week from now at any distance up to a mile and one half," Martin said. "We'll go as short as a mile and one eighth again and run for any price they want."

Because of his suspension, any match race held during the final days of the Santa Anita meet would not include Laffit Pincay. The point proved to be moot as the race was never held. Sham headed East for the Wood Memorial at Aqueduct while Linda's Chief remained in California.

## Chapter 14

## The Field Takes Shape

In addition to the players involved with the Santa Anita Derby out West and Secretariat in the East, early spring prep races began to shed light on other Kentucky Derby challengers. March 31 was a busy day in setting the stage. In addition to the Santa Anita Derby, the Florida Derby and the Louisiana Derby were run the same day.

Strolling musicians roamed the grounds of Gulfstream Park in Hallandale, Florida, while the University of Miami band also accompanied the Florida Derby. A fashion show and water skiers set up a festive day of events, capped by a half-furlong race of aoudads—wild bovines native to North Africa, related to goats and sheep. For the exhibition, exercise boys dressed in Arabian attire seemed to have their hands full in trying to stay aboard their mounts. No report was found whether or not the winning aoudad was considered a Derby prospect.

In the featured event, Royal and Regal earned the blanket of flowers in the "Run for the Orchids." The mahogany-colored bay went to the front in his first few strides, drew away under the whip in the upper stretch, and finished a wire-to-wire, three-length victory.

"I bent over at the five-sixteenth pole and I knew damn well he was going to go sailing," jockey Walter Blum on Royal and Regal said. "I hadn't asked him to run yet."

In his write-up in *The Blood-Horse*, Art Grace reported Royal and Regal "ran himself right into the Kentucky Derby." Like Secretariat, Royal and Regal had already been syndicated for breeding, with shares selling at the much more economical price of $50,000.

Forego, the Florida Derby favorite, took second and Restless Jet, bred in Florida by Liz Tippett, finished third. The three finishing in the money in the Florida Derby were Kentucky Derby hopefuls for fans and handicappers to consider.

In the Louisiana Derby at the New Orleans Fair Grounds, Angle Light was made the even money favorite in another "Run for the Orchids." He held the lead turning for home, but longshot Leo's Pisces (off at odds of 54 to 1) found room in the middle of the track and charged past Angle Light deep in the stretch for the win.

Trainer Herb Paley had entered Leo's Pisces only as a favor to Fair Grounds management. The field had been short and needed another horse. "I think I have a chance possibly to finish third," Paley had said before the race. He had removed the blinkers from Leo's Pisces earlier in March and had quipped he'd done it so his colt could get a better look at the tough competition with the hope "maybe he'd learn something."

The late-rallying Navajo took second place, while a tiring Angle Light dropped to third. "His race in the Louisiana Derby was a disappointment," trainer Lucien Laurin said of Angle Light's finish, "but the track that day was very sticky. He likes to hear his feet rattle."

After crossing the finish, jockey Bobby Breen on Leo's Pisces looked back and over his right shoulder at the second and third place finishers where he met the glance of jockey Weston Soirez who was standing in the saddle on Navajo. It was as if Breen was asking for confirmation over what had just happened, and a disbelieving Soirez was asking the same. A joyous Abe Simoff, Leo's Pisces owner, was in tears.

The colt's victory wasn't his only recent stroke of fortune. He was able to avoid injury while being flown in from Miami when strong ground winds hit his airplane causing it to skid off the runway in New Orleans. Perhaps Leo's Pisces' horoscope had indicated safe and prosperous travel.

Fresh off his Santa Anita Derby win, Sham was made the second favorite in the Kentucky Derby future book by the Reno Turf Club at 4 to 1. Secretariat, still the favorite, was pared from 6 to 5 to even money. Linda's Chief lost his place as second choice to Sham, going from 9 to 2 up to 6 to 1. Royal and Regal's win in the Florida Derby made him the fourth choice at 8 to 1. Newsmen already began asking questions regarding Secretariat's chances of taking the Triple Crown. The future book put him at odds of 5 to 2 to make the sweep.

Secretariat's next race, the one-mile Gotham Stakes, was over a fast track in the afternoon wind at Aqueduct. Secretariat again faced Champagne Charlie who had trailed him in second place in their prior match-up in the Bay Shore.

Secretariat was made the overwhelming favorite at odds of 1 to 10 by Aqueduct's biggest crowd of the year, 41,998 strong. NYRA president Jack Krumpe had conservatively estimated Secretariat's appearance alone would bring 5,000 additional fans to the track and increase the wagering handle by half a million dollars.

Out of the starting gate Secretariat hit the side of the stall and momentarily wobbled. Jockey Ron Turcotte let him regain his stride, and the colt recovered quickly. Secretariat ran third by the quarter-mile mark.

Secretariat picked up speed. As planned, he went to the lead, taking the position by the half mile. It was the earliest he had ever been sent to the front. Into the final stretch, Champagne Charlie made a move, gaining ground, cutting into Secretariat's lead. He moved to within a length of the leader. Turcotte was unaware Champagne Charlie had gotten so close. The reaction from the crowd alerted him to the challenge. The place exploded in excitement.

Turcotte caught a glimpse of roan to his right and recognized the challenge from Champagne Charlie on the outside. Secretariat took the rail. Champagne Charlie got within a neck of the leader, but Turcotte prompted Secretariat with the whip. "I reached down and tapped him twice," Turcotte said.

Secretariat accelerated to shut out the challenger, winning by three lengths and equaling the track record of 1:33⅖ set in 1968 by Plucky Pan. His disqualification in the Champagne Stakes aside, Secretariat had won his tenth consecutive race.

"He must have an unusually big stride," Red Smith of *The New York Times* wrote, "for he runs with so little show of effort that he does not seem to be hitting the speed the teletimer registers."

Secretariat showed he could set the pace as well as come from behind to win. He had won by passing horses on the outside and had won by taking them on the rail. He had won by plowing through them. He had won over fast tracks and had won in puddles and mud. "He again proved that nothing around here at this time can beat him," Mike Casale told readers in *The Thoroughbred Record*. The question remained if something around California could beat him.

Sham and Secretariat were both products of stallions standing at Claiborne Farm. Claiborne also owned Sham's dam, putting Seth Hancock in an enviable position. "Sure, it's a nice spot to be in," he said, "but I guess it's a little precarious, too. Assuming Sham and Secretariat meet, I just hope both horses have good racing luck and the best one wins."

Sham and Secretariat were both on course for the Wood Memorial on April 21 at Aqueduct. "I'll be there to see it," Hancock assured.

The Wood Memorial was perhaps the most important Eastern prep race for the Kentucky Derby. Seven victors from the Wood went on to win the Derby, 10 went on to win the Preakness Stakes, and 11 went on to win the Belmont Stakes. Pancho

Martin had won the race with Manassa Mauler in 1959. Lucien Laurin had won it three times, with Amberoid in 1966, Dike in 1969, and Upper Case in 1972.

Martin wasn't shy to face his East coast rival. "When you get a good horse like Sham, you don't avoid anybody," he declared.

Laffit Pincay, however, expressed some reservations. He had ridden against Secretariat three times. "I've seen Secretariat go around five or six horses with one enormous move," he said. "He is truly fantastic. I don't know if Sham is in his class."

With Hancock in the role of diplomat, Martin was the optimist, while Pincay wore the hat of the pessimist, or was it simply that of a realist? Another realist was Bobby Frankel. He had no plans for Linda's Chief to travel east. Linda's Chief's next scheduled race, the California Derby at Golden Gate Fields, was to be run on April 21, the same day as the Wood Memorial.

Laffit Pincay remained in California for a prior commitment to ride a highly touted filly, Susan's Girl, in the Long Beach Handicap at Hollywood Park. The Eclipse Award-winning Champion Filly of 1972 was the race's favorite. For the Wood Memorial, Jorge Velasquez would be back on Sham. Velasquez had won the Wood in 1969 on Dike while riding for Lucien Laurin.

Since Secretariat had proven his ability to set the pace or close in a race, setting a strategy would be difficult for Velasquez and every other jockey in the Wood Memorial. Velasquez was aware of the challenge, commenting years later in reflection that Secretariat was like "Samson the horse, strong all the way." And if his work weren't already cut out for him, Velasquez hadn't ridden Sham in a race since his two-year-old season.

Secretariat collected nicknames as plentiful as winning purses. Followers tagged him Superhorse, Red, Big Red, the Red Horse, Super Red, and the Big Red Machine. His size, his girth, and the length of his stride had caused a stir.

"I don't know how big he is and I don't want to know," Pancho Martin said. "I'm superstitious."

Secretariat's sire, Bold Ruler, won the Wood Memorial in 1957 while setting the record for the stakes race in 1:48⅘.

After Sham's Santa Anita Derby victory, he was sent to Belmont Park. He arrived on an early April Sunday and was stabled in Barn 52, the place Pancho Martin called his "headquarters." Other Santa Anita Derby winners who went on to win the Kentucky Derby, Swaps, Lucky Debonair, Majestic Prince, had been sent to Kentucky, either Churchill Downs or Keeneland, for final works before the Kentucky Derby. Sham would run an additional prep race in the mile-and-one-eighth Wood Memorial before his Kentucky journey.

"We want to get a true line on our colt," Martin said, "and the best way to do that is to run against Secretariat." But Martin knew what he was up against. "They are two good horses running," he said. "It's going to be a good race. … This is the best horse Sham will meet in his career."

## Chapter 15
## High Pressure Before the Storm

Sham's celebrity might not have equaled the shine of Secretariat's stardom, but Pancho Martin roped off the area surrounding Sham's stall as if the colt were making his Broadway debut. A red cord supported by stanchions, the type used in theaters, ran the perimeter around Sigmund Sommer's star performer. It was an honor Martin had bestowed upon other good horses he had trained, Hitchcock and Autobiography.

Martin explained the practicality of the rope. "I put that there so that all the people who go by, he don't bite them," he said, giving no credence to what some perceived as the star treatment. Martin did, however, take to calling the colt "Champ."

Pancho Martin rubbed Sham's dark brown nose, telling him, "You're the champion." He opened Sham's mouth to remove a strand of straw and pulled his head down to remove a speck of dirt from his eye. Sham made no objection. He behaved like a gentleman, with a trust in his trainer. "Got the disposition of a baby," Martin said.

Not only Sham's demeanor, but his work ethic made life easier for his trainer. Martin said Sham was agreeable to working fast or slow and would do anything he asked of him in a race, whether it was to go to the lead or to come from behind as a closer. Sham's earlier problem of drifting wide had long been resolved.

"I put an extension blinker on him," Martin said. "He runs straight now. I don't even have to use it now, he runs in a closed-cup blinker."

On a Thursday two days before the Wood Memorial, as Sham nosed through a tub of oats, Martin held court with reporters. "I think my horse is a superhorse, too," he said. "If Secretariat can beat Sham, then I give credit to him. Then I give him all the credit he deserves. I think Secretariat is a good horse—that everybody knows—but I know one thing: Secretariat has never run with a horse like Sham. He has not beaten horses the type like Sham. If Sham had to run with horses like Secretariat ran against, Sham would beat them, too."

Martin's confidence held true as the race day neared. "At this moment, I think Sham is the best horse in the race," he declared. "Secretariat has a big job ahead of him if he expects to beat my colt." Further, he said, "Sham is the most perfect thoroughbred I've ever been around. ... He is a magnificent individual, is perfectly sound, eats all the oats you can put before him, and does everything else well."

As early as February, General Manager Bob Gorman of

Churchill Downs (home of the Kentucky Derby) had visited Santa Anita during an annual promotional tour. After watching Sham win the Santa Catalina Stakes, Gorman had predicted, "Looks like a battle of S's for the Kentucky Derby." Gorman clarified, "Sham and Secretariat."

Angle Light was another tough competitor Sham would face in the Wood Memorial. He had defeated Sham in his debut in August of 1972 but that had been in a six-furlong sprint.

"Actually he was a faster horse than Sham," Jorge Velasquez recalled years later. "I wouldn't say that he [Angle Light] was a better horse," Velasquez added, "but he was faster." Velasquez liked Angle Light in sprint or for a mile, but would give the nod to Sham in longer races.

Because Lucien Laurin trained both Secretariat and Angle Light, the two were coupled as an entry for wagering purposes. Pancho Martin initially responded to the coupled entry by upping the headcount. "If he runs two," he said, "I'll run three. If he runs only Secretariat, I'll run only Sham." Laurin couldn't reciprocate, however. His colts had different owners. He couldn't tell one or the other not to run their horse.

Martin pondered what the pace might be in the Wood Memorial. Along with Sham, Martin's strategy was to run Knightly Dawn and another Sigmund Sommer horse named Beautiful Music, a wire-to-wire winner by 10 lengths in his only career start. Martin hoped to ensure a speedy pace by adding the extra two. But with the mention of Knightly Dawn's name, old speculations arose regarding his Santa Anita Derby controversy. The flames were fanned by Charles Hatton, an ardent Secretariat supporter, who wrote in his *Daily Racing Form* column, "It is not as if horses have not ganged up on Secretariat before, if it comes to that, and he is the best alley fighter of his species we have ever seen." Hatton seemingly expected a tag-team match or street rumble.

When Hatton wrote, people noticed, including Pancho Martin and Sigmund Sommer. Hatton was generally respected for his insight and intellect regarding the racing scene. He had seen every winner of the Wood Memorial, which was inaugurated in 1925, in person and had seen three of them (Gallant Fox, Count Fleet, and Assault) win the Triple Crown. With his own eyes he had seen the glory of Man o' War. The byline for Hatton's column pictured the writer in an inset photo, a stern-looking, mature gentleman who looked as though he could pass for a court prosecutor. He employed a distinctive power of persuasion while commenting in the first person plural voice, employing the editorial "we."

As if half cheerleader, half gossip columnist, Hatton lamented the draw when Secretariat was assigned an outside starting gate. With only 330 feet until the first turn at Aqueduct, post-position could be a factor in establishing early running position. Traffic might hinder a horse from an outside post. Hatton predicted the type of traffic Secretariat might encounter going into the first turn and stated of the competition, "Some of them having little more to recommend than their registration papers." He further stated, "In our perhaps astigmatic view, if Secretariat is given a shot, he can break from out in row 12 of the parking lot and win this Wood."

In addition to Sham, Knightly Dawn, Beautiful Music, Secretariat, and Angle Light, the field included the wonderboy of the Louisiana Derby Leo's Pisces, Champagne Charlie, Flush, Expropriate, and Step Nicely. Like Secretariat and Angle Light, Flush and Expropriate were a coupled entry; both colts were owned by Buckland Farm. Flush had been purchased on the same day as Sham from the Hancock dispersal sale, collecting a hefty sum of $135,000. Flush had one victory for the year in five starts, with a second- and third-place finish. In seven starts as a three-year-old, Expropriate had won twice. Champagne Charlie had won an allowance race at Aqueduct on April 14 since his performance in the Gotham Stakes. Step Nicely was a dark bay colt with a win, a second-place finish, and a third-place finish in four starts for the year.

In his review of past performances, Charles Hatton might have concluded Secretariat's opponents were sub-par, their times were nothing impressive, they hadn't run at this level of competition before—in short, they didn't belong on the same track with the "Superhorse." Even Angle Light, it was predicted by several writers, would have gone off with odds in the neighborhood of 20 to 1 for the Wood Memorial if he weren't coupled with Secretariat. The problem with relying solely on a racing form, however, is a horse can't read. Ignoring a horse's heart neglects the heroic aspect of the sport. A figure can't be attached to such an abstract. The track condition, the ratings, the statistics may add up to say a horse won't win, but in the flash of the track photographer's camera in the winner's circle, most overachievers don't seem to mind they're not good at math. Leo's Pisces victory in the Louisiana Derby provided recent evidence.

Lucien Laurin had himself said of Secretariat, "The only way they can beat him is to steal it." On face value, the remark might have appeared more inciting than intended. But in racing terminology, a horse steals a race when he sets a slow, uncontested pace, thus saving his energy to hold off closing bids by challengers down the stretch. It might also be noted Sham was not a pace-setter in the traditional sense, so a false pace would tend to hinder, not help him. By entering Knightly Dawn and Beautiful Music, Pancho Martin was trying to prevent precisely that, a false pace.

Laurin's quote about "stealing" the race was set as the headline of Charles Hatton's column in one edition of the *Daily Racing Form*. Hatton hadn't helped matters by implying a rather sinister meaning to Laurin's statement. Hatton wrote the track stewards were "assurance that nobody is going to purloin the race," as if a referee would be needed to rule on an infraction.

Despite all the fuss, a stable running more than one entry in a race was nothing new to the sport. The horse used to ensure a fast pace was commonly referred to as a "rabbit." A rabbit, in fact, won the very first Kentucky Derby in 1875, when Aristides set the early pace and ran to victory. His stablemate, Chesapeake, had gotten off to a bad start and failed to make a move, and as the racing chart called it, Aristides' owner, H.P. McGrath, "standing near the head of the stretch, waved to jockey [Oliver] Lewis on the little red horse to go on because Chesapeake, supposedly the better of the McGrath horses, was far back and had no chance."

*Washington Post* columnist Gerald Strine noted Charles Hatton didn't have a problem when one of the "Establishment barns," meaning members of New York society's in-crowd, sent out more than one horse. By Strine's account, Sigmund Sommer was not a member of this clique, and Pancho Martin was not a society trainer. At Belmont Park, Martin's barn stood in a far corner sometimes referred to as "Spanish Town." Lucien Laurin's barn was among those regarded as "Society Row."

Understandably angry over Hatton's remarks, Pancho Martin scratched both Knightly Dawn and Beautiful Music. "I became infuriated," Martin said. "I have never taken advantage of any man's horse during my career in racing." Martin was also upset with Lucien Laurin, who had inadvertently started the fireworks. "Let me tell you, my reputation on the race track is a million per cent honest," Martin said. "It was very cheap to say that about me."

Angle Light was now the only speed horse left in the race to set the pace. Had Martin been goaded into a mistake? "I don't like to run against cry babies," Martin said. "They were crying before the race."

Viola Sommer was also in on the decision to scratch Sham's stablemates. She didn't care for coupled entries when Martin had employed the strategy in California.

"I'm tickled to death he took them out," Sigmund Sommer said of the move. "Now they can't say they had a bad post position." Sommer was also upset by the Hatton story. "I think Laurin put him up to it," he said.

"I did not write the story," Laurin replied to the remark. "I don't want to get involved in all this," he said, "other than to say I never accused Martin of attempting to steal the Wood. I never said that to anybody." Laurin clarified what he had meant. "I just didn't want some horse to get to the front unchallenged and sneak home before the others had a chance. I warned Ronnie [Turcotte] about it."

Laurin assured his two colts would run as individuals, not partners. Laurin declared Secretariat didn't need any help and Angle Light was also capable of winning himself.

"He is a free-running colt who sometimes opens long leads when the pace is slow," Laurin said in describing Angle Light. "The jockey has been told that he is on his own, that he is to try to conserve his horse so he will have something left in the stretch."

It sounded much like the strategy was to "steal" the race. It was unlikely Laurin would use Angle Light in any capacity except to run his own race. "I couldn't use one to help the other if it hurt him," Laurin said. Angle Light and Secretariat were the property of separate owners. Secretariat was the property of Penny Tweedy, while Angle Light was owned by Edwin Whittaker, an electronics executive and president of the Toronto-based Canadian Admiral Corporation, Ltd., makers of televisions and refrigerators.

At a glance, the 59-year-old, white-haired, bespectacled Whittaker had the appearance of a man more concerned with the hundredth place of pi rather than the win, place, or show of a racehorse. Whittaker had purchased Angle Light as a yearling for the bargain price of $15,500 at the Keeneland summer sales in 1971. He traveled to watch all of Angle Light's 13 career starts, with stops in Maryland, New York, New Jersey, Florida, and Louisiana. He planned to be there for the Wood Memorial. The English-born Whittaker came from a family of horsemen. His father and grandfather had owned Clydesdales in England, and his brother had owned and trained horses in Ontario. Whittaker's first hobby was boat building, which waned when his serious interest in horses grew. A self-avowed "punter," Whittaker borrowed $20,000 and told himself when it was gone he was through with racing. Though he admitted to coming close, he never lost the sum.

"I've enjoyed every minute of racing," Whittaker declared. "I'm down at the track at 6:30-7:00 o'clock in the morning, and you couldn't find a nicer group of people than on the backstretch."

Angle Light was Whittaker's best horse, though not as highly regarded as Sham or Secretariat. Angle Light had faced Secretariat three times as a two-year-old, improving his finish each time, though Secretariat won each race. Angle Light had finished eighth in the Champagne Stakes on October 14, 1972, third in the Laurel Futurity on October 28, and second in the Garden State Stakes on November 18.

Angle Light had won only one race in six starts in 1973. Though chart callers had noted past performances when he had tired or weakened near the end of a race, it was evident Angle Light did have speed. It was, however, a natural speed that didn't necessarily carry over with stamina.

Angle Light's sire, Quadrangle, had won the Wood Memorial in 1964, as well as the Belmont Stakes that year. In preparing to attempt to follow in his father's footsteps, Angle Light worked a blistering four furlongs in :45 on April 7 and a brisk six furlongs in 1:11⅕ on April 12.

Sham worked a mile in 1:37⅖ on April 12. "It was a beautiful work," Pancho Martin said, "and the best part was that he finished strongly." Adding the exercise rider and the heavy saddle, he estimated Sham carried 140 pounds for his workout. Sham had carried 120 pounds in the Santa Anita Derby, and would be assigned 126 for the Wood. Martin made plans for a subsequent breeze with his colt and predicted Sham would run "a hell of a race" in the Wood and would give Secretariat "something to think about."

Sham worked a fast five furlongs in :58 on April 17 before being eased up at six furlongs in 1:10⅗. Lucien Laurin also sent Secretariat out on April 17. He planned a moderately paced workout.

As Ron Turcotte led Secretariat to the Belmont oval, a riderless horse bolted, running past them. Turcotte knew a riderless horse was unpredictable and could be dangerous. Throughout the workout, Turcotte kept an eye open for its possible return. "There was a loose horse on the track, and a bunch of green horses galloping, and I just didn't want to take any chances of hurting the horse," he said.

The subsequent work was slower than Laurin had wanted. He planned to get in a brisk blow-out before the Wood Memorial, but two lackluster works followed on April 19 and April 20.

Sham, with the quality of his workouts, began to shift the spotlight from Secretariat, though both colts were considered by more than a few to be head and shoulders above their competition. Pancho Martin praised Sham's works and his having not missed a step in training since arriving in New York.

"Secretariat is, indeed, a great colt and, naturally, I have the utmost respect for him," Martin said. "But at this moment I am not conceding anything. I feel confident that we'll win the Wood with Sham, and I'm not ready to admit Secretariat's superiority until he proves me wrong." He added, "They say Secretariat is a great one. I think Sham is a great one, too."

On race day during a routine physical, a NYRA veterinarian discovered an abscess under Secretariat's upper lip. Just prior to the Wood Memorial, Secretariat refused to open his mouth and shied away when groom Eddie Sweat tried to place the bit. Raising his snout, Secretariat backed away, offering more resistance to the bit than he ever had before.

## Chapter 16

## Rivals Finally Meet

Aqueduct's largest crowd of the year witnessed the 49th running of the Wood Memorial. The 43,416 surpassed the mark of 41,998 set only two weeks earlier during Secretariat's run in the Gotham Stakes. Secretariat walked into the circle of the paddock, around the potted geraniums and daffodils, to the applause of spectators. Bettors made the entry of Secretariat and Angle Light the 3 to 10 favorites with Sham the second at roughly 5 to 2. Most of the money seemed to sit on their three noses as the third favorite, Champagne Charlie, went off at the generous odds of 13 to 1.

A nervous Lucien Laurin waited in the saddling area before the race. When a dark bay took his place near him, the trainer looked at the horse. It wasn't the chestnut colt he was expecting. "Who's this?" he asked. Sham stood beside him.

Laurin had gone to the wrong stall.

Laurin later found the right owner and stood alongside Penny Tweedy to watch the race. She often watched in the company of a cheering section of friends and relatives. For the Gotham Stakes, her entourage overwhelmed two boxes and overflowed to a third. For the Wood Memorial, she welcomed as her guests bankers from Chase Manhattan Bank, the co-executors of the Chenery estate. Seth Hancock was also on hand, as he had promised. Since Hancock had brokered the $6-million-dollar syndication of Secretariat, his reputation as successor of Claiborne Farm could well be on trial as much as the reputation of the Superhorse himself.

Originally, Secretariat had been assigned the number eight post-position, Angle Light the ten. Sham was given the number three post. But with the scratch of Knightly Dawn and Beautiful Music, the remaining horses would move to gates further inside. The starting gates were now filled by Flush in the one position, Sham in two, Champagne Charlie in three, Expropriate in four, Leo's Pisces in five, Secretariat in six, Step Nicely in seven, and Angle Light taking the outside in eight.

After the break, Angle Light sprinted clear to take the lead, followed by Sham and Leo's Pisces. Secretariat was seventh. Jacinto Vasquez on Angle Light pointed his horse to the rail and relaxed the pace once he had established a front-running position.

By the quarter mile Angle Light led by one length over Sham, who led by one and a half lengths over third-place Champagne Charlie. Secretariat chased the field from the seventh position.

Ron Turcotte tried to prompt a response from his horse, but Secretariat didn't answer.

At the half mile Angle Light and Sham still held one-two with each colt's margin increased by a half length. Angle Light ran one and a half lengths in front of Sham; Sham ran two lengths in front of Champagne Charlie in third. Secretariat, unhurried, took an outside course along the backstretch and moved to sixth.

At three-quarters of a mile Angle Light and Sham continued to hold the same margins in the one and two positions, respectively. "I was in striking distance of Angle Light all the way," Velasquez recalled later.

Champagne Charlie still clung to the third position and made a move along the rail at the final turn. He eased to the outside as he neared the stretch. Secretariat, continuing wide, worked his way to fifth.

Making the final turn Turcotte put the whip to Secretariat. Sham still trailed behind Angle Light, Velasquez not yet asking Sham for a closing move. An invested observer, Sigmund Sommer looked on and yelled to Velasquez, "Let 'im go!"

Jorge Velasquez, however, was in a nearly impossible position. He had to make a run at the leader, but in the meantime, he had to hold off a closing charge from Secretariat. Velasquez was between a proverbial rock and a hard place, or as he colorfully put it in recalling the situation, "Now I was like in between the knife and the wall." He said of the predicament, "Angle Light was fast and Secretariat was closing. ... I have to be careful Angle Light don't steal the race and the other one that was the favorite, the big favorite, was coming off the pace. So I was a length and a half off Angle Light."

Sham seemed ready to move when asked, but Velasquez didn't want to use up his colt battling with Angle Light, leaving Sham too tired to counter Secretariat. "I was trying to save him when Secretariat was coming," Velasquez said. "What I wanna do is be in striking distance that I can get Angle Light at the end and hold Secretariat's big move."

Velasquez considered Secretariat his biggest threat. "I gotta watch out for Secretariat. If he fire at the end. He's the one to beat. He's the monster." But Velasquez hadn't discounted the leader, either. "I was worried about Angle Light. He's a nice horse. And he was the speed of the race so I couldn't chase him, being head-to-head with him 'cause I know I won't finish anyway." He knew Sham couldn't fight one battle with Angle Light, then follow with enough left in the tank to take on Secretariat in a closing duel. "I'm gonna kill him [Sham] and it's gonna kill my chances too," he said. "So that's why I was in striking distance."

Secretariat was failing to menace, however, and time was running out for Velasquez to wait any longer. "Velasquez! Let 'im go!" Sommer called. Halfway through the turn Velasquez made the move and put Sham to task on Angle Light. But Angle Light himself kicked it up a notch. Turcotte lashed Secretariat to stir him. Velasquez went to the whip with Sham.

Into the stretch it was still Angle Light by one and a half lengths over Sham with Sham still two lengths over Champagne Charlie. Secretariat now took the fourth position.

Secretariat moved in closer to the rail for the final furlong. Jacinto Vasquez pushed Angle Light, driving him to the finish.

Jacinto Vasquez was riding a brilliant race. He had set an easy pace to help Angle Light conserve himself. The fractions hadn't even bettered a 12-second furlong pace, :24⅗ for a quarter mile, :48⅕ for a half mile, and 1:12⅕ at three-quarters. Vasquez hoped his horse had enough left to hold off the closing Sham.

Sham moved on the leader, who was tiring. Sham cut the advantage to a length and worked closer from there. Quick, powerful strides drove Sham closer and closer to the front. Only a half length separated him from Angle Light, then a neck. Angle Light pinned his ears back in exertion. His head bobbed with his step, flashing the star on his forehead and white snip between his nostrils. Sham's ears poked straight up from his green and gold hood. He moved within a head of Angle Light, the two so close they nearly rubbed saddle cloths. The white chevrons on dark green sleeves of Jacinto Vasquez's silks pointed forward and upward, leading the way. Sham fought to pounce on the leader. The colors of the two combatants blurred in action as the finish line met them at a mile and one-eighth.

The wire came before Sham could finish the job. He ran out of room, two or three strides short. In those steps after the finish, Sham pushed his head past Angle Light, but it was too late. Angle Light first, then Sham, crossed the finish line with the whips of Jacinto Vasquez and Jorge Velasquez looking like the aerial antennas on speeding cars. Angle Light lasted to take the race by a head.

"My horse closed real good when I asked him to go and,

if the race were a little longer, we would have passed the winner," Jorge Velasquez said. "My horse would have won in another couple of jumps."

Secretariat never made the closing drive on Sham and finished four lengths behind him in third. "He just didn't have his punch today," Turcotte said later. "He finished pretty good, but not with his usual kick."

A hail of boos greeted Turcotte and Secretariat when they returned to the unsaddling area along the Aqueduct surface and followed Turcotte to the scales. Angle Light had covered the bets in their coupled entry, so the display wasn't one of pecuniary disgust.

Lucien Laurin had watched Secretariat during the stretch run and was not even certain who had won the race. From behind, an observer congratulated Laurin with a slap on the back. Laurin turned to ask, "Congratulations for what? Who won?"

"You did," he was told. "With the wrong horse!"

Jacinto Vasquez greeted the trainer with delight. "We did it, Mr. Laurin, we won," he said.

"Yeah, yeah… good, good," Laurin replied, in his only offer of congratulations for the tremendous upset his jockey had pulled.

In the most unlikely of places, the winner's circle, Lucien Laurin looked like a beaten man aside Angle Light, Jacinto Vasquez, and Edwin Whittaker. Dave Carnahan, the director of admissions at Aqueduct, organized the trophy presentation. He put his hand on Laurin's shoulder, likely one of the few times he felt the urge to console a winner. Laurin posed somberly for the traditional photograph looking as if he were a convicted felon awaiting sentencing. In a way, he was. He would soon face the ire of a livid Penny Tweedy.

"It looked to me," Mrs. Tweedy complained to Laurin, "as though we were racing one horse, Sham, and forgetting the rest of the field."

"What's the difference?" Laurin replied. "We got beat by Sham, too."

Blame was passed from one culprit to another. Turcotte should have responded to the slow pace ("They were walking," Laurin said.); Laurin should not have divided his loyalty between Secretariat and Angle Light.

The abscess, however, was still an issue. Turcotte said Secretariat never seemed to take hold and push against the bit as he normally did when he accelerated. Neither Turcotte nor Mrs. Tweedy knew about the abscess.

Ron Turcotte sat slumped on a couch in the jockeys' room watching the Wood Memorial's rerun on closed-circuit television. He shook his head in apparent disbelief as the inevitable played out on-screen. The same result ensued.

"He just didn't run his race," Turcotte said, and repeated again and again to the flock of reporters who came looking for an explanation. When the tape of the race was over, Turcotte stayed focused on the blank screen.

Turcotte admitted he hadn't really noticed how slow the pace had been, but he discounted its effect. "If he had run the way he always has, the pace wouldn't have made any difference," he said. "Just before the half-mile pole," he explained, "I thought he was lagging so I hit him. Nothing happened. I don't know how many times I hit him, I should have counted on the rerun."

Bobby Ussery was aboard Flush. Regarding the leisurely pace, he commented, "When they went the 6 furlongs in 1:12, I said, 'Good night, Secretariat.'"

Secretariat, the seemingly invincible champ, had been knocked to the canvas by two opponents. With a little more room, Sham could have taken Angle Light. Mike Casale reported in *The Thoroughbred Record*, "If they'd gone another 20 yards Sham definitely would have won."

Angle Light had been uncontested early. He had done precisely what Pancho Martin had hoped to prevent and what Lucien Laurin had predicted would need to be done in order to beat Secretariat. Angle Light had stolen the race. Sham hadn't relied on that strategy, but had suffered for it—if only for Knightly Dawn and/or Beautiful Music.

In a follow-up column, Charles Hatton graciously called Sham the race's "hero in defeat." He praised Pancho Martin's "exemplary sportsmanship" and show of confidence in Sham by scratching Sham's stablemates. He also wrote the race was a "Hesitation Waltz into the stretch, with nobody venturing to make an issue of the pace," and "Sham had dead aim all the way, and only just missed vindicating the popular trainer."

In the wake of the Wood Memorial, Pancho Martin was thrilled to have beaten Secretariat, yet angry Sham hadn't won. Perhaps Martin didn't want to criticize his jockey openly, but he removed Velasquez from Sham for future races with no explanation.

"Maybe because he felt that he shoulda win the race," Velasquez considered. "Maybe he thought that I rode a bad race. I don't know what it was."

Laffit Pincay had been Sham's regular rider prior to the Wood, so Martin's choice may have been one of convention. "Maybe he thought that the horse run better for Laffit," Velasquez said. "But I don't think I rode a bad race either." Velasquez also mentioned Sham had tried to lug in during the race. "He never lugged in before," Velasquez explained, "he used to lug out."

Martin repeated the phrase "lugged in" with emphasis and dismissed the remark.

Velasquez considered his strategy, "I was trying to press the pace and at the same time watch out for Secretariat who was coming. So I think I did what was right. But it didn't work out because I didn't win. I know one thing, that I did beat Secretariat."

Publicly Pancho Martin took the blame for the loss, citing his change in strategy in scratching Knightly Dawn and Beautiful Music. "Against my better judgment, I decided to run only Sham. I didn't want possible victory to be tainted," he said. "As it turned out, I played right into Lucien Laurin's hands." Martin felt he had been conned. "Had I run Knightly Dawn or Beautiful Music to assure a real pace," Martin said, "Sham would have won easily."

Sigmund Sommer felt the same way. "I should have put Knightly Dawn in," he said. "This slow pace killed us." Sommer thought Pincay's familiarity with Sham also would have given him the victory. "He knows the horse better than anybody." Pancho Martin vowed Knightly Dawn would run the Derby.

In his column, following another lament regarding Secretariat's starting position and a comment about Aqueduct's banked turns favoring speed horses, Hatton stated, "Secretariat's whimsy turned off many fans," while noting, "Sham came out of the race smelling might lak a rose."

Momentum was shifting, allowing Pancho Martin to state boldly (not as though he needed permission), "Sham is a better horse than Secretariat or any other three-year-old in America."

With the Wood Memorial history, Sham and Secretariat faced three more upcoming battles, the Kentucky Derby, the Preakness Stakes, and the Belmont Stakes—the three jewels of the Triple Crown. With one defeat of Secretariat in hand, Pancho Martin predicted, "I'm going to beat him every time I run against him. But," he added of Lucien Laurin, "if he beats me three out of four, I'll take my hat off and congratulate him and say, 'You got the best horse.'"

Sham was now lauded in some arenas as the Kentucky Derby favorite. The *Louisville Courier-Journal and Times* Derby Ratings on April 22 reflected the opinion: Sham topped the list. Angle Light had been dropped from the poll a week earlier when Lucien Laurin stated he would rest the colt and pass on the Kentucky Derby, but the result of the Wood Memorial would likely change that plan. Secretariat, coincidentally, was now rated in the same position as his Wood finish, third. Royal and Regal took the number two slot.

*Daily News* columnist Gene Ward commented the results of the Wood Memorial "transformed a nice, tidy Kentucky Derby picture into something resembling a painting by Salvador Dali." A nationwide survey by the *Daily Racing Form* listed 23 leading candidates for the Derby.

Martin Kivel of the *Pasadena Star News* stated, "The feeling is that Laffit Pincay would have brought Sham home a winner in the Wood had he elected to travel to New York instead of remaining in California to ride Susan's Girl. Pinky knows Sham well. He's a tough horse to ride, but a winner when you know how to handle him. That's what should make him tough to best when he goes at Louisville under the guidance of Pincay. In any event, we like him in the Derby over Secretariat and any other entry in the race."

Though Sham might have been getting the respect he deserved from some avenues, his name, and that of his trainer, were still not household words. Just as an unfortunate typo had butchered Sham's name in the *Los Angeles Herald-Examiner* by referring to him as "Shaw," an April 22 newspaper article referred to one "Frank (Punch) Martinez." Had the misnomer appeared in the lifestyles section of a far-off publication covering the event as a human interest story, the error could be dismissed. But the story appeared among the sports pages of the *Daily News*, in Pancho Martin's backyard. Martin and Sham might well have felt like the ill-treated Rodney Dangerfield in getting no respect.

Following the Wood, Lucien Laurin refused to return phone calls, including those from Secretariat's $190,000 shareholders. On Monday, April 23, Secretariat was flown to Louisville, Kentucky to prepare for the Derby. On Tuesday, Laurin sipped a cup of bouillon at Belmont Park prior to his own trip to Louisville. "This is my breakfast and last night's dinner, too. I am disgusted," he said. "I am tired and I am not feeling well."

Pancho Martin, still angry, was also waiting for a Louisville trip. Sham and Knightly Dawn were waiting to be vanned to the airport amidst Martin's complaints about the media and their "cheap stories."

Upsets prevailed as Laffit Pincay fared no better in California than Jorge Velasquez did in New York. Pincay's favored Susan's Girl lost to Bird Boots in the Long Beach Handicap in a similar ride and by the same margin Sham had lost to Angle Light. When the mile-and-one-eighth turf race was over, Pincay found himself short by a head after a late challenge on the leader who led wire-to-wire. A visit from Miss Port of Long Beach, Vickie Eddington, might have inspired Bird Boots to victory, as the two posed for a newspaper photographer the day of the race with Miss Eddington grasping both sides of the brown filly's bridle and staring her in the eye, appearing to offer an encouraging pep talk.

"She really tried hard, it was a tough one to lose," Pincay said, defending Susan's Girl's performance, while placing no blame for the loss on Miss Port of Long Beach.

## Chapter 17

## Other Contenders

In the media swell following the Wood Memorial, Edwin Whittaker maintained a guarded perspective. He still had no definite plans for Angle Light to enter the Kentucky Derby, saying he'd leave the final decision to Lucien Laurin.

Whittaker realized his colt had lasted only a head at the mile-and-one-eighth distance and the track condition was fast. The Derby's extra furlong and possible off track conditions could be his undoing. For recent proof, the New Orleans Fair Grounds was rated as good for the Louisiana Derby when Angle Light dropped to third.

"One swallow doesn't make a summer," Whittaker said. "One race doesn't change reality," he added with tempered optimism. "Secretariat is still the super horse and every horse, like every person, has an off day. I still think he'll win the Derby."

Whittaker also noted, with his sense of humor intact, the Wood Memorial was portrayed as a Secretariat loss rather than an Angle Light win.

There was, of course, no question Sham had earned the right to run for the roses, the first ever Kentucky Derby starter for Sigmund Sommer. Likewise, Pancho Martin had never saddled a horse for the Kentucky Derby, nor had he ever seen one. He couldn't even recall having seen one on television.

Sommer's confidence in his trainer remained high nonetheless. "He is simply a genius," Sommer said. "I guess there is no better illustration as to his ability than Sham."

Absent from the Kentucky Derby picture was Linda's Chief. Owner Neil Hellman had stated in order for Linda's Chief to convince him to make the trip to Louisville, he would have to win impressively in the California Derby. He won by less than a length. Another point figured in Hellman's decision. Before the Wood Memorial, Hellman stated in a manner as guilty as Charles Hatton of favoring the favorite, "The second factor depends on how easily Secretariat wins in New York." Further he said, "If, for any reason, Sham beats Secretariat, we will definitely go to the Derby." Hellman later amended his declaration, stating a mile-and-a-quarter distance was too demanding for a three-year-old in May. "I think it's too early in the season for *any* horse, at three, to go that distance."

Bobby Frankel kept Linda's Chief in California for the season at Hollywood Park. But that didn't keep him from voicing his opinion on those who would make the Derby trip.

"Some 40-1 shot will win it," he quipped. "I was mildly surprised Secretariat couldn't beat Sham and Angle Light in the Wood, but I didn't buy all that superhorse stuff you heard about him. If you cut through all the baloney what you saw was that he beats a horse called Champagne Charlie. Knightly Dawn and Settecento can run with Champagne Charlie and they're no hell, so I didn't come unglued when Secretariat got beat."

One of the final important prep races for the Kentucky Derby was the mile-and-one-eighth Blue Grass Stakes at Keeneland in Lexington, Kentucky on April 26. With the fall of Secretariat's stock in the Wood Memorial, the Blue Grass Stakes took on greater importance as a potential source of Derby candidates. Nine of the previous 14 Kentucky Derby winners had either won or finished second in the Blue Grass.

Off at the long odds of 15 to 1, My Gallant, a big chestnut colt, ran at the fourth-place position until the top of the stretch where he was rushed to the lead. Coming from far back, he closed the gap and caught Our Native with his final few strides to win by a head. Warbucks and Impecunious finished in a dead heat for third.

With his Blue Grass victory, My Gallant also had to his credit a second-place finish in the Flamingo Stakes at Hialeah Park, in Hialeah, Florida, on March 3, having lost by just a head, despite having encountered traffic problems and having been blocked three times during the race. Jockey Carlos Marquez on My Gallant had claimed interference in the upper stretch on the winner, Jacinto Vasquez and Our Native, but after reviews of the incident, the foul claim had not been allowed.

"The Flamingo might have been by fault," My Gallant's trainer, Lou Goldfine, said. "At Hialeah, the rail was dynamite, so I told the boy to stay in there. He could not get clear until late."

My Gallant carried the reputation of a strong runner in the stretch, able to come from far back in the field. "I believe he can give you that big run after a mile, or after 1¼ miles," Goldfine said.

Our Native had won the Flamingo Stakes on a balmy afternoon at Hialeah Park. He had taken the lead in the stretch turn by running on the outside and had held off My Gallant's strong closing effort. Our Native had finished second in the Hibiscus Stakes on January 20 and Everglades Stakes on February 14, both run at Hialeah Park.

*The Thoroughbred Record*'s Dave Goldman classified Our Native as a hard-running colt and stated, "Our Native strikes one as an honest competitor that may be short of championship caliber, but no equine with championship hopes had better make a mistake with him around."

"He's just like a cannon," trainer Bill Resseguet once described Our Native. "When you pull the string, you know he's going to explode."

Our Native brought the most experience to the Kentucky Derby with 23 prior career starts. His 11 wins also led all Derby starters.

"Some of the writers have criticized me for running him too often," Resseguet said, "but if I don't run him I have to work him, and he is not a particularly good work horse. If you run him, they say it is too much, if you don't they say he is short." Resseguet also commented, "You can't win a fight unless you get in the ring."

Louisville breeder E.W. Thomas had sold Our Native for $44,000 at the 1971 Keeneland fall yearling sales to Bill Resseguet and Mrs. M.J. Pritchard. Resseguet, heavy-set and long haired, had a taste for colorful clothing and loud sports coats. He represented the fourth-generation of a New Orleans horse racing family. Mrs. Pritchard was the owner of the Jockey Oats Company of Minneapolis, Minnesota. In March of the colt's three-year-old season, Resseguet had sold a partial interest in Our Native back to Thomas. By this time, however, the colt's value had jumped. A mere one-quarter interest carried the price tag of $200,000.

Blue Grass third-place finisher Warbucks had won a mile-and-70-yard allowance race on March 31 at Oaklawn Park prior to finishing third in the Arkansas Derby. He was a short (15.3 hands), muscular bay colt. His effort in the Blue Grass might have been his best. Trapped behind horses in the upper stretch, Warbucks was forced to wait until a hole opened up. He was still able to make a solid challenge for the dead heat third.

Warbucks would make the trip to Louisville with the added advantage of jockey Bill Hartack up. Hartack, with five victories, had ridden more Kentucky Derby winners than any other active jockey. Warbucks' trainer, Don Combs, had also tasted Derby success as the youngest man to saddle a Kentucky Derby winner. At age 32, he sent Dust Commander to victory in 1970.

Joe Kellman, a glass company owner and fight promoter out of Chicago, also owned a Kentucky Derby candidate. Kellman befriended several nightclub comics and named the foals from one of his broodmares (Lester's Pride) after them. The foals included Phil Foster, Pat Henry, Totie Fields, Ivy Hackett (for Buddy Hackett's daughter), and Shecky Greene.

Shecky Greene took center stage in the winner's circle in five of six starts in 1973. His performances were hardly laughable. He set the six-furlong track record with an eight-length victory at Hialeah Park in an allowance race on Valentine's Day and equaled the seven-furlong track record at Gulfstream Park on March 7 in winning the Hutcheson Stakes despite a slight bobble at the start. In between the two record-setting performances, Shecky Greene had managed to win the seven-furlong Florida Breeder's Handicap on February 21 at Hialeah Park with little trouble.

Primarily a sprinter, Shecky Greene had run a route course over a mile only twice in his career. He had won the mile-and-one-sixteenth Fountain of Youth Stakes on March 21, but after setting the pace in the mile-and-one-eighth Arkansas Derby on April 7, he finished a dismal tenth, and last, in a race in which he reportedly didn't like the track. There was little doubt Shecky Greene was one of the fastest sprinters around, but his pedigree indicated distance could be a problem.

Shecky Greene's trainer, Lou Goldfine (who also trained My Gallant), certainly had his doubts regarding the colt's stamina. "As far as I'm concerned, I would just pass the race with Shecky Greene," he said. "I don't think he's a 1¼–mile horse." He also pointed out, "Everything out of that mare [Lester's Pride] has been very quick—and very short." Columnist Gene Ward of the *Daily News* wrote Shecky Greene's critics claimed the colt could "travel a mile-and-a-quarter only in a van."

Though Goldfine said Shecky Greene might be able to relax on the lead to save something for the final stretch, he noted the colt would have to be fairly clear of nearby competitors. "As soon as Shecky hears feet behind him, when he's right, he just takes off." It was unlikely Shecky Greene would be allowed to relax in the Kentucky Derby, and the early speed in the race could prove problematic. "It's likely to take our colt too far, too early," Goldfine said.

Groom Bob Richie thought his bruise, courtesy of Shecky Greene, might be a lucky sign. "He kicked me before he won the Hutcheson and he kicked me before he won the Fountain of Youth," Richie said. "And, man, he just kicked me again yesterday."

When Secretariat was beaten in the Wood Memorial, owners and trainers who might have otherwise passed on the Kentucky Derby reconsidered their options. Randy Sechrest, trainer of Gold Bag, was one. "Why not?" he asked. "When that big horse got beat it opened it up like a raffle."

Gold Bag was coming off some poor finishes. He won the mile-and-one-sixteenth Coronado Stakes by a neck under Laffit Pincay at Hollywood Park on April 15 on a cool, overcast afternoon. Gold Bag's win in 1:41 was the fastest mile and one-sixteenth of the Hollywood Park meeting. But prior to that start, he was coming off races in which he managed only a third-place finish in a six-and-a-half-furlong sprint on turf sandwiched between an eighth- and ninth-place finish.

Pincay and Sechrest thought the colt tried to pull up in the stretch in the Coronado Stakes after getting the lead in a back-and-forth battle with second-place finisher Pontoise. "If I can correct that," Sechrest said, "I think I'll have a real top colt." The stooped, yet rugged Missouri-born veteran of 40 years explained, "This is a good little horse with just one bad habit. He likes to run at horses but when he catches up to them he has a habit of pulling up. He doesn't like to go past them."

The Florida-bred Royal and Regal was an emerging star. He had finished in the money in six of his seven starts as a two-year-old and won an impressive four of seven starts as a three-year-old. He won the Bahamas Stakes at Hialeah Park on January 31. He managed the victory after overcoming a stumble at the start and later being bumped and knocked sideways off-course. Showing his versatility, Royal and Regal also won over the grass at Calder Race Course in Miami in the Dade Turf Classic. He left his nearest rival behind by a margin of 10 lengths and missed the course record by only one-fifth of a second.

Royal and Regal followed his Florida Derby victory with a win in the seven-furlong Forerunner Purse at Keeneland on April 19 with a strong close despite unfavorable track conditions that had been tiring horses due to recent rains.

With Royal and Regal's potential came no high-strung demeanor. "He's so placid, he doesn't care about anything," trainer Jimmy Croll said. Royal and Regal had a habit of lying down in his stall, which scared the trainer, leading him to believe the horse was ill. "I must have taken his temperature 100 times," Croll said. "Last year, I bet he would be down 18 or 20 hours a day, and he still lies down a lot. He's so easy-going he'll embarrass you in the paddock before a race."

Jockey Walter Blum also found the colt to be calm and easy

to ride. "He seemed to be a little smarter than the average horse," Blum said years later, "which makes a good horse." Though Blum believed the colt liked to compete against other horses, race fans wouldn't necessarily know it by observing his relaxed manner in the paddock. "He looked like a dead-head," Blum commented. "But when we got to the gate and I tapped him on his ass a couple of times, let him know, hey, it's time to run, he walked in that gate and he was ready to go." Blum said, "In the middle of competition he knew what he was doing. He understood when it was time to go with a flick of the whip, and he was on his way."

Another likely Kentucky Derby candidate was Forego. The bay gelding was the biggest (17 hands) in the Derby field. "He's so big," jockey Pete Anderson said, "he has legs like a giraffe."

Ankle problems had kept Forego from racing as a two-year-old, but he won three of seven starts in 1973, with a second-place finish in both the Hutcheson Stakes, while coming from last with a strong rush on the turn before the stretch, and the Florida Derby.

When Royal and Regal's trainer, Jimmy Croll, was asked if he thought Secretariat was the horse to beat in the Kentucky Derby, he grinned his assent and added to the list. "I think there are two or three horses in the race who are tough. Sham is going to be tough and Forego is strictly on the improve."

Restless Jet, winner of the Everglades Stakes, by splitting horses mid-stretch, and third in the Florida Derby, had also earned a spot. With a fifth-, third-, and second-place finish, respectively, in his last three races since March, Restless Jet was getting closer to a stakes race victory with each outing. The colt was trained by Carter Thornton under the supervision of horse racing icon Jimmy Jones. "I'm sort of an unofficial manager without portfolio," Jones quipped. "I'm working on a commission basis. I get zero."

Jimmy Jones had saddled Citation, the last horse to win the Triple Crown (1948), and Kentucky Derby winners Iron Liege (1957) and Tim Tam (1958). Including Jones' wife, Peggy, Restless Jet was the property of four female owners. Deanna Gross, Norma Hess, and Betty Iselin were the others. Norma Hess was the wife of Leon Hess, president of Hess Oil Company. Betty Iselin's husband was Phil Iselin, president of the New York Jets football team.

"They claim Restless Jet has no chance," Phil Iselin said. "But that's what they said about the New York Jets when we played the Baltimore Colts in the Super Bowl. We were 17-point underdogs."

The Kentucky Derby field was rounded out by Navajo and Twice a Prince. Navajo was a dark gray Indiana-bred colt who had only one win in six tries in 1973. In his last 10 starts going back to November of 1972, however, he did manage four wins, three second-place finishes, and one third-place finish to be in the money eight of ten times. He was second in the Louisiana Derby, beaten by only a half length. Navajo was the first Indiana-bred ever to be entered in the Kentucky Derby, but the colt's birthplace didn't trouble trainer Jimmy Keefer. "Ol' Navajo don't know he's a Hoosier," he said. "All he thinks about is working and eating."

Twice a Prince was owned and bred by Max Gluck, former ambassador to Ceylon. Twice a Prince had not raced as a two-year-old. As a three-year-old, he finished second in the Fountain of Youth Stakes on March 21, only a length behind winner Shecky Greene. In April, he won a mile-and-one-eighth contest at Aqueduct by five and a half lengths. "I don't know if he's seasoned enough, but I'm going with him," trainer Johnny Campo said.

Photo Gallery ◆ 1

BOB COGLIANESE

Heliodoro Gustines on 1968 Belmont Stakes winner Stage Door Johnny.

BILL MOCHON ARCHIVAL PHOTO

Jockey Jorge Velasquez.

2 ♦ SHAM: Great Was Second Best

George Andrus, Bill Mochon Archival Photo

Sham after the Fleet Nasrullah Purse.

Bill Mochon Archival Photo

Laffit Pincay on the scale at Santa Anita Park.

Photo Gallery ♦ 3

BILL MOCHON ARCHIVAL PHOTO

Laffit Pincay accepts the George Woolf Memorial Jockey Award at the Santa Anita paddock garden in 1970.

BILL MOCHON ARCHIVAL PHOTO

Sham and groom Secundino Gato in the walking circle.

SANTA ANITA PARK

Sham (center) is sandwiched at the start of the Santa Catalina Stakes.

GEORGE ANDRUS, BILL MOCHON ARCHIVAL PHOTO

Left to right, Isadore Martin, assistant trainer Dagoberto Perez, L. Wilbert Rydbeck of the Los Angeles Turf Club, Laffit Pincay, and Pancho Martin after the Santa Catalina Stakes.

Photo Gallery ♦ 5

BILL MOCHON ARCHIVAL PHOTO

Santa Anita Park.

COURTESY OF THE CALIFORNIA THOROUGHBRED BREEDERS ASSOCIATION (CTBA)

Viola Sommer accepts the Eclipse Award for Autobiography as Champion Handicap Horse. NYRA chairman Alfred G. Vanderbilt presents the award.

Sham (No. 1), Laffit Pincay up, and Knightly Dawn (No. 1A), Milo Valenzuela up, in the Santa Anita Derby post parade.

Knightly Dawn (No. 1A) with Ancient Title (on the rail) in the Santa Anita Derby. Groshawk (striped hood) and Linda's Chief (No. 5) follow.

Photo Gallery ♦ 7

Sham (No. 1) holds the lead in the Santa Anita Derby over Linda's Chief (No. 5).

Sham in the Santa Anita Derby.

Sham after the Santa Anita Derby, Laffit Pincay up.

Left to right, Sigmund Sommer, Pancho Martin, Laffit Pincay, Pincay's wife, Linda, and Isadore Martin (below) after the Santa Anita Derby.

Sham (left) and Angle Light (right) battle down the stretch of the Wood Memorial. Secretariat (background, left) gives chase.

The Louisville, Kentucky Marriott makes its Kentucky Derby prediction.

10 ◆ SHAM: Great Was Second Best

COURTESY OF JIM MELIA

Ten dollars to win on Sham (No. 5) in the Kentucky Derby.

© THE COURIER-JOURNAL

The final stretch of the Kentucky Derby, Sham in front. Shecky Greene (rail) and Secretariat (outside) give chase.

Photo Gallery ♦ 11

FRANK ANDERSON—LEXINGTON HERALD-LEADER

Secretariat, then Sham, then the rest in the Kentucky Derby.

© COURIER-JOURNAL

National Guardsmen separate the crowd and Secretariat, with help from groom Eddie Sweat. Ron Turcotte up.

12 ◆ SHAM: Great Was Second Best

STAFF PHOTO—Lexington Herald-Leader

Secretariat, Ron Turcotte up, in the Kentucky Derby winner's circle before a full house.

© Cappy Jackson Photos, Inc.

Sham works at Pimlico for the Preakness Stakes.

Photo Gallery ♦ 13

© Cappy Jackson Photos, Inc.

Left to right, Jack Sommer, Sigmund Sommer, Laffit Pincay, and Pancho Martin await the Preakness Stakes.

© Cappy Jackson Photos, Inc.

Sham in the Preakness Stakes post parade.

14 ◆ SHAM: Great Was Second Best

© Cappy Jackson Photos, Inc.

They're off at the Preakness Stakes, Sham (No.1), with Deadly Dream to his right, then Secretariat.

© Cappy Jackson Photos, Inc.

Secretariat on the rail leads in the Preakness Stakes, Sham in pursuit with Our Native third, Ecole Etage fourth.

Photo Gallery ♦ 15

Sham in the paddock before the Belmont Stakes, Laffit Pincay up.

Virginia Governor Linwood Holton (left) and Penny Tweedy (center) at the Belmont Stakes.

Early going in the Belmont Stakes. From the top: Secretariat (No. 2), Pvt. Smiles (No. 3), My Gallant (No. 4), Twice a Prince (No. 5), Sham (No. 1A).

Forego, Heliodoro Gustines up. After Sham, Gustines rode Forego with success in winning multiple stakes races.

## Chapter 18

# Prep for the Roses

Sham stood at the opposite end of Churchill Downs' Barn 42 where Angle Light and Secretariat were stabled in stalls 20 and 21. The set-up was ideal for reporters and media personnel to fan the embers of Pancho Martin's temper and to send them smoldering to Lucien Laurin's side of the barn. The press provoked Martin with stories they'd heard, or in some cases fabricated, to prompt a response. They pointed out attributes or perceived advantages Secretariat held over Sham and claimed Lucien Laurin had made the boast. The fiery Martin wasn't hesitant to respond. The press then rushed to Laurin's end of the barn and reported what Martin had said.

Pancho Martin vented ongoing feelings regarding the Wood Memorial. "Lucien is always looking for excuses," he said. "He doesn't know how to take defeat. He kicks his feet in the air when he wins. When he loses, he sulks—and excuses." Martin told reporters, "It's funny, the only day Secretariat didn't want to run was the day he met Sham."

A story relayed by the press had Martin offering Laurin a $5,000 wager on the outcome of the Derby, Sham versus Secretariat straight up. Upon reflection years later, Martin denied he had ever made the offer. "That's why most time I don't want to talk to a person like that," Martin said, critical of certain members of the press.

Lucien Laurin began to lose patience when reporters continued repeating the story, asking him if he'd accept the challenge. Laurin refused to talk about it, threatening to walk away from persistent writers. And he did follow up on the threat, leaving them with empty pads of paper. Of the over zealous media's instigation, Laurin commented, "This whole thing is ridiculous, and I don't like it."

Reports of Pancho Martin's anger escalated. One story had Martin stating he no longer wanted to be Lucien Laurin's friend after knowing the man for nearly twenty years. Martin allegedly said he'd never speak to him again. As for any intense rivalry with Laurin, years later Pancho Martin denied that too, though time might have mellowed his emotions. "I know Lucien for all my life," Martin said. "A nice guy, you know. He tried to do the same thing I tried to do. Win."

Laurin stated he was a long-time friend of Martin, calling him "a damn good horseman, one of the best."

When questioned about it years later, Viola Sommer didn't recall the media's hype of the supposed rivalry between Martin and Laurin. "Actually I was not aware of that at all in the

Derby," she said. "The press seemed to be pretty confident that Sham would win the Derby, having come off such a nice win with the Santa Anita Derby."

Mrs. Sommer, however, was less enthusiastic than her husband and Pancho Martin regarding the Kentucky Derby. As Charles Hatton had lamented the full field of the Wood Memorial, Mrs. Sommer felt the even larger field the Derby was likely to bring with Secretariat's fall from grace could cause Sham injury if he were to get caught in the rush to the clubhouse turn.

With reporters in tow between the Louisville barns, Martin led Sham to the Churchill Downs track. Martin continued to give Sham the red carpet treatment as he stooped to clear stones and errant pebbles from Sham's path, tossing them aside. Two stable hands also worked the detail, one armed with a broom, the other with a rake to clear the stones. Martin might have appeared to be pampering his colt, but he didn't want to risk a hoof injury to Sham. A lesson on the matter could be learned from Royal and Regal. To win the Florida Derby on March 31, he had had to overcome a bruised right front foot, an injury he had originally suffered back in February when he stepped on a nail. Royal and Regal had worn a heavy steel bar shoe to protect the foot before being switched to an aluminum bar shoe for the Florida Derby.

The Churchill Downs oval was busy with pre-Derby works, though track conditions weren't ideal. Twice a Prince breezed four furlongs on Thursday, April 26 over a surface sloppy with puddles and mud. On Friday, Angle Light and Secretariat went out together for a six-furlong work with both turning out a respectable

1:12⅗ under sloppy track conditions.

On Saturday, April 28, Shecky Greene, Restless Jet, and Twice a Prince ran the Stepping Stone Purse, getting in seven furlongs over an improved track rated as fast. Shecky Greene won the race with Restless Jet coming in second, five lengths behind. Twice a Prince ran poorly, finishing sixth in a field of seven. Sham's stablemate Knightly Dawn also ran the Stepping Stone Purse. He faded in the stretch from third to finish fifth. Pancho Martin said the race took something out of his colt. He remarked Knightly Dawn had backed away from his feed, another sign Martin didn't like. He pulled Knightly Dawn out of the Derby. Again, Sham would be on his own.

Pancho Martin took Sham out for calisthenics on Monday with a television camera and roughly fifty newsmen enveloping the colt and his trainer. Martin headed to the clocker's shed midway along the backstretch to watch his colt run. Sham started in a slow canter, but when exercise rider Pedro Cachola set him to task, Sham picked up speed near the turn, gunning through five furlongs in :59. He finished six furlongs in 1:11⅕. During the workout, Sham carried 136 pounds (10 more than he would be assigned for the Kentucky Derby). Nearly pulling Cachola from the saddle, Sham won the approval of curious horsemen who gathered along the rail to watch. More important, Martin was thrilled with the work.

Martin analyzed Sham's strong finish, noting he ran his first three furlongs in :36⅖ and went his last three in :34⅗. "He finished full of run. That's what I liked so much." Sham galloped out a seventh furlong, finishing in a nice 1:24. "He rated beautifully and the boy held him hard at the start," Martin said, indicating Sham could have run even faster had Cachola let him.

Back at Barn 42, Martin declared, "I can beat him," referring to his big red neighbor, though he never looked in the direction of Secretariat. He believed Sham's chances of winning not only the Kentucky Derby, but the Triple Crown, were at least as good as Secretariat's. Beneath a blue raincoat and Tyrolian hat, Martin entertained newsmen with stories of his days at Oriental Park in Havana while waving a cigar. "I don't say I'm the best trainer. Just say 95 per cent of the trainers are worse than me," Martin told the crowd.

Forego's Tuesday morning work on the first of the month produced a tremendous five furlongs over a fast track in :57 before he galloped the sixth furlong in an impressive :1:10⅕. Forego left clockers scratching their heads trying to recall the last time they had seen such a speedy work by a Derby contender. "I never had a horse prepare himself for a race as well as he has," trainer Sherrill Ward said. "He wants to run."

The Churchill Downs surface was sloppy again on Wednesday, May 2 when Royal and Regal galloped. He reportedly struck his foot, the same one he had injured in February. Though troubled with soreness that evening, he appeared to have recovered adequately while walking the next day.

Secretariat also worked five furlongs on Wednesday. Turcotte pointed him to the backstretch in a light rain with reporters following their celebrity. Secretariat ran five furlongs in a sharp :58⅗ and galloped out the sixth furlong in 1:12. The Thursday headline of an Associated Press column summed it up succinctly: "Secretariat Drill Pleases Laurin."

## Chapter 19

## It's Official

Most candidates went through light works in final preparation for the Derby. Sham, Secretariat, Angle Light, My Gallant, Our Native, Shecky Greene, Restless Jet, Twice a Prince, and Gold Bag all took it relatively easy. Secretariat reared and acted up a bit during his work. Lucien Laurin, who accompanied him riding another horse nearby, grabbed Secretariat's reins to settle the horse. Warbucks breezed, but covered three furlongs in a brisk :35 and galloped a half mile in :48.

"I couldn't want him to come up to the Derby any better than he is now," trainer Dan Combs said. Pleased with Warbucks' workout and his Blue Grass Stakes performance, Combs added, "I think he has a chance to win, particularly with Bill Hartack as his rider."

Forego worked three furlongs in :35 ⅕. Trainer Sherrill

Ward commented, "I was looking for him to go in about 36 and change, but he wanted to run." Forego finished a half mile in a speedy :47⅕.

Navajo tore over three furlongs in :34⅘. Trainer Jim Keefer compared the Churchill Downs surface with that of the New Orleans Fair Grounds, where his colt rallied for second place in the Louisiana Derby. "He handled the Fair Grounds beautifully this winter," Keefer noted. "This track is similar in many respects to the one at the Fair Grounds so he might run well in the Derby."

Royal and Regal breezed three furlongs in :36⅕ before finishing a gallop of a half mile. Upon returning to the barn, exercise rider Milt Conner reported Royal and Regal ran very well. In fact, he had to hold the colt back from overdoing it.

After his final gallop before the Derby, Secretariat appeared to be napping in his stall, rolling his eyes, nodding his head. Perhaps playing the entertainer, he quickly came to, as if he had been pretending, when an onlooker called his name. He seemed to enjoy the publicity the pre-Derby fanfare bestowed. With a unique camera presence, he seemingly posed for photographers as if preparing for a studio publicity shot. When other horses displayed a distant, glassy-eyed appearance, Secretariat charmed the camera with a gaze that looked to greet fans and to say, "Thanks for coming out today." Penny Tweedy, in describing her horse, once said Secretariat loved "attention, carrots, photographers, and winning."

In the neighborhood of Barn 42, Pancho Martin promoted his own colt, praising Sham's great intelligence. "He communicates with his groom and the exercise boy and he cooperates with me," he said. "He's gutty and determined," Martin added.

After his workout impressed local horsemen, Martin declared Sham "about fit as he can be." The track, Sham's running style, and his ability to adapt also suited his trainer. "He doesn't have to carry his own track around with him. He has won twice in the mud and has trained well on all sorts of tracks," Martin explained. "He has many things in his favor. He has the gait of a natural router, along with the speed to escape the type of traffic jams that usually develop in big fields going into that first turn in the Derby. But they have a good run before they hit there and those with enough speed have a chance to get a good position."

Martin's heraldry might have been biased, but it couldn't be called false praise. Whitney Tower, in his *Sports Illustrated* column, picked Sham to win the Kentucky Derby. *Daily News* columnist Gene Ward also made his picks: Sham to win, My Gallant second, and Secretariat third. *Daily News* handicapper Joe Gelardi rated the field and said of Sham, "Here is the colt they have to beat." Gelardi summarized his comments on Secretariat by stating, "Can be had." For race fans trying to exclude horses from contention and narrow their choices, Gelardi threw more confusion into any potential choice. His comments listed the strengths and weaknesses of Derby candidates, were fair in their appraisal, and likely left the reader thinking what many had already known—many of these horses could win it. Gelardi did go on record, however, with his picks: in order, Sham, My Gallant, and Secretariat, which agreed with Gene Ward's choices. Maybe the New Yorkers knew something.

Had the Kentucky Derby been a handicap race instead of all entrants being assigned equal weight, Churchill Downs racing secretary and handicapper Allan W. "Doc" Lavin stated he would have assigned the top weight of 126 pounds to Sham. Secretariat would have been a close second at 125 pounds, Royal and Regal third at 124 pounds, and Warbucks fourth at 123 pounds. "This is one of the best balanced fields in recent Derby history," Lavin said. "Sham has a slight edge with me, but it could be close."

When official entries were made for the Kentucky Derby, Johnny Campo, trainer of Twice a Prince, was the first to drop his colt's name into the entry box. He waited a little more than an hour after entries were first being accepted. Other trainers seemed to be in no hurry. Thirty minutes before the closing deadline, Navajo's name was dropped into the box, yet he was only the third entry. Joe Kellman telephoned his orders to Lou Goldfine—Shecky Greene was entered with the instructions to scratch the colt if the track turned up anything but fast on Derby Day.

With the deadline approaching, names were entered in a rush to fill out the field. Don Combs was late, and officially his colt Warbucks was entered after the deadline, an infraction overlooked by officials. After all entries were made, the field was complete at 13—comprising 12 colts and one gelding.

Track officials were pleased to keep the number of entries below fourteen. The starting gate had fourteen stalls. More horses would require adding a second gate, a six-stall addition. To keep the number down, an alternative to the Derby was offered to trainers who were on the fence about entering their horses. The $20,000 Twin Spires Purse for three-year-olds was put on the Derby Day program and probably looked good to the owners whose horses might not get a piece of the Derby winnings.

At 10 AM Thursday before Saturday's Kentucky Derby, the traditional drawing of post-positions took place in the racing secretary's office under the watch of Doc Lavin. Lavin wore the little remaining hair on his balding head long, and with his spectacles added to the look, it appeared as if Benjamin Franklin were overseeing the proceedings.

For the drawing, ivory pellets numbered for each horse were dropped into a leather-covered bottle. Mrs. W. A. Croll, wife of trainer Jimmy Croll, drew the names and Charlen Resseguet, wife of trainer Bill Resseguet, shook the bottle and rolled the numbers. The fatigued Mrs. Resseguet had been beginning her days early by going to the barn to see Our Native and considered the Derby experience "hectic but exciting." Each ivory number was withdrawn and with it a horse was assigned his post position.

Restless Jet drew the rail, assigned the number one post-position. Gold Bag took the outermost post, number thirteen. It was the Kentucky Derby's first 13-horse field in 13 years. Gold Bag, coincidentally, was quartered in stall 13 of Barn 42. Triskaidekaphobia might cause other trainers to cringe, but Randy Sechrest wasn't concerned for Gold Bag.

"I don't know any horses that can read tote boards and I ain't a bit superstitious," the curmudgeonly trainer growled. "My wife was born on the 13th," he said, "and I've been living with her for 30-odd years."

Navajo experienced a different sort of luck. He was put in the number five post, pleasing Jane Stevenson, wife of co-owner Joe Stevenson. The week before the Derby, Mrs. Stevenson had found five four-leaf clovers, one on the grounds of Churchill Downs.

Sham was assigned the number four post-position. Secretariat was given an outside post, number 10. One of the horses between them was Twice a Prince in the number seven stall. The assignment of post positions appeared routine enough, but post positions and bad luck would play a big role in the upcoming race.

Theories and rumors plagued the Secretariat camp since the Wood Memorial. Questions were asked and, in some minds, answered. They included observations such as Bold Ruler's progeny being unable to go the Derby distance of a mile and a quarter. Bold Ruler himself had finished fourth in the 1957 Kentucky Derby.

Lucien Laurin relayed the doubts of Warner Jones, one of the investors in Secretariat's breeding syndication. "He'd call me two or three times a night," Laurin said. "He didn't want him to go to the Kentucky Derby. He'd say, pardon the expression, 'Don't bring that son-of-a-bitch to the Derby. There's no Bold Ruler that can go that far.'"

Few of Bold Ruler's sons had won at that distance as three-year-olds, and none had ever won the Kentucky Derby. Considering the Wood was Secretariat's first race at a mile and one-eighth, critics speculated how he would fare at the Derby distance two weeks later, which was one-eighth mile longer. Additionally, some felt Secretariat was the moody son of a moody father—He sulked if things didn't go his way.

By his own admission, Lucien Laurin was feeling more pressure in the week preceding the Derby than he had ever felt in his life. It was all taking a toll on Laurin, the Martin-Laurin feud, the pressure of living up to the $6 million syndication deal, the theories of Secretariat's pending failure, and the Wood Memorial disappointment. Penny Tweedy was still angry over Secretariat's loss at Aqueduct.

"You know, I couldn't believe what happened in the Wood," she would later say. "It hurt. It hurt terribly."

Earlier in the week, Mrs. Tweedy had met Lucien Laurin and Edwin Whittaker at the dining room of the Executive Inn in Louisville, where Laurin was staying. The five-star Executive Dining Room featured chandeliers, tables formally set for red and white wine, a live orchestra, raised dance floor, and strolling violinists. Customarily there was dancing from 11 PM to 1 AM, but such wasn't the only entertainment that evening.

Mrs. Tweedy began gesturing and pointing a finger at Laurin. Jockey Walter Blum was also staying at the Executive Inn and saw the confrontation. Though he didn't hear the specifics, he couldn't miss the tone of her argument.

"When Angle Light beat Secretariat she came apart, man. I mean she flipped out. And she stayed flipped out," Blum said. "When things went wrong with Secretariat or Lucien Laurin and Secretariat, well, shit, she let him know it, man," he said. "She thought Secretariat was, nobody could beat him. And nobody *should* beat him. And if anybody beat him it was Lucien Laurin's fault or Ronny Turcotte's fault or whatever."

With a laugh Blum recalled, "She was at the table reading him the *riot act*. I mean she was all over top of him. And he was so embarrassed. He was like looking around, and people looking to see what the hell she was hollering at." Lucien Laurin could only take the punishment. "He just wanted to crawl under the table," Blum said. Blum averted his eyes during the exchange hoping to remain unseen. The Kurt Seigert Orchestra closed the evening at the Executive Dining Room with a Can-Can.

Even the calendar seemed to be against Lucien Laurin. Forced to wait for Secretariat's syndication deal to be completed, he had had time for only three races to prepare his colt for the Kentucky Derby.

Lucien Laurin made a surprise move in pulling Jacinto Vasquez off of Angle Light for the Derby. Vasquez had ridden Angle Light to the biggest win of the colt's career in a masterful trip in the Wood Memorial, but Laurin announced Canadian jockey John LeBlanc would ride. No definitive answer was given for the switch, and speculation rose.

One report had Laurin stating owner Edwin Whittaker, a Canadian, wanted a fellow Canadian in the saddle. Another story was Jacinto Vasquez was feeling effects of a fall he had suffered after the first race at Aqueduct on May 1, even though Vasquez was able to ride three winners two days later on May 3. Another claimed Laurin made the switch at the request of a fellow trainer whose Eclipse Award-winning filly, La Prevoyante, was stabled next to Secretariat, the reason being La Prevoyante was scheduled to run in the Kentucky Oaks the Friday before the Derby and LeBlanc would be at Churchill Downs anyway to ride her.

It wasn't as if Vasquez had refused to make the trip to Louisville. He had been there on Friday, April 27, for Angle Light's workout. He was given no answer for the switch in riders.

"I don't know what's going on," Vasquez said. "I don't know what the hell happened."

Vasquez's agent, Harold Wiseman, got a call telling him Angle Light wouldn't be running in the Derby. Wiseman reported this to his client and signed him up for another mount at Aqueduct on Derby Day.

Some felt it was Vasquez's own doing, his unwillingness to commit to riding Angle Light, that got him released. The thought was he feared the colt would be scratched if the track were muddy on Derby Day. Another possibility was the threat of an impending sale of Angle Light, which eventually fell through, might have affected Vasquez.

Whatever the cause, Vasquez reported, "I won't be going down for the Derby under any circumstances."

With Derby Day fast approaching, bettors continued to support their picks. In the *Daily Racing Form*'s overnight line, the coupled entry of Angle Light and Secretariat was favored at even money. Sham was the second choice at 5 to 1 odds, with the coupled entry of My Gallant and Shecky Greene (both trained by Lou Goldfine) third at 6 to 1.

Heavy advanced wagering on Friday, Derby Eve, however, told a different story. Sham was made the slight favorite over Angle Light-Secretariat. Sham and the Secretariat-Angle Light entry were both quoted at odds of 2 to 1, but Sham drew more bets to win. The total amount wagered topped the record amount set the previous year. Bettors put the third choice My Gallant-Shecky Greene entry at 5 to 1. Warbucks was also at 5 to 1.

Confidence in each individual horse might have been better illustrated by off-track betting handles. Off-track betting wagers were based on individual horses—there was no coupling of entries. The *Daily News* reported a close duel between Sham and Secretariat. Secretariat was the favorite at 2 to 1 odds with Sham at 3 to 1. My Gallant came in third at 6 to 1 with Warbucks fourth at 10 to 1. Forced to stand on their own, Angle Light and Shecky Greene didn't fare as well. Shecky Greene was at 11 to 1 and Angle Light was at 17 to 1.

The *Louisville Courier-Journal*'s Derby Poll Contest earned the interest of nearly 100 writers covering the Derby from around the country. They too made Sham their pick, outpolling Secretariat by a 2 to 1 ratio in first-place votes. Forty percent of the responding writers put Sham at the top of the list, and he appeared on all but three ballots. Secretariat was the second choice with My Gallant third.

Perhaps Seth Hancock was covering his own bets as well. He hadn't forgotten the pricey syndication deal he had arranged for Secretariat. "We, of course, have a big interest in this running of the Derby," he said. "Secretariat will stand here next season."

But ulterior motives might have prompted his remarks if Sham were to embarrass Secretariat again. "Naturally, we are all very happy at his success and we would like it if he would win today and bring honor to the farm," he said of Sham. "It would be the ultimate in irony if Sham would win this Derby," he said. "Dad always wanted to have a Derby winner. It was one of the few aims in his life that he failed to realize. Now there is a colt with a genuine chance to get the job done and we bred, broke, raised him."

Along with the *Louisville Courier-Journal*, another publication seemed to give Sham his due. A Derby Day ad for the John J. McCabe Agency in the *Daily Racing Form* read like the page of a racing program listing the names of horses it had delivered by air to the Kentucky Derby. Nine Derby winners, beginning in 1951, had flown with the McCabe Agency according to the ad. "Flying must agree with horses—they win!" the copy declared. Contenders for the 1973 Derby flying with the McCabe Agency included Royal and Regal, Our Native, Twice a Prince, and Sham. Sham had finally made the big time with an endorsement ad, though it wasn't an exclusive.

A suggestion was made to Pancho Martin along the Churchill Downs backstretch that Sham would have to better the two-minute mark in order to win the Kentucky Derby. It had never been done. The record, at two minutes even, was set in 1964 by Northern Dancer.

"He can do it," Martin responded.

## Chapter 20

# The Day Arrives

*Sham showed me he's really a runner.*
—Laffit Pincay

In the May 5 issue, the *Lexington-Herald and the Lexington Leader* featured photographs of the Kentucky Derby lineup. Thirteen faces, not jockeys, but horses, were set above and below a headline that closed with the charge, "Derby Field is Wide Open." Side by side, the photo of each face appeared in the paper like mug shots on a police blotter. Some looked coolly ahead, others turned to the side in photos characteristic of accused criminals. Some horses looked tough, some looked distant and disinterested, some looked as innocent as a kitten asking a passerby to tussle the tuft of hair over his head. But could a bettor rely on any of these mugs to come through when a wager was on the line? Nothing was clear-cut. It was like the headline said, any one of these guys could pull it off. In his *Daily Racing Form* column, Joe Hirsch predicted an exciting race with "perhaps the most contentious finish in recent Derby history."

With the day beginning before dawn for most, horses went through pre-race routines in Saturday's dusk. They ate their morning meals and were brushed, walked, and rubbed down as the sun rose. Stable hands swept and raked the stalls and laid a new cover of straw. The 99th running of the Kentucky Derby was just hours away. Though the competitors could not have appreciated the magnitude of the race, many likely knew what was expected of them later that afternoon.

"Most horses, they know, because the day they run, they do different things," Pancho Martin said. Martin, for one, preferred not to feed Sham too much the day of a race. Likewise, Secretariat, at the opposite end of the barn, was given just two quarts of oats for breakfast. Normally he'd enjoy four quarts with an additional quart of sweet feed and perhaps some carrots.

Though he understood each trainer had his own way of doing things, Martin commented, "Good horses run no matter what you do to him."

Breakfast for Derby patrons was hosted by Governor Wendell Ford at the executive mansion in Frankfort during the traditional Derby Day breakfast. Guests were offered a menu of country ham, bacon, sausage, eggs, grits, honey and hot biscuits, after which, they were transported by bus, or limousine for the lucky ones, to Churchill Downs.

A harried Lucien Laurin, beneath a topcoat and gray fedora, arrived at the Churchill Downs barn. He managed to display a sense of humor as Ron Turcotte walked Secretariat around the barn.

"You have an expensive hot walker," Laurin told his horse.

Addressing reporters from his end of Barn 42, Pancho Martin assured in a worn voice Sham was doing fine. "By the time we get to the Belmont Stakes," a restrained Martin said, patting his midsection to support his remark, "I'll be ready to ride this horse myself."

Lucien Laurin stopped by at 2 PM to check on Secretariat. "He was laying down flat in his stall like he's dead," Laurin remarked. "Two o'clock in the afternoon, and he's going to run a couple of hours later."

Laurin asked groom Eddie Sweat what the problem was. Sweat had been working with race horses for 18 of his 35 years, ever since Laurin hired him to work at his Holly Hill, South Carolina training facility.

"Boss, he does that every day," Sweat replied.

On Derby Day's undercard, Knightly Dawn won the Twin Spires Purse by two lengths with Laffit Pincay aboard. "The 'rabbit' hopped into Kentucky Derby festivities after all," columnist Bob Adair later reported in the *Louisville Courier-Journal*. The Twin Spires was the day's eighth race, off at 4:30 PM. After his trip to the winner's circle, Pincay dismounted hoping to return there roughly an hour later following the ninth race, The Kentucky Derby.

CBS began its nationwide telecast at 5:30 PM, obviously uninterested in earlier competition. Jack Whitaker and Haywood Hale

Broun handled commentary and interviews. CBS radio likewise focused on the main event and broadcast from 5:15 to 5:44 PM.

When the time arrived, Laffit Pincay met Pancho Martin in the paddock. Martin told his rider, "You know the horse. Lay close to the pace. Don't be too far off it. Don't worry about Secretariat. Last time we did we got beat."

Lucien Laurin's advice was similar to Ron Turcotte regarding the jockey's familiarity with the horse. "You know the horse, Ronnie. Just try to keep clear. Don't worry about a thing. Ride the race the way it comes up." Laurin then added in their native French, "*Use ton propre judgment.*"

Lucien Laurin took his seat at the finish line with Penny Tweedy and next to the skeptical investor Warner Jones. Jones looked at Laurin and said, "You damn Frenchman, you don't have any sense. When he gets to the quarter pole, he'll leave you."

"I don't think he will," Laurin replied.

Sigmund and Viola Sommer were just a row away. Sigmund Sommer left for the clubhouse bar, not wanting to remain in his seat until Sham's race. When the time arrived and he tried to return to his seat, an usher stopped him. Sommer wore no identification, no badge or emblem to signify he was with the Sommer stable. But he had tipped the same usher $20 and told him to remember who he was. The usher didn't remember him. Sommer's son Jack was called to come with the tickets to get his father. They made it back just in time to see the horses come onto the track.

Strains of "My Old Kentucky Home" filled the air during the post parade, and thousands sang. Even veterans like Lucien Laurin were not immune to the effect. "This is the greatest race in the world and you really get the chills when you see your horse out there and hear that song," he said.

At post time bettors showed their confidence in Secretariat, making him (along with Angle Light) the 3 to 2 favorite. Sham was second at 5 to 2. The Shecky Greene-My Gallant entry was off at 6 to 1 with Warbucks close behind at 7 to 1. Our Native was off at 11 to 1, while Forego, Royal and Regal, and Restless Jet all came in around the neighborhood of 28 to 1. The longest odds belonged to Navajo at 52 to 1, Twice a Prince at 63 to 1, and Gold Bag at 68 to 1.

After Twice a Prince's starting gate antics left Sham closed in his stall for five minutes, after the gate's assault and battery on him, after his collision with Navajo at the start, and after getting cut in the leg, Sham was still game to contend with a late-charging Secretariat.

At the quarter-mile pole, Sham and Secretariat had flashed past a homemade banner visible from the infield. Fans clutched the cloth colored with squares of blue over a white background, a checkerboard pattern in support of Meadow Stable. The number "72" was written in the top left corner to represent Riva Ridge's Kentucky Derby win; "73" was written in the lower right corner to call for Secretariat's. Sham had blown past the banner in the lead, setting the stage to spoil the party.

But in the final stretch, Secretariat inched to an advantage. Sham still wanted to come on, but he eventually tired from the prolonged exertion. Pincay later said he "still had some horse at the finish," but admitted Secretariat was too much that day. "My horse gave him a fight," Pincay later said of his persistent mount.

Secretariat increased his lead to half a length, then further extended the lead across the wire, winning by two and a half lengths. Pincay could only lament Sham's fate. "He ran perfectly," he said. "He just got tired, I guess. I mean he wasn't really that tired, he was trying, but you know the other horse."

Competing jockeys congratulated Turcotte, offering hearty handshakes. With a victorious grin, Turcotte doffed his cap to the crowd's thunderous tribute, his goggles still clinging to the edge as if holding on for dear life after the ride they'd had. A regal-looking outrider in a red jacket, white shirt, and black bow tie led him to the winner's circle.

While Turcotte collected due praise, Pincay led the defeated Sham to the edge of the grandstand. Pancho Martin gathered the reins and led his horse to be unsaddled. Pincay dismounted, uncinched the girth, and lugged his riding tack to the scales for the post-race weigh-in. He and Martin exchanged few words.

Secretariat's heavy breathing betrayed the effects of a battle hard fought. Photographers on and along the track snapped rapid-fire pictures of the victor. From the grandstands and the infield, from box seats and along the rails, thousands of voices roared in response to the battle they had seen. By the winner's circle on the infield side of the track, followers wrapped around the horse and his jockey, trainer, owner, groom, and various Meadow Stable personnel. National Guardsmen on duty crouched and braced themselves to hold back the swelling mass of onlookers. In tight formation, they looked as though they had prepared a skirmish line. Their helmets dotted the area near Secretariat and Ron Turcotte. In the intense atmosphere, Secretariat became spooked; he jumped and trotted a step to the side.

Eddie Sweat struggled to contain Secretariat, who after his clash with Sham seemed ready to battle again. The groom leaned in, driving his legs, trying to contain his horse, while Turcotte grasped the reins. But Secretariat pushed back harder, hitting with his powerful chest the rope that had been secured as a barrier by National Guardsmen for crowd control. People in Secretariat's line of fire scattered, fearing he'd break free and trample them.

After Secretariat's dance with Eddie Sweat and the rope, Sweat steadied the horse and directed him toward the winner's circle. They were met on the way by Lucien Laurin and joined their party for the winner's circle photograph.

Situated outside the trumpeter's quarters, this particular winner's circle was used just once a year, after the conclusion of the Kentucky Derby. Secretariat had earned the right to use it. The traditional blanket of roses was draped over Secretariat's neck while red of a different source flowed from Sham's mouth. Secretariat seemed not to care for his adornment, quickly shaking the roses off.

Governor Wendell Ford made the trophy presentation. The cup itself was a testimony to the day's triumph, 14-karat gold on a marble base with a horse and rider at its peak represented in 18-karat gold. A decorative horseshoe on the side of the trophy pointed downward, however, perhaps an indication of how the day would turn out for at least one hard-luck competitor. According to racing superstition, if a horseshoe is turned down, all the luck runs out.

Pancho Martin struggled to stop the heavy bleeding from the deep gashes in Sham's mouth. In the process, one of Martin's grooms grew faint, sickened by the sight, and was carried from the area.

"His two teeth were dangling by a thin strip of gum," Martin said, "and he was bleeding so hard it took us three-quarters of an hour to cauterize the wound." He later described, "It was hanging there like this in his head," he said, bending a finger to represent one of the teeth. "They had to cut him in his gum." The teeth would need to be extracted and a fair amount of dental work performed while torn tissue was snipped from the colt's mouth. The wound would later bleed again, continuing for more than half an hour before the wound was re-cauterized.

Mrs. Tweedy accepted the cup from Governor Ford, leaving Sham and Pancho Martin to pace the stables, Laffit Pincay to take a locker room bench, and owner Sigmund Sommer to ponder the race's outcome, offering the sporting remark, "Secretariat won it fair and square."

Pincay was forced to move sooner than he had wanted on leader Shecky Greene. Did this result in precisely what Jorge Velasquez had feared in the Wood Memorial? Velasquez's instincts might have been correct. He had no way of knowing Secretariat wouldn't fire that day in the Wood Memorial. Secretariat was indeed the "monster."

It was a day for records at Churchill Downs, including the record attendance of 134,476, which didn't include the several thousand fans who had crashed the rear gate, bringing the unofficial attendance to approximately 140,000. A record handle was wagered on the day's races ($7,627,965) and on the Kentucky Derby race itself ($3,284,962). A record Kentucky Derby purse ($198,800) was paid and a record value was paid to the winner ($155,050).

There were also record times: at the mile-and-a-quarter distance, no horse had ever bettered the two-minute barrier. On that afternoon, Sham, with a time of 1:59⅘, broke Northern Dancer's record of two minutes even. Pancho Martin was right when he predicted Sham could do it. Unfortunately for Sham, the effort wasn't enough. Northern Dancer's mark fell twice that first Saturday in May. Sham's performance left him two and a half lengths behind Secretariat's 1:59⅖.

Times for non-winners of the Kentucky Derby were not recorded, but Sham's time could be determined by comparing his finish with Secretariat's. Using the thoroughbred racing convention of one length equaling one-fifth of a second, the time of a non-winner is calculated by taking the distance in lengths a horse finished behind the winner and adding that number in fifths of a second to the winner's time.

But taking into account Secretariat's brisk final quarter (which he ran in 23 seconds), considering a length to equal one-fifth of a second might not be accurate. Calculations would differ depending on how one defined a length, whether the horse was standing still or running, and, if running, at what speed. A "length" in horse racing terms refers to the horse's body length (not including the neck and head) and is taken to be approximately eight feet. Since Secretariat ran his final Derby quarter mile in 23 seconds, he ran 1,320 feet in 23 seconds.

The corresponding time for Secretariat's "length" in the final quarter of the Kentucky Derby, therefore, didn't equal one-fifth second (0.2 seconds), but averaged 0.139 seconds.

Determining Sham's time based on his two-and-a-half-length margin behind the winner (with one length equaling 0.139 seconds), the result would add 0.348 seconds to Secretariat's time of 1:59⅖. Sham's resulting time would be a shade under 1:59⅘ (Secretariat's time of 1:59.4 + 0.348 = Sham's time of 1:59.748).

The Kentucky Derby, "the most exciting two minutes in sports," wasn't quite so time consuming for two competitors. But history remembers the winners. Sham's name did not appear on lists of the fastest Kentucky Derbies ever run, where it should have been listed second, just a shade behind Secretariat.

"Remember," Pancho Martin said in recognizing the accomplishment, "Sham ran faster in losing the Derby than any horse had ever done in winning."

Lucien Laurin considered Secretariat's performance one of the most powerful races he'd ever seen a horse run. After the race, Laurin praised Secretariat's nearest competitor and his jockey. "Pincay was riding a good race on Sham too," he said. "He had a lot of horse under him, and he tried to get away on that last turn and steal it." Laurin quickly realized his unfortunate choice of words. "Oops, I shouldn't say that again."

When prompted to comment on his feud with Lucien Laurin, Pancho Martin replied, "I have too much headache to talk."

Riders gathered in the jockeys' room to relive their defeat for the sake of the media.

"You guys ain't lookin' for me," Earlie Fires, the first jockey to arrive acknowledged to converging reporters. Fires' Gold Bag had shown good early speed, but by three-quarters of a mile, had dropped to ninth before finishing eleventh. "He ran up there second and third at the start, but he just couldn't do it," Fires said.

Failure to catch Sham and Secretariat was not unique. Our Native finished third, eight full lengths behind second-place Sham. "He wasn't making up any ground on the first two," Don Brumfield remarked of Our Native, the closest witness to the match race the Kentucky Derby had become. Secretariat and Sham had exploded to separate themselves from the remaining field in the final two furlongs.

Pete Anderson shook his head, recalling his close call against the rail with Forego, who finished fourth. "He hit the inside fence so hard, he almost tore it down. I was moving up on the rail then and was committed to go. I couldn't change my mind. I got by one horse but I was too close to the fence."

Anderson ignored the cost in terms of his own life and limb to suggest how it affected the race results. "I'm not saying it would have changed the outcome, but it would have had some bearing. It cost him third place money, there's no doubt about that." Anderson later confessed Forego wasn't the most agile of horses. "I don't want to use the word clumsy, but he wasn't Fred Astaire." Luckily, the only rider thrown was Angel Santiago in his mishap at the starting gate, courtesy of Twice a Prince.

Restless Jet, with Mike Hole up, took fifth. Hole, with succinct logic, clarified the difficult question of who truly had the better horse and where his fit in relation to the others. He declared the horses in front of him were better and those behind him weren't.

Larry Adams said of Shecky Greene, who weakened near the final turn to finish in sixth place, "He ran a good race—as far as he ran." Adams added, "He did everything the trainer wanted but win."

Navajo, after his brush with Sham, was outrun and finished seventh. Royal and Regal was competitive early in the race, taking third at the start and holding fourth at three-quarters of a mile, but failed in his final drive and finished eighth. My Gallant was never a threat to the leaders, hovering around tenth, eleventh, twelfth, before making up a little ground to finish ninth.

John LeBlanc ran into trouble on Angle Light. "Gold Bag buried me," he said. LeBlanc and Angle Light were crowded behind Gold Bag, where LeBlanc was forced to check his horse's momentum. "The pace kind of backed up into me and I was running into horses' heels around the first turn," LeBlanc said.

Overall, Angle Light's performance lacked punch as he fell further back, fourth at the start, to fifth, seventh, eventually finishing tenth. LeBlanc felt his colt didn't handle the track well, which had been a concern of Lucien Laurin's. Gold Bag finished eleventh.

Perhaps justice was served to a misbehaved prince. Twice a Prince might have spent his energy at the gate, running last for most of the race before passing a dull Warbucks in the final stretch.

Ron Turcotte displayed little emotion after arriving from the presentation ceremony. Laffit Pincay offered his congratulations. Turcotte told him he was sorry it had to be him he beat, but it didn't really matter who it was—he wanted to win regardless. Turcotte was quickly off to discuss Secretariat's bloodline with a writer who had expressed doubts.

"Bold Rulers won't go a mile and a quarter, eh?" Turcotte delivered with a grin.

A television crew called to Laffit Pincay for an interview, a bit of recognition for a great performance. "This will be short and sweet," an announcer told Pincay, as if to remind him the world cared only for winners.

But before the interview could begin, a member of the broadcasting crew gestured to the announcer. It was another cruel blow for Pincay, who perhaps could have predicted it by this time.

"I'm sorry, really sorry," the announcer apologized, "we're clean out of time."

The gracious Pincay smiled. He'd have another chance. He'd face Secretariat again in two weeks in the Preakness Stakes. Competitors had barely cooled off from the Derby's exertion when the Reno Turf Club made Secretariat the 4 to 5 favorite to win the Preakness. His Derby performance was expected to scare off most of the competition, but not Pincay, the lifetime winner of nearly 2,000 races and $18 million in purse money. "Sham," Pincay said, "is as good a three-year-old as I've ever sat on."

## Chapter 21

# The Derby Dust Settles

*The only apology the beaten can offer is that they happened to be contemporaries of a special and thrilling animal.*
—Whitney Tower, *Sports Illustrated*

*What a big race he ran in the Derby! We're very proud of him.*
—Pancho Martin on Sham

Lucien Laurin and Penny Tweedy left the winner's circle and followed the celebration to the Churchill Downs press box, then to the barn. For Laurin, a modest man not prone to displays of pride, the festivities were likely a sigh of relief more than a cause for merriment.

Celebrants gathered for a Derby winner's party in the Churchill Downs director's suite with live music and champagne. The recipient of a congratulatory toast, Mrs. Tweedy commented, "I imagine I'll wake up smiling all night long!" She sipped a mint julep in the company of Governor Ford.

A waitress handed Lucien Laurin a glass of champagne. He took the drink and watched the Kentucky Derby replayed on a television monitor inside the buffet room. With Secretariat gaining ground in a sustained charge, Laurin called his shot.

"He's going after the other horse now," he told the audience, and with a slightly trembling right hand spilled his drink onto his shirt sleeve. It had been a torturous two weeks for the trainer.

"There were all those rumors about the horse, and they were even going around this morning," Laurin said. He had met Royal and Regal's owner, Butch Savin, the morning of the Derby, and Savin had asked if it was true Secretariat had been scratched. "If I hadn't just come from the barn and seen him myself, I would have dropped dead," Laurin said. The evening wasn't a complete exercise in anxiety for Laurin, however. He did manage to enjoy the thrill of winning his second consecutive Kentucky Derby.

Lucien Laurin became one of only four trainers to saddle back-to-back Kentucky Derby winners with Riva Ridge and Secretariat. Ron Turcotte was only the third jockey to ride back-to-back Kentucky Derby winners. Penny Tweedy and Meadow Stable became only the third owner and fourth breeder with consecutive Kentucky Derby winners. It was the first time the same combination of owner, trainer, and jockey won the Kentucky Derby in consecutive years. When Mrs. Tweedy was warned in jest the Justice Department might be after her for attempting to establish a monopoly in the Kentucky Derby, she played along.

"I guess they could crack down on me," she said. "But right now, that's the least of my worries."

By Sunday morning, Eddie Sweat was sweeping the remnants of the Derby celebration from the front of Secretariat's stall, stray American Beauty rose petals that had fallen from the winner's blanket. Broken glasses and empty bottles of champagne littered the ground. On Monday Secretariat flew to Baltimore. Angle Light flew with him, but continued on to Belmont Park.

Pancho Martin gave Sham a careful examination at the barn before putting the colt on a Baltimore-bound plane that same Monday. Martin turned Sham's upper lip, taking a look at the wound he sustained when head met starting gate. "He also grabbed his left quarter but fortunately the wound isn't too deep and he will be all right for the Preakness," Martin concluded. "He was a very game horse to run as well as he did."

Martin didn't let Sham out of his sight. He accompanied the colt on his flight.

After the Kentucky Derby battle, only Warbucks remained at Churchill Downs. Forego was flown to New York. Pete Anderson admitted how difficult it would be to catch Secretariat and Sham in the Preakness Stakes, stating, "It's hard to make up eight or nine lengths."

Twice a Prince would be allowed time in New York to heal from the cuts he suffered on his legs in his altercation with the starting gate. Restless Jet fractured an ankle in the right foreleg. He was put in a cast and was out of action for the rest of the season. My Gallant, who bruised his ankle banging the starting gate, Shecky Greene, and Royal and Regal were sent to Monmouth Park in New Jersey. Navajo, who suffered a small cut to his left hock, was shipped to Thistle Downs in Cleveland, Ohio. Gold Bag was sent to Hollywood Park.

Other than Pancho Martin, Bill Resseguet was the only trainer considering squaring off again with Secretariat in the Preakness Stakes. Our Native was sent by van to Chicago while Resseguet decided. Though their horses' destinations varied, most trainers agreed on one thing, to avoid Secretariat and Sham.

The *Pasadena Star News* ran an Associated Press article recapping the race, stating, "The Derby, as it has for all those years, was run most importantly down the Churchill Downs stretch where thousands of dreams have gone up in dust and sweat." The article neglected to mention for Sham, blood.

In Baltimore Pancho Martin was still upset over the events surrounding Sham's injury. "When all that trouble started at the gate, the man who was supposed to stay with the horse disappeared and never came back," Martin said, complaining about the handling of the incident with Twice a Prince. "Such a big race as that and they don't have enough men to handle every horse," he said. "I would pay the money myself if that's the problem." Martin also observed, "When that horse acted up, they made my horse stay in the gate all that time and Secretariat's outside the gate, walking round and round. All that didn't help any."

A trainer, however, was required to file a request with the Churchill Downs starter to get an assistant starter in the stall with the horse. Ironically, Twice a Prince's trainer, Johnny Campo, had not wanted an assistant starter for Twice a Prince. Campo claimed it was the presence of an assistant starter in the stall that had upset his colt.

"If they'd have left him alone, he wouldn't have become upset and would have started without incident," he said.

What Campo didn't seem to notice was Twice a Prince began acting up before he got into the gate, which was the reason an assistant starter went into the stall with him.

"Hell, that type doesn't belong in the Derby," starter Jim Thomson said. "The way he was rearing, kicking and fussing, it was lucky he didn't hurt one of the other horses." In defense of his crew, using the track vernacular "bad actor" to describe a misbehaved horse, Thomson added, "They're supposed to warn us in advance about a bad actor. Nobody said anything."

Though Twice a Prince might have influenced the outcome of the Kentucky Derby, he hadn't ruined the race outright. If that had been the case, *Daily News* columnist Gene Ward wrote, "Watergate would have lost the front page spotlight to the Starting Gate Scandal."

"You can see that all a guy wants at the race track is an even shake, such as his horse coming out of the starting gate with all his teeth," Melvin Durslag quipped in the *Los Angeles Herald-Examiner*. "Horses before had lost their riders, and others had lost their stirrups," Durslag wrote. "But it had been a long time since one had been asked to go a mile and a quarter without all his teeth."

Whitney Tower, in his *Sports Illustrated* column, noted the incident at the gate "left Sham looking like a four-legged hockey player."

Pancho Martin suggested Sham and Secretariat might have come to the wire in a photo finish had Sham not banged his head. "The gate episode hurt Sham," Martin said. "He came out shaking his head and stunned. He usually breaks well on his own, but this time Laffit had to use him right away to get position. His whole race plan was affected."

Laffit Pincay had no definitive answer regarding the effect of Sham's accident. "I really don't know how to answer that," he said candidly. "It's difficult to see how he could have run much better than almost 1:59⅘, and yet, logically, hitting his head on the gate and losing the teeth couldn't have helped him."

Pincay liked Sham's chances in the mile-and-three-sixteenths Preakness. "I feel we have a chance to beat him at Baltimore. My horse has more speed than Secretariat and probably will have an advantage at the shorter distance. And he's much handier. I can do anything I want with him," he said. "Another point to remember is that Sham is improving with every race. The way the Preakness comes up I should be able to place him second or third to whoever wants the lead. And when you have a situation like that, and a horse with Sham's class, you have to be given a chance to win."

## Chapter 22

## Round Two in Baltimore

*The Derby is a race of aristocratic sleekness,
for horses of birth
to prove their worth
to run in the Preakness.*
—Ogden Nash

Laffit Pincay felt Sham ran better in the Derby than he had in the Wood Memorial when he had beaten Secretariat. "He keeps improving," Pincay said, "he's been improving ever since the Santa Anita. I think Sham and Secretariat gonna keep beating each other, you know?"

Pancho Martin didn't think Sham's Derby Day injuries would affect him for the Preakness. The cut on his leg wasn't deep, and Martin said the injury to Sham's mouth didn't bother him when the bit was inserted. He thought Sham was able to get his usual grip on the bit during a race. "He can't pick grass right now," Martin said about Sham's missing front teeth, "but outside of that he is fine and is regaining his energies."

Still, the possibility remained Sham might not participate in the Preakness. "If there is any question at all, he is not going to run," Martin declared. "We are not going to hurt this horse just to race against Secretariat. He can beat him later in the Belmont."

If meetings between Sham and Secretariat had been rounds in a boxing match, Sham would be ahead by points on Pancho Martin's scorecard (blows to the head aside). "We're going to meet four times," Martin said. "We won the first round by four lengths in New York. He wins the second by two in Kentucky. Let's see about Maryland."

Of the match-up, Gene Ward wrote, "Secretariat is going to have to work for his Triple Crown. He's not about to win it by default, not if Pancho Martin and Sham can help it."

Martin indicated he had no plans to run Knightly Dawn in the Preakness. Sigmund Sommer agreed with the strategy. "What is the sense of using a good colt for nothing more than a rabbit?" Sommer asked, adding Knightly Dawn was a proven stakes winner and noting his Twin Spires Purse victory on Derby Day. "I think we showed in the Derby that Sham doesn't need any pacemakers. He was beaten fairly by Secretariat, but he was out there by himself," he said. The next round would be another one-on-one duel, but with a field of challengers gunning for them both.

After their arrival in Baltimore, both Sham and Secretariat walked around the shedrow on Tuesday, May 8. It was the first full morning there for both horses. Both appeared to be relaxed, having escaped the commotion of Louisville. Again, they were stabled in the same barn, Barn EE this time, Sham in stall 32, Secretariat half a barn away in stall 41. But reporters didn't hound the respective teams as badly as they had before the Kentucky Derby.

Sham walked with a cloth shoe over his right front foot to protect the cut. Pancho Martin had made quick work with hammer and nails the day before, attaching padding to the walls of Sham's stall. Nearby, Martin's office was stacked with five-gallon containers of Mountain Valley mineral water, 15 of them, the product of Hot Springs, Arkansas. Martin also brought in his own hay, oats, and straw bedding for Sham. The red theater ropes and stanchions were back, separating Sham's stall from anyone wandering by.

Though the atmosphere in Baltimore was not nearly as hectic as it had been in Louisville, the relationship between rival trainers remained strained. Lucien Laurin and Pancho Martin continued to be the media's center of attention. Both trainers talked with the same writers who had interviewed them in Louisville two weeks earlier. In their first gallops on the Pimlico Race Course surface, Sham and Secretariat both went out for mile works on Wednesday morning, May 9, on a track muddy from evening rain.

While Secretariat was cooling out after his workout, Lucien Laurin said, "Look at him! He just keeps getting bigger. He's so thick that Ron may have to have a special saddle made just to ride him." Several days later, Ron Turcotte did have a special girth made to accommodate his growing horse.

On Saturday, May 12, again the rival colts both galloped once around the one-mile Pimlico oval. Secretariat stated his case that he hadn't yet had enough when he completed his run still full of vigor. He fought his exercise rider George "Charlie" Davis when the rider tried to bring him back to the barn. Lucien Laurin and Eddie Sweat both had to assist in convincing the colt to get off the track.

While Secretariat and Sham worked, Baltimore played. On Saturday, a balloon race was held across Chesapeake Bay. The Preakness Parade followed on Sunday. An ensemble including 23 bands passed through center-city Baltimore, with an estimated 10,000 crowding City Hall plaza to watch.

Pimlico Race Course, first opened in 1870, was the second oldest racetrack in the country, just after Saratoga. In 1873, Pimlico introduced a stakes race honoring the winner of the 1870 Dinner Party Stakes held at Pimlico during its inaugural season. Named after the winning colt, Preakness, the Preakness Stakes was born. After Preakness' victory in that Dinner Party Stakes, jockey Billy Hayward followed the racing tradition of the day by claiming his winnings (gold coins) by untying a silk bag from a wire that stretched across the track from the judges' stand. This was the supposed manner in which the "wire" at the finish line was introduced, as was the awarding of "purse" money.

For many years Pimlico's sloped infield provided a gathering place for fans to watch the races, spawning the nickname "Old Hilltop." The site was a fashionable venue for visitors to park their carriages and meet for a champagne lunch. The hill was removed in 1938 to provide a better view of the backstretch.

As the Kentucky Derby had its run for the roses, the Preakness Stakes had its black-eyed susans, the Maryland state flower. The mysterious entity known only as the Phantom of Pimlico had promoted the black and yellow flower, and what it represented, in Louisville prior to Sham and Secretariat's battle in the Kentucky Derby. Black-eyed susan stickers left their mark at the Churchill Downs stable area. Plastic representations of the flower found their way onto jacket lapels. Yellow balloons with the message "Pimlico Race Course" and "Home of the Preakness" filled the air.

The 1973 Kentucky Derby was not the Phantom of Pimlico's first visit. The Phantom had been visiting Louisville for years promoting the Preakness Stakes. Past gimmicks included fliers disguised as $10 bills. The advertisements, posing as money on one side, were folded over and revealed the message "Go Where the Real Money Is—Baltimore, Preakness" on the other. The bills were scattered along the floor and grounds of Churchill Downs. In another stunt, the Phantom projected a slide onto the side of a Louisville Bank like a giant billboard. "Next Stop: Preakness, Pimlico," it announced.

The leading suspect was the crew-cut sporting, stocky six-footer, Charles "Chick" Lang, Pimlico's general manager. The outgoing, mischievous, 46-year-old Lang, a former agent to jockey Bill Hartack and a personal friend to vice-president Spiro T. Agnew, denied the Phantom of Pimlico was his alter ego. Lang did admit he knew who the Phantom was, however. Coincidentally, Lang arrived at Pimlico in 1960. The Phantom of Pimlico first appeared in 1961, and no one seemed to suspect Spiro T. Agnew.

Not everyone appreciated Chick Lang's pranks. Churchill Downs management once sent a letter of protest to Pimlico over his stunts. "Chick's enthusiasm can get downright sickening," Nathan Cohen, vice-president of Pimlico commented. But old friend Spiro T. Agnew seemed to understand how Lang worked.

"I could have used him in a staff position, but he needs a less structured existence," Vice-President Agnew said. "He could always see the humor in things."

Applying the label "people person" to Lang would not be cliché, as the man embodied the description. "I never dislike more than three people at the same time," Lang once said. "I just don't have the time. Actually, one of my three passed away, so now I have one slot open."

Lang had been improving the track since he took over. He rallied Baltimore's civic leaders to support a Preakness Festival Week, with celebrations similar to those held in Louisville prior to the Kentucky Derby.

"It takes a little of the old show biz," Lang declared. "Some of the P.T. Barnum to put the proper life into the game." Lang undoubtedly took his job to heart. The morning of Preakness Day 1972, he sat at the foot of his bed and cried when he saw it was raining.

Challengers willing to face Secretariat and Sham dwindled to four for the 98th Preakness Stakes. The field was the smallest since 1964, the year Northern Dancer won it—the same colt whose

Kentucky Derby record was bested by Secretariat (and Sham).

Of the six competing, Secretariat, Sham, and Our Native were back from the Kentucky Derby, while several local horsemen got into the act. Local Baltimore contractors Robert and Harry Meyerhoff entered Ecole Etage.

Ecole Etage was coming off a win in the Preakness Prep at Pimlico on May 12. He set the pace to lead all the way and finished with a three-and-a-half-length victory, drawing away from the pack at the end. His 1:42⅕ time over a fast surface was the season's best for a mile-and-one-sixteenth contest. Ecole Etage had also won the General George Stakes by eight lengths at Maryland's Bowie Race Course in February after leading the whole way. Ecole Etage was familiar with the Pimlico track. His last three races had been run there, as well as quality workouts on May 10 and May 17.

It looked as though the front-running colt aimed to set the pace for the Preakness, the role that had been filled by Shecky Greene in the Derby. If Sham and Secretariat invested their attention in each other and ignored the remaining field, Ecole Etage might be allowed to set his own pace. When he established a clear lead early, Ecole Etage was tough to beat.

Local Maryland auto dealer (Pontiacs to be precise) Fredrick R. Menke put Deadly Dream's name into the ring to represent his Wide Track Farms. The bay gelding had won four of nine starts in 1973, including a win over Ecole Etage by a neck in the Militia Handicap at Liberty Bell in Philadelphia on January 27. Deadly Dream had also beaten older horses over a mile and one-sixteenth on May 5 in a handicap race at Penn National

Race Course in Grantville, Pennsylvania. Deadly Dream was also familiar with the Pimlico surface, having run there twice as a two-year-old in May of 1972.

The field was completed by another longshot trained by Johnny Campo. Campo didn't enter Twice a Prince, but a colt named Torsion, a winner of only one race in seven starts for the year. "No race like the Preakness should be allowed to get off with only two horses in it," Johnny Campo stated as one of his reasons for entering. "If an owner or a trainer has a horse with even half the talent of a Secretariat, and he's a real horseman, he shouldn't allow a walkover or a two-horse race." Torsion was the property of owner Thomas Mellon Evans of Buckland Farm.

As a three-year-old, Torsion had battled with Secretariat in his 1973 debut at the Bay Shore Stakes. Torsion was the colt who had broken badly from the gate and had slammed into Secretariat. Torsion had finished fifth in that race, behind the winning Secretariat.

Torsion had finished fifth of six in the Preakness Prep. Johnny Campo believed the colt was a late bloomer and would improve over his Preakness Prep performance. Torsion worked 4 furlongs in a quick :46⅕ on May 17, galloping out 5 furlongs in :59.

"Torsion can run," Campo declared to newsmen at his barn after his colt's run. "He went his last eighth in 11 seconds and that ain't bad." Meanwhile, Campo checked his enthusiasm. "He can't beat any Secretariats or Shams now, but he will improve." As for the Preakness, Campo said, "If he gets any part of it, I'll be happy." Hopefully this time a Campo entry wouldn't get a part of another horse.

Our Native worked a mile in Illinois at Arlington Park on May 13. The following day, Bill Resseguet announced Our Native was out of the Preakness. He would opt instead for the Jersey Derby on May 28 at Garden State Park in Cherry Hill, New Jersey.

Despite Resseguet's hedging, Our Native did make the trip to Baltimore. The day following the announcement that Our Native was out, Resseguet called Pimlico racing secretary Larry Abbundi from Chicago to say his colt was back in. Resseguet still had plans in New Jersey, but decided to give Our Native a shot at the Preakness while using it as a prep for the Jersey Derby.

Our Native's departure got delayed at the airport in Chicago until after midnight Monday morning. By the time the colt arrived at his barn in Pimlico, it was 3 AM.

Resseguet didn't push Our Native for speed during a May 17 four-furlong work. "He's run 10 times this year," Resseguet said, "and if he isn't fit now, it's too late to worry about it."

Resseguet predicted Our Native would finish closer to the front in the Preakness. He pointed to the melee with Twice a Prince in the Kentucky Derby as a factor in getting his colt excited and making him hard to handle for the first half mile of the race. "Whether he will improve enough to threaten Secretariat and Sham remains to be seen," he said.

## Chapter 23

# Facing the Phantom of Pimlico

*There are interesting days ahead.
Racing needs a superstar, and now it may have two.*
—Arnold Kirkpatrick, *The Thoroughbred Record*

The Preakness was one-half furlong shorter than the Kentucky Derby's mile and a quarter. The final stretch at Pimlico Race Course ran 1,152 feet, a bit shorter than Churchill Downs' stretch of 1,234½ feet. With the shorter stretch run, if the race played out as the Derby did, there would be less room for Secretariat to make a closing move on Sham and the likely pace-setter Ecole Etage.

"We'll just have to hurry up a little sooner," Lucien Laurin said.

Laurin hinted he might work on Secretariat's speed and instruct Ron Turcotte to go to the front during the race as he had in the Gotham Stakes, when Secretariat won after going to the lead early.

Meanwhile, Laurin couldn't escape reminders of his own personal Phantom of Pimlico. The trainer was well aware of the trouble a local horse with Pimlico track experience could stir. In 1972, after Riva Ridge had won the Kentucky Derby, a practically unknown Maryland-bred Bee Bee Bee upset the Derby winner in the Preakness Stakes. Bee Bee Bee had won by racing in front, setting the pace under muddy track conditions.

On Sunday, May 13, Secretariat took the track before an audience of some 500 eager onlookers. It had become commonplace for crowds to gather in the morning just to watch him gallop. Though it was Mother's Day, fans lined the rail of Pimlico Race Course at 10 AM to witness his workout. "We could have sold tickets if we'd promoted it," Chick Lang said about the turnout.

Secretariat's normal workout time of 7:30 AM was delayed to 10 AM so the Pimlico track could be harrowed for a fresh running surface. Chick Lang and Arnold Kirkpatrick of *The Thoroughbred Record* had made arrangements to measure Secretariat's stride. Secretariat ran a blistering five furlongs in :57⅖. The crowd broke into spontaneous applause as Ron Turcotte turned Secretariat around to meet Penny Tweedy and Lucien Laurin before heading back to the barn.

"Can you imagine a horse running a mile and a quarter in 1:59⅖, as he did in the Derby, and then coming back a week later with a work like this?" a pleased Lucien Laurin asked after the work. "He didn't have blinkers on for the work," Laurin said.

"He'd have gone in :56 with blinkers." Secretariat galloped out a sixth furlong in a remarkable 1:10. The Pimlico track record for five furlongs was :57, and the record for six furlongs was 1:09⅕. In a single workout, Secretariat nearly equaled two records.

Ron Turcotte noted the lack of blinkers as if to explain why Secretariat hadn't broken the records. "He was kind of gawking at the crowd through the stretch, and I had a little trouble keeping his mind on his business," Turcotte said.

Secretariat's stride was determined to be 24 feet 11 inches. Contemporary accounts reported Man o' War's stride to be 25 feet, only an inch longer. It was noted in a NYRA press release, however, Secretariat's shorter, sprinting stride had been measured, rather than his longer, distance-running type of stride. Ron Turcotte added, "When he's relaxed and going easy on his own, he stretches out and covers an awful lot of ground. When he digs in and goes all out for speed—that's when he shortens his stride."

Beginning his work week early Monday morning, like the average working man, Sham ran a fast :58⅖ over five furlongs on May 14. Only a sparse following from the media was present, perhaps due to Sham's lack of celebrity or perhaps due to the early hour of 7:30 AM. His run was a full second slower than Secretariat's the day before. Sham also galloped out the sixth furlong, finishing with a great time of 1:10⅘, but still nearly a full second slower than his rival. Secretariat walked around the shedrow, marching circles with an air of confidence, as if Sham's work were hardly a cause for concern.

Secretariat's workout caught the attention of Frank Robinson, the *Daily Racing Form*'s head clocker at Pimlico. Secretariat's time of :45⅕ at the half-mile mark was the second fastest Robinson had ever seen. "Very, very impressive," Robinson commented.

Sham's time at the same distance was a very respectable :46⅘. The remarkable note regarding Sham's effort, however, was the strong finish. His first two furlongs were run in 12 seconds, followed by brisk times bettering the 12-second mark coming in at :11⅗, :11⅕, and :11⅗, for the third, fourth, and fifth furlongs, respectively. Sham's final two eighth-mile ticks of :11⅗ and :12⅖ bested Secretariat's effort of :12⅕ and :12⅗ at the same distance. Again Sham was lugging the extra weight of exercise rider Pedro Cachola, approximately 136 pounds in total including tack, which was 10 more than he'd be carrying during the race. Pancho Martin was pleased with Sham's run, particularly the finish.

"He didn't have his usual punch through the stretch of the Derby," Martin said. "There was a good reason, for he got off to a bad start, was used up a little in getting a position, and was laying closer to the pace than planned." Martin again noted Sham's mishap at the Derby start, commenting similarly on events that still troubled him. "That's in the past, though," he said. "Now we are looking forward to the Preakness." Martin said barring bad luck, Sham would have no excuses for not winning. "He's ready," Martin assured. "Anybody that beats him will have [to] do some running."

Secretariat grazed not far from Sham. When Secretariat began to roughhouse with Eddie Sweat, he returned him to his stall. Other than roughhousing, Sham passed the time with another favorite pursuit of young males, girl watching. A filly grazed near his stall, and it was obvious to Pancho Martin Sham was checking her out. As if in a scene from the movie *Rocky* (though not to be released for another three years), with trainer Mickey watching over his fighter, Martin wanted none of his star athlete dividing his attention while in training. Unlike Mickey, Martin didn't insist, "Women weaken legs!" But he did insist a security guard have the filly moved.

On May 15, despite earlier showers, mist, and overcast skies, Sham and Secretariat both galloped once around the Pimlico track. The usually reserved Lucien Laurin voiced the opinion that Secretariat's chances of winning the Triple Crown were at least 50-50. "It's got to be tough for any kind of a horse, but I think we have one big edge," he said. "This big fellow loves the mud."

Pancho Martin was likewise unconcerned about the possibility of a muddy surface. "Sham has won the only two times he started on an off-track."

On Thursday, May 17, Sham galloped a mile and three-eighths in a spring morning chill of 40 degrees, finishing just as strongly as he began, according to his trainer. "I think Sham finishes stronger than any horse in the country—any horse," Pancho Martin said.

Though Sham's versatility allowed him to handle tracks of different composition, Pancho Martin felt the Pimlico track was little different from that of Santa Anita and Churchill Downs. The three had firm surfaces to produce fast races, but of Pimlico, Martin observed, "A number of horses have been winning on the lead here. The leaders don't seem to get tired, so

I expect the Preakness to be run in fast time."

With flashes of a pre-Wood Memorial workout, a loose horse ran free on a path between the barn and racetrack as Secretariat was heading out for his Thursday gallop. Lucien Laurin maneuvered his horse between Secretariat and the loose horse to avoid any problems. Secretariat went for two miles around the Pimlico oval, running the final two furlongs down the stretch in :25 ⅕ after two passes around the track.

"He has come up to the Preakness perfectly," Laurin said after the workout. In as close to a boast as he could muster, he added, "Frankly, barring bad racing luck, I don't see how they can beat him Saturday." Laurin did note, however, he had felt the same way the previous year when Riva Ridge ultimately finished fourth.

Penny Tweedy was present for Secretariat's work. When he finished, she walked the dividing yards between her barn and Pancho Martin's. After an exchange of pleasant greetings, Mrs. Tweedy asked to see Sham. Martin, playing the gracious host, led her to his colt. Sham poked his head from the stall, having watched the two exchange greetings. He stood behind his gold-colored stall gate, embossed with the Sommer "S" inside a green diamond. As Mrs. Tweedy neared, he angled his head and neck over the gate. She patted his nose, telling Martin what a nice horse he had. Martin turned Sham's upper lip to show her the missing teeth. As if offering a handshake, Sham touched his snout to Mrs. Tweedy's upturned palm. Before Mrs. Tweedy left, she thanked Martin with the hope both colts should run well that coming Saturday and with a call for racing luck. Martin smiled and agreed.

The drawing of post positions was held on Thursday, May 17 at 10 AM in the office of Larry Abbundi. One competitor whose name was entered the previous Tuesday was withdrawn the following day. The colt was The Lark Twist, a longshot who had won only one race, a $14,000 claimer, in fourteen attempts in 1973 and two races in a career of 26 starts. But with purse values of $129,900 to the winner, $30,000 for second place, and $15,000 for third in such a small field, the odds weren't looking so long for a nice payday, even if conceding the first two positions.

When The Lark Twist's owner-trainer Larry Boyce learned Our Native would be in the race, however, he scratched The Lark Twist on Wednesday. He reconsidered and changed his mind on Thursday, but track officials told him the scratch was irrevocable. The field was minus one more.

The Lark Twist had drawn the rail, but with his scratch, Sham, originally assigned the number two post position, was moved to the number one. Secretariat was put in the number three stall.

The *Daily Racing Form*'s overnight line had Secretariat at odds of 2 to 5, Sham at 5 to 2, and Our Native at 10 to 1. Racing secretary and handicapper Larry Abbundi said if he were adding weight to the field, he would assign Secretariat 130 pounds, Sham 126 pounds, Our Native 118 pounds, Ecole Etage 113 pounds, Deadly Dream 112 pounds, and Torsion 107 pounds.

Ecole Etage, Deadly Dream, and Torsion had never attempted a mile and three-sixteenths, the distance of the Preakness Stakes. All horses would carry 126 pounds.

Thursday evening's nip in the air with temperatures in the

30s didn't cool Mayor Donald Schaefer's enthusiasm to entertain at a crabcake feast held at the newly restored Babe Ruth House on Emory Street in center-city Baltimore. The event was held for the press and those involved in the Preakness Stakes. As part of the festivities, Sam McCracken of the *Boston Globe* sang, accompanied on the spoons by Bill Resseguet. According to Joe Hirsch in the *Daily Racing Form*, "The two men were besieged by requests, but insisted on finishing."

Friday morning before the Preakness, the Pimlico clubhouse hosted the annual Alibi Breakfast, a longstanding tradition since the 1930s. It provided trainers, owners, and racing enthusiasts the opportunity to swap horse stories and offer prescient predictions. The idea was to exchange information regarding Preakness Stakes entries and the teams involved—with no alibis. The spurious nature of some of the tales exchanged allowed the perfect opportunity for braggarts to expel some hot air.

Though the modern version of the Alibi Breakfast served roughly the same good-natured purpose, it was also an occasion for the Maryland Jockey Club to recognize significant contributions made to thoroughbred racing. The turnout prior to the 98th running included owners, trainers, and jockeys participating in the Preakness Stakes, as well as press, radio, and television personalities, Pimlico track officials, and representatives from the Maryland Racing Commission.

In a relaxed moment, Lucien Laurin shared a laugh with attendees. "This is my fourth time in the race," he stated. "I was third with Amberoid in 1966, was third with Jay Ray in 1969, and fourth last year with Riva Ridge. If I don't do it tomorrow, gentlemen, you've lost a customer for sure."

The Sham camp was not represented at the breakfast. Pancho Martin, Sigmund Sommer, and Laffit Pincay didn't attend the event. Martin spent the morning of the Alibi Breakfast with his horse.

Martin strode quietly to the barn, as if not to awaken a sleeping baby, and told his brother Isadore, who was watching the colt, "Let no one here! … No one!" Sham lay comfortably on the straw bedding in his stall. Pancho Martin said, "I want no one bothering this horse." He added, "He needs all the rest he can get."

Martin was happy with Sham's preparation coming into the event. "He has trained perfectly for the Preakness and has never been better in his life. If he doesn't beat Secretariat tomorrow then he just can't handle the other horse. I think he can beat him."

## Chapter 24

## Daisies on Old Hilltop

The first page of the May 19 Preakness Day issue of the *Daily Racing Form* featured an article by Joe Hirsch. Perhaps sensing the magnitude of the battle to come, Hirsch wrote as if it were an epic on the scale of *The Iliad* of Homer. Hirsch praised "Meadow Stable's record-breaking Kentucky Derby winner, Secretariat," in terms fit to describe Achilles, while describing "Sigmund Sommer's fleet and courageous Sham" as if he were the fleet and courageous Hector. Hirsch might not have been far off with his words. As Hector clashed with Achilles, hero of the Greeks, Sham clashed with Secretariat, America's new hero. Of their respective riders, Laffit Pincay had never before ridden in a Preakness Stakes. Ron Turcotte had won in 1965 on Tom Rolfe. *Time* magazine sent a photographer and reporter to the race in anticipation of a Secretariat cover story.

The gates at Old Hilltop opened at 9 AM with the first post time scheduled for 1:10 PM. The early morning gray that had threatened rain gave the day over to clear skies. The Preakness Stakes was scheduled for 5:40 PM. It would again be telecast by CBS and broadcast on radio from 5:25 to 5:45 PM. The tight focus of the day's racing was again on one race. But the contest would not be limited to an audience secured behind the walls of Pimlico. A constant stream of motorists created the biggest traffic jam Baltimore had ever seen.

Loud and wild shouts from partygoers, as well as disciplined voices in harmony from a choral group, filled the grounds. Strains of music joined in from brass bands. Local celebrities including Miss Preakness (18-year-old Johns Hopkins University freshman Mimi Kelly) and football legends Johnny Unitas, Weeb Ewbank, and Don Shula mingled among the picnics, cotton-candy, dance contest, and lacrosse game held within the 25-acre infield. Footballs and Frisbees took to the air. Though the Preakness Stakes didn't have a drink to rival the Kentucky Derby's mint julep, the Preakness did have its crab cakes. Chick Lang pointed out something else that Baltimore held over Louisville. "Never forget that the Preakness has one thing that the Derby does not have," he said. "We have the Derby winner."

The largest racing crowd in Maryland history showed up for the event, bettering the old mark by approximately 13,000. Some of the infield crowd had spent the night. The *Lexington Herald-Leader* said the record crowd, "turned the grandstand area into one big sardine can."

Jim Nabors, of television's Gomer Pyle fame, sang the National Anthem to begin the day of racing. The second race on the card was the Johnny Unitas Purse. The 19th of May was set to honor number 19 for his 17 years as the quarterback of the Baltimore Colts. Unitas entered the fanfare in an Indianapolis 500 pace car driven along the home stretch of the Pimlico racetrack. With the crowd calling his name, he made his way to the infield attired in colors flashier than the brightest jockey silks—a gold jacket with black polka dots, green trousers, and white shoes. A large area of the Pimlico infield was fenced off for the Unitas party, recognized by a sign reading "The Golden Arm Corral." A hanging banner saluted the quarterback, offering, "Thanks for the Memories Johnny." From a tent inside the corral, Unitas joked with friends and former Colts teammates and signed autographs for fans.

Among multiple awards, a bronze bust, the key to the city, a street sign with the name "Unitas Pass" (which was to be erected in Timonium, Maryland where he had recently bought a house), Unitas was handed a check in the amount of $20,000 for his favorite charity. Maryland Governor Marvin Mandel and Mayor Donald Schaefer addressed the crowd, and Unitas' football locker and uniform were presented to a representative of the Football Hall of Fame. Unitas thanked the fans, and a band broke into "Thanks for the Memories."

The jockeys' room at Pimlico stood at the top of a flight of stairs beginning at trackside, leading up to the second story quarters. Unitas' Baltimore Colts teammates had greeted him from a balcony in front of the jockeys' room before meeting him on the track. Laffit Pincay had also stood on the balcony trying to get a look at the track to judge its condition and see where the winners had run down the stretch.

"How am I going to see anything?" the 112-pound jockey asked among 250-pound, and bigger, bodies. Pincay edged his way to the rail, as if fighting for position in a stakes race, slipping past Colts of a different nature.

Pancho Martin wanted Pincay to ride at least one race on Preakness Day to familiarize himself with the track before the Preakness Stakes. Martin had shipped the Sigmund Sommer horse Banderlog to Pimlico for the sixth race. Pincay had the opportunity to ride the fifth race for another owner, finishing fourth on a horse named Gold Landing. In the sixth race, Banderlog finished second with a strong closing effort, only three-quarter lengths behind the winner. Pincay, Martin, and Sommer would soon learn if finishing second after a strong effort would become a habit. Coincidentally, it was Ron Turcotte on a horse named Spanish Riddle who finished third, just behind Banderlog. The second- and third-place finish of the Wood Memorial might have sprung to mind to those hoping to see Turcotte again finish behind Pincay.

As the time for the main event neared, Pancho Martin waited by Sham's stall. The director of the television broadcast cued Pimlico personnel, who in turn cued Martin and Sham's handlers to take Sham to the turf course near the finish line. Rather than saddling the horses in the regular paddock, Preakness tradition had them brought to the grass just inside the main track to be saddled, allowing more people to see them and their jockeys during their pre-race ritual.

Isadore Martin walked along with Sham, carrying the colt's green and gold hood. Pancho Martin filed in behind his brother. Upon passing Secretariat's stall, neither of the Martins looked. The showdown would come soon enough, and they'd have ample opportunity to see him. Secretariat and Eddie Sweat followed Sham in line, his blue and white checkered hood carried by a member of the Meadow Stable entourage. Secretariat rolled the bit in his mouth like a gunfighter wiggling his fingers to keep them nimble.

On a wooden fence by the barn, the names of the eight Triple Crown winners were nailed to individual posts: Sir Barton, the first, followed by Gallant Fox, Omaha, War Admiral, Whirlaway, Count Fleet, Assault, and Citation. Martin knew Sham couldn't be the ninth, but he could prevent Secretariat from taking his place on the next post.

Pimlico grooms and hot walkers shouted support for the local boy, Ecole Etage, as the entrants made their way to the track. The horses lined the trackside turf, along a row of yellow and black signs listing the names and numbers of the Preakness entries. Seth Hancock was in attendance and said he wasn't as nervous as he was before the Derby.

If the day's earlier goings were any indication, Hancock and Penny Tweedy might be in for a disappointment. Stopping for a lunch of Maryland crab cakes at the Pimlico Hotel, Mrs. Tweedy had learned a parking attendant had damaged her car along with three others, causing some $5,000 damage. She had walked two blocks to the track. Upon her arrival at the clubhouse gate, she had learned no credentials had been left for Meadow Stable. She had had to buy a ticket to see her own horse run in the Preakness.

Sham, Deadly Dream, Secretariat, Our Native, Torsion, and Ecole Etage were saddled on the turf as the crowd swarmed as tightly around Secretariat as security allowed. A cigarette from the mob of onlookers burned Mrs. Tweedy on the arm.

The contenders took the track in the post parade. The crowd might have questioned the playing of a Christmas song, strains of "Oh, Tannenbaum" filling the air, but the song, accompanied by the same melody, was "Maryland, My Maryland," the state song and a Preakness Stakes institution since 1909.

Secretariat got a rousing ovation. They had come to see him run, and the heavy favorite at 3 to 10 odds could do no wrong. He got wild cheers and applause when he stopped, lifted his tail, and dropped a pile of manure on the track.

Sham was off at odds of 3 to 1. Interest in Ecole Etage put his odds at 11 to 1, favored just ahead of Our Native at 12 to 1. Deadly Dream and Torsion went off as longshots at 36 to 1 and 39 to 1, respectively. The record Preakness Day attendance set a new mark for Preakness Day wagers (and a Maryland record), betting close to $4 million ($3,792,076). Nearly $1 million ($922,989) of that money was bet on the Preakness Stakes alone.

The horses were loaded into the starting gate without serious incident. Secretariat was a little hesitant entering and had to be pushed from the rear by an assistant starter for the final few feet before the gate could be closed behind him. Ron Turcotte hadn't tipped his hand regarding Secretariat's strategy, whether or not he'd send the red colt to the front, or lay back as he did in the

Kentucky Derby. "We'll play it by ear and see what happens once the race starts," Turcotte had said.

Pancho Martin had commented if either Sham or Secretariat were to try for the lead, it would be Sham. "He breaks from the gate a lot better than Secretariat."

But it was Ecole Etage who got the jump out of the gate, followed by Torsion and Deadly Dream. Sham was fourth followed by Our Native. Secretariat broke slowly, sixth, and last. When the horses passed the grandstand for the first time with Secretariat at the rear, a nervous Lucien Laurin told Mrs. Tweedy, "I can't stand it. I don't want to see the race."

"You sit right here," she replied. She later commented, "Lucien's heart was pounding so hard he couldn't hold his glasses."

Secretariat didn't have the worst of it, however. Deadly Dream stumbled after the start. Then trouble again found Sham, or perhaps this time he found it. Leaving the gate, Sham broke to his right and brushed Deadly Dream coming from the number two post-position. Sham then drifted in toward the rail and caromed off it as he entered the clubhouse turn. He recovered to continue the chase.

After a quarter mile Ecole Etage, to the surprise of few, set the pace. He ran one and a half lengths in front of second-place Torsion. Torsion moved toward the rail, squeezing out Sham who trailed by a half length. Secretariat moved to fourth, three and a half lengths behind Sham.

George Cusimano aboard Ecole Etage set a slow pace at :24⅖, only a ⅕-second tick faster than Angle Light had set in the Wood Memorial. Was Ecole Etage setting his own stage for an upset? The question seemed to cross Secretariat's mind. He had enough of this leisurely pace and took action. "He soon let me know that the pace was slow and so we started to roll," Turcotte said after the race.

With a smooth twist of his wrists, "like a gentleman straightening the cuffs on his dress shirt," William C. Phillips reported in the *Daily Racing Form*, Turcotte moved the reins to signal Secretariat it was okay to move. Turcotte steered Secretariat outside at the clubhouse turn.

Cusimano saw a shadow creeping up and knew it wasn't Ecole Etage's shadow. Cusimano urged his horse to move, but the shadow kept coming until the jockey could hear a pair of nostrils blowing beside him. Going into the turn Ecole Etage was in front by one and a half lengths. By the time he came out of the turn, Secretariat had taken command. "When he came by, it felt like a freight train passing—blew the number right off my sleeve," Cusimano said afterward.

Anthony Black, on Deadly Dream, got a bird's eye view of the move. He later reported, "I was on the inside, with Our Native next to me and Secretariat on the outside. Next thing I know, I look over—and Secretariat was gone."

Laffit Pincay hadn't expected Secretariat to move so soon. By the half-mile mark Secretariat ran in front with Ecole Etage a half length behind in second. Torsion ran third, two lengths behind Ecole Etage. Sham dropped to fourth. Pincay was forced to back off when Torsion nearly pinned Sham to the rail.

Pincay now pointed Sham outside to challenge, and the colt responded. He overtook Torsion then Ecole Etage by the three-quarter-mile mark. Sham ran second, two and a half lengths behind Secretariat. In contrast to the Kentucky Derby, Sham pursued Secretariat this time. Pincay didn't want Secretariat to get too far ahead. He felt confident as Sham ran strongly and still had something left in reserve. "At the three-eighths pole my horse was running pretty strong, and I really hadn't asked him to run yet," Pincay later said.

On the final turn Pincay went to the stick to make his move on Secretariat. Pincay continued aggressively with the whip throughout the turn and into the stretch. Secretariat wasn't extending his lead over Sham by the top of the stretch, and Pincay thought Sham was gaining on him. Sham held fast, but the only gain he was making was on the third place horse, who was now Our Native, five lengths behind. In fourth, Ecole Etage trailed Our Native by three lengths. Torsion and Deadly Dream followed.

The gap between Ecole Etage and Torsion was 10 lengths as the field separated into two divisions. The match race some had predicted was coming to fruition. Pincay liked his chances. He felt Secretariat had extended himself making his big move to the front along the backstretch. But Turcotte believed Secretariat had come into this race even sharper than he had been for the Kentucky Derby.

The overzealous infield crowd broke through security lines, overtook retaining fences, and cut through the hedges that ran along the turf course. They rushed the inner rail of the track halfway down the final stretch. They cheered a mere ten feet from where the horses would pass during their final move. Some spectators still weren't satisfied with their view of the battle. They stood or sat themselves on the rail, endangering themselves, the horses, and the jockeys. In the hype, they screamed, shouted, waved papers and balloons. One fan reached out across the rail with a handkerchief and nearly touched the passing horses. In the hysteria of the moment, some misguided individuals dared to lean over the rail trying to lay a hand on Secretariat as he ran past. They were witnessing another Sham and Secretariat duel down the closing furlongs.

Ron Turcotte saw the people along the rail to his left and turned Secretariat's head to the right so he wouldn't become spooked or distracted. "He wasn't bothered by them at all," Turcotte later said. Either Secretariat hadn't seen the devotees, or he was used to the adoration.

Sham chased the leader down the home stretch, but Sham could gain no ground. Nor did Secretariat gain any ground on Sham. Pincay worked the whip, swatting Sham with a left-handed delivery. Pincay watched Turcotte, waiting for him to cock his whip, but Turcotte kept it tucked away. Instead he kept a watch on Sham. Twice Turcotte looked over his shoulder to check Sham's progress. The second time came at the eighth-mile pole when he looked to his left to see if Sham was trying to sneak up on the rail in the final yards. But Sham ran to the outside of Secretariat, still two and a half lengths back. Confident with Secretariat's lead, Turcotte took the colt to the wire in a hand ride, never going to the whip.

Secretariat won by the identical two and a half lengths by which he had taken the Kentucky Derby. Ironically, Sham's second-place margin over third-place Our Native was the identical eight-length advantage Sham had held in the Kentucky Derby. Ecole Etage finished a length behind Our Native to take fourth place over Deadly Dream, who closed to fifth, with Torsion sixth. After the horses cleared the finish line, a few unrestrained youths darted across the track.

It was the first time the first-, second-, and third-place horses from the Kentucky Derby finished in the same order for the Preakness. The blanket of flowers that stood in for a blanket of black-eyed susans was draped across Secretariat. Maryland's state flower didn't bloom until June, so Viking daisies with the centers painted with black lacquer served in the post-Preakness ceremony in the winner's circle. Secretariat stood much more relaxed for the Preakness festivities that he had after the Kentucky Derby when it had appeared he would charge the crowd.

After the daisies were presented to Secretariat, the Woodlawn Vase was presented to Mrs. Tweedy. Armed security guards had delivered the vase, one of the most valuable trophies in American sports, 34 inches tall in 29 pounds, 12 ounces of silver. It stood atop a circular base decorated in shields, horseshoes, a saddle, whip, and jockey cap. Four representations of winged Victory clutching wreaths in hands held overhead encircled the vase. The champion horse Lexington stood at the peak with a jockey up. Governor Marvin Mandel made the presentation with Miss Preakness standing by.

Secretariat hadn't even left the winner's circle nor had the blanket of daisies been removed from his withers before a maintenance man climbed a ladder to paint the weathervane on the

Pimlico cupola in the winning colors of Meadow Stable. Fifteen minutes after the race, Laffit Pincay was watching a replay of the Preakness Stakes in the jockey's dressing room. "The hell with it," he said, walking away from the re-run of defeat.

Other jockeys shared in praising the winner. Don Brumfield, on Our Native, called Secretariat "a helluva horse." Brumfield himself had ridden to victory in the 1966 Kentucky Derby and Preakness Stakes on Kauai King. When asked if he'd ever seen a better horse, he replied, "Not that I can recall."

"I knew Secretariat was some kind of good horse," George Cusimano commented.

"He's unreal," Anthony Black said. "I've never seen anything like the horse, to move so early and still have so much left."

Pincay was asked if Sham could take Secretariat in the Belmont Stakes, the final jewel of the Triple Crown. "It doesn't seem like it but I don't know," he replied. "That other horse is just too much," he said. "He was running so easy and I kept looking for Ron to hit him but he never did. He went by us flying and I tried to keep close."

The jockey of "that other horse" praised his rival. "Sham ran a very good race," Ron Turcotte said. "Pincay is a hell of a rider. But my horse ran real big." Turcotte summed up the prevailing attitude: "Once this colt is rolling nobody can catch him."

Pincay also recognized Sham's game effort. "My horse ran a powerful race," he said. "Sham kept trying."

Likewise, Don Brumfield recognized Our Native's effort. "My horse ran a good race. He just ain't good enough—not for those two, anyway."

Just as he was asked after his hard-luck Kentucky Derby effort, Pincay was again asked for a post-race broadcast interview. CBS broadcaster Chic Anderson, in wild plaid and wide lapels, introduced Pincay to the television audience. And rather than having the clock run out on him, Pincay was at least afforded roughly one minute to summarize the race. When asked if Sham could go a mile and a half, Pincay assured, "My horse is the type of horse that he could go any distance." But as to whether he could go that distance ahead of Secretariat, Pincay wasn't so sure. "My horse, he tries, you know what I mean. He, he, he," Pincay stammered, trying to explain and adding a laugh, "I don't know how to put it."

"He's a fine horse," Anderson cut in to finish the thought for him.

"That's right. He's really good horse," Pincay agreed, though his last words were muffled by Anderson in closing the interview.

"Well we'll see you in the Belmont Stakes. And hopefully another shot for you to try the big horse," Anderson said.

Chapter 25

# Broken Record and Broken Clock?

Secretariat followed in the hoofprints of his father, Bold Ruler, who had won the Preakness in 1957. Pimlico's Visumatic electric timer caught Secretariat in 1:55 for the mile and three-sixteenths. It went as the third fastest Preakness Stakes ever run: Canonero II ran in 1:54 in 1971 and Nashua ran in 1:54⅗ in 1955. Ron Turcotte, however, questioned the time. He knew Secretariat had run faster. Lucien Laurin and Penny Tweedy disputed the time as well.

"I thought he was running faster than the fractions showed on the board," Laurin said. "I was surprised when his time came up 1:55. I thought he would be close to the record."

They weren't mistaken. The *Daily Racing Form*'s head clocker at Pimlico, Frank Robinson, timed Secretariat in 1:53⅖. In a separate timing, Gene "Frenchy" Schwartz, chief of clockers for the *Daily Racing Form,* standing at the other end of the press box some 100 feet away, caught Secretariat in exactly the same time. Both men had nearly 50 years experience clocking horses.

"If my horse broke the record, he should have the credit," Laurin told reporters from the Pimlico shedrow amid Sunday morning rainfall. "You can bet your sweet life we'll ask for a review by the track, the stewards and the Maryland Racing Commission, if necessary."

Eddie Sweat walked Secretariat in circles around the shedrow. The colt kicked his heels and tossed his head as if he knew he was the topic of conversation. "This race didn't take anything out of him compared to the Derby," Sweat said.

At the far end of the barn, Sham's stall was empty. He had been shipped out by van at 4 AM to New York. Our Native was sent to Garden State Park in New Jersey. Our Native would not contest the Belmont Stakes, nor would Sham, Pancho Martin indicated. "I have no plans for my horse, and that includes the Belmont Stakes," he said in a huff, apparently upset over the Preakness start when Sham and Deadly Dream collided, sending Sham into the rail.

On the case of the disputed time, Chick Lang contacted Pimlico's official timer, E.T. McLean Jr., who reported his own clocking of 1:54 2/5. Lang talked with Visumatic executive William Sallee, along with Maryland's presiding steward, J. Fred Colwill, to set up a test of the timer. Colwill agreed to conduct an investigation.

The Monday following the Preakness Stakes, columnist Gene Ward of the *Daily News* reported the Visumatic timer had malfunctioned three previous times during the present Pimlico meeting, but all three times the races had been on the turf course. The 25-second first quarter of the Preakness Stakes recorded by the Visumatic timer was the slowest for any race on the card that Saturday. Ecole Etage was the leader at that point in the race, which put Secretariat's time at :26 1/5.

"No way," Laurin responded to the proposed time. "I don't think Ronnie could hold him that slow."

Clem Florio, handicapper for the *News American*, timed the race three times, each time coming up with 1:53 4/5. Though his clockings didn't match those of Schwartz or Robinson, the time still bettered that of Canonero II by one-fifth of a second. Two days after the Preakness Stakes was run, the Maryland Racing Commission lowered Secretariat's time by one second to 1:54 2/5, the time E.T. McLean had recorded. Secretariat still didn't have the record he had earned.

In the Pimlico press box, reviews of the videotaped race showed at least two people from the infield crowd had gotten close to the Visumatic timer's electric eye attached to the inner rail. The movement of these people might have broken the electronic beam and started the timer prematurely. In reviewing kinescope re-runs of the race, Chick Lang said he couldn't accurately determine the start of the race. The tapes did show, however, a man raking the track in front of the gate, which also might have tripped the timer.

On the CBS *Sports Illustrated* television show, simultaneous films were run on split-screen of Canonero II's 1971 Preakness race and Secretariat's race. The films showed Secretariat winning by three lengths. With a three-length margin of victory, Secretariat's calculated time would be 1:53⅖, agreeing with that of Gene Schwartz and Frank Robinson. CBS did not attempt to present a time for Secretariat's race, only to show he had crossed the finish line before Canonero II.

What CBS failed to note, however, was the starting gate might not have been placed in the exact same position each year. Pimlico Race Course sources said the gate's placement could vary from 10 to 15 feet. A conflicting source reported there was a mark on the rail to guide the gate's location, so the difference shouldn't have been more than two feet. Regardless, nearly everything seemed to be pointing to another Secretariat record—everything but the Maryland Racing Commission.

Racing commission chairman J. Newton Brewer said, "We are not people to close our eyes and stay with the rules just because they are in the book." But arguing it was bound by its rules and regulations, the Maryland Racing Commission stated, "The official time of any race is that which is clocked by the official timer."

Though he didn't fault CBS for its involvement, Brewer pointed out CBS had no official position regarding the matter. The racing commission further noted in its statement, "It was acknowledged by several of the witnesses including those persons representing CBS that to change records established by the official timer because of later electronic analyses of such events would be destructive of the integrity of all sporting events." Apparently the opinion of CBS had standing when it supported the Maryland Racing Commission.

Sandy Grossman, who prepared the tapes for CBS, concluded Secretariat had run faster by four-fifths of a second. In a *Daily*

*Racing Form* article, the publication reported Secretariat had finished ahead of Canonero II by approximately two lengths. The *Lexington Leader* said Secretariat had won by a margin of "about three lengths." Such discrepancies would put Secretariat's time somewhere between 1:53 1/5 and 1:53 3/5. William Sallee reported his personal timing of 1:54 4/5, which disagreed with his Visumatic timer's 1:55. Sallee explained, however, it wasn't unusual to have a one-fifth second variation. Throw in Clem Florio's triplicate 1:53 4/5 timings, Gene Schwartz's and Frank Robinson's identical 1:53 2/5 timings, and pinpointing any one official time would be difficult. J. Newton Brewer admitted, "We're having some difficulty trying to pin down a time."

There seemed to be little doubt Secretariat had beaten Canonero II, just to what extent he had done it. The Maryland Racing Commission acknowledged Secretariat might have run faster than Canonero II, but the official time would still stand at 1:54 2/5. The *Daily Racing Form*, however, still disputed it and went with the time their clockers reported, 1:53 2/5. The *Daily Racing Form*'s time was not only a Preakness Stakes record, but a Pimlico track record.

Penny Tweedy accepted the racing commission's decision gracefully. "I realize your problem," she told a member of the five-member commission. "You're stuck."

The Preakness victory still belonged to Secretariat, and he would have the second fastest Preakness time, moving just ahead of Nashua.

Accepting the 1:53 2/5 time recorded by Frank Robinson and Gene Schwartz, and using that same time reported by the *Daily Racing Form* as the standard, Secretariat alone did not break the Preakness Stakes record. Sham, two and a half lengths behind, would have come in at 1:53⅘, a tick ahead of Canonero II's 1:54. Sham had set two records in Triple Crown races, yet had nothing to show for it.

While the champagne flowed again at the Secretariat barn, Pancho Martin reportedly announced, "The hell with the Belmont. I don't want any more part of my horse looking at that big behind. Maybe we go to the Jersey Derby."

Martin later denied his plans didn't include the Belmont. "I never said that," Martin said in complaining of writers and misquotes. "It's no fair to put things in the paper something I don't say. If I say it I don't care. But if I don't say it…" Martin insisted his plans always included the Belmont. "Who wanna go to anyplace else? I'm from New York. I'm not from anyplace else. That's why I wanna win in New York."

By now, Secretariat had become a social phenomenon, conquering the imagination of the American public. Ads for Secretariat mementos flooded the media. Souvenir vendors began peddling memorabilia honoring the Meadow Stable icon. Some sold traditional items, like t-shirts and photographs, while one entrepreneur would offer brown paper bags of Secretariat's manure, which sold for $3. Secretariat's pause to relieve himself along the stretch of Pimlico might have had considerable retail value.

An estimated 28 million people had seen the televised broadcast of the Kentucky Derby and Preakness Stakes. Secretariat was receiving 200 fan letters a day. Some were addressed merely "Secretariat, New York," but his renown got the mail delivered just the same. Other letters were sent to owner Helen "Penny" Tweedy at her farm in Virginia. She recalled one letter she opened that read, "I think you're wonderful, I'd like to put my arms around you." The writer might have seemed overly familiar to Mrs. Tweedy, but she soon realized the letter wasn't addressed to her—it began, "Dear Secretariat." Another letter touched upon the awe Secretariat inspired, stating, "I'm just glad I was born in his lifetime."

Sham got letters too. But lately, after the Preakness, letters were coming addressed to Pancho Martin. "People tell me how I should train him," Martin said.

The Belmont Stakes would offer Sham another chance to challenge and to deny his rival. Confidence in Sham, however, was waning. In the May 7 issue of *Sports Illustrated*, columnist Whitney Tower had praised Secretariat but had made the prediction regarding the Kentucky Derby, "I think the winner is going to be an equally beautiful colt named Sham." By the May 28 issue, Tower conceded the Belmont Stakes and the Triple Crown to Secretariat. In referring to the chances of Secretariat's opponents he declared, "June 9 will rout them all. This is the day when, by winning the mile-and-a-half Belmont Stakes, Secretariat will become only the ninth Triple Crown horse ever."

Martin Kivel of the *Pasadena Star News* had also picked Sham to win the Kentucky Derby. But a day after the Preakness, he too changed his view on Secretariat, of whom he wrote, "They might just as well mail him the crown now." He also wrote, "The only horse that looked like he had a chance of spoiling Secretariat's bid for immortality," making his statement in the past tense of lost opportunity, "was Sham."

Though Arnold Kirkpatrick and Ashbel Green in *The Thoroughbred Record* were clearly in agreement with the prevailing opinion of the class of Secretariat, they also put Sham's status in perspective. "Meadow Stable's Secretariat ranks 2½ lengths above the second best of the 24,137 registered foals of 1970. That horse is Sigmond Sommer's Sham." But like Sham and Pancho Martin before him, Sommer was now having his name misspelled in print.

Kirkpatrick and Green went on to voice what was becoming painfully clear to the Sigmund Sommer-Pancho Martin camp: "Sham, the beautiful dappled bay… in any other year would be far and away the best colt around."

In the pages of the *Daily Racing Form*, Joe Hirsch's "fleet and courageous Sham" became "courageous but outgunned Sham."

Viola Sommer had seen enough of Secretariat. In fact, after the Kentucky Derby, "Not being such a good sport as my husband," as she once put it, Mrs. Sommer didn't want to go to the Preakness Stakes. Her husband, however, had convinced her it was an opportunity for great competition and was, she said, "The sportsman-like thing to do." But after the Preakness she "certainly didn't want to go to Belmont," she stated years later.

Despite Viola Sommer's opposition, Sigmund Sommer and Pancho Martin made the decision to put Sham in the 105th running of the Belmont Stakes. Martin noted Sham had had problems in both the Kentucky Derby and the Preakness Stakes. He wanted the colt to have another chance in the longest of the

Triple Crown races, at one and a half miles.

"It's tough enough to beat a horse like Secretariat without having trouble," Martin said. "I want to see him in a race like the Belmont with plenty of room." Sham's run-in with the rail during the Preakness had caused no injury. "He came out of the race just fine and his next race will be the Belmont," Martin said.

After Sham had been sent to New York the Sunday after the Preakness Stakes, Secretariat was sent later the same day. He was in his Barn 5 stall at Belmont Park by 2:30 PM, stabled among 18 other Meadow Stable horses. The names of his stablemates such as Riva Ridge, along with Lucien Laurin and Ron Turcotte, were spelled out near the stalls. Secretariat's name appeared too, only in much bigger, eight-inch letters. Reporters and photographers were already waiting for him when he arrived.

The renown might have been bothersome to Lucien Laurin and his training routine, but Penny Tweedy enjoyed the attention and her role in public relations for Meadow Stable. "I love the prestige, the notoriety, the excitement and the money," she noted. "There are times in crowds like the Derby when you feel like Joe DiMaggio, but the object is to be pleasant and visibly there and not let the horse down." She drove home in her red Mercedes Benz with faux black-eyed susans in a plastic bag behind the seat, the blanket from Secretariat's Preakness victory.

Sham, still a star in Pancho Martin's eyes, took his place of honor behind the red theater ropes and stanchions at Barn 52 on the far side of the Belmont Park backstretch.

"Sham is by far the best horse I've ever trained," Martin said. "His disposition is the best part of him. He has a good disposition. No matter what happens to him he still runs his race, and you can't say that about 90 per cent of the horses."

Still, Martin couldn't help but feel his horse hadn't gotten a fair shake. "I never get disappointed," he said. "I don't get disappointed because I know he didn't get the best of it. In fact, this horse is a very lucky horse after what happened to him. He came back sound." Martin considered the starting gate mishap in the Derby and Sham's hitting the rail in the Preakness. "I'm not using these as excuses but everything has to go right when you run against a horse like Secretariat," he said. "You can make no mistakes."

## Chapter 26

## The Test of Champions

Martin Kivel wrote in the *Pasadena Star News* what many were likely thinking: "If more than three or four horses show up to offer an argument in the Belmont Stakes, the final jewel in the Triple Crown, it will be a surprise." Entries for the June 9 contest would close on Thursday, June 7 at 10 AM.

Pancho Martin's immediate plan was to give Sham a few days of rest and then "begin to crank him up," as the trainer put it, the following week. After two meetings with Secretariat, Bill Resseguet wasn't eager to find Our Native a third.

"We've had enough of Secretariat for a while," he said. "He [Our Native] ran well in the Preakness but he just wasn't good enough to beat Secretariat and Sham." Resseguet put Our Native in a van for Garden State Park with plans for the Jersey Derby.

Trainer Henry "Buzz" Worchester felt Deadly Dream was

bred for turf and scheduled him to run on the grass in Delaware. Worchester also thought Deadly Dream might have taken third in the Preakness had he not collided with Sham. "Normally our colt would have been laying much closer to the pace," Worchester said. "He finished well, but by that time he was out of the race, for all practical purposes. He's not really a top stakes horse, like Secretariat or Sham, but he has been a useful individual who won two stakes this season, and I felt he might have beaten Ecole Etage again. He beat him before."

Ecole Etage remained at Pimlico with plans for the Ohio Derby at Thistledown in North Randall, Ohio in his future, though ultimately he wasn't entered. Other than Sham, Torsion was the only other Preakness horse to be stabled in the same state as Secretariat, let alone share the same track. Torsion was vanned to Belmont Park, but not for the Belmont Stakes.

Angle Light occupied a stall near Secretariat at Belmont and got a daily show of his neighbor's media attention. But Angle Light wouldn't contest the Belmont Stakes either.

In the *Daily News*, Gene Ward wrote, "The Triple Crown may be a *fait accompli* to Secretariat's huge following, but he still has to run around the race track... and finish ahead of Sham in the mile-and-a-half Belmont Stakes."

Arnold Kirkpatrick and Ashbel Green in *The Thoroughbred Record* identified Sham as one of only "two legitimate obstacles to Secretariat becoming the ninth Triple Crown Winner." The other was Stop the Music, a colt who had defeated Secretariat as a two-year-old in the Champagne Stakes (with the help of a foul, placing Secretariat second). On the same day as the Preakness Stakes, Stop the Music had run a mile at Belmont Park and taken four-fifths of a second off the track record.

In the event Sham were the only challenger to face Big Red, the *Lexington Herald* noted the last Belmont Stakes match race had been in 1920, when the old Big Red, Man o' War himself, had beaten Donnacona. But Pancho Martin found another potential challenger for Secretariat. Knightly Dawn's name came up again.

Martin said Knightly Dawn would run in the Belmont only if the track condition was muddy or sloppy. His role would be to run as the rabbit, allowing Sham to stay off the pace and challenge with a strong closing bid. "It will be fun to see what happens when someone opens up five or six lengths," Martin said, anticipating Knightly Dawn's lead.

Lucien Laurin didn't seem concerned for Secretariat's sake. "It just means another horse for him to get around," he said.

Milo Valenzuela was again assigned to ride Knightly Dawn. Valenzuela's most recent Belmont Stakes was in 1968 on Forward Pass when he finished second to Heliodoro Gustines and Stage Door Johnny. Knightly Dawn would be Valenzuela's fourth career Belmont Stakes mount.

Knightly Dawn was riding a winning streak after his Twin Spires Purse victory on Kentucky Derby Day. On May 28 at Garden State Park, he won the Jersey Derby in dramatic fashion on a sloppy track over a field that included the favorite Our Native and Warbucks. Knightly Dawn stalked the leader, Hearts of Lettuce, to the three-eighths pole, flinging mud in pursuit before taking the lead. Knightly Dawn extended his lead to four lengths with only a furlong to go to the finish, but with the heavy running surface he began to tire. Pvt. Smiles, who had been eight lengths back with a quarter mile to go, challenged with a strong closing move. Knightly Dawn held on by a nose for the win. It was the second time he had won a stakes race valued at $100,000.

"Maybe I should run him in only $100,000 races," Pancho Martin said with a laugh. "He runs real good when he runs for big money."

Linda's Chief was mentioned as a possible Belmont Stakes starter. He was running well out West, taking 5 of 7 starts in California with two second-place finishes. He also won the Withers Stakes at Belmont Park on May 30. Owner Neil Hellman said he'd wait to see how the colt responded after that race before deciding. Other notable possibilities were Forego, Champagne Charlie, and Sham's old rivals from his two-year-old campaign in New York, Dick's Boots (also a Hellman-owned colt), Broadway Playboy, and Timeless Moment.

The Belmont Stakes was the oldest of the Triple Crown races, first run in 1867, though not always at the Elmont, New York site of the present-day Belmont Park. The first running of the Belmont Stakes held at Belmont Park was in 1905, with respites in subsequent years, such as those due to anti-betting legislation that shut racing down in New York in 1911 and 1912, and the demolition and rebuilding of the track from 1963 to 1967 when the Belmont Stakes was run at Aqueduct.

Though Belmont Park's one-and-a-half-mile main track was the longest in the country, the stretch run to the finish line was only 1,097 feet, which was shorter than the stretch run at both

Churchill Downs and Pimlico. The mile-and-a-half distance could do in a pace-setter, but the intimidating sight of the Belmont stretch, which extended another 843 feet past the finish line, could also do in a closer, even though the horse wouldn't be required to run the entire length to finish the race.

Jockey Jesse Davidson, who had experience on the Belmont surface said, "A horse coming into the Belmont stretch sees that endless straightaway, and, if he's easily discouraged, he'll chuck it." Davidson explained, "His eye takes in the whole stretch, not just to the finish line. And a horse trying to come from behind can get discouraged the same way."

Secretariat was contending not only with Sham and whatever field dared face him in the Belmont Stakes, but with history. Nine horses had won the Kentucky Derby and Preakness Stakes, only to fail to win the Belmont Stakes. They were Burgoo King in 1932, Bold Venture in 1936, Tim Tam in 1958, Carry Back in 1961, Northern Dancer in 1964, Kauai King in 1966, Forward Pass in 1968 (with the aid of a disqualification of Dancer's Image in the Kentucky Derby), Majestic Prince in 1969, and Canonero II in 1971.

Considering everything working against a horse, it was easy to see why so many had failed to win that third race. It wasn't just the year's three-year-olds a Triple Crown hopeful had to contend with, but the challenge of mastering different courses. The Kentucky Derby at one and a quarter miles, followed by the one-and-three-sixteenths-mile Preakness Stakes, followed by the grueling one-and-a-half-mile Belmont, a true test of a horse's stamina. The Belmont Stakes was known as the "test of champions."

Against top-notch competition, a Triple Crown candidate needed to stay in top form and stay sound for the Derby, and just two weeks later the Preakness, and then three weeks after that, the Belmont. A horse might look good after the Kentucky Derby, but it was entirely possible several fresh horses would be waiting for him in the Preakness, horses who hadn't run the Derby and were better rested. The same was true in the Belmont. A horse finishing the grind of Triple Crown competition might find fresh opponents in the Belmont who hadn't raced for a month or longer.

Neither Burgoo King nor Bold Venture was able to start in the Belmont due to injury. Tim Tam looked like a strong contender with an excellent chance to follow Citation to the Crown. But a broken leg at the top of the stretch ended not only his bid, but nearly his life. Sheer guts brought him home second, an amazing feat considering he did it on only three sound legs. Fortunately, his life was saved. The Belmont distance did in Carry Back (finishing seventh), Northern Dancer (finishing third), and Kauai King (finishing fourth). Forward Pass managed a second-place finish. Majestic Prince had peaked and wasn't in best form. That, plus injury, prevented his bid when he finished second. A sick and injured Canonero II did his best to finish fourth. He would recover and race as a four-year-old, but the Triple Crown was lost.

Charles Hatton originated the term "Triple Crown." Omaha was the first to win the series under that name in 1935. The three races were unrelated events prior to that year. When Sir Barton won all three in 1919, and Gallant Fox won the three in 1930, they won the races simply as individual contests. In 1973, only Secretariat and Sham would endure the challenge of all three races.

Lucien Laurin was asked about a possible Belmont Stakes jinx, the failure to capture the Triple Crown after winning the first two races. "Sure I think about it," he replied, "but I'm not superstitious. I'm just a little nervous and I'll be glad when it's over."

"It's not really a jinx," Pancho Martin said. "If there is a jinx it is the extra quarter of a mile. The horse can be a champion at the Derby distance and yet fail at a mile-and-a-half." As for the upcoming contest, Martin said, "I tell you this, I think Secretariat can go the mile-and-a-half as easy as he go the mile-and-a-quarter, but so can my horse."

In prior Belmont Stakes experience, Pancho Martin had finished fourth with Manassa Mauler in 1959. Laurin had two winners, Riva Ridge in 1972 and Amberoid in 1966. Incidentally, Amberoid had been one of the horses that had foiled Kauai King's attempt for the Triple Crown that year. Ron Turcotte had one previous Belmont Stakes victory with Riva Ridge. Laffit Pincay was riding in his first Belmont Stakes.

Near a path the horses took to and from the stables, a walkway ran between the front entrance of Belmont Park and the walking circle. The walkway led to the racing secretary's office where trainers, riders, and jockey agents congregated at various times throughout their workday. Pancho Martin sat on a bench outside the office near an umbrella of overhanging trees and stared at the latest issue of *Time* magazine. Secretariat, wearing his familiar blue and white hood, stared back at him. Secretariat appeared in a full head shot, with a glance as if he truly were a

Hollywood screen idol. Few words were needed to say what his image couldn't. "Super Horse" and "Secretariat" were the only explanation on the cover, as if the editors granted everyone knew who he was by now.

"*If* he beats me in the Belmont Stakes on Saturday, *then* I'll call him a super horse," Martin responded to the magazine, or perhaps the cover subject himself. Martin remained confident, noting Secretariat had yet to beat Sham in a manner Martin considered "fair and square."

In racing circles there are stories of broken-hearted horses who were demoralized by tough losses. Pancho Martin was a skeptic of that belief. He didn't see Sham getting discouraged.

"C'mon," he told a visitor to Barn 52, "I gonna show you how discourage he is." Martin took Sham by the halter and turned back his upper lip to reveal the missing teeth. "This son of a gun, he impress me," Martin said.

The phone in his office rang, and Martin told the caller, "I don't do no business transactions till Monday." It was a real-estate broker offering a horse farm on Long Island. "I'm gonna be busy. Call me Monday," Martin replied. He described the property to his visitor; it was a small farm, a few horses to give his family something to do. "I gotta look for a hobby," he said, "'cause I don't drink no more, I don't go out."

Some horsemen did believe the defeats might hurt Sham's confidence, leaving his willingness to fight shaken. Some felt Sham might have lost heart, while others felt the defeats would not adversely affect a horse of his caliber.

Charles Hatton wrote Sham had not shown any signs of

nervousness, but possessed "the aplomb one looks for in good horses." He noted, "Sham must be what horsemen call 'a good whip horse.' He was subjected to severe punishment through the stretch in the Preakness. But he goes about his daily chores cheerfully and dutifully."

Jockey agent Ralph Theroux said of Sham, "He's been in three big wars," adding the Wood Memorial to the mix, "and he was always trying at the end." He observed, "He was always stridin' out and doin' the best he could. He didn't chuck the bit and pull back." Theroux's confidence in Sham nearly equaled Pancho Martin's. "If Secretariat has an off day, Sham will swallow him," Theroux declared.

Trainer Allen Jerkins also believed Secretariat wouldn't have it easy. "He is facing a very grim competitor in Sham," Jerkins said. "He hung on like a bull dog in those other two races and I have a great deal of respect for him. We could have quite a horse race here Saturday."

Steve Cady, however, wrote in the *New York Times*, "If ever a horse deserved to have a nervous breakdown, it's Sham."

Heliodoro Gustines had had experience with Sham and was asked years later to consider Sham's situation. Gustines was familiar with both types of horses, the type that quit, and the type that continued to battle regardless of tough defeats. "Some horses, they don't care," he said. "They just keep going. But some horses, they're very moody. They're all different. Some give up. Some keep trying. They keep trying, trying, trying."

Gustines felt Sham might have been a bit down-hearted for the Belmont Stakes. "I remember Carmen Basilio, the fighter," he said. "He used to get beat up, but he kept on fighting. You beat me up once, I won't go back again," he said with a laugh. Sham could have taken heart that Carmen Basilio eventually did become champion.

## Chapter 27

# Sham Refuses to Yield the Crown

Sham's workouts indicated no lack of confidence, no lack of effort. "My horse has enough confidence to beat three Secretariats," Pancho Martin announced. "He knows he got two teeth knocked out in the starting gate and he knows he got knocked against the rail in the Preakness. Oh, he knows he didn't get beat fair and square."

Sham ran a strong seven furlongs in 1:23 on May 30. He was prompted for speed during the work, with Jules Watson of the *Daily Racing Form* noting, "The boy did tap him lightly a couple of times." Two days later, Secretariat followed up with a June 1 work over a mile in a fast 1:34⅘. It was as if he wanted to keep Sham in check after his impressive workout.

By June 4, Neil Hellman decided Linda's Chief would not run in the Belmont Stakes. He was pointed toward the Pontiac-

Grand Prix at Arlington Park in Chicago. Hellman's colt Dick's Boots would pass on the Belmont as well.

At 7 AM on Tuesday, June 5, Sham went a brisk six furlongs in 1:12, while not being asked to run full out. He eased a final seventh furlong in a sharp 1:24 1/5 with a note from the clockers stating, "Went easy and evenly." But Pancho Martin reported Sham did seven furlongs in 1:25. He said they missed the start of the workout and the colt ran 1:25 with a final five furlongs in :59, which would be a very strong finish. "He start very slow," Martin said, "and the clockers miss him because they maybe think he's just galloping."

Quality workouts continued to be the norm for Sham and Secretariat. Rider Pedro Cachola said he never really had Sham run full out during a work. "Go too fast," he said, "I might fall off."

On Wednesday, Lucien Laurin hoped to beat the day's humidity with a 6:40 AM workout. Despite the early hour, a party of photographers, writers, and onlookers followed. The workout was delayed when Ron Turcotte couldn't get to his horse. He had spent half an hour looking for a parking spot. The rush of media had been filing in to the facility, bumper to bumper, practically since daybreak. Bus service had also been provided from the Biltmore Hotel for visiting newsmen. The bus had arrived at 5:15 AM for early risers who wanted to see Secretariat's work.

Secretariat breezed a speedy four furlongs in :46 3/5. Again, he wasn't asked for speed, yet showed it anyway. Penny Tweedy and Lucien Laurin watched from the stands. After the run, Turcotte said the colt didn't want to pull up, finishing a fifth furlong in :59 2/5. Mrs. Tweedy thought the effort "marvelous."

"He came back playing," Mrs. Tweedy said. "He just loves to run. It is as if he thinks racing is a game we thought up for his amusement."

That same Wednesday, Sham's routine limited him to walking the barn shedrow. "Walk Wednesday," Pancho Martin outlined the strategy, "gallop Thursday, gallop Friday, walk Saturday—and then run." Hopefully, Sham would run well on Saturday, on Belmont Day.

Martin spent much of his time with Sham, either during workouts or around the barn. He was often too busy to mingle with other horsemen, and his attitude reflected his work ethic. "I get up at 5 a.m. every day," Martin was known to say. "I don't need an alarm clock. If a man has trouble getting up at 5 o'clock, he has no business being a trainer."

The betting crowd maintained confidence in Sham. The early line reported on June 6 had Sham at the low odds of 5 to 2. Secretariat, however, was at the exceedingly low 2 to 5.

Forego was still being considered a possibility for the Belmont, though trainer Sherrill Ward said, "I'm not sure he is a distance horse." Forego had finished a disappointing third in the Withers Stakes on May 30, but on Wednesday, June 6, he ran a scalding four furlongs in :45, faster than even his trainer wanted him to go. Ward didn't fear a detrimental effect from the work, later pointing out Forego hadn't lost his appetite: "There he is now, picking away at this grass as if he is afraid it won't be here tomorrow."

On Wednesday evening, Pancho Martin declined the racing association's invitation to their annual party. "I don't drink,"

Martin said when asked if he planned on going. Upon declining the Belmont Ball the following evening as well, Martin said he didn't dance. "All I want to do is be with Sham," he said, surrounded by Sham's five-gallon jugs of Mountain Valley mineral water.

In his 44-horse stable, only Sham drank the mineral water. "At four and a quarter a jug," Martin explained the preferential treatment, "you'd go out of business."

"Only 24 hours more," Lucien Laurin said on Thursday, nervously miscalculating the race's Saturday start. His plans for Secretariat had the colt walking Thursday, followed by a light gallop on Friday, when there really would be only 24 hours more. "He's been raising hell, ready to go," Laurin said of Secretariat's eagerness to run. "Let's hope he stays that way until Saturday."

Covering the Belmont Stakes were visiting local press and faraway representatives from Massachusetts to Hawaii, Canada, Puerto Rico, and Venezuela, totaling approximately 300. Adding television and radio personnel from local stations and major networks, the number increased to approximately 500. According to a NYRA press release, the newspaper and magazine still photographers were "legion—and uncounted."

"They make such a fuss about this horse, if we got beat I guess I would hide in a hole like a groundhog," Lucien Laurin said.

Secretariat seemed to be taking it all in stride. Eddie Sweat reported Secretariat was relaxed despite the building hype. "And playful, man, is he playful. He is always grabbing my shirt with his teeth and yanking me to him. And sometimes he hits me with his nose and almost decks me," Sweat said.

Nor did Secretariat have a problem with the media who crowded around him as if fighting for standing room at a sold-out show. During a television interview with one of his handlers, Secretariat casually nibbled on the microphone. When he heard the click of a camera, he'd put up his head and strike a pose, "looking grand," Mrs. Tweedy reported. "He's quite a ham," she said. But arranging a meeting with the equine celebrity wasn't the easiest assignment.

"Getting to see Secretariat might be more difficult than arranging an audience with the Pope. Or perhaps, a chat with President Nixon. And your credentials—they better be in order," wrote Tom Cunningham of the *Albany Times-Union*. "I took a walk over to Barn 5 Thursday. I was stopped by six Pinkertons and a German shepard."

In the New York City area, Sham also had his fans, particularly the thousands of supporters in the Latin community. A bumper sticker declaring, "I like Ky.-Bred Sham," was affixed to the vehicle of Sham's blacksmith, Ray Amato.

"I pull up at a stop light," Amato said, "and people in cars around holler 'Show 'em, Sham' and 'You can do it, Sham.'"

Sham also appeared to be at ease with the mounting tension. He stretched out on the floor of his stall for a nap. "Like clockwork, every day at noon he lies down and conks off," Martin said. "The darndest thing… the most relaxed horse I ever had."

Meanwhile, in his *Daily News* column, Gene Ward was calling Sham "the most dangerous challenger any champion ever had."

"You can't make a mistake against Secretariat," Pancho Martin noted. "But they can't afford to make a mistake against us, either, not even a little one."

Nominations had closed for the Belmont Stakes on February 15, 1973 with 187 names entered. As it turned out, of those 187 hopefuls, only three would actually face Sham and Secretariat. As potential Belmont challengers dropped from consideration, Pvt. Smiles, a chestnut colt owned and bred by Cornelius Vanderbilt (C.V.) Whitney, joined the field. Whitney was from one of the old families of racing. He had taken over the family stable in 1930, and had twice won the Belmont Stakes, with Phalanx in 1947 and with Counterpoint in 1951. The 1973 Belmont Stakes would be Whitney's eighteenth.

A stretch-running colt, Pvt. Smiles had won only once in seven starts for 1973, but had earned two second-place finishes. Trainer George Poole felt he was improving race by race. "He was kind of dumb at the outset of the season, but he is beginning to learn what racing is all about and I think he may turn out to be something special," Poole said.

Pvt. Smiles had run the Stepping Stone Purse at Churchill Downs in Louisville on April 28 finishing fourth, some nine lengths ahead of Knightly Dawn. On May 28, Pvt. Smiles closed strongly in the Jersey Derby, making up a distance of four lengths in the last furlong to finish second to Knightly Dawn. The race led many to believe Pvt. Smiles might be a serious challenger to Secretariat.

"The Jersey Derby was quite a race," George Poole said. "I sat with Pancho [Martin] and it was so close that he congratulated me. Naturally, I would have liked to have won it but Pvt. Smiles' race was so good that it took a lot of the sting out of dropping a cliff-hanger." After the race, Poole pronounced, "He's ready now."

On June 2, Pvt. Smiles breezed a quick three furlongs in :36 at Belmont on a fast track. "I think we have a chance," George Poole said. "Mr. Whitney is a sportsman and he isn't running a horse in the Belmont just to see his name in the program." C.V. Whitney had indeed enjoyed success on the racetrack, having bred more than 150 stakes winners.

Whitney's latest Belmont Stakes contender got his name from an historic circumstance. C.V. Whitney had been a lieutenant colonel during World War II. His wife, Mary Lou Whitney, had worked during the war at a Kansas City radio station broadcasting to the troops. She used the name Pvt. Smiles for her broadcasts. According to her husband, the former Pvt. Smiles "had a higher rating than Bob Hope." C.V. Whitney added, "My hope is that my horse can get a higher rating than Secretariat before the year is out."

On June 6, Pvt. Smiles galloped the main track with the trainer's son Timmy Poole riding. Timmy Poole commented the horse took hold of the bit near the wire as if he could have circled the mile-and-a-half track again. Outside the Whitney barn, George Poole acknowledged Secretariat's popularity and his hope in playing the role of spoiler. "I'd like to be the most hated man in America Saturday," he said.

Joining Sham, Secretariat, and Pvt. Smiles in the Belmont Stakes were My Gallant and Twice a Prince. Since the Kentucky Derby, My Gallant had worked out at Monmouth Park in Oceanport, New Jersey. He had run a blistering three furlongs in :34 ⅘ on May 30, having not even been pressed for speed, and had followed up on May 31 by defeating older horses in the Alibhai Purse at Belmont Park. On June 6, My Gallant worked a nice five furlongs in :59 ⅘ at Monmouth Park. Jockey Angel Cordero, however, didn't express the greatest optimism for his mount. "I feel sorry for my colt," he said. "He has to run against Secretariat."

Twice a Prince worked at Belmont Park since the Kentucky Derby. On May 26 he had run a fast four furlongs :47 ⅗ over a sloppy track. In an allowance race on June 2 at Belmont, he had finished fourth, but only three and a quarter lengths back. But he had again caused trouble at the start by breaking through the starting gate.

While entering Twice a Prince in the Belmont, Campo questioned Secretariat's ability to go a mile and a half. "He was all out to win the Derby," he said. "Turcotte had to get into him pretty good, and that was only a mile and a quarter. With six horses there'll be an honest pace. Knightly Dawn and Sham will be rattling and I think Secretariat will be along with them. My horse likes to come from off the pace."

On Thursday, June 7, an 8:30 AM bus took newsmen to the Trustees Lounge at Belmont Park for the annual press breakfast for owners, trainers, and jockeys participating in the Belmont Stakes. Apparently, it was to be a working breakfast. The Belmont Park press release providing the information noted, "Sorry no wives." Racing secretary Kenneth Noe Jr. drew post positions for the race.

Penny Tweedy clutched her Kentucky Derby trophy and

Woodland Vase for photographers while eyeing the August Belmont Memorial Cup set on a table beside her. The silver bowl, 18 inches high and 15 inches across, displayed a figure of Fenian, winner of the 1869 Belmont Stakes on its lid. Representatives of the thoroughbred foundation sires, Eclipse, Herod, and Matchem surrounded and supported the bowl. With a bent knee in checkered slacks, Mrs. Tweedy held the Kentucky Derby trophy in her right hand, the Woodlawn Vase in her left. Near the Belmont Cup was the Thoroughbred Racing Association's Triple Crown trophy—a silver triangle representing the three jewels of the Triple Crown. By Saturday, Mrs. Tweedy might need a bigger trophy case.

The draw for the Belmont put Sham and Twice a Prince in adjacent stalls, Sham at six with Twice a Prince at five. Pancho Martin suggested Twice a Prince be left in the barn.

Johnny Campo, trainer of Twice a Prince, was running his fourth Belmont Stakes. Braulio Baeza, hired to ride Twice a Prince when Linda's Chief was withdrawn, had missed riding in only one Belmont Stakes since 1961. Baeza had won in his Belmont Stakes debut on 65 to 1 long-shot Sherluck in 1961, had won in 1963 on Chateaugay, and had won in 1969 on Arts and Letters, spoiling Majestic Prince's Triple Crown bid. Baeza had the unusual distinction of winning three Belmont Stakes over three different surfaces. In 1961 he had won at the old Belmont Park, in 1963 he had won when the race was run at Aqueduct, and in 1969 he had won at the new Belmont Park.

Lucien Laurin was more relaxed prior to the Belmont than he had been for the Kentucky Derby and wasn't as shy in expressing his confidence in Secretariat. Each subsequent race since the Derby had gotten easier, according to the trainer. "The Derby had to be the toughest because of the large field; you don't know what kind of racing luck you'll get." With the smaller field, Laurin considered the Preakness an easier race than the Derby. He figured the trend to continue for the Belmont. "There will be a small field and the turns on this mile-and-a-half track are sweeping, so if you are on the outside you lose little ground," Laurin's said. "I think he'll win the Belmont easier than the other two," he predicted.

George Poole had different ideas. "If a match race develops, and it could, Secretariat and Sham *might* be awfully tired at the end of a mile and a quarter. And then a late runner like Pvt. Smiles would have a chance of catching them."

Owner C.V. Whitney also expressed his optimism. "Anything can happen in this race, and who knows if Secretariat can handle that last quarter of a mile?"

"I don't think they can beat him," Laurin said of Secretariat's challengers. "He can do it all. If he has to come from behind, he will. If he has to go to the lead, he will. He's sharp as he can be, and I don't have the slightest doubt he will be able to stay the mile and a half." Laurin also said, with Pancho Martin-like bravado, "He will stay as far as horses are asked to run in this country."

With Secretariat having run two completely different races in the Kentucky Derby and Preakness Stakes, both with resounding success, Pancho Martin was left to guess what type of strategy Meadow Stable would employ for the Belmont Stakes.

He also considered whether Knightly Dawn would be part of his own strategy. Knightly Dawn ran a fast four furlongs at Belmont in :47 ⅕ on June 7.

The weather forecast called for mostly sunny, warm weather with only a ten percent chance of rain. "The track has been fast here this meeting," Martin said. "Ordinary horses are running fast, and Secretariat and Sham are no ordinary horses. If the pace is real, a record may be set."

If Sham and Secretariat were up to their previous two performances, it looked as though the Belmont Stakes record was ready for the taking. During the spring meeting six new track records had been broken over the Belmont Park surface by late May. New marks had been set at both six and at six and a half furlongs on May 15, at seven furlongs on May 16, and at one mile on May 19. The records set at six and a half and seven furlongs hadn't stood long. They were both broken again on May 19.

On Thursday, Laffit Pincay won at Hollywood Park for the 500th time in his career. He was one of only six jockeys to win 500 or more at that track. But Pincay's luck didn't hold. His flight to New York that evening was fogged in at Los Angeles International Airport. He caught an afternoon flight on Friday.

Both Sham and Secretariat were out for easy gallops on Friday. Sham went once around the main track. Secretariat went twice around the one-mile training track, much to the chagrin of television crews who had set up near the main track.

After the gallop, Pancho Martin led Sham back to Barn 52, crossing paths with Lucien Laurin on his way from the training track with Secretariat to Barn 5.

"Hello," Martin said.

"Hello," Laurin returned.

It was the first time the two had spoken since just after the Wood Memorial.

Another Belmont track record fell that Friday. This time it was the five-and-a-half-furlong mark. It was the seventh track record to be broken that spring.

## Chapter 28

# Battling a Tremendous Machine

*And scarcely had he Maggie rallied
When out the hellish legion sallied...*

*Now, do thy speedy-utmost, Meg,
And win the key-stone o' the brig;
There, at them thou thy tail may toss,
A running stream they dare na cross.
But ere the keystane she could make,
The fient a tail she had to shake!*

*For Nannie, far before the rest,
Hard upon noble Maggie prest,
And flew at Tam wi' furious ettle;
But little wist she Maggie's mettle!
Ae spring brought off her master hale,
But left behind her ain grey tail:
The carlin claught her by the rump,
And left poor Maggie scarce a stump.*
—Robert Burns, "Tam o'Shanter: A Tale"

Eddie Sweat arrived at the Belmont barns just after 5 AM on Saturday. He called to Secretariat, who poked his head from out of his stall. By 5:57, exercise rider Charlie Davis weaved through the Pinkerton men standing watch. Davis took Secretariat around a walking circle for about 20 minutes. The colt jumped and played to the din of feed tubs being filled for the morning meal on Belmont Day.

"The only thing he knows is eat, relax and run," Eddie Sweat said.

The Pinkerton men were not so at ease. "It worries me, watching something worth that much," one guard admitted. "This is my first big assignment. I've been with Pinkerton three weeks."

Ron Turcotte made time early in the day for a haircut beneath the Belmont stands. Just before 10 AM, Pancho Martin scratched Knightly Dawn. Weather conditions hadn't created a muddy track, and Martin didn't want to run an entry with Sham, wasting Knightly Dawn as a rabbit.

"If Sham runs true, he does not need any help, I think," Martin said. "If he does not have any trouble in the Belmont, maybe he will beat Secretariat—finally—but alone."

That left only Sham, My Gallant, Twice a Prince, and Pvt. Smiles as Secretariat's Belmont competition. Martin said Knightly Dawn would instead be reserved for the Ohio Derby.

Sham poked his head from his stall while an electric fan set on the ground blew a quiet breeze over him. He closed his eyes, seemingly relaxed, enjoying the rush of air as it fluffed his mane. That morning, the *Albany Times-Union* reported Secretariat still at 2 to 5 odds on the early line, but the public's confidence in Sham had grown to lower his odds to 2 to 1.

Penny and John Tweedy had lunch with New York Governor Nelson Rockefeller and his wife, Happy Rockefeller, Virginia Governor Linwood Holton, and New York Senator Jacob Javits and his wife, Marion. Henry Kissinger was scheduled to join them, but was detained in Paris in talks with the North Vietnamese.

Throngs pushed through the Belmont Park gates in a rush for available seats. The gates had opened at 9:15 AM with the first race scheduled for 1:30 PM. The Belmont Stakes would be off at 5:38 PM. In a scene resembling the sidewalks of Disneyland, a crowd gathered along the streets outside the gates of the racetrack. An overflow of race fans and curiosity seekers collected on Hempstead Avenue. Campers lined the avenue in front of Belmont Park and along adjacent blocks.

Inside, a Dixieland band performed at the clubhouse, a steel band played by the eighth pole near the final stretch, another band played marches, and among it all, a rock band called Fresh Garbage also played. There was no infield crowd as there had been for the Kentucky Derby and Preakness Stakes. Spectators weren't allowed in the Belmont Park infield. "We have two turf tracks out there which must be protected and a couple of lakes," a track spokesman said. "We don't want any soused customers falling into the water."

Throughout the day, people from the standing room crowd stopped by to offer Mrs. Tweedy best wishes, shake her hand, or request an autograph. In a pastel blue and white flowered dress with blue and white shoes to match, she greeted well-wishers, acknowledged an ovation by standing and raising both hands above her head like a prize fighter, shook hands, and continued to smile. "I feel like a Roman emperor or something," she said. "The people all are very nice."

A colorful John Tweedy, in a green jacket and pink shirt, wore a black button with a heart on it. The button said, "Breed More Secretariats." Governor Holton wore one too.

Both Laffit Pincay and Ron Turcotte rode several mounts prior to the Belmont Stakes. Pincay rode Stet in the first race and Golden Palace in the fourth. Neither horse found success, finishing seventh and fifth, respectively. Turcotte was busier. He won the second race on Mister Fantasy, rode Sharp Quill to a fourth-place finish in the third race, and won the fifth race, the High Gun Purse, on Spanish Riddle, the horse he had ridden at Pimlico prior to the Preakness Stakes. Turcotte also rode Angle Light in the seventh race, the Phalanx Purse, but finished ninth in a field of ten after Angle Light tired, having fought for the early lead. Forego won the Phalanx Purse, drawing away by nine lengths with old friend Heliodoro Gustines aboard.

Onlookers crowded the Belmont walking circle. To get within sight of it, they ignored earlier races to stake a claim on the tiniest plots of ground. Two girls wearing t-shirts decorated in blue and white checks across the sleeves and "Secretariat" printed across their backs in block letters waited among the thousands for a glimpse of their hero. The girls were done up, appropriately, in pony tails. By the seventh race, the terrace surrounding the walking circle was packed even tighter, though the Belmont Stakes was the eighth race and wouldn't be run for another 45 minutes. Balconies behind, on the red brick clubhouse, also filled up.

Despite the hot, humid 90-degree weather, despite the number diverted to New York's 120 off-track betting parlors, despite the local television broadcast not being blacked out, and despite the Mets-Dodgers game at Shea Stadium drawing the venue's biggest crowd of the year, the second largest crowd ever to see a Belmont Stakes made it to the track. A tally just short of 70,000 came to catch a glimpse of Secretariat's attempt to make history. CBS televised nationally from 5 to 6 PM and broadcast on radio from 5:25 to 5:45 PM. According to Nielsen ratings, the televised spectacle drew a 60 percent share locally with an estimated 2.17 million television viewers, which didn't include people watching in bars, restaurants, and country clubs.

Secretariat had gained mass appeal unlimited by followers' age, sex, race, political affiliation, or economic standing. He transcended limits and divisive categories. He had no ulterior motive or hidden agenda—he ran to win. Sham was just as honest, just as earnest. But it was Secretariat who had reached the populace, the Rolling Stones crowd, the Grateful Dead crowd, the Duke Ellington, Lawrence Welk, Mantovani, and Mozart crowds. The fan club was all inclusive. No initiation fee or registration was required—you just had to watch.

Prior to the long awaited eighth race, the walking circle filled with horse owners, some not particularly schooled in the sport of thoroughbred racing. They eagerly snapped the picture of the first horse to enter the paddock. They were after a chestnut colt and they got one. It was, however, Pvt. Smiles, not "Big Red."

In the paddock, the formerly calm Sham now seemed on edge. Pancho Martin knew his horse was not the type to get nervous or anxious before a race, but Sham was visibly sweating while Secretariat appeared cool and dry. "I've never seen Sham so nervous as before the Belmont," Martin commented later. "He was wringing wet, it was a very hot day, and the long walk from his barn to the paddock in all that heat and humidity took a lot out of him. Sure it was hot for Secretariat, too, but different horses react differently to conditions."

Viola Sommer also noticed Sham's condition, recalling years later, "Normally when he was being saddled he was just as cool and calm and collected as could be." Though she acknowledged the day's heat, she added, "When he was being saddled for the Belmont... he was sweating, which was unusual for him."

One could only guess what Sham was thinking. He had been battered and beaten in two previous races. He'd lost teeth, been cut, and had caromed off a rail at high speed. With the madding crowd and zealous circumstance, it looked to be another Kentucky Derby or Preakness Stakes. Could he really expect the upcoming race, or its result, to be any different? Would he again be battered and spent, exerted and whipped for a no more than second best?

Mrs. Tweedy and Lucien Laurin edged their way through the swarm to reach the paddock. Among the calls of "Bravo, Secretariat" and "Triple Crown, baby," a few assorted boos were thrown into the mix. During his walk around the paddock, Secretariat seemed to defy the critics with a toss of his head. Governor Rockefeller, on hand to present the Belmont Cup to the winner, also got his share of boos throughout the day.

The five competitors completed their stroll around the walking circle beneath Norwegian maples and headed for the tunnel that would bring them onto the track. Sham emerged first. The crowd applauded his appearance, which grew in waves when Secretariat appeared. The applause swelled continually as the band played "The Sidewalks of New York" during the post parade. Fans jumped up and down and waved their hands in anticipation. A helicopter hovered overhead by the first turn. "I'm scared to death," Mrs. Tweedy admitted.

The odds on Secretariat flashed 1 to 9, but only because the tote board couldn't accommodate three digits. The odds were, in fact, 1 to 10. Sham was the second favorite at 5 to 1. My Gallant went off at 12 to 1, Pvt. Smiles at 14 to 1, and Twice a Prince at 17 to 1.

Lucien Laurin's instructions to Ron Turcotte were succinct. Laurin would not allow a slow pace such as that in the Wood Memorial and one that might have developed in the Preakness had Secretariat not taken command early. Laurin expected Sham to go to the lead. "Just sit on him," he told Turcotte, "take a long hold, I want him on the lead all the way. And I hope to God he gets to the wire."

Laurin had gotten into Pancho Martin's head. Martin instructed Laffit Pincay to go to the front to avoid a repeat of the Preakness.

The horses gathered before the finish line, lining up at the starting gate. Secretariat was loaded first, followed by Pvt. Smiles and My Gallant. Twice a Prince was led in, blindfolded to reduce the risk of bad behavior. This time the colt, as Whitney Tower described in his *Sports Illustrated* column, "behaved like a lamb." Sham, loaded last, suffered nothing from his neighbor.

With the bell and the gates bursting open, Sham was off without trouble. Secretariat broke a bit off balance, angling toward the rail, but quickly recovered. My Gallant had broken from the gate first, but jockey Angel Cordero thought he had little chance to pull away as he looked to his left and saw Secretariat grabbing the bit, "Coming up like a dam [sic] lion," as he described it.

To avoid getting shuffled back at the start, Ron Turcotte sent Secretariat along the rail to challenge Sham for the lead. Sham worked the outside. During the Derby and Preakness, it was Sham who worked the rail with Secretariat on the outside. The rivals would see the race, and each other, from a different perspective. After one furlong Sham led by a head.

By the quarter mile Secretariat reversed the order. He held the lead by a head over Sham. With each step the anticipation of the crowd increased. They buzzed, then roared when Sham pulled alongside the leader. The two began to pull away from the other horses. They went after each other as if they were running a sprint rather than a mile-and-a-half course. Sham led five lengths over third-place My Gallant. Twice a Prince and Pvt. Smiles trailed further back. Pincay knew the early pace was too fast and looked for Turcotte to slow Secretariat down. Turcotte did nothing of the sort.

Lucien Laurin and Penny Tweedy watched through binoculars from a second tier box as Secretariat took the lead near the first turn. "I'm worried," Laurin said. "He may be running too fast."

Entering the first turn Secretariat led by a head over Sham as they further separated themselves from the pack. The lead Sham was unable to take back in the Derby, the gap he was unable to close in the Preakness, he overtook now. He grabbed back the head separating him from Secretariat. Sham poked his nose in front, and he wasn't through yet. He came on for more, extending the advantage to a head, then a neck. Further he went in a fury of slashing black legs, gaining half a length over Secretariat. Big Red, America's Horse, the Superhorse might finally be bested by the hard working everyman's horse. Sham ran strongly.

Then it was Secretariat's turn. The chestnut colt, whose coat had darkened a shade since the spring, as if to signify an increase in supernatural power, took back the half-length, then the neck, then the head, then the lead.

Only Sham contested Secretariat's running away with the race, and it was shaping up as Pancho Martin had predicted. "The Belmont will be a match race, just Secretariat and Sham," he had said. "The rest will be nowhere."

My Gallant was somewhere, though far back, 10 lengths behind Sham. My Gallant held a slight lead of a head over Twice a Prince with Pvt. Smiles another 10 lengths further back in the fifth position.

Noting the suicidal pace Secretariat and Sham were setting, :23 3/5 for the quarter mile and :46 1/5 for a half mile, Penny Tweedy said, "Oh, oh! I'm scared."

Secretariat ran so smoothly, Turcotte was not aware how fast his colt was going. But the scalding furlong splits caused concern for many whose experience told them Secretariat and Sham were running too fast too soon.

The already deafening crowd exploded. "When he [Secretariat] and Sham hooked up around the clubhouse turn, I thought I might have a shot to come on and get them both," Angel Cordero said afterward. "Maybe they'll run each other into the ground."

On Twice a Prince, Braulio Baeza said the early Secretariat-Sham duel gave him "a bag full of hopes, but not to win—not at that pace."

As My Gallant and Twice a Prince battled for third, Cordero looked over to Braulio Baeza. "None of us going to be second now," Cordero said.

Sham and Secretariat stayed together until midway through the backstretch. By three-quarters of a mile Secretariat began to pull away, extending his lead over Sham to two and a half lengths—the margin that seemed to curse the bay. "Once he got inside of Sham he wasn't about to give anything away," Ron Turcotte said after the race. "He drew off on his own down the backstretch."

Turcotte was still unaware just how fast Secretariat was moving. "I thought we were doing something like 1:11 for the first 6 furlongs," Turcotte later commented. "As it turned out, he was going in 1:09 ⅘. His action is so smooth it's hard to tell."

"Secretariat is blazing along!" track and CBS broadcast announcer Chic Anderson called in excitement over what he was witnessing, declaring the chestnut colt's time of 1:09 ⅘ for three-quarters of a mile. "Secretariat is widening now. He is moving like a tremendous machine!"

Secretariat had run the fastest six furlongs ever in the Belmont Stakes by nearly a full second. Lucien Laurin watched with nervous concern. Secretariat's father, Bold Ruler, had also set a fast pace for six furlongs in the 1957 Belmont Stakes, only to fade in the stretch, coasting on fumes to finish third. The tote board told the present story as it unfolded but with no hint of Secretariat's demise. On the contrary, Secretariat continued to run strongly, firing on all cylinders.

He extended his lead to seven lengths over Sham at the one-mile mark. It was the fastest mile in Belmont Stakes history. Sham held second by seven lengths over Twice a Prince, who had overtaken My Gallant for third.

Turcotte looked back at Sham once, then again, as if he couldn't locate his competition. "All of a sudden Sham started to drop back," Turcotte said later. "That's when I looked around. I wanted to see what happened. I didn't expect him to drop out of it that soon."

Secretariat entered the final turn leading by seven lengths. Coming out of the turn, he increased the lead by *another 13 lengths*. By a mile and a quarter, Secretariat led an incredible 20 lengths. And Turcotte hadn't even asked him to run yet. "Shoot, no," Turcotte later remarked, "I didn't even cock my whip."

Sham was spent. The impossible early fractions had done him in. "We couldn't keep up in a pace like that," Laffit Pincay said afterward. Twice a Prince passed Sham for second place with My Gallant close behind.

Seeing his horse easily dominate the field, Lucien Laurin leaned over to Mrs. Tweedy and told her, "He'll have to fall on his face now to lose."

Pincay knew the race was over for Sham. My Gallant passed him to take third. Only Pvt. Smiles, eight lengths back, trailed Sham.

Into the stretch Secretariat charged ahead, increasing his lead to an unthinkable 28 lengths. The remaining field hadn't yet cleared the turn as Secretariat entered the final stretch alone. CBS television struggled with its widest-angle lens to keep him in the same shot as his nearest competitor as Secretariat tore down the stretch.

The sustained crescendo of the crowd was the only thing closely following Secretariat. "Wow! What a horse!" Mrs. Tweedy declared.

Catherine "Cappy" Jackson was an 18-year-old freelance photographer covering the event. She had positioned herself on the roof at Belmont, snapping photos at the eighth poles throughout the race.

"I was on the roof, and the noise was coming up to me," she recalled years later. "The crowd was so intense." Even after years of experience photographing NFL football games she said, "I never heard anything like it before or since." As Secretariat pulled clear, she focused her camera on him, though capturing his image in the lens proved difficult. "It was hard to shoot," she said. "I was in tears."

She wasn't alone. Writer George Plimpton once commented, "There were these co-eds lining the rail. This sounds hard to believe, but I swear, half of them were weeping as he went by."

Jack Whitaker of CBS Sports recalled, "Everybody was speechless. And then, when it set in, people were crying. I actually saw people crying at this event. I mean, it was such an overwhelming thing."

Only upon seeing the fractions flash on the infield board was Turcotte fully aware of Secretariat's feat. "I knew we had a record made and I didn't want to blow it," Turcotte reported later. He never went to the whip, but urged Secretariat in a hand ride in the final 70 yards of the stretch. "He had been fast… but he still had more left when I asked him to go get the record," Turcotte said. "We both must have wanted the record."

My Gallant continued his battle for second, taking the position by a head from Twice a Prince. A 12-length gap separated Twice a Prince from the further fading Sham as Pvt. Smiles was moving in, closing to within one and a half lengths. Pincay didn't ask anything from his battle-weary colt down the stretch. Sham had had enough. "There was no reason to punish him trying for fourth," Pincay said after the race.

Secretariat finished in full stride, an unfathomable 31 lengths in front. Arnold Kirkpatrick described the Belmont scene in *The Thoroughbred Record*: "People were crying, others were speechless, others were jumping around like mad hooligans waving both fists in the air, others were hugging and kissing."

Twice a Prince retook second, finishing a half length over My Gallant. Thirteen lengths separated third-place My Gallant from Pvt. Smiles. He had finally closed on Sham to finish fourth, three-quarter lengths ahead.

Sham trotted home last, 45¼ lengths behind Secretariat. The racing chart stated Sham "stopped badly."

Tom Cunningham wrote about Sham in the *Albany Times-Union*, "The game animal gave Secretariat a tussle, and many, including myself, feel the horse ran just one too many times against the Man O' War of the jet age."

Laffit Pincay was apparently one of Cunningham's "many" in sharing his thoughts on Sham. "He was not the same horse that ran in the Kentucky Derby and Preakness."

Ron Turcotte's assessment agreed nearly verbatim with Pincay's. "I don't believe he was quite the same horse in the Belmont that he was in the Derby and Preakness," Turcotte said.

Twice a Prince earned a degree of redemption from his Kentucky Derby tantrum and poor performance. Johnny Campo said, "I hope you notice he acted perfectly in the gate." Campo said he thought the people in the infield had set him off prior to the Derby. "He is not used to people. He broke out in the paddock Saturday, but once he got on the track and was by himself, he calmed right down. He'll get over that sort of thing with maturity and seasoning."

"My horse ran a better race than was expected," Braulio Baeza said of Twice a Prince, "but Secretariat is a super horse."

My Gallant trainer Lou Goldfine said taking on Secretariat was "a little like going after an elephant with a BB gun."

Jockey Dan Gargan on Pvt. Smiles joked of the winner's margin of victory, and how the last he'd seen of Secretariat was in the starting gate. "The closest I got to him was when I stood beside him," he said.

Mike Barry commented in the *Louisville Courier-Journal*, "When a horse wins by an utterly unbelievable 31 lengths, as Secretariat did, the next finisher should be listed as fourth."

## Chapter 29

# All Over but the Shouting

*Let us aspire to the highest excellence, for, by this means, we shall either attain the summit, or at least see many below us.*
—Quintilian

Penny Tweedy leapt into the air. "Whee! Marvelous! Marvelous!" she exclaimed. A rush of photographers followed her to the winner's circle along with the ubiquitous Pinkertons. "Back up, back up, please," Mrs. Tweedy asked, hoping to avoid a replay of the Kentucky Derby winner's circle incident.

"I was afraid they'd crush me," Ron Turcotte said. "They're all biggern'n me."

After the photograph, Mrs. Tweedy and Lucien Laurin were off to accept the August Belmont Memorial Cup from Governor Rockefeller. The Governor also awarded the Triple Crown trophy, which had been brought to Belmont Park several times over past years, only to be packed up and stored for the next time. From the winner's circle, owner and trainer left for the Belmont Park Trustees' Room for the traditional winners' glass of champagne.

It took several moments for an emotional Lucien Laurin to compose himself. "He won… I feel great… lightheaded… no weight pushing me down."

Bettors had shown such confidence in a Secretariat victory, his 1 to 10 odds paid only $2.20 to win, while bets to place paid higher at $2.40.

"This is the greatest moment of my life," Laurin said. "Nobody had any excuses today," he added. "The best horse won."

"It was perfectly marvelous," Mrs. Tweedy said. "I loved the ending."

Joe Hendrickson wrote in the *Pasadena Star News*, "Hardened writers and fans of any description went batty as mighty Secretariat unleashed his power. Emotion exploded at Belmont this hot day."

Roberto Landa, winner on *The Dating Game* television show, was at the race with his date. He was a winner on the track as well, holding a $10 win ticket on Secretariat. He decided not to cash it. "I'm just glad to be here at a time like this—to be part of it," he said.

Secretariat's margin of victory exceeded the previous Belmont Stakes record of 25 lengths set by Count Fleet in 1943. Secretariat's final time of 2:24 for one and a half miles was a new record not only for the Belmont Stakes, but a world record on a dirt surface. He shattered the old Belmont Stakes record of

2:26 ⅗ by 2 ⅗ seconds, the equivalent of 13 lengths.

"I never saw anything like that in all my years on the race track," Lucien Laurin said. "I didn't think any horse could run that far that fast."

After winning the Triple Crown, Ron Turcotte rode the ninth race. He finished fifth on a colt named Head of the River. After Turcotte returned to the jockeys' room, racing steward Warren Mehrtens met him there. Turcotte grinned when he saw him and thrust out his hand. Mehrtens wasn't there to reprimand Turcotte for an infraction. Instead, he shook Turcotte's hand, then grabbed him in a bearhug. Mehrtens had just welcomed the latest member to an exclusive club. Warren Mehrtens was the jockey who had ridden Assault to his Triple Crown in 1946.

In revisiting Pancho Martin and Laffit Pincay's Belmont Stakes strategy, if they had chosen to pace Sham, or if Sham had given up in challenging Secretariat, Sham likely could have coasted to a second-place finish, completing the Triple Crown route as runner-up in all three races. But Pincay had ridden Sham, and Sham had run, to win, not to secure second place.

Sham hadn't shied from Secretariat, but had taken the lead from him early in the race. Nose to nose, he had slugged it out with an invincible opponent, equal to the impossible pace until too many too fast quarters had finished him.

Lucien Laurin had a different read on the situation. He felt it wasn't fast early fractions that had beaten Sham. He said Sham didn't know he would be asked to run a mile and a half, and he didn't know he had to pace himself. Sham could handle three-quarters of a mile in 1:09 with little trouble if pacing weren't an issue. Laurin thought Sham quit when he realized it was Secretariat running easily with him. But if Sham's confidence had been shaken going into Belmont, if he had been overly nervous before the race, he had fought hard nonetheless, whether it was for three-quarters of a mile or for as long as he could maintain the pace.

"Sham had nothing left to give," Gene Ward wrote in the *Daily News*. "You cannot run with a whirlwind and not get hurt."

Secretariat was not expected to race for at least a month following the Belmont. "He might not need a vacation," Laurin said, "but I do." Pancho Martin indicated Sham, who clearly did need a vacation, would also rest after the Belmont. Martin had no future plans regarding Sham's next race.

Reams of print media lauded "America's Horse" after what Whitney Tower in *Sports Illustrated* called, "the greatest performance by a racehorse in this century." Secretariat drew numerous references to Pegasus. Associated Press writer Wick Temple denied the Belmont Stakes was a race at all, but instead called it "a one-horse stampede." Columnist Dave Anderson noted the margin of victory in declaring, "Secretariat pounded across the finish line, more alone than Greta Garbo ever was." Melvin Durslag also noted the margin in the *Los Angeles Herald-Examiner*, commenting Secretariat crossed the finish line at Belmont, "and discovered the rest of the field in Queens." Bud Furillo made a similar observation in the same paper: "They gave him a margin of victory as 31 lengths but it was difficult to be certain. He won from here to Watts." Furillo also imagined a dialogue between Laffit Pincay and Sham as Secretariat pulled away, writing, "Secretariat opened up and Sham shouted: 'Use the lariat. Rope the big galoot.'"

*Washington Post* sports writer Tom Callahan reported a more melodramatic turn of events. He stated Braulio Baeza and Angel Cordero from 10 lengths behind "could actually see Sham's heart breaking. They glanced at each other in unjaded astonishment. Sham's legs were splaying apart. He was swimming instead of running. He was crying out in frustration." Secretariat's Belmont romp had that effect on people.

Golfer Jack Nicklaus told the story of how he watched the race on TV alone in Florida. He pounded his fists into the carpet and cried as Secretariat raced down the final stretch.

"I don't know why I did that," he told writer Heywood Hale Broun.

"It's because you've spent your entire life searching for absolute perfection," Broun told him, "and you finally saw it."

Viola Sommer years later said she had felt a bit of frustration at the time of the Triple Crown races, but concluded, "It was just one of those things." Mrs. Sommer wasn't interested in redemption for Sham, but was only interested in winning. "It was not personal to me at all. I just wanted to win, because I thought he was a great horse and I loved him. I loved him, my children loved him."

Mrs. Sommer believed a horse could become broken-hearted, down-spirited, demoralized by loss, but didn't know if that were the case with Sham. "It's hard to tell if a horse is disappointed," she said. "I suppose that's very possible. Going into the Belmont, he was not his usual composed self. Maybe he wasn't feeling well, or maybe he just didn't want to take another beating."

"Sham looks and feels fine," Pancho Martin reported from Belmont Park. "Horses don't get broken hearts from losing a tough race, even a couple of tough races to the same winner," he said. "When he's ready to run again, and the right race comes up, Sham will be in it. Sure, even against Secretariat." Martin acknowledged Sham would benefit from some time off, but had his eye on the Travers at Saratoga in August.

"Secretariat is a great horse. He's already proved that," Martin admitted. "One horse against another, that's a matter of their condition in a particular race. Secretariat was at his peak in the Belmont and he gave the greatest exhibition most of us have ever seen. Sham wasn't at his best, far from it, the way things came up. Maybe if they meet again in the Travers, Sham will be at his peak, Secretariat below it, that's the way horses are."

Martin called it as he saw it. "Sham finished ahead of Secretariat in the Wood even though Angle Light won the race, and was beaten only two and a half lengths by Secretariat in the Derby and Preakness. And he was in trouble in both races. So his race in the Belmont has to mean he wasn't at his best, the way he stopped. It happens to a lot of horses, even the best. Secretariat threw in a poor race in the Wood, but look how he came back." Martin said he had to "throw out" Sham's Belmont. "He's much better than that," he concluded.

"Some horse ain't he?" Lucien Laurin asked rhetorically about his own horse upon meeting with reporters on Sunday following the Belmont Stakes. Laurin guaranteed Secretariat would race again, probably at Saratoga in August in the Jim Dandy Stakes and Travers Stakes. "He definitely will race again unless something happens to him—God forbid," Laurin said. The words would prove prophetic for Sham.

Sigmund and Viola Sommer were also at Belmont Park on Sunday. They came to see Sham at his barn. Sigmund Sommer's response to Saturday's event wasn't as cordial as Laurin's. "I went home last night and got drunk and cried," Sommer said.

## Chapter 30

## Sham's Biggest Challenge

Pancho Martin prepared Sham for a possible return to California, specifically Hollywood Park in Inglewood for the Hollywood Derby on July 15. It would be Sham's debut on grass in the mile-and-a-half turf race.

On or about June 20, eleven days after the Belmont Stakes, Martin noticed Sham limping following a workout. He immediately had Sham's right front leg put in a cast. X-rays revealed a fracture.

Sham had fractured the third metacarpal bone (commonly called the cannon bone), which extends between the horse's knee and fetlock. The fracture started in Sham's ankle joint and extended upward, approximately four inches. Dr. William O. Reed, who examined the colt, said, "This type of fracture always concerns us because in addition to the visible fracture on X-ray a continuation of the fracture may occur in the form of microfractures which may not be visible on X-ray."

"I've been feeling bad ever since this happened," Sigmund Sommer commented. "I'm emotionally involved with the horse. In construction you can put something back together again with manpower and machinery, but no amount of manpower or machinery can put a horse back together."

On July 6, Dr. Reed operated at the Veterinarian's Equine Hospital, just across the street from the Belmont Park backstretch. He inserted three screws during a two-hour surgery.

Countering the grim looks of concern from those waiting in the recovery room for word on Sham's condition, Dr. Reed emerged with a smile to pronounce the operation a success. "I think the operation went very well," he told reporters. "I'm almost certain Sham will race again. I've done the same kind of surgery on many horses who returned to racing following such an injury." Dr. Reed predicted Sham could return to racing after six months of rest.

Sham lay on his left side on the recovery room floor over a cover of California hay. He wore a hood over his head and a fiberglass cast on his right foreleg. Dr. Reed grasped the hood, and with his hand spread over Sham's snout, attempted to wake him. A few hours after the operation, Sham was moving under his own power. Sham ate the hay from the recovery room floor and nuzzled Dr. Reed as he trimmed the cast. Later that evening, Sham returned to his stall at Belmont Park.

Within a week following the surgery, Leslie Brownell Combs, representing Spendthrift Farm in Lexington, Kentucky, finalized a deal to acquire Sham. On July 13, Combs' father and owner of Spendthrift Farm, Leslie Combs II, announced he was syndicating Sham for breeding. Sham's racing career was over.

The elder Combs said, "In any other year he would have been a champion, and I have wanted this horse for a long time. It's just a shame that he had to run against the horse of the century, Secretariat."

Dr. Reed commented on Sham's situation. "As a patient Sham is ideal," he said. "He has a marvelous disposition, is extremely intelligent and certainly has all of the gameness in the world. In some ways I regret that he is being syndicated for breeding as I am confident that he would return to his original racing form."

Within two weeks following the announcement of Sham's syndication, the deal was completed. Thirty-two shares at $90,000 per share were sold for a total of $2,880,000. Sigmund Sommer retained three shares. Sham's purchase price in November of 1972 had been $200,000. His value increased greater than ten-fold less than a year later.

"I am especially pleased with the people comprising this syndicate," Leslie Combs II said, "and the quality of mares the members own virtually assures that Sham will be an overwhelming success at stud." Members of the syndicate were not announced.

Combs noted Sham's pedigree offered a complete outcross for mares with Nasrullah blood. This could potentially exploit a Nasrullah-Princequillo nick. "Sham is the second best three-year-old in America," Combs declared. In noting the share price for both Secretariat and Sham, he added, "I think both colts are a bargain. Sham pushed Secretariat to greatness."

If Sham missed the beauty of Claiborne Farm he had enjoyed in his youth, Spendthrift Farm was no less idyllic. Spendthrift had a reputation for its grazing pastures. Their beauty was no mere accident of nature, but the result of study, hard work, and care.

Prior to purchase, grazing lands were developed to Spendthrift standards after extensive soil testing and landscaping. Leslie Combs was known to work with engineers from the Agriculture Stabilization and Conservation Service (a division of the Department of Agriculture) to determine water tables, re-route streams, and create ponds and lakes. The land was smoothed, dragged, and harrowed to a surface safe for horses. Fields were spread with fertilizer and seeded with bluegrass and clover. The fields were maintained with the help of soil scientists and pasture specialists from the University of Kentucky and the Farm Clinic of the U.S. This involved processes such as surveys, soil sampling, and observation by aerial photography.

"We spend a fortune on pasture control, but it's one of our cheapest investments," Brownell Combs said. Coincidentally, the name of the farm was not in recognition of the money put into its development and operation, but after the stallion Spendthrift, winner of the 1879 Belmont Stakes, Jersey Derby, and Travers Stakes, who had stood there.

Sham began stud duty at Spendthrift in 1974. Father joined son as Sham's sire, Pretense, who had stood at Claiborne Farm, was moved to Spendthrift for the 1974 breeding season. Knightly Dawn was also retired to stud for the 1974 season, but he wouldn't be joining Sham. Knightly Dawn was sent to Hill 'N' Dale Farms in Ontario, Canada. An ad announcing his availability in *The Blood-Horse* made it known Knightly Dawn was not only a stakes winner, but "half-brother to Secretariat." Both had Somethingroyal as their dam.

Sham's career winnings tallied $204,808. His record, on paper, didn't appear overly impressive. In 13 starts, Sham won five, placed second in five, and finished third in one. His only finishes out of the money were the San Felipe Handicap, when he finished fourth, and the ill-fated Belmont Stakes. Sham's best efforts, however, couldn't really be captured on a racing chart, nor could his heart.

In a *Daily Racing Form* column, Joe Hirsh noted of Sham's Belmont Stakes effort, "Sham attacked early, gave it everything he had for six furlongs, and then faded into history… Sham was all through for practical purposes but he left the scene with dignity and stature."

While Sham retired relatively unseen, Secretariat left the stage with much more fanfare. He raced six more times before the year was over and before his retirement to stud. After the Belmont, his next event was the Arlington Invitational Stakes on June 30 at Arlington Park. Chicago Mayor Richard Daley proclaimed the day Secretariat Day. The horse was awarded the key to the city. He went off in the Arlington Invitational at the astoundingly low odds of 1 to 20. He won by nine lengths.

The *New York Times* reported 15,508 winning tickets from Secretariat's last four races (the Kentucky Derby, Preakness Stakes, Belmont Stakes, and Arlington Invitational), were uncashed, totaling a value of $63,644.10. The tickets were likely kept as souvenirs by winning bettors. Reportedly one entrepreneur bought $2 win tickets in the three Triple Crown races and was selling them framed with a picture of Secretariat for $300. Considering the tickets cost $6 and their total redeemable value was $9.80 ($5, $2.60, and $2.20 for the Derby, Preakness, and Belmont, respectively), the cost of materials left room for a healthy profit.

In the *Daily Racing Form*, Charles Hatton got into the capitalist spirit, stating, "It is noted Secretariat's tail has become a bit long and bosky. Perhaps Lucien Laurin is missing a bet if he does not pull it to the modish hock length and go into the souvenir business."

Secretariat's popularity was not limited to commercial appeal. Columnist Art Buchwald suggested President Nixon should hire Secretariat as an aide, that the White House needed someone who had "the complete and unequivocal backing of all the American people." When a skeptical member of the White House press corps told him there had been horses in the White House before, Buchwald replied, "But this one has a head."

On August 4, Secretariat proved he wasn't infallible. In the Whitney Stakes, a horse named Onion pulled off an upset, defeating second-place Secretariat by a length. Ridden by Jacinto Vasquez, Onion led wire to wire, just as Vasquez had ridden Angle Light when they upset Secretariat in the Wood Memorial. Secretariat reportedly suffered from a virus and fever during the running of the Whitney.

Secretariat came back on September 15 to win the Marlboro Cup Handicap, an invitational event at Belmont Park. His stablemate Riva Ridge finished second, three and a half lengths behind.

On September 29 Secretariat was beaten again in the Woodward Stakes at Belmont Park. A horse named Prove Out finished four and a half lengths in front of second-place Secretariat. This time Jorge Velasquez rode the winner. He too had beaten Secretariat in the Wood Memorial when Sham finished second in front of third-place Secretariat. With the win, Jorge Velasquez joined Jacinto Vasquez in becoming the only other jockey to beat Secretariat twice. Pancho Martin had said if Sham and Secretariat were to meet again, the situation might be reversed regarding peak conditioning. Secretariat was obviously not at his best. One can speculate what a healthy, rested Sham could have done.

Secretariat ran his last two races on turf. He won by five lengths on the grass at Belmont Park on October 8 in the Man o' War Stakes before flying out to Toronto's International Airport, where admirers, photographers, reporters, and television crews gathered to watch his arrival. He won the Canadian International Championship Stakes by five and a half lengths on October 28.

November 6, 1973 was "Farewell to Secretariat" Day at Aqueduct. A gathering of 32,900 watched their hero led by a pony to the winner's circle. Pancho Martin was near the paddock during the event. "I'm just sorry it's not Sham," he said upon departing. A band played "Auld Lang Syne" as Secretariat galloped the Aqueduct stretch.

Secretariat's show biz appeal remained intact upon retirement. He was offered an appearance on *The Sonny and Cher Show*, and a Las Vegas nightclub offered him $15,000 a performance for just walking on stage, quite a fee considering $15,000 was the average value paid to the winner of stakes and feature races run that year.

For 1973, Secretariat was voted Horse of the Year, in addition to Champion Three-Year-Old Male. His two turf victories were enough for him to be voted Champion Turf Horse. Secretariat was honored as "the man who did the most for racing" in 1973 at the 51st annual dinner of the New York Turf Writers Association. In *The American Racing Manual*, Charles Hatton wrote in his year-end review for 1973, "Secretariat was a Superhorse, rather than a transient Horse of the Year. Veteran turfmen, sophisticates of deep experience and broad, informed tastes, pronounced him 'The Horse of the Century.' He is the only thoroughbred ever given this identity on an official program. ... Secretariat is the most capable horse we ever saw, and geriatrics defeat any thought of seeing his like again."

Hatton also gave Sham his due. In recognizing his efforts in the Sham-Secretariat match-ups he stated, "For one thing, we shouldn't limit the possibilities to one great horse each year." Hatton reflected upon past Triple Crown winners and their rivals. "Some of the Triple Crown winners, to be frank with you, didn't have much to beat," he said. "Count Fleet beat Fairy Manhurst by 25 lengths in the Belmont Stakes, beat him after bowing a tendon in the first turn. ... The best horse Citation beat in the Belmont was Vulcan's Forge and that's not much. ... Lord Boswell was no hell of a horse. That was the second favorite the day Assault got the Crown. Neither Whirlaway nor Omaha had to beat Sham."

Hatton noted Sham's Triple Crown run. "The way he's lost, at first I didn't know whether to be glad Bull [Hancock] didn't see it or to wish he had. But I wish he had. Bull would've seen he's a great horse."

Many noted what might have been, had Sham been born any other year. The June 11, 1973 issue of *Newsweek* stated in its story on Secretariat, "It is conceivable that he will not only capture the Triple Crown but shatter still another track record in doing it. In fact, he may find it necessary to break a record just to beat Sham, a colt who might have won a Triple Crown of his own if he had not been unfortunate enough to be born in the same year as Secretariat."

In its "Super Horse" coverage, the June 11, 1973 issue of *Time* stated, "Few three-year-olds will even dare take the track against him at Belmont but he will again have to face Sham, the horse that ran second in both the Derby and Preakness in efforts good enough to win in most years."

In his write-up following the Belmont Stakes, Arnold Kirkpatrick said in *The Thoroughbred Record*, "Going into the race Sham was a truly superb horse who… would be the best around in any other year." Kirkpatrick also called Sham, "a horse of great beauty, speed and heart, who was, far and away, the best of the others of his generation."

Similarly, Steve Cady wrote in the *New York Times*, "Take Secretariat out of the 1973 picture, and Sham would be going into the Belmont on Saturday as a superhorse—an eight-length winner of both the Derby and Preakness and an overwhelming favorite to become the first Triple Crown winner in 25 years."

Gene Ward, in the *Daily News*, wrote, "In any other year but the year of Secretariat this strapping son of Pretense… would be the one to have dead aim on the Triple Crown."

Joe Hirsch wrote in his *Daily Racing Form* column, "Sham, it is widely conceded, would be a champion in any other year."

Barry H. Irwin, in *The Thoroughbred of California*, stated, "It is conceivable that Sham would have carried off the Triple Crown himself (and perhaps easily) had Secretariat not been born in the same generation."

With the close of 1973, Laffit Pincay won his fourth consecutive title as the nation's leading money-winning rider, passing $4 million in winnings on December 1. Pincay finished the year with $4,093,492, this time leaving Ron Turcotte in second at $3,393,368. On January 11, 1974, Pincay received the Eclipse Award as the outstanding jockey for 1973.

## Chapter 31

# Adding to the Princequillo Legacy

Sham took well to retirement. Stallion groom Butch Simpson looked after him in his daily routine. He turned Sham loose to run the fields at Spendthrift, but now his runs came without a jockey, saddle, or any additional weight assigned by racing secretaries. Every day Sham roamed a private paddock.

"All the stallions have their own paddock," Simpson explained. "Can't put 'em together or they'll fight."

Sham maintained his good nature after his racing days, but in Simpson's experience, the horse did have his limits. If Sham were annoyed, Simpson recalled years later, "He'd nip at you."

Simpson recalled Sham's partiality to mud. After a rain, Sham liked to get out and find a puddle to roll in. Simpson called him "Bandit," since Sham often came back covered in a mask of mud over his head and around his eyes. After Sham had had his fun,

Simpson hosed him down and gave him a bath.

In his duties, Simpson saw first-hand the odd behavior Viola Sommer had described when Sham slept. He'd lie down with his legs stretched out, and he snored. Simpson described a high-pitched whinny Sham made while asleep: "Like they're coming after or racing after another horse, or whatever."

Simpson was close to Sham and got to know him well over some 20 years together. "He's a special horse," Simpson said emphatically. "He chased Secretariat for all those races, and when he come off the racetrack he was just special to everybody, and he was a kind, nice horse to be around."

Sigmund and Viola Sommer made it out to Spendthrift to visit. And it wasn't just the Sommers and Butch Simpson who were fond of Sham. "Everybody kinda, they loved the horse," Simpson said.

Sham's success at stud didn't take long, nor did his influence on European soil. From his first crop, a colt named Jaazeiro won as a two-year-old in France in 1977. Jaazeiro followed up with a victory in the 1978 Irish Two Thousand Guineas, having gone off as the favorite. He also won the Sussex Stakes and St. James' Palace Stakes in England, and the Prix des Chenes in France.

Also from Sham's first crop was the filly Sherry Peppers, winner of the 1977 Spinaway Stakes. She followed in the footsteps of her grandmother (Sham's dam), Sequoia, in winning that same race.

One of Sigmund Sommer's successes as a breeder with Sham came from a colt named Bottled Water, a tribute to his sire's beverage of choice (or at least Pancho Martin's beverage of choice for him). The dark bay, foaled in 1978, also looked like Sham. Bottled Water won 11 races and finished in the money in 21 of 38 career starts.

Sham's other stakes winning offspring included Shamgo (winner of the El Cajon Stakes in 1979 and Yankee Valor Handicap in 1981); Colonel Moran (winner of the Gotham Stakes, Withers Stakes, Bay Shore Stakes, Salvator Mile Handicap, and [like his father] finished second in the Wood Memorial in 1980, along with a third-place finish in the Preakness Stakes that same year); Safe Play (winner of the La Canada Stakes and Falls City Handicap in 1982); Arewehavingfunyet (winner of the Oak Leaf Stakes, Del Mar Debutante Stakes, Landaluce Stakes, Sorrento Stakes, and Time to Leave Stakes in 1985); and Mexican Champion Diablotain (winner of the Jockey Club Mexicano and the Derby Mexicano in 1988 and the Clasico de las Americas in 1990).

Sham, like his grandfather Princequillo, was a successful broodmare sire. Stakes winners produced by Sham's daughters included Sham Say (winner of the Maryland Juvenile Filly Championship, Smart Angle Stakes, Cameo Stakes, and What a Summer Stakes in 1987, and winner of the Ruffian Handicap, Dancealot Stakes, and Jameela Stakes in 1988); Defensive Play (winner of the Man o' War Stakes and Guardian Classic trial in England in 1990, winner of the Charles H. Strub Stakes in 1991, and winner of the Excelsior Handicap, Oak Tree Invitational, San Bernardino Handicap, Californian Stakes, Suburban Handicap, and San Gabriel Handicap in 1992 with career earnings of $1,695,557); and Dixie Brass (winner of the Metropolitan Mile Handicap, Withers Stakes, Swift Stakes, and Cherry Hill Mile Stakes in 1992).

On November 30, 1992, Sham was moved from Spendthrift Farm to nearby Walmac Farm, also in Lexington, Kentucky. He settled in without trouble as his familiar stallion groom Butch Simpson also made the move to Walmac. By the time the twentieth anniversary of Sham's Triple Crown battles with Secretariat neared in 1993, Sham had sired 74 stakes horses and 44 stakes winners and had sired earners of more than $13.8 million. Sham's daughters produced more than 25 stakes winners. He covered five mares for breeding in 1993.

Early Saturday morning on April 3, 1993, Sham was fed by a night watchman at 3 AM. When Sham was next checked at 4 AM, he was lying in his stall. Butch Simpson found him. Sham had died in the early morning hours, having suffered an apparent heart attack.

Upon Secretariat's death in 1989, Dr. Thomas Swerczek, a professor of veterinary science at the University of Kentucky, performed a necropsy revealing Secretariat's heart was more than twice the normal size for a horse. Dr. Swerczek and the assisting veterinarians stood around looking at the heart. Dr. Swerczek noted, "The heart was perfect—there were no defects. It was simply the largest heart I've ever seen. We didn't weigh it, but we visually estimated it between 21 and 22 pounds," he said. "This was a heart completely out of anybody's league."

By comparison, the Australian champion Phar Lap was also known to have a very large heart. It weighed 13.4 pounds.

Eclipse, the great 18th century thoroughbred, was said to have had a heart that weighed 14 pounds. The heart of the average racehorse of the early 1990s weighed approximately 8½ pounds.

"Looking back to what he had done, it was easy to put a connection to it," Dr. Swerczek said of Secretariat. "It was just this huge engine."

When announcer Chic Anderson had made the call on Secretariat during his Belmont Stakes run, Anderson had proclaimed, "He is moving like a tremendous machine!"

Secretariat may well have been a racing machine. This would have put Sham at a substantial disadvantage. Sham was merely mortal horseflesh.

Following Sham's death, Dr. Swerczek also performed the necropsy. He found the *second*-largest thoroughbred heart he'd ever seen. "I thought it was ironic," he said, "Sham was still finishing second to Secretariat." Dr. Swerczek did weigh Sham's heart, which was 18 pounds.

In the traditional manner of honoring a horse, Sham's head, heart, and hooves were buried at Walmac. Pancho Martin was at his office in Hialeah, Florida when he heard of Sham's death. "I was very sad, felt very bad when I heard about him," he said. "He was a good horse, a special horse, and I had feelings for him."

Butch Simpson didn't forget Sham. Ten years after Sham's death, he said, "I still got his halter hanging on the wall." Simpson kept it at his home rather than at the barn. "The last halter to come off of him," he said.

Sham's *Thoroughbred Times* obituary called him "an exceptional racehorse ironically better remembered for the races he lost than for his own successes."

The headline from a Tom Callahan column stated, "Sham had heart of a champ," while the article detailed his hard-luck history. Callahan described Sham as a "dark, leggy, elegant bay who rode alongside history instead of into it."

Pancho Martin also recalled his horse's tough luck. "There's no question Sham would have won the Triple Crown if it wasn't for Secretariat," he said.

Nearly thirty years after the Sham-Secretariat duels, Jorge Velasquez reflected, "Sham was a nice horse. And he was born in the wrong time, I guess, the wrong year. The year of Secretariat."

Heliodoro Gustines felt the same way. "He come with the wrong year," he said. "Secretariat was there. Secretariat was a fantastic animal."

Even Ron Turcotte commented on what Sham might have accomplished in another time, "We'll never know because he came along in the wrong year."

In a November 19, 2000 *Daily Racing Form* column, Joe Hirsch announced Sham would be honored at Santa Anita with a stakes race bearing his name, the Sham Stakes. Hirsch wrote, of the honoree, "Sham... has always ranked high on our list of unappreciated or underappreciated horses. That is easy to understand, because no matter what he did or the magnitude of his accomplishments, he was competing against one of the most popular and successful Thoroughbreds of all time: Secretariat."

The Secretariat phenomenon cannot be fully explained out of its social context. Secretariat did more than win a Triple Crown.

He won a nation's adulation. To understand fully what Sham was up against in the hearts of fans, one should consider his battles were not limited to the racetrack. Secretariat's popularity comprised new followers outside of racing circles who had never seen a horse race before hearing of the "Superhorse." While challenging a racing legend, Sham was contending with a social force and rhetorical circumstances.

By early 1973, peace talks with the North Vietnamese had begun, stalled, and resumed with the eventual U.S. withdrawal of combat soldiers by March of that year. Many felt the U.S. had not only failed to win the war, but lost it. Many were of the opinion the U.S. didn't belong in Vietnam at all. Regardless, morale was low in a good portion of the U.S. population. People were tired of the war. People were tired of protesting the war. For its involvement, the U.S. had no military victory and nearly 58,000 killed, more than 1,000 missing in action, and approximately 150,000 seriously wounded to show for it.

The political waters were further muddied by a lack of confidence in government with the Watergate scandal. Inflation and the economic situation also added to the frustration of the American people. For Americans to feel good about America again solutions had to be sought, as they were not forthcoming from government or from a sense of national pride. The creation of Secretariat hype was one response to these conditions, though Secretariat hype providing some form of relief from these conditions is only one partial interpretation of the phenomenon.

Secretariat provided a substitute, an outlet for erstwhile Vietnam protests, for complaints about the political situation, and for concerns over the economy. Finding pride in the accomplishments of Secretariat was an alternate way of finding pride in America. Secretariat was a metaphor for credibility, integrity, and patriotism, all the while representing the American flag—Big Red running under white and blue silks. Secretariat hype was a positive reaction to the low morale of post-Vietnam America. Secretariat's success represented a renewed hope for the success of America. The image of "America's Horse" was adopted as the image for America.

Sham could have answered the call had Secretariat come along in a different year. Sham would not have represented the colors of the red, white, and blue so literally, but his green and gold silks could have just as easily provided a satirical metaphor for the economy. In the hands of entertaining copy writers, headlines could have proclaimed Sham Sets New Gold Standard, with a reference to greenbacks thrown in for good measure.

When a horse wins a race by five, six, or seven lengths, it can look to be a rather impressive margin. Those who have seen a horse win a race by 10 lengths could call the performance dominating, more so at 15 lengths and still more so at 20 lengths (Man o' War's margin of victory in the 1920 Belmont Stakes). Picture Count Fleet's victory in the 1943 Belmont Stakes when he won by 25 lengths. Extend the lead farther to 27, then 28, 29 lengths. Put a colt 30 lengths ahead of the field in the 1973 Belmont Stakes and he still wouldn't find the winner's circle. Secretariat's incredible 31-length victory was considered by some to be the single best performance by a race horse ever. And, of course, there was the record 2:24 time.

When considering Secretariat's feats, combined with records in the other two legs of the Triple Crown (though unofficially in the Preakness Stakes), it's hard to imagine any horse could get as close to him as two and a half lengths in the Kentucky Derby and Preakness. In recognizing the accomplishments of Secretariat, one can appreciate Sham.

After Sham, Secretariat's nearest challenger in both the Kentucky Derby and Preakness Stakes was Our Native (a fine stakes-winning colt in his own right), who trailed 11 lengths behind. Without Sham in those races, Secretariat could have coasted to easy victories with mediocre performances. Ron Turcotte would have likely saved Secretariat for both the Preakness and Belmont, only letting him go in the Belmont once the Triple Crown was assured. Had that been the case, instead of earning legendary status, Secretariat might be remembered as just another horse in a long list of past winners of the previous 98 Kentucky Derbies, 97 Preakness Stakes, and 104 Belmont Stakes—historic, yet hardly exclusive, company. It was unlikely he would have run the Kentucky Derby and Preakness in record times if there were no need for Turcotte to push him to keep clear of Sham. Had Sham not challenged Secretariat for the early lead in the Belmont Stakes, Secretariat might not have run opening fractions so quickly and attained a victory so stunning. As Leslie Combs II observed, "Sham pushed Secretariat to greatness."

Secretariat still would have won the Triple Crown, but it was unlikely he would have done so with any more flair than any of the other previous eight horses to win it. The Superhorse would have likely been forgotten three years later in the Affirmed-Alydar series. During the run for 1978 Triple Crown, Affirmed beat Alydar in each of the three events, but with Alydar creeping closer with each race, a one-and-a-half-length margin in the Kentucky Derby, a neck in the Preakness, and a head in the Belmont. But Affirmed didn't win in the same awe-inspiring, record-smashing manner in which Secretariat had won, nor did Affirmed's victories come with the social impact of Secretariat's.

In order for Secretariat to win races and sustain nationwide admiration, he was forced to break a few records in order to beat Sham. As for leaving his mark in thoroughbred racing history, it took a Superhorse—arguably the greatest horse of the 20th century (protests of Man o' War supporters duly noted)—to keep Sham from his place among the greats of thoroughbred racing and to keep Sham from being embraced as America's Horse.

Charles Hatton once noted of Secretariat, "His only point of reference is himself." Truth be told, Secretariat's point of reference was Sham.

# Bibliography

Some of the articles used in researching this project were clipped from various publications and filed in folders at sites such as the Belmont Park Press Office. For this reason, complete information wasn't always available to cite fully the article. In the case of unidentified articles, best efforts were made to identify the missing information. Sources that could not be identified are noted as "unknown source from [site]."

1. 1972 Eclipse Awards. *The Thoroughbred of California*. March 1973. pp. 120-121.
2. The 1972 Horse of the Year: Secretariat. *The Thoroughbred Record*. April 14, 1973. pp. 894-895.
3. [*1974 Media Guide?*]. from Belmont Park Press Office.
4. *1980 Media Guide*. from Belmont Park Press Office.
5. *1992 Stallion Directory*. *Thoroughbred Times*. Thoroughbred Publications, Inc. 1991.
6. A.B. Hancock Jr. Dies at 62. *The Thoroughbred of California*. October 1972. p. 84.
7. Adair, Bob. Fall of 'Big Horse' Makes 99th Derby Wide-Open Affair. *Louisville Courier-Journal and Times*. April 22, 1973. p. C3.
8. Adair, Bob. No Laughing, Shecky Greene Still 'in' Kentucky Derby. *Louisville Courier-Journal*. May 1, 1973. p. B7.
9. Adair, Bob. Settecento Overtakes Mr. Prospector in Trial: Winner's Derby Status Cloudy; I'm Guaranteed a Distant Third. *Louisville Courier-Journal*. May 2, 1973. p. B4.
10. Adair, Bob. 16 May Enter Derby, but Fewer Likely to Start. *Louisville Courier-Journal*. May 3, 1973. pp. C1, C5.
11. Adair, Bob. Keefer Happy with Progress of Hoosier Hopeful Navajo. *Louisville Courier-Journal*. May 3, 1973. p. C2.
12. Adair, Bob. 99th Derby: Roses, Riches, Records. *Louisville Courier-Journal*. May 5, 1973. pp. 1, 12.
13. Adair, Bob. Sham's 'Rabbit' Wins by Two in Twin Spires. *Louisville Courier-Journal*. May 6, 1973. p. C6.
14. *The American Racing Manual: 1974 Edition*. Highstown, New Jersey: Triangle Publications. 1974.
15. Ancient Title Charges Back; Nips Linda's Chief by Neck. Arcadia, Calif. *Louisville Courier-Journal*. Associated Press. February 2, 1973. p. B4.
16. Anderson, Dave. Bravo, Secretariat…: They All Cheer as Super Horse Does His Thing. *Lexington Herald-Leader*. *New York Times* News Service. June

10, 1973. pp. 25, 38.

17. Anderson, Dave. Move Over Elvis… Secretariat Now Challenging Show Biz Celebrities for Fame. *Louisville Courier-Journal. New York Times* News Service. June 30, 1973. p. B7.

18. Anderson, Dave. Secretariat Ranks with the Best of Clients Now that William Morris Is His Agency. *Lexington Herald and the Lexington Leader. New York Times* News Service. June 30, 1973.

19. Angle Light Dropped from Preakness List. *Lexington Herald.* Associated Press. May 10, 1973. pp. 31, 35.

20. Angle Light, 'Regal' Ready for Derby: Pre-Derby Betting Backs Sham. *Albany Times-Union.* Associated Press. May 5, 1973. p. 19.

21. Arcaro, Eddie. Hickcok Sports.com. http://www.hickoksports.com.

22. Aristides. Racing Chart of 1st Kentucky Derby. http://www.kentuckyderby.com/. Derby History. http://d3b4lt1s53xf6k.cloudfront.net/sites/kentuckyderby.com/files/charts/1875.pdf.

23. Arthur Boyd Hancock Jr. *The Thoroughbred Record.* September 23, 1972. pp. 983, 984D.

24. Arrive at Pimlico. *Albany Times-Union.* Associated Press. May 8, 1973.

25. Axthelm, Pete. Woody Stephens Quits Cain Hoy. *New York Herald Tribune.* August 21, 1965. p. 16.

26. Axthelm, Pete. Superhorse—Secretariat. *Newsweek.* June 11, 1973. 81(24). pp. 62-69.

27. Ayres, Ray. Secretariat Odds-On Favorite to Win Triple Crown. *Lexington Herald.* United Press International. June 8, 1973. p. 43.

28. Ayres, Ray. Amazing Secretariat Forges Racing Legend: Wins Triple Crown, Sets World Record in 31-Length Romp. *Lexington Herald-Leader.* United Press International. June 10, 1973. pp. 1, 24.

29. Bailey, Logan. Secretariat, Sham Put Hancock in Enviable Ky. Derby Position. *Daily Racing Form.* April 5, 1973. pp. 4, 12.

30. Bailey, Rick. This Sporting Life. *Lexington Herald-Leader.* May 6, 1973. p. 26.

31. Barry, Mike. Claiborne's Seth Hancock: He's a Chip off the Old Block. *Louisville Courier-Journal.* May 6, 1973. p. C2.

32. Barry, Mike. Secretariat a BIG Favorite to Capture Belmont Today. *Louisville Courier-Journal.* June 9, 1973. p. B4.

33. Barry, Mike. Band Operates on Belmont Day—But All This One Does Is Play Music. *Louisville Courier-Journal and Times.* June 10, 1973.

34. Barry, Mike. Secretariat Makes Sham-bles of Triple Crown. *Louisville Courier-Journal and Times.* June 10, 1973. pp. C1, C3.

35. Battlefield: Vietnam. http://www.pbs.org/battlefieldvietnam.
36. Beard, Gordon. Mrs. Tweedy Requests Review of Secretariat's Time in Preakness. *Lexington Leader*. Associated Press. June 18, 1973. p. 12.
37. Beard, Gordon. Secretariat Loses! (To Race Commission). *Lexington Leader*. Associated Press. July 11, 1973.
38. Beardsley, Dick. Derby's Losing Jockeys Agree: Secretariat Ran a Super Race. *Louisville Courier-Journal*. May 6, 1973.
39. Becker, Bill. Sham Is Victor at Santa Anita. *New York Times*. April 1, 1973. Section 5. pp. 1, 8.
40. Belmont's Biggest Sale. *The Thoroughbred Record*. December 2, 1972. pp. 1767-1770.
41. Bernstein, Ralph. Knightly Dawn Nips 'Smiles'. *Lexington Herald*. May 29, 1973. p. 11.
42. Beyer, Andrew. Martin A Special Case. *Washington Star*. December 4, 1974.
43. Biles, Deirdre B. Sham Dead at 23. *The Blood-Horse*. April 17, 1993. p. 1833.
44. Biles, Deirdre B. Pinnacle Pursuit. *The Blood-Horse*. June 26, 1999. pp. 3704-3708.
45. Blair, Carole and Michel, Neil. Commemorating in the Theme Park Zone: Reading the Astronauts Memorial. *At the Intersection: Cultural Studies and Rhetorical Studies*. Thomas Rosteck, Editor. New York: The Guilford Press. 1999.
46. Blankney Village. Henry Chaplin. macla.co.uk. http://www.macla.co.uk/blankney/index.php.
47. *The Blood-Horse Stallion Register for 1992*. The Blood-Horse, Inc. November 23, 1991.
48. *The Bloodstock Breeders Review*. Volume XI. 1922. p. 37.
49. Bloodstock Research Information Services, Inc. 2008. National Museum of Racing and Hall of Fame, Saratoga Springs, New York.
50. Blum, Walter. telephone interview with author. January 7, 2005.
51. Boling, Dave. Derby Winner is Short of Secretariat and Sham. *Tacoma News Tribune*. Nando Media. Scripps Howard News Service. 2001.
52. Bolus, Jim. Angle Light Stuns Sham, Secretariat in Wood. *Louisville Courier-Journal and Times*. April 22, 1973. pp. C1, C3.
53. Bolus, Jim. Martin Raps 'Cheap Talk,' Drops Laurin as a Friend. *Louisville Courier-Journal*. May 1, 1973. p. B3.
54. Bolus, Jim. Settecento Sees 'Sights' First, Then Races for Home and Win. *Louisville Courier-Journal*. May 2, 1973. p. B4.
55. Bolus, Jim. If Royal and Regal Wins Derby, Croll Would Be a Little Ahead. *Louisville Courier-Journal*. May 3, 1973. p. C3.
56. Bolus, Jim. If Lucien's Lucky… Secretariat Will Win and Squelch His Critics Again.

*Louisville Courier-Journal.* May 5, 1973. p. C1.

57. Bolus, Jim. *Kentucky Derby Stories.* Gretna, Louisiana: Pelican Publishing Company. 1993.

58. [Bowen, Edward L.]. What's Going on Here. *The Blood-Horse.* April 9, 1973. p. 1257.

59. Bowen, Edward L. Kentucky Derby Preps. *The Blood-Horse.* April 23, 1973. p. 1396.

60. Bowen, Edward L. Ten Days Before. *The Blood-Horse.* April 30, 1973. pp. 1480-1481.

61. Bowen, Edward L. Prologue to the 99th Running. *The Blood-Horse.* May 7, 1973. pp. 1592-1596.

62. Bowen, Edward L. Resumption of a Legend. The Blood-Horse. May 14, 1973. pp. 1659+

63. Bowen, Edward L. At the Threshold of Giants. *The Blood-Horse.* May 28, 1973. pp. 1832-1841.

64. Bowen, Edward L. Joining the Giants. *The Blood-Horse.* June 18, 1973. pp. 2074-2081

65. Bowen, Edward L. A Prince, A Derby, and Susan's Girl. *The Blood-Horse.* October 8, 1973. pp. 3890-3894.

66. Bowmar III, Dan. Clocking the Candidates. *The Thoroughbred Record.* May 5, 1973. pp. 1110+.

67. Bowmar III, Dan M. Background of the Derby Winner. *The Thoroughbred Record.* May 12, 1973. pp. 1166, 1178.

68. Broken Bone Sidelines Sham; My Gallant, Our Native Vie. *Louisville Courier-Journal.* Associated Press. July 7, 1973. p. B7.

69. Broken Cannon Bone Will Sideline Sham. *Lexington Herald.* Associated Press. July 7, 1973.

70. Buchwald, Art. Nixon Should Hire Secretariat as Aide. *Lexington Herald.* June 19, 1973.

71. Burns, Robert. Tam o' Shanter: A Tale. www.robertburns.org.

72. Byles, Anthony. Hermit (GB). Thoroughbred Bloodlines. http://www.bloodlines.net/TB.

73. Byles, Anthony. Tristan (GB). Thoroughbred Bloodlines. http://www.bloodlines.net/TB.

74. Byron, George Gordon, Lord. *Beppo.* Stanza 27. Bartlett's Quotations online.

75. Cade. Thoroughbred Bloodlines. http://www.bloodlines.net/TB.

76. Cady, Steve. Next Best to Triple Crown: Three Times as No. 2. *New York Times.* June 6, 1973. p. 55.

77. Callahan, Tom. Not All Great Horses Win the Triple Crown. [*Washington*

*Post?*]. March 7, 1979.

78. Callahan, Tom. In '73, Sham Had Heart of a Champ but Lacked Greatness of Secretariat. *Lexington Herald-Leader*. *Washington Post* byline. April 29, 1993. pp. C1, C6.

79. Capps, Timothy T. *Secretariat*. Lexington, Kentucky: Eclipse Press. 2003.

80. Carlson, Frank. Good-Bye Kisses. *The Blood-Horse*. January 10, 1998. p. 162.

81. Carlson, Frank. Silver Anniversary. *Thoroughbred Daily News*. April 28, 1998. p. 6.

82. Carlson, Frank. Silver Anniversary (Part 2). *Thoroughbred Daily News*. May 12, 1998. p. 6.

83. Carlson, Frank. Silver Anniversary (Part 3). *Thoroughbred Daily News*. May 28, 1998. p. 5.

84. Casale, Mike. Sigmund Sommer Strikes Again. *The Thoroughbred Record*. December 23, 1972. pp. 1954, 1959.

85. Casale, Mike. Still the Best. *The Thoroughbred Record*. March 24, 1973. p. 733.

86. Casale, Mike. He's Fast, Too. *The Thoroughbred Record*. April 14, 1973. pp. 980-981.

87. Casale, Mike. New Light on the Derby Picture. *The Thoroughbred Record*. April 28, 1973. pp. 1070, 1072.

88. Census.gov. http://www.census.gov/const/uspricemon.pdf.

89. 'Chief' Gets Challenge. *Albany Times-Union*. Associated Press. March 31, 1973. p. 17

90. Christopher T. Chenery. *The Thoroughbred Record*. January 13, 1973. p. 107.

91. http://www.churchilldowns.com.

92. City of Hialeah, Florida. http://www.hialeahfl.gov/about/history.aspx.

93. Claiborne Consignment Heads Belmont Vendue. *Daily Racing Form*. November 20, 1972. pp. 1, 12.

94. Claiborne Dispersal. *The Thoroughbred of California*. November 1972. p. 142.

95. Claiborne Sale Grosses $2,580,000. *The Blood-Horse*. November 27, 1972. p. 4617.

96. The Claiborne-Perry Consignments. *The Blood-Horse*. December 4, 1972. p. 4725+.

97. Claiborne Farm. http://www.claibornefarm.com.

98. Claiborne Farm advertisement. "The Pretenses Are Popular". *The Thoroughbred Record*. November 25, 1972. p. 1684.

99. Clippinger, Don. So Long, Big Red. *The Thoroughbred Record*. October 1989. pp. 1212-1216, 1218.

100. Clippinger, Don, editor. *Thoroughbred Times Racing Almanac 2003*. Lexington, Kentucky: Thoroughbred Times Books. 2002.

101. Cobb, Irvin S. Hickcok Sports.com. http://www.hickoksports.com.

102. Cochran, Kent. He's the Real Thing. *Daily Racing Form*. February 5, 1973. p. 4.

103. Cochran, Kent. Ain't No Sham! *Daily Racing Form*. February 13, 1973. p.8.

104. Connell, Thornton. Why Hancock Yearlings Get the Top Price. *Louisville Courier-Journal*. December 27, 1936.

105. Cooper, Bob. Few Derby Trainers Plan Challenge of 'Super Horse' in Preakness Bid. *Lexington Herald-Leader*. Associated Press. p. 10.

106. Cooper. Bob. Triple Crown the Greatest Yet for Turcotte. *Lexington Herald-Leader*. Associated Press. June 10, 1973. p. 25.

107. Cooper, Ron. Santa Anita* Gets Its Mud Mark. *The Thoroughbred of California*. March 1973. pp. 138+.

108. Cox, Teddy. Martin by Himself as Trainer. *Daily Racing Form*. March 1, 1972.

109. Cox, Teddy. Pancho: Perfect Man for a Problem Horse. *Daily Racing Form*. December 27, 1972. p. 26.

110. Cox, Teddy. Sommers a Winning Pair. *Daily Racing Form*. December 27, 1972. p. 27.

111. Cox, Teddy. Sham Impressive in Wood Tune-up. *Daily Racing Form*. April 18, 1973. pp. 2, 29.

112. Cox, Teddy. Secretariat Encounters Sham in $116,400 Wood Memorial. *Daily Racing Form*. April 21, 1973. pp. 1, 5, 48.

113. Cox, Teddy. No Primrose Lane for the Sommers. *Daily Racing Form*. May 5, 1973. p. D8.

114. Cox, Teddy. Sham Is the Real Thing. *Daily Racing Form*. May 5, 1973. pp. 5D-6D.

115. Cox, Teddy. Sham Perfect Thoroughbred Says Proud 'Pancho' Martin. *Daily Racing Form*. May 5, 1973. pp. 12D, 19D.

116. Cox, Teddy. Sommers Accept Fortunes of Racing: Top Money-Winning Owners Lost Fine Horses in Tragedies. *Daily Racing Form*. May 5, 1973. p. 10D.

117. Cox, Teddy. Sommers Pass the Test of the 'Greatest' Game. *Daily Racing Form*. May 5, 1973. p. 5D.

118. Craine, Carl. Astrological Contradiction. *The Thoroughbred Record*. April 7, 1973. p. 820.

119. Crist, Steven. More to Stephens Than Met the Eye. *Daily Racing Form*. August 24, 1998. p. 5.

120. Cunningham, Tom. Belmont's Barn 5 Guarded Well. *Albany Times-Union*. June 8, 1973. p. 21.

121. Cunningham, Tom. Secretariat 2-5 Favorite. *Albany Times-Union*. June 9, 1973. p. 19.

122. Cunningham, Tom. Secretariat's Triumph Popular with Fans. *Albany Times-Union*.

June 10, 1973. p. C1.

123. Cunningham, Tom. Frank Martin Finally Gets Racing Dues. *Albany Times-Union.* July 23, 1981. p. 27.

124. Curtis, Charlotte. We Got the Horse Right Here. *Vogue.* August 1973. p. 102, 148.

125. *Daily Racing Form Chart Book.* Belmont Park, third race, August 28, 1972. Highstown, New Jersey: Triangle Publications. 1973.

126. *Daily Racing Form Chart Book.* Belmont Park, third race, September 13, 1972; Belmont Park, third race. September 23, 1972. Highstown, New Jersey: Triangle Publications. 1973.

127. *Daily Racing Form Chart Book.* Aqueduct, second race. December 9, 1972. Highstown, New Jersey: Triangle Publications. 1973.

128. *Daily Racing Form Chart Book.* Santa Anita, sixth race, January 1, 1973. Highstown, New Jersey: Triangle Publications. 1974.

129. *Daily Racing Form Chart Book.* Santa Anita, eighth race, February 2, 1973; Santa Anita, eighth race: Santa Catalina Stakes, February 12, 1973. Highstown, New Jersey: Triangle Publications. 1974.

130. *Daily Racing Form Chart Book.* Santa Anita, eighth race: The San Felipe Handicap, March 17, 1973; Santa Anita, eighth race: The Santa Anita Derby, March 31, 1973. Highstown, New Jersey: Triangle Publications. 1974.

131. *Daily Racing Form Chart Book.* Aqueduct, seventh race: Wood Memorial, April 21, 1973. Highstown, New Jersey: Triangle Publications. 1974.

132. *Daily Racing Form Chart Book.* Churchill Downs, eighth race: Twin Spires Purse, May 5, 1973; Churchill Downs, ninth race: Kentucky Derby, May 5, 1973; Pimlico, eighth race: Preakness Stakes, May 19, 1973. Highstown, New Jersey: Triangle Publications. 1974.

133. *Daily Racing Form Chart Book.* Belmont Park, sixth race: Alibhai Purse, May 31, 1973. Highstown, New Jersey: Triangle Publications. 1974.

134. *Daily Racing Form Chart Book.* Belmont Park, seventh race: Phalanx Purse, June 9, 1973; Belmont Park, eighth race: Belmont Stakes, June 9, 1973. Highstown, New Jersey: Triangle Publications. 1974.

135. Daley, Arthur. Colonel Called It Long Ago. *Louisville Courier-Journal. New York Times* News Service. May 6, 1973. p. C7.

136. Daley, Arthur. 'Peaceful' Derby Eve Gives Way to Race Where Excitement Builds, Funmakers Revel. *Lexington Herald-Leader.* May 6, 1973. p. 26.

137. Daley, Arthur. Turcotte Relatively Silent, But Pleased. *Lexington Herald-Leader.* May 6, 1973. p. 26.

138. Day, Joe. No Secretariat Record—It's 1:54.2. *Daily News.* May 22, 1973. p. 82.

139. Day, John I. Bullish Horse Market. *Lexington Leader.* July 30, 1973.
140. DeFord, Frank. Man in the Middle Jewel. *Sports Illustrated.* May 21, 1973. Vol 38. No. 20. pp. 59-66.
141. Denlinger, Kenneth. More Carrots: On the Most Important Day of His Life, Secretariat Stays Calm through It All. *Louisville Courier-Journal and Times.* June 10, 1973.
142. Duffy, Martha. Boss Tweedy: Lady with a Lot of Horse. *Sports Illustrated.* June 11, 1973. 38(23). pp. 34-39.
143. Durslag, Melvin. Pressure Was on Secretariat. *Los Angeles Herald-Examiner.* May 6, 1973. pp. C1-C2.
144. Durslag, Mel. Secretariat. *Albany Times-Union.* May 8, 1973.
145. Durslag, Melvin. Sham in Need of New Plan. *Los Angeles Herald-Examiner.* May 20, 1973.
146. Durslag, Melvin. Super Horse Should Hide In New York. *Los Angeles Herald-Examiner.* June 10, 1973. pp. B1, B4.
147. Eagle, Dean. Secretariat, Worth Four Times Weight in Gold, Defends Honor. *Louisville Courier-Journal.* April 20, 1973.
148. Early OTB Odds. *Daily News.* May 5, 1973. p. 29.
149. Easterling, Tom. Dispersal of Hancock Racing Stable Set Today at Belmont. *Lexington Herald.* November 20, 1972. p. 14.
150. Easterling, Tom. Record $2.58 Million Paid in Hancock Dispersal Sale. *Lexington Herald.* November 21, 1972. p. 9.
151. Edbauer, Jenny. Unframing Models of Public Distribution: From Rhetorical Situation to Rhetorical Ecologies. *Rhetoric Society Quarterly.* Fall 2005. 35(4). pp. 5-24.
152. Elevate Sham to Second Choice in Future Book. *Daily Racing Form.* April 4, 1973.
153. Ellis, Ercel. Sham Syndicated, Race Career Over. *Daily Racing Form.* July 14, 1973. pp. 9, 53.
154. Engelhard, Jack. *The Horsemen.* Chicago: Henry Regnery Company. 1974.
155. Ennor, George and Mooney, Bill. *The World Encyclopedia of Horse Racing: An Illustrated Guide to Flat Racing and Steeplechasing.* [Dubai?]: Carlton Books Limited. 2001.
156. Extra Care a Stone's Throw Away for Martin's Sham. *Louisville Courier-Journal.* May 5, 1973. p. C2.
157. Fairfax Morocco Barb. Thoroughbred Bloodlines. http://www.bloodlines.net/TB.
158. Fenlon, Dick. 'Nicest Thrill in World' Ends an Ordeal for Lucien Laurin. *Louisville Courier-Journal.* May 6, 1973. p. C2.

159. Finley, Bill. Trainer Loved Life in Winner's Circle. *Daily News*. August 23, 1998.

160. Finley, Bill. Woody Stephens Dies at 84. *Daily News*. August 23, 1998.

161. Five for Martin. *The Blood-Horse*. January 3, 1972. p. 85.

162. Fla. Derby King Is Wire-to-Wire; Forego Runs 2nd. *Lexington Herald-Leader*. Associated Press. p. 33.

163. Flatter, Ron. Secretariat Remains No. 1 Name in Racing. Special to ESPN.com. ESPN.com. http://espn.go.com.

164. Flynn, John. 50 to 1… Indiana Horse Races a Derby 'Dream'. *Louisville Courier-Journal*. May 5, 1973. p. A5.

165. Forego Upset Victim. *Los Angeles Herald-Examiner*. United Press International. April 1, 1973. p. D8.

166. Fountaine, Ed. Woody Stephens: Belmont Streak among Trainer's Top Feats. *Daily Racing Form*. September 27, 1997. p. 9.

167. Frank Martin Named Harbor View Trainer. *Racing Digest*. August 8, 1983. pp. 3, 8.

168. Furillo, Bud. Frankel Doesn't Talk to Horses. *Los Angeles Herald-Examiner*. May 20, 1973. p. C2.

169. Furillo, Bud. The Price of Horsemeat (Secretariat), $40, 533.33 a Pound. *Los Angeles Herald-Examiner*. June 10, 1973. p. B1.

170. Gaffer, Wes. Turcotte: I Pushed Him for Mark. *Daily News*. June 10, 1973. p. 156.

171. Gaffer, Wes. Pancho Martin Has Big Secret: Hard Work. *Daily News*.

172. Gallaher, Mary Jane. Where Champs Are Born. *Louisville Courier-Journal Magazine*. May 7, 1972. pp. 71+.

173. Gay Jr., Marvin N. And Now Turcotte Sets His Sights on No. 100. *Louisville Courier-Journal*. May 6, 1973. pp. C1, C3.

174. Gay Jr., Marvin N. 'Rabbit' May Trigger a Secretariat Record. *Louisville Courier-Journal*. May 19, 1973. p. B4.

175. Gay Jr., Marvin N. Secretariat Ends Laurin Jinx in Derby Replay. *Louisville Courier-Journal*. May 20, 1973. pp. C1, C3.

176. Gelardi, Joe. Joe Gelardi's Derby Preview. *Daily News*. May 5, 1973. p. 29.

177. Gilcoyne, Tom. interview with author. National Museum of Racing and Hall of Fame, Saratoga Springs, New York. August 2004.

178. Goldman, Dave. Good News and Bad News for Darby Dan. *The Thoroughbred Record*. February 10, 1973. pp. 406-407.

179. Goldman, Dave. Busier and Better. *The Thoroughbred Record*. March 10, 1973. pp. 605, 618.

180. Goldman, Dave. Triumphant Tactics. *The Thoroughbred Record*. March 17, 1973. pp. 676, 693.

181. Goldman, Dave. Living up to His Name. *The Thoroughbred Record*. April 7, 1973. pp. 821, 824.

182. Goldstein, Herb. Fasig-Tipton Sale Smashes Records: Claiborne Group Averages $73,714. *Daily Racing Form*. November 21, 1972. pp. 1, 7.

183. Goldstein, Herb. Sham's Campaign Mapped Out. *Daily Racing Form*. March 5, 1973.

184. Goldstein, Herb. Claiborne Brand Rides with Sham. *Daily Racing Form*. May 5, 1973 p. 10D, 12D.

185. Goldstein, Herb. Preakness Regarded as 'Match' by Sommer. *Daily Racing Form*. May 13, 1973. pp. 1, 15.

186. Goldstein, Herb. Martin Hoping for Preakness Luck After Derby Misfortune. *Daily Racing Form*. May 19, 1973. p. 5.

187. Goldstein, Herb. Pancho Hoping for the Breaks. *Daily Racing Form*. May 19, 1973. p. 5.

188. Goldstein, Herb. Turcotte Is Back—with Secretariat and Another Chance at Triple Crown. *Daily Racing Form*. May 19, 1973. p. 5.

189. Goldstein, Herb. Sham Turns in Sharp Move for June 9 Belmont Stakes. *Daily Racing Form*. May 31, 1973. pp. 1, 30.

190. Goldstein, Herb. Leading Horsemen Pick Secretariat. *Daily Racing Form*. June 9, 1973.

191. Goldstein, Herb. Sommer Typified N.Y. Racing. *Daily Racing Form*. May 9, 1979.

192. Good-Bye Jorge. *The Jockey News*. February/March 1998. p. 22.

193. Grace, Art. Confirmation in the Bahamas. *The Blood-Horse*. February 12, 1973. pp. 612-613.

194. Grace, Art. 'Not looking for Secretariat, but We'll Try When the Time Comes.' *The Blood-Horse*. March 12, 1973. pp. 918-919.

195. Grace, Art. The Revitalization of Shecky. *The Blood-Horse*. March 19, 1973. pp. 1008-1009.

196. Grace, Art. The Florida Derby. *The Blood-Horse*. April 9, 1973. pp. 1262-1263.

197. Grace, Art. Black Type for Leo's Dam. *The Blood-Horse*. April 16, 1973. pp. 1347, 1349.

198. Green, Ashbel. A Threat to Secretariat. *The Thoroughbred Record*. June 2, 1973. p. 1322.

199. Grimsley, Will. Martin and Laurin—There's No Love Lost among These Trainers. [unknown source from Belmont Park Press Office]. Associated Press. May 3, 1973.

200. Grimsley, Will. Martin and Laurin—There's No Love Lost between Derby Foes. *Louisville Courier-Journal*. May 3, 1973. p. C5.

201. Grimsley, Will. Don't Overlook Unlucky Mr. 13 in Derby Field. *Louisville Courier-Journal*. Associated Press. May 4, 1973. p. C5.

202. Grimsley, Will. Secretariat's Win Not Bad for 'Ailing' Colt. *Lexington Herald-Leader*. Associated Press. pp. 10, 12.

203. Grimsley, Will. Losing Tickets? A Costly Cap for Derby Day. *Lexington Herald-Leader*. Associated Press. May 6, 1973. p. 25.

204. Grimsley, Will. While World Awaits Secretariat's Belmont, New York Yawns. *Lexington Herald*. Associated Press. June 7, 1973. p. 22.

205. Grimsley, Will. Amazing Secretariat Forges Racing Legend: Happy Mrs. Tweedy Quite a Champion in Her Own Right. *Lexington Herald-Leader*. Associated Press. June 10, 1973. pp. 1, 24.

206. Grimsley, Will. Laurin Thought Secretariat Was Going Too Fast. *Los Angeles Herald-Examiner*. Associated Press. June 10, 1973. p. B2.

207. Grimsley, Will. Mrs. Tweedy Dances for Joy—All the Way to Winner's Circle. *Louisville Courier-Journal and Times*. Associated Press. June 10, 1973. p. C3.

208. Two-Year-Olds of 1972: Groshawk. *The Thoroughbred Record*. April 14, 1973. pp. 893, 896.

209. Guilliams, Cliff. Woody Stephens: Love of the Horse Fueled Legend's Long Career. *Daily Racing Form*. September 27, 1997. p. 8.

210. Gustines, Heliodoro. interview with author. Aqueduct, Jamaica, New York. March 30, 2003.

211. Gustines, Heliodoro. telephone interview with author. September 10, 2003.

212. Gustines, Heliodoro. interview with author. Belmont Park, Elmont, New York. September 20, 2003.

213. Gustines, Heliodoro. telephone interview with author. May 5, 2004.

214. Gustines, Heliodoro. telephone interview with author. October 5, 2004.

215. Gustines, Heliodoro. telephone interview with author. June 21, 2005.

216. Hall of Fame Selections. *The Blood-Horse*. May 21, 1973. p. 1786.

217. Hancock Horses Sold. *The Thoroughbred Record*. November 25, 1972. p. 1721.

218. Hancock, Seth. telephone interview with author. April 21, 2003.

219. Harvin, Al. Obituaries: Sigmund Sommer, 62, Real Estate Dealer. *New York Times*. May 1, 1979.

220. Haskin, Steve. Quiet Stephens Taught by Example. *Daily Racing Form*.

December 9, 1995. p. 8.

221. Haskin, Steve. Woody Stephens Dead at 84. *Daily Racing Form*. August 24, 1998. pp. 1, 3.

222. Hatton, Charles. Hancock Sale Points Out Strong International Market. *Daily Racing Form*. November 22, 1972. p. 3.

223. Hatton, Charles. Secretariat's Mere Presence Guarantees Drama, Suspense. *Daily Racing Form*. April 2, 1973.

224. Hatton, Charles. Frank Martin Insists Sham Can Do It. *Daily Racing Form*. April 13, 1973. p. 36.

225. Hatton, Charles. The Only Way They Can Beat Him Is Steal It: Lucien Laurin. *Daily Racing Form*. April 21, 1973. pp. 3, 38.

226. Hatton, Charles. Secretariat Takes on Sham, Big Field in $100,000 Wood. *Daily Racing Form*. April 21, 1973.

227. Hatton, Charles. It Just Wasn't Secretariat's Day. *Daily Racing Form*. April 24, 1973. p. 24.

228. Hatton, Charles. Secretariat Had His Shot—But He Failed to Fire. *Daily Racing Form*. April 24, 1973.

229. Hatton, Charles. Wood Survivors Derbytown Bound. *Daily Racing Form*. April 24, 1973.

230. Hatton, Charles. Secretariat Rates All Superlatives: Champion Bigger, Better than Ever. *Daily Racing Form*. May 5, 1973. pp. 4D, 19D.

231. Hatton, Charles. Three Marks Tumble on Week End: Reduce Secretariat's Time to 154⅖: Champion Is Infallibly a Good Show. *Daily Racing Form*. May 22, 1973. p. 3.

232. Hatton, Charles. SRO to Watch Secretariat Train. *Daily Racing Form*. June 7, 1973.

233. Hatton, Charles. Triple Crown Author Expects to Witness Ninth Coronation. *Daily Racing Form*. June 9, 1973.

234. Hatton, Charles. Writer Agrees with Kenny Noe: Secretariat Horse of Century. *Daily Racing Form*. June 12, 1973. p. 2.

235. Hatton, Charles. Aqueduct. *Daily Racing Form*. July 16, 1973.

236. Hatton, Charles. Aqueduct. *Daily Racing Form*. July 26, 1973.

237. Hatton, Charles. Profiles of Best Horses. *The American Racing Manual: 1974 Edition*. Highstown, New Jersey: Triangle Publications. 1974.

238. Haun, Marianna. Great Heart: Secretariat Had an Enormous Engine Pumping His "Big Red Machine". *Thoroughbred Times*. April 23, 1993. p. 16.

239. Haun, Marianna. The X-Factor: Heart of the Matter. HorsesOnly.com. www.

premierpub.com.

240. Hebert, Bob. Sham's Targets: Wood and Derby. *Los Angeles Times*. April 1, 1973. p. 2.

241. Hebert, Robert. Looking for a Derby Winner. *The Blood-Horse*. February 12, 1973. pp. 606-607.

242. [Hebert, Robert?]. Victory and Death. *The Blood-Horse*. February 26, 1973. pp. 784+

243. Hebert, Robert. At Her Absolute Peak. *The Blood-Horse*. March 12, 1973. pp. 922-923.

244. [Hebert, Robert?]. Linda's Chief and Belle Marie. *The Blood-Horse*. March 26, 1973.

245. Hebert, Robert. The Santa Anita Derby. *The Blood-Horse*. April 9, 1973. pp. 1263-1264.

246. Hebert, Robert. In Front for 14 Furlongs. *The Blood-Horse*. April 16, 1973. pp. 1344, 1346.

247. Hebert, Robert. Sundays in the Stands. *The Blood-Horse*. April 23, 1973. pp. 1394-1395.

248. Heller, Bill. *Forego*. Lexington, Kentucky: Eclipse Press. 2000.

249. Henderson, Jon. The 10 Greatest Comebacks of All Time. The Observer. October 7, 2001. http://observer.guardian.co.uk.

250. Hendrickson, Joe. Secretariat… Incredible. *Pasadena Star News*. June 10, 1973. pp. S-1, S-2.

251. Herman, Robin. Improved Surgery Helping Horses Live to Race Again. *New York Times*. July 8, 1973. pp. 1, 6.

252. Herman, Robin. Two-Hour Operation on Sham Deemed 'a Success' by Doctor. *Lexington Herald*. *New York Times* News Service. July 9, 1973.

253. Heywood, John. Bartlett's Quotations online.

254. Hialeah History: History of the City of Hialeah. http://www.ci.hialeah.fl.us.

255. Hirsch, Joe. Never Bend Latest Ace for W. Stephens. *Daily Racing Form*. November 10, 1962.

256. Hirsch, Joe. Easy 4-Panel Move by Secretariat Is Just What Laurin Had in Mind. *Daily Racing Form*. April 14, 1973. pp. 4, 34.

257. Hirsch, Joe. Secretariat's Wood Defeat Sure to Swell Derby Line-up. *Daily Racing Form*. April 24, 1973. pp. 1, 4.

258. Hirsch, Joe. Six Fillies Vie for Arlington Honors; Probable Derby Field Swells to 23: Secretariat's Loss Prompts Changes. *Daily Racing Form*. April 24, 1973. pp. 1, 4.

259. Hirsch, Joe. Forego Reels off 5 Panels in :57; Derby Field Remains Static at 18. *Daily Racing Form*. May 2, 1973. pp. 1, 30.

260. Hirsch, Joe. Secretariat and Angle Light Sparkle in 'Rose Run' Works. *Daily Racing Form*. May 3, 1973. pp. 1, 31.

261. Hirsch, Joe. Post Positions Assigned 13 for Derby; Secretariat Gets 10. *Daily Racing Form.* May 4, 1973. pp. 1, 29.

262. Hirsch, Joe. Straight Shooter. *Daily Racing Form.* May 4, 1973. p. 32.

263. Hirsch, Joe. Coming Up Roses. *Daily Racing Form.* May 5, 1973. p. D24.

264. Hirsch, Joe. Concern over Angle Light's Status Clouds Derby Picture. *Daily Racing Form.* May 5, 1973. pp. 3, 35.

265. Hirsch, Joe. Favor Secretariat over Sham in $198,800 Kentucky Derby: Enter 13 for Richest Running of Historic Churchill Classic. *Daily Racing Form.* May 5, 1973. pp. 1, 16D.

266. Hirsch, Joe. A Man with Good Ideas: Gov. Ford Awaits Centennial. *Daily Racing Form.* May 5, 1973. p. 28D.

267. Hirsch, Joe. Martin Has Sham Ready to Run. *Daily Racing Form.* May 5, 1973. p. 29D.

268. Hirsch, Joe. Secretariat Entry, Sham Top 13 In Record $198,800 Ky. Derby. *Daily Racing Form.* May 5, 1973. pp. 1, 3.

269. Hirsch, Joe. Sham Topweight at 126 If Derby Were Handicap. *Daily Racing Form.* May 5, 1973. pp. 3, 36.

270. Hirsch, Joe. Derby Day Notes. *Daily Racing Form.* May 7, 1973. p. 3.

271. Hirsch, Joe. Derby Day Sidelights. *Daily Racing Form.* May 7, 1973. pp. 4, 5.

272. Hirsch, Joe. Secretariat Smashes Record in Magnificent Derby Score: Champion Clocked in 1:59 २/५; Game Sham Two, Half Away. *Daily Racing Form.* May 7, 1973. pp. 1, 4.

273. Hirsch, Joe. Fabulous Last Quarter. *Daily Racing Form.* May 8, 1973. p. 48.

274. Hirsch, Joe. Secretariat Continues on Triple Crown Path. *Daily Racing Form.* May 8, 1973. pp. 1, 5.

275. Hirsch, Joe. Secretariat and Sham Limber Up at Pimlico. *Daily Racing Form.* May 11, 1973. pp. 1, 30.

276. Hirsch, Joe. Torsion Added to Preakness Line-Up: Buckland Colt Goes in Saturday's Prep. *Daily Racing Form.* May 11, 1973. pp. 3-4.

277. Hirsch, Joe. Preakness Field Begins to Shrink. *Daily Racing Form.* May 14, 1973. pp. 2, 24.

278. Hirsch, Joe. Secretariat, Sham Extremely Sharp: Respective 5-Panel Preps of :57 २/५, :58 ३/५. *Daily Racing Form.* May 15, 1973. pp. 1, 5.

279. Hirsch, Joe. Secretariat, Sham Impressive in Drills. *Daily Racing Form.* May 15, 1973. pp. 1, 3.

280. Hirsch, Joe. Secretariat, Sham, 5 Others Expected to Vie in Preakness. *Daily Racing*

*Form.* May 16, 1973. pp. 1, 27.

281. [Hirsch, Joe?].Our Native's Arrival for Preakness Makes Deadly Dream's Status 'Doubtful'. *Daily Racing Form.* May 17, 1973. p. 34.

282. Hirsch, Joe. Secretariat, Sham Head Preakness Saturday. *Daily Racing Form.* May 18, 1973. pp. 1, 5.

283. Hirsch, Joe. Seven Enter Preakness, But Only Six to Compete. *Daily Racing Form.* May 18, 1973. pp. 1, 32.

284. Hirsch, Joe. '72 Preakness Upset Haunts Laurin: Pimlico Loss Cost Riva Ridge Crown. *Daily Racing Form.* May 19, 1973. p. 3.

285. Hirsch, Joe. Laurin Remembers, and Is Concerned. *Daily Racing Form.* May 19, 1973. p. 5.

286. Hirsch, Joe. Secretariat Encounters Sham, 4 Others in Preakness Stakes. *Daily Racing Form.* May 19, 1973. pp. 1-4.

287. Hirsch, Joe. Secretariat Heads Preakness: Choice over Sham and Four Others in $182,400 Stakes. *Daily Racing Form.* May 19, 1973. pp. 1, 6, 57.

288. Hirsch, Joe. Secretariat is 2-5 in Preakness. *Daily Racing Form.* May 19, 1973. pp. 1, 8.

289. Hirsch, Joe. Preakness Sidelights. *Daily Racing Form.* May 21, 1973. p. 4.

290. Hirsch, Joe. Secretariat Adds Preakness: Takes Lead Early, Easily Holds Sham. *Daily Racing Form.* May 21, 1973. pp. 1, 4.

291. Hirsch, Joe. Secretariat Vans to New York in Pursuit of Triple Crown. *Daily Racing Form.* May 22, 1973. pp. 1, 4.

292. Hirsch, Joe. Secretariat's Brilliant Effort Should Dispel Slightest Doubt. *Daily Racing Form.* May 22, 1973. p. 5.

293. Hirsch, Joe. Two Down and One More to Go; Belmont Next for Secretariat. *Daily Racing Form.* May 22, 1973. pp. 1, 5.

294. Hirsch, Joe. Without a Doubt. *Daily Racing Form.* May 22, 1973. p. 24.

295. Hirsch, Joe. Secretariat Next. *Daily Racing Form.* May 30, 1973. p. 24.

296. Hirsch, Joe. Secretariat Completes Belmont Preparation with Half in :46⅗. *Daily Racing Form.* June 7, 1973. pp. 1, 4, 41.

297. Hirsch, Joe. Confident Laurin Awaits Act Three. *Daily Racing Form.* June 9, 1973. pp. 9, 11.

298. Hirsch, Joe. Secretariat Bids for Lasting Fame in $151,200 Belmont: Five Block Way to Triple Crown. *Daily Racing Form.* June 9, 1973. pp. 1, 6.

299. Hirsch, Joe. Belmont Stakes Sidelights. *Daily Racing Form.* June 11, 1973. p. 4.

300. Hirsch, Joe. Secretariat Achieves 'Triple': Astonishing 31 Lengths Best in 2:24

Belmont Stakes Romp. *Daily Racing Form.* June 11, 1973. pp. 1, 4.

301. Hirsch, Joe. Secretariat Begins Short Vacation: Aug. 8 Jim Dandy May Be Next Start. *Daily Racing Form.* June 12, 1973. pp. 1, 5, 11.

302. Hirsch, Joe. Another Long-Winded One for Martin? *Daily Racing Form.* December 12, 1987.

303. Hirsch, Joe. Sham Wasn't, but Who Remembers? *Daily Racing Form.* November 19, 2000. p. 5.

304. Hirsch, Joe. Secretariat Achieves a Triple. http://www.drf.com.

305. Hirt, Clyde. Secretariat Made Quick 1-to-5 Belmont Favorite. *Daily Racing Form.* June 9, 1973.

306. Hold Sigmund Sommer Funeral. *Daily Racing Form.* May 3, 1979.

307. [Hollingsworth, Kent?]. A.B. Hancock Jr.: (1910-1972). *The Blood-Horse.* September 25, 1972. pp. 3524-3526.

308. [Hollingsworth, Kent]. What's Going on Here. *The Blood-Horse.* October 2, 1972. p. 3623.

309. [Hollingsworth, Kent]. What's Going on Here. *The Blood-Horse.* February 5, 1973. p. 533.

310. Hollingsworth, Kent. The Boom at Hot Springs. *The Blood-Horse.* April 16, 1973. pp. 1322-1326.

311. [Hollingsworth, Kent?]. The Fastest Closing Half-Mile. *The Blood-Horse.* May 14, 1973. p. 1671.

312. Hollingsworth, Kent. Kentucky Derby Notes. *The Blood-Horse.* May 14, 1973. p. 1672.

313. [Hollingsworth, Kent]. What's Going on Here. *The Blood-Horse.* May 28, 1973. p. 1831.

314. [Hollingsworth, Kent]. What's Going on Here. *The Blood-Horse.* June 4, 1973. p. 1927.

315. Hollingsworth, Kent. Belmont Thoughts. *The Blood-Horse.* June 18, 1973. pp. 2082-2085.

316. [Hollingsworth, Kent]. What's Going on Here. *The Blood-Horse.* July 23, 1973. p. 2661.

317. [Hollingsworth, Kent]. What's Going on Here. *The Blood-Horse.* December 10, 1973. p. 5077.

318. Horse of the Year Secretariat, Champions Typecast and *Cougar II Top Eclipse Award Balloting. *The Thoroughbred of California.* January 1973. pp. 5-8.

319. Hotaling, Edward. *They're Off! Horse Racing at Saratoga.* Syracuse University Press. 1995.

320. How Fast Is Secretariat? *Albany Times-Union.* Associated Press. May 21, 1973.

321. Iandoli, Dean. Jockey Journal: with Laffit Pincay, Jr. *Horseplayer Magazine.* May 1994.

322. In Riding Strategy, What Goes at Big A Might Not Go at Belmont. *New York Times*. May 13, 1973. p. 7.

323. Irwin, Barry H. The (*)Cougar (II) Revisited. *The Thoroughbred of California*. April 1973. pp. 4-6, 8.

324. Irwin, Barry H. Western Derbys to New York Runners. *The Thoroughbred of California*. May 1973. pp. 6-8.

325. Irwin, Barry H. Yes, Kentucky, There Is a Virginia… Yes, Man O' War, There Is Another Big Red. *The Thoroughbred of California*. June 1973. pp. 26-38.

326. Irwin, Barry H. The Big Red Machine Rolls to Triple Crown. *The Thoroughbred of California*. July 1973. pp. 10+.

327. Isaak, W. Georg. Plenty of Honor, in Many Countries. *The Thoroughbred Record*. October 30, 1965. pp. 1368+.

328. Isinglass (GB). Thoroughbred Bloodlines. http://www.bloodlines.net/TB.

329. Jackson, Catherine "Cappy". telephone interview with author. July 21, 2010.

330. Jacobson, Steve. Stephens Looks Back. *Knickerbocker News*. June, 5, 1986.

331. Jacobson, Steve. A Venerable Stephens Puts Tale Before Horse. *Newsday*. pp. 183, 154.

332. Jacobson, Steve. History Still with Stephens. *Newsday*. June 7, 1987. p. 4.

333. Jitters at Louisville. *Pasadena Star News*. Associated Press. May 5, 1973.

334. Jones, Gordon. Secretariat Is No Cinch in Derby. *Los Angeles Herald-Examiner*. February 3, 1973.

335. Jones, Gordon. Frankel Cries Foul. *Los Angeles Herald-Examiner*. April 1, 1973. pp. D1, D8.

336. Jones, Gordon. Record 134, 476 at Downs. *Los Angeles Herald-Examiner*. May 6, 1973. pp. C1-C2.

337. Jones, Gordon. Secretariat: Last to First. *Los Angeles Herald-Examiner*. May 6, 1973. pp. C1-C2.

338. Jones, Kathleen. Princequillo. http://www.thoroughbredchampions.com.

339. Kaukas, Dick. Record Crowd Turns Out in Warm-up for Derby. *Louisville Courier-Journal*. May 5, 1973. pp. 1, 12.

340. Kazickas, Jurate. A Lady in a Man's World: That's Penny Tweedy, Who May Own a Triple Crown Winner. *Lexington Herald-Leader*. May 27, 1973. pp. 27, 29.

341. Kelly, Joe. The Baltimore Posture. *The Blood-Horse*. May 21, 1973. p. 1775.

342. Kenny, Dan. Leo's Pisces Shows Punch in La. Derby. *Daily Racing Form*. April 3, 1973. p. 4.

343. http://www.kentuckyderby.com.

344. Kindred, Dave. Pincay Resigned to Secretariat's 'Super' Handle. *Louisville Courier-Journal and Times.* May 20, 1973. p. C3.

345. Kindred, Dave. Secretariat: The Successor to Citation also Surpasses Gallant Man. *Louisville Courier-Journal and Times.* June 10, 1973.

346. Kirkpatrick, Arnold. Grass-Roots Foundation. *The Thoroughbred Record.* October 30, 1965. pp. 1376-1380.

347. Kirkpatrick, Arnold. Doubts Dispelled. *The Thoroughbred Record.* May 12, 1973. pp. 1158-1164.

348. Kirkpatrick, Arnold. Secretariat's Stride. *The Thoroughbred Record.* May 19, 73. p. 1216B.

349. Kirkpatrick, Arnold; Green, Ashbel. The Name of the Game Is Class. *The Thoroughbred Record.* May 26, 1973. pp. 1256-1261.

350. Kirkpatrick, Arnold. Secretariat: The Ultimate Superlative. *The Thoroughbred Record.* June 16, 1973. pp. 1438-1443.

351. Kirkpatrick, Arnold. A Panamanian Festival. *The Thoroughbred Record.* December 29, 1973. pp. 2067-2068.

352. Kivel, Martin. Hot Stretch Run by Kentuckian. *Pasadena Star News.* January 2, 1973. pp. 7, 10.

353. Kivel, Martin. Sham Proves He's Classy. *Pasadena Star News.* February 13, 1973. pp. 18, 20.

354. Kivel, Martin. Sham Routs Doubt with Derby Triumph. *Pasadena Star News.* April 1, 1973. pp. S-1, S-4.

355. Kivel, Martin. Susan's Girl Favored. *Pasadena Star News.* April 21, 1973.

356. Kivel, Martin. Bird Boots New Racing Heroine. *Pasadena Star News.* April 22, 1973. pp. S-1, S-4.

357. Kivel, Martin. OK for Sunday Racing Near: Deby Wide Open. *Pasadena Star News.* April 22, 1973. p. S-4.

358. Kivel, Martin. Don't Give Up on Sham Yet. *Pasadena Star News.* May 6, 1973.

359. Kivel, Martin. Secretariat for Real. *Pasadena Star News.* May 20, 1973. p. S-4.

360. Knightly Dawn. Hill 'N' Dale Farms advertisement. The Blood-Horse. November 19, 1973.

361. Kram, Mark. Watching a Different Race. *Sports Illustrated.* May 28, 1973. p. 27.

362. Krulik, Stephanie. Woody's Way. *The Florida Horse.* April 1988. pp. 354+.

363. LaBelle Jr., Francis. For Woody, Racing's the Best Medicine. *Daily Racing Form.* May 11, 1991.

364. LaBelle Jr., Francis. Pancho Martin Remembers Sham. *Daily Racing Form.* April 13, 1993.

*365. Laffit: All About Winning.* Six Furlongs LLC. 2005.

366. Late Items. *The Blood-Horse.* December 26, 1973.

367. Laurin under Plenty of Pressure. *Albany Times-Union.* Associated Press. May 6, 1973.

368. Laurin's Entry Favored in Derby. *Albany Times-Union.* Associated Press. May 4, 1973. p. 26.

369. Leo's Pisces Romps to Victory in LA. Derby. *Los Angeles Herald-Examiner.* Associated Press. April 1, 1973. p. D8.

370. Lewin, Leonard. Pancho, Like Stevie, Got an Early Start. *New York Post.* February 25, 1977. p. 56.

371. Liebman, Dan. Big Weekend for Author Stephens. *Daily Racing Form.* November 28, 1985.

372. Linda's Chief 'Anita' Pick. *Albany Times-Union.* Associated Press. March 30, 1973. p. 25.

373. Linda's Chief Beaten by Sham in Anita Derby. *Albany Times-Union.* Associated Press. April 1, 1973.

374. Linda's Chief Likely to Race in Preakness. *Albany Times-Union.* United Press International. May 10, 1973. p. 34.

375. Linda's Chief out of Belmont. *Knickerbocker News Union Star.* June 4, 1973.

376. Linda's Chief Rated Heavy California Derby Favorite. *Lexington Herald and the Lexington Leader.* Associated Press. April 21, 1973. p. 9.

377. Linda's Chief, Sham Top San Felipe 'Cap. *Lexington Herald and the Lexington Leader.* March 17, 1973. p. 9.

378. Linda's Chief Still a Question. *Knickerbocker News Union Star.* June 1, 1973.

379. Lister Turk. Thoroughbred Bloodlines. http://www.bloodlines.net/TB.

380. Longrigg, Roger. *The History of Horse Racing.* New York: Stein and Day. 1972.

381. Longshot Cops Blue Grass Stakes: 'Gallant' Posts Win by Nose. *Albany Times-Union.* Associated Press. April 27, 1973.

382. Lowitt, Bruce. Secretariat Proves He's a Unique Breed. *St. Petersburg Times.* Online Sports. http://www.sptimes.com. December 19, 1999.

383. Macaroni (GB). Thoroughbred Bloodlines. http://www.bloodlines.net/TB.

384. Manser, David. Isinglass. The Pedigree Post. http://www.pedigreepost.com.

385. Martin, Frank (Pancho). interview with author. Belmont Park, Elmont, New York. March 21, 2003.

386. Martin, Valerie. This Is Findon Village. Racing Stables in Findon. http://www.findonvillage.com.

387. Martiniak, Elizabeth. Hermit. Thoroughbred Heritage. http://www.tbheritage.com/index.html.

388. Maryland Commission to Study Preakness Time. *Daily Racing Form.* June 21, 1973.

389. John J. McCabe Agency, Inc. advertisement. *Daily Racing Form.* May 5, 1973.

390. McCulley, Jim. Handicap for Secretariat: Post 8 in Today's Wood. *Daily News.* April 21, 1973.

391. McCulley, Jim. Secretariat Winds Up 3rd in Wood. *Daily News.* April 22, 1973. pp. 115, 132.

392. McCulley, Jim. Preakness: You Gotta Have Heart. *Daily News.* May 18, 1973. p. 100.

393. McCulley, Jim. Sham Works 6-7 Furlongs. *Daily News.* June 6, 1973.

394. McCulley, Jim. Knightly Dawn May Be Scratched. *Daily News.* June 9, 1973. p. 29.

395. McCulley, Jim. Secretariat Breezes by 31 Lengths. *Daily News.* June 10, 1973. pp. 134, 156.

396. McCulley, Jim. Will Secretariat Run Again? *Daily News.* June 11, 1973.

397. McGuire, Hugh J. Arthur B. Hancock III to Operate Stone Farm. *Daily Racing Form.* February 1, 1973. p. 2.

398. McKerrow, Raymie E. Critical Rhetoric: Theory and Practice. In *Contemporary Rhetorical Theory: A Reader.* Eds. John Louis Lucaites, Celeste Michelle Condit, Sally Caudill. Guilford Press: New York. 1999. pp. 441+.

399. Meier, Ted. Forego, Linda's Chief Morning Line Favorites in Major Derby Preps. *Lexington Herald and the Lexington Leader.* March 31, 1973. p. 12.

400. Miller, Norm. When Winning Isn't Everything. *Daily News.* April 22, 1973. pp. 115, 132.

401. Mills, Jeffrey. Much Headache Moans Martin. *Lexington Herald-Leader.* May 6, 1973. p. 26.

402. Mochon, Bill. letter to the author. June 18, 2004.

403. Mochon, Bill. telephone interview with author. July 5, 2004.

404. Mrs. Tweedy: 'What a Horse!' *Albany Times-Union.* Associated Press. June 10, 1973. p. C1.

405. Munn, William G. Pedigree Profiles…: Sham. *The Thoroughbred Record.* May 24, 1978. pp. 1564-1565.

406. Murray, William. *Horse Fever.* New York: Dodd, Mead, and Company. 1976.

407. Nack, Bill. Not an Unguarded Moment for Sham. *Newsday.* May 18, 1973. p. 143.

408. Nack, Bill. Real Threat Or a Sham? *Newsday*. April 20, 1973.

409. Nack, Bill. Martin's Sparing No Expense for Sham. *The Miami Herald*. Newsday Service. May 19, 1973. pp. 1F, 4F.

410. Nack, Bill. Secretariat Hasn't Convinced Martin. *Newsday*. June 5, 1973.

411. Nack, Bill. Sham Undergoes Surgery. *Newsday*. July 7, 1973. p. 27.

412. Nack, William. He's Got the Horse Right Here. *Sports Illustrated*. March 5, 1984. pp. 26+.

413. Nack, William. *Secretariat: The Making of a Champion*. Cambridge, Massachusetts: Da Capo Press. 2002.

414. Nack, William. Saratoga. *My Turf: Horses, Boxers, Blood Money, and the Sporting Life*. Cambridge, Massachusetts: Da Capo Press. 2003. pp. 18-29.

415. Nagler, Barney. A Look Back with Woody.... *Daily Racing Form*. October 10, 1985. pp. 3-4.

416. National Baseball Hall of Fame and Museum. A. Bartlett Giamatti Research Library.

417. National Museum of Racing and Hall of Fame. http://www.racingmuseum.org.

418. Never Bow Destroyed. *The Blood-Horse*. December 20, 1971. p. 4805.

419. Nichols, Joe. Christopher T. Chenery Is Dead; Meadow Stable Founder Was 86. *New York Times*. January 5, 1973. p. 34.

420. Nichols, Joe. Shecky Greene Takes Stepping Stone; Poker Night Triumphs. *New York Times*. April 29, 1973. Section V, pp. 1, 6.

421. Nichols, Joe. Derby Champ Heads for Preakness. *Lexington Herald-Leader*. *New York Times* News Service. p. 10.

422. No Way. *Lexington Herald-Leader*. United Press International. May 20, 1973. p. 35.

423. Nolan, Irene. Derby Celebrations Are on Despite the High Prices. *Louisville Courier-Journal*. May 4, 1973. p. A11.

424. http://www.nyra.com.

425. Obituary. Sigmund Sommer. *The Blood-Horse*. May 14, 1979. p. 2378.

426. O'Day, Joe. No Secretariat Record—It's 1:54.2. *Daily News*. May 22, 1973. p. 82.

427. On Bloodlines, Sham Should Stay. *Daily Racing Form*. May 5, 1973. p. 6D.

428. Only Supersteed Can Stop Secretariat's Bid for Triple Crown Sweep. *Lexington Herald*. *New York Times* News Service. June 4, 1973. p. 10.

429. Ormonde (GB). Thoroughbred Bloodlines. http://www.bloodlines.net/TB.

430. Our Native Eyes Florida Derby Win. *Albany Times-Union*. Associated Press. March 31, 1973. p. 19.

431. Pancho Martin Scratches at Laurin. *Daily News*. United Press International. May 1, 1973. p. 68.

432. Parker, Ron. Wire to Wire Winner. *The Thoroughbred Record*. April 28, 1973. pp. 1071-1072.

433. Past performances. Belmont Park, third race. *Daily Racing Form*. Highstown, New Jersey: Triangle Publications. August 28, 1972.

434. Past performances. Belmont Park, third race. *Daily Racing Form*. Highstown, New Jersey: Triangle Publications. September 13, 1972.

435. Past performances. Belmont Park, third race. *Daily Racing Form*. Highstown, New Jersey: Triangle Publications. September 23, 1972.

436. Past performances. Aqueduct, second race. *Daily Racing Form*. Highstown, New Jersey: Triangle Publications. December 9, 1972.

437. Past performances. Santa Anita, sixth race. *Daily Racing Form*. Los Angeles, California: Triangle Publications. January 1, 1973.

438. Past performances. Santa Anita, eighth race. *Daily Racing Form*. Los Angeles, California: Triangle Publications. February 2, 1973.

439. Past performances. Santa Anita, eighth race: Santa Catalina Stakes. *Daily Racing Form*. Los Angeles, California: Triangle Publications. February 12, 1973.

440. Past performances. Santa Anita, eighth race: The San Felipe Handicap. *Daily Racing Form*. Los Angeles, California: Triangle Publications. March 17, 1973.

441. Past performances. Santa Anita, eighth race: The Santa Anita Derby. *Daily Racing Form*. Los Angeles, California: Triangle Publications. March 31, 1973.

442. Past performances. Aqueduct, seventh race: Wood Memorial. *Daily Racing Form*. Highstown, New Jersey: Triangle Publications. April 21, 1973.

443. Past performances. Churchill Downs, ninth race: Kentucky Derby. *Daily Racing Form*. Chicago, Illinois: Triangle Publications. May 5, 1973.

444. Past performances. Pimlico, eighth race: Preakness Stakes. *Daily Racing Form*. Highstown, New Jersey: Triangle Publications. May 19, 1973.

445. Past performances. Belmont Park, eighth race: Belmont Stakes. *Daily Racing Form*. Highstown, New Jersey: Triangle Publications. June 9, 1973.

446. Pedigree Online: Thoroughbred Database. http://www.pedigreequery.com.

447. The People History. http://www.thepeoplehistory.com.

448. Phelps, Frank T. Secretariat Draws 10th Post Position. *Lexington Herald*. May 4, 1973. pp. 17, 19.

449. Phelps, Frank T. Secretariat, Angle Light Draw Even Odds, but Derby Field Is Wide Open. *Lexington Herald and the Lexington Leader*. May 5, 1973. pp. 13, 16.

450. Phelps, Frank T. Is Secretariat Worth $6 Million? *Lexington Herald-Leader*. May 7, 1973. p. 10.

451. Phelps, Frank T. The Claiborne Connection Forms Link Between Secretariat and Sham. *Lexington Herald*. May 9, 1973. p. 29.

452. Phelps, Frank T. Will Preakness Turn Into a Match Race? *Lexington Herald*. May 10, 1973. p. 31.

453. Phelps, Frank T. Sham Is the Only Certain Foe for Secretariat in Preakness. *Lexington Herald Leader*. May 13, 1973. pp. 25, 32.

454. Phelps, Frank T. Four State-Breds to Oppose Secretariat in Belmont. *Lexington Herald*. June 5, 1973. p. 10.

455. Phelps, Frank T. Standing in the Presence of Immortality…: Secretariat Gives Same Thrill as Natural Beauty, Work of Art. *Lexington Herald*. June 11, 1973. p. 10.

456. Phillips, William C. Secretariat to Test Pimlico Strip Today. *Daily Racing Form*. May 9, 1973. p. 1.

457. Phillips, William C. Racing's 'Giant' Has Stride to Match. *Daily Racing Form*. May 15, 1973.

458. Phillips, William C. Chick Lang Top Preakness Booster. *Daily Racing Form*. May 19, 1973. pp. 4, 8.

459. Phillips, William C. Strategy is Important Factor to Preakness Stakes Outcome. *Daily Racing Form*. May 19, 1973. p. 8.

460. Phillips, William C. A Superlative Performance. *Daily Racing Form*. May 22, 1973. p. 24.

461. Pincay Aboard 500th Hollywood Park Winner. *Daily Racing Form*. June 9, 1973.

462. Pincay Rejects Sham for Filly Champion. *Lexington Herald and Lexington Leader*. Associated Press. April 21, 1973. p. 9.

463. Pocahontas (GB). Thoroughbred Bloodlines. http://www.bloodlines.net/TB.

464. Point Our Native to Jersey Derby. *Daily Racing Form*. May 22, 1973. p. 5.

465. Potoooooooo (GB). Thoroughbred Bloodlines. http://www.bloodlines.net/TB.

466. Poulakos, John. Toward a Sophistic Definition of Rhetoric. In *Contemporary Rhetorical Theory: A Reader*. Eds. John Louis Lucaites, Celeste Michelle Condit, Sally Caudill. Guilford Press: New York. 1999. pp. 25-34.

467. http://www.preakness.com.

468. Preakness Official Time Is Changed to 1:54⅖. *Daily Racing Form*. May 22, 1973. p. 1.

469. Press release. [Add Notes…]. June 15, 1961. from Belmont Park Press Office.

470. Press release. [Feb '59]. from Belmont Park Press Office.

471. Press release. Frank (Pancho) Martin. from Belmont Park Press Office.

472. Press release. Information for Visiting Newsmen: Bus Schedule from Biltmore Hotel. from Belmont Park Press Office.

473. Press release. New York Racing Association. 1973 Belmont Stakes Fact Sheet. from Belmont Park Press Office. June 9, 1973.

474. Press release. New York Racing Association. Belmont Stakes—1973. from Belmont Park Press Office.

475. Press release. The New York Racing Association. The Belmont Stakes: Agenda and Oddenda. from Belmont Stakes Press Office. June 4, 1973.

476. Press release. New York Racing Association. How Pvt. Smiles Got His Name. from Belmont Park Press Office. June 7, 1973.

477. Press release. New York Racing Association. Jockey Quotes. from Belmont Park Press Office. June 9, 1973.

478. Press release. Jockey Quotes [1973 Belmont Stakes]. from Belmont Park Press Office.

479. Press release. New York Racing Association. Kanchuger, Sam, Director of Press Relations. Record Press Coverage for Today's Belmont Stakes. from Belmont Park Press Office. June 9, 1973.

480. Press release. New York Racing Association. Pancho Martin's 25 Years on Big Apple. from the Belmont Press Office. November 24, 1974.

481. Press release. New York Racing Association. For Release to Papers of Wednesday, March 7. from Belmont Park Press Office. March 7, 1973.

482. Press release. No 'Broken Heart' for Sham—Martin. from Belmont Park Press Office.

483. Press release. Pimlico Race Course Press Release. Siciliano, Sam, Public Relations Director. Sham Impresses His Trainer with Fast Preakness Workout. from Belmont Park Press Office. May 14, 1973.

484. Press release. A Statement from Frank Martin. from Belmont Park Press Office. April 23, 1973.

485. Press release. New York Racing Association. Sommer Elected to NYRA Board of Trustees. from Belmont Park Press Office. February 8, 1984.

486. Press release. Stephens, Woodford C. (Woody). from Belmont Park Press Office. May 1987.

487. Press release. Trainer—Frank (Pancho) Martin [Preakness '73]. from Belmont Park Press Office.

488. Press release. Trainer—Frank (Pancho) Martin [Preakness 1974]. from Belmont Park Press Office.

489. Press release. Trainer—W. C. (Woody) Stephens. [May '71]. from Belmont Park

Press Office.

490. Press release. Trainer: Woody Stephens. [Belmont '71]. from Belmont Park Press Office.

491. Pretense. *The Stallion Register for 1969. The Blood-Horse.* Lexington, Kentucky: The Blood-Horse, Inc. November 2, 1968. p. 352.

492. Pretense, Restless Wind Moved. *The Thoroughbred Record.* July 21, 1973. p. 301.

493. Quintilian. *Institutes of Oratory.* in *The Rhetorical Tradition: Readings from Classical Times to the Present.* 2nd Edition. Bizzell, Patricia and Herzberg, Bruce, editors. Boston: Bedford/St. Martins. 2001. pp. 364-428.

494. Ramsey, Sy. Laurin Felt Pressure. *Los Angeles Herald-Examiner.* Associated Press. May 6, 1973. p. C1.

495. Rasmussen, Leon. Still a Champion. *The Thoroughbred Record.* February 24, 1973. pp. 490-492.

496. Rasmussen, Leon. Doubts Dispelled. *The Thoroughbred Record.* March 24, 1973. pp. 729, 740.

497. Rasmussen, Leon. Point, Counterpoint. *The Thoroughbred Record.* April 7, 1973. pp. 819, 832.

498. Rasmussen, Leon. Kentucky Derby Preview. *The Thoroughbred of California.* May 1973. pp. 30-36.

499. Rasmussen, Leon. Secretariat over Sham—'Bloodlines': Latter Could Take Deep Stretch Duel. *Daily Racing Form.* May 5, 1973. p. 47D.

500. Rasmussen, Leon. Derby Winner Secretariat's Pedigree. *The Thoroughbred of California.* June 1973. pp. 40-46.

501. Rasmussen, Leon. Sham Becomes Classic Sire with Jaazeiro's Irish Win. *Daily Racing Form.* May 18, 1978.

502. Reed, Billy, One-Track Mind... Phantom of Pimlico Strikes Again at Churchill. *Louisville Courier-Journal.* May 4, 1973. p. B1.

503. Reed, Billy. The Hancock Connection, and Secretariat's Future. *Louisville Courier-Journal.* November 14, 1973 p. A21.

504. Reed, Dr. William O. Sham's Fracture a Classic Case. [unknown source from Belmont Park Press Office]. August 6, 1973. p. 26-S.

505. Retro Fashion History. http://retro-fashion-history.com/index.html.

506. Richman, Milton. 'Worried' Laurin Relaxed after Lead Was 20 Lengths. *Lexington Herald-Leader.* United Press International. June 10, 1973 p. 25.

507. Rivals Call Secretariat Super Horse. *Albany Times-Union.* Associated Press. May 7, 1973.

508. Robertson, William. The Making of a Stallion. *The Thoroughbred Record*. October 30, 1965. pp. 1342-1347.

509. *Rocky*. Director John G. Avildsen. Performer Burgess Meredith. United Artists. 1976.

510. Rogerson, Pat. Sham Firm Choice at Santa Anita: Faces Table Run at Mile, Sixteenth. *Daily Racing Form*. February 2, 1973. pp. 1, 34.

511. Rogerson, Pat. Exciting Sham Engages 7 at Anita: Prohibitive Favorite in Santa Catalina. *Daily Racing Form*. February 12, 1973. pp. 1, 34.

512. Rogerson, Pat. Sham in Field of Eight Seeking Santa Catalina. *Daily Racing Form*. February 12, 1973. pp. 1, 3.

513. Rogerson, Pat. Mrs. Tippett Casts Covetous Eyes on Sham: Langollen Owner Underbidder at $195,000: Chalk Players Shudder at Colt's Rough Trip. *Daily Racing Form*. February 14, 1973. p. 5.

514. Rogerson, Pat. Linda's Chief vs. Sham in San Felipe: Eight Others also in $70,300 Stakes. *Daily Racing Form*. March 17, 1973.

515. Rogerson, Pat. Run Derbys at Fair Grounds, Gulfstream and Santa Anita: Linda's Chief has Only Five Rivals. *Daily Racing Form*. March 31, 1973. pp. 1, 5.

516. Rogerson, Pat. A Shamful Heart. *Daily Racing Form*. March 31, 1973. p. 44.

517. Rogerson, Pat. Score Tied at One All. *Daily Racing Form*. April 3, 1973. p. 32.

518. Rogerson, Pat. Bright, Rich Future. *Daily Racing Form*. April 27, 1973. p. 40.

519. Rogerson, Pat. Pincay Has the Touch. *Daily Racing Form*. May 5, 1973. p. 6D.

520. Rogerson, Pat. Pincay's Ride on Sham Follows Soul Searching. *Daily Racing Form*. May 5, 1973. p. D8.

521. Rogerson, Pat. Sham Being Ridden by 'Agent's Dream'. *Daily Racing Form*. May 5, 1973. p. 13D.

522. Rogerson, Pat. Pincay Believes Sham Can Beat Secretariat. *Daily Racing Form*. May 19, 1973. pp. 5, 12.

523. Royal and Regal Scores by Three Lengths in Florida Derby, Returns $15.20. *New York Times*. April 1, 1973. Section 5. p. 8.

524. Rudy, William H. Calling It a Season. *The Blood-Horse*. January 1, 1973. p. 29.

525. Rudy, William H. 'Champ'. [unknown source from Belmont Park Press Office]. April 11, 1973.

526. Rudy, William H. The Hatton Angle. *The Blood-Horse*. April 30, 1973 pp. 1478, 1479.

527. Rudy, William H. Reactions. *The Blood-Horse*. June 18, 1973. p. 2086.

528. Runyon, Keith. Derby Boxes: All of Them Are Long Gone. *Louisville Courier-Journal*. May 3, 1973. p. B1.

529. http://www.santaanita.com.

530. Santa Anita Derby Hero Considered Fine Example of Selective Breeding. *Daily Racing Form*. May 5, 1973. p. D10.

531. Santa Anita Derby Hero Sham Syndicated by Combs. *The Thoroughbred of California*. September 1973. p. 132.

532. http://www.saratoga.com/aboutsaratoga/history/.

533. Schmitz, David. Sham Dead. *The Blood-Horse*. April 24, 1993. p. 1983.

534. Schmitz, David. A Handful of Belmonts. *The Blood-Horse*. August 29, 1998. pp. 4678-4680.

535. Schultz, Gary. Twice a Prince, Once a Bad Actor: Colt that 'Didn't Belong in Race' Throws Jockey, Delays Derby. *Louisville Courier-Journal*. May 6, 1973. p. C4.

536. Schuyler Jr., Ed. Secretariat Gets No. 8 in Wood. *Lexington Herald and the Lexington Leader*. Associated Press. April 21, 1973. p. 9.

537. Schuyler Jr., Ed. Angle Light Stuns Sham, Secretariat in Wood. *Lexington Herald-Leader*. April 22, 1973. p. 29.

538. Schuyler Jr., Ed. Most Preakness Entries Eye Third Place; Field of Six Is Expected. *Lexington Herald*. May 17, 1973. p. 25.

539. Schuyler Jr., Ed. Sham Disappointing? Not to Pancho Martin. *Lexington Herald*. May 31, 1973. p. 17.

540. Schuyler Jr., Ed. Five Try to Thwart Secretariat's Triple Crown Bid Today. *Lexington Herald and Lexington Leader*. Associated Press. June 9, 1973. p. 10.

541. Schuyler Jr., Ed. Merchandising Is Topic as Secretariat Returns to New York. *Lexington Leader*. Associated Press. July 2, 1973.

542. Schwartz, Larry. Big Red Comet. ESPN.com. http://espn.go.com/sportscentury/features/00016467.html.

543. Secretariat Achieves 'Triple': Grand Prix Nominations Number 22. *Daily Racing Form*. June 11, 1973.

544. Secretariat—1973 Preakness Stakes—Laffit Pincay, Jr., Sham's Jockey, Interviewed! [CBS broadcast]. YouTube.com. http://www.youtube.com/watch?v=hVOqm67DBt4.

545. Secretariat Assured of Challenger—Sham. *Lexington Herald*. Associated Press. May 22, 1973. p. 9.

546. Secretariat Bid for Mark Foiled. *New York Times*. Associated Press. July 11, 1973. pp. 29, 31.

547. Secretariat Changes Style but Not Result in Easy Preakness Victory. *Lexington Herald-Leader*. United Press International. May 20, 1973. pp. 25, 35.

548. Secretariat Confirms Derby Form in Preakness Stakes. *Daily Racing Form*. May 22, 1973. pp. 2, 21.

549. Secretariat Drew 2,170,000 TV Fans in N.Y. [unknown source from Belmont Park Press Office]. June 13, 1973.

550. Secretariat Drill Pleases Laurin. *Albany Times-Union*. Associated Press. May 3, 1973. p. 25.

551. Secretariat 4-5 for Preakness. *Los Angeles Herald-Examiner*. May 6, 1973. p. C 5.

552. Secretariat in Belmont Drill; Knightly Dawn Joins Field. *Lexington Herald*. Associated Press. June 7, 1973. p. 21.

553. Secretariat Honored at N.Y. Scribes Dinner. *Daily Racing Form*. September 14, 1974.

554. Secretariat in 'Speedy' Belmont? *Knickerbocker News Union Star*. Associated Press. June 8, 1973. pp. 1C, 5C.

555. Secretariat No Proletariat—Wins Belmont by 31 Lengths! *Los Angeles Herald-Examiner*. United Press International. June 10, 1973. pp. B1-B2.

556. Secretariat Outrun in Record Bid by Maryland Racing Commission. *Lexington Herald*. Associated Press. July 11, 1973.

557. Secretariat Romps in Belmont: Captures 3rd Jewel of Triple Crown. *Albany Times-Union*. Associated Press. June 10, 1973 pp. C1, C13.

558. Secretariat, Sham End Major Drills. *Albany Times-Union*. AP, Baltimore. May 15, 1973. p. 15.

559. Secretariat to Race Again: Laurin. *Louisville Courier-Journal*. Associated Press. June 11, 1973.

560. Secretariat to Race in August. *Pasadena Star News*. Associated Press. June 11, 1973.

561. Secretariat 2-5 Belmont Favorite. *Pasadena Star News*. Associated Press. June 9, 1973.

562. Secretariat… Two-Thirds a Triple Crown King. *Pasadena Star News*. Associated Press. May 20, 1973. p. S-1.

563. Secretariat Waltzes to Preakness Win: Plucks Second Jewel of Triple Crown. *Albany Times-Union*. Associated Press. May 20, 1973 p. C1.

564. Secretariat Writes Record. *Pasadena Star News*. Associated Press. May 6, 1973. pp. S-1, S-2.

565. Secretariat.com. Ask Penny. http://secretariat.com.

566. Secretariat's Triple Crown Chances 50-50, Says Laurin. *Los Angeles Herald-Examiner*. United Press International. May 6, 1973. p. C2.

567. Secretariat's Triple Crown—Part 2—Belmont Stakes. Sports Century. ESPN Classic. Youtube.com. http://www.youtube.com/watch?v=k-KvaeuIIsw&feature=related.

568. Seven More Stallions to Leave Spendthrift. *The Blood-Horse*. December 12, 1992. p. 5652.

569. Sham. *The Stallion Register for 1992*. *The Blood-Horse*. Lexington, Kentucky: The Blood-Horse, Inc. 1991. pp. 888-889.

570. Sham, 1970-1993. *Thoroughbred Times*. April 16, 1993. p. 12.

571. Sham Among 12 'Catalina Nominees. *Daily Racing Form*. February 9, 1973. p. 3.

572. Sham and 'Chief' Go Separate Ways. *Daily Racing Form*. April 3, 1973. p. 3.

573. Sham Early Bet Choice. *Daily News*. Associated Press. May 5, 1973. p. 29.

574. Sham Has Operation; Doc: Will Race Again. *Daily News*. July 7, 1973.

575. Sham Has Strong Preakness Drill. *Lexington Herald*. Associated Press. May 15, 1973. p. 11.

576. Sham Is the Favorite in Early Betting. *Louisville Courier-Journal*. May 5, 1973. p. A5.

577. Sham Is the Favorite in Early Betting. [*New York Post?*]. May 5, 1973.

578. Sham Not Suffering from a 'Broken Heart'. *Lexington Leader*. June 19, 1973. p. 9.

579. Sham Overcomes Mud, Trouble and 4 Foes in Catalina. *Louisville Courier-Journal*. Associated Press and Special Dispatches. February 13, 1973. p. B5.

580. Sham, Royal and Regal, Leo's Pisces in Derby Spotlight: Fla. Derby King Is Wire-to-Wire; Forego Runs 2nd. *Lexington Herald-Leader*. Associated Press. April 1, 1973. p. 33.

581. Sham, Royal and Regal, Leo's Pisces in Derby Spotlight: Linda's Chief 2½ behind Winner in 'Anita Derby. *Lexington Herald-Leader*. Associated Press. April 1, 1973. p. 33.

582. Sham Stamps Himself Potential Derby Threat. *Daily Racing Form*. February 5, 1973. pp. 3, 29.

583. Sham Survives Claim of Foul Against Entrymate to Take Down Winner's Share of $124,400 Santa Anita Derby. *Daily Racing Form*. April 3, 1973. p. 2.

584. Sham Syndicated. *The Blood-Horse*. July 23, 1973. p. 2767.

585. Sham Syndicated. *The Thoroughbred Record*. July 21, 1973. p. 301.

586. Sham's Breeding Stresses Stamina. *Daily Racing Form*. May 5, 1973. p. 11D.

587. Sham's Trainer Sees Derby Victory. *Albany Times-Union*. Associated Press. May 3, 1973.

588. Shulman, Lenny. The Finish Line: Laffit Pincay Jr. Retires at the Top of His Game. *The Blood-Horse*. May 10, 2003. pp. 2682-2683.

589. Simpson, Butch. interview with author. Walmac Farm, Lexington, Kentucky. May 8, 2003.

590. Simpson, Butch. telephone interview with author. May 15, 2003.

591. Simpson, Butch. telephone interview with author. May 22, 2003.

592. Smith, Red. The Good Horses of Chris Chenery. *New York Times*. February 16, 1973. p. 27.

593. Smith, Red. Secretariat's Gotham Win Puts Him in Fast Company. *Lexington Leader. New York Times* News Service. April 9, 1973.

594. Smith, Red. He's Only Human. *Lexington Leader. New York Times* News Service. April 23, 1973.

595. Smith, Red. Barn 42: Where the Favorites Are. *New York Times*. May 1, 1974. p.51.

596. Smith, Red. Sweat Reduces Oats, But Secretariat Feels His in Record Gallop. *Louisville Courier-Journal. New York Times* News Service. May 6, 1973. p. C7.

597. Smith, Red. Twin Bill: Secretariat's Smashing Victory Must Share Spotlight with Fans' Salute to Johnny Unitas. *Louisville Courier-Journal and Times. New York Times* News Service. May 20, 1973. p. C3.

598. Smith, Red. Countdown... Laurin Will Be Glad When It's Over. *Louisville Courier-Journal. New York Times* News Service. June 9, 1973. p. B4.

599. Soffian, Seth. Laffit & Mr. Hooper. *The Florida Horse*. January 2000. pp. 55+.

600. Sommer Set Earnings Record. *The Thoroughbred Record*. January 13, 1973. p. 158.

601. Sommer, Viola. interview with author. Aqueduct, Jamaica, New York. March 29, 2003.

602. Springstead, Will. Hall of Famer Stephens Dies. *The Saratogian*. August 23, 1998. p. 1C.

603. Sprint Champion Shecky Greene. *The Blood-Horse*. December 24, 1973. p. 5303.

604. St. Simon (GB). Thoroughbred Bloodlines. http://www.bloodlines.net/TB.

605. Stakes and Horses. Linda's Chief. *The Blood-Horse*. January 29, 1973. p. 505.

606. Stakes and Horses. Linda's Chief. *The Blood-Horse*. March 12, 1973. pp. 943-944.

607. Stakes and Horses. Our Native. *The Blood-Horse*. March 12, 1973. pp. 941-942.

608. Stakes and Horses. Linda's Chief. *The Blood-Horse*. March 26, 1973. pp. 1154-1155.

609. Stakes and Horses. Sham. *The Blood-Horse*. April 9, 1973. pp. 1289-1290.

610. Stakes and Horses. Leo's Pisces, Louisiana Derby. *The Blood-Horse*. April 9, 1973. p. 1290.

611. Stakes and Horses. Royal and Regal, Florida Derby. *The Blood-Horse*. April 9, 1973. p. 1289.

612. Stakes and Horses. Impecunious. April 16, 1973. *The Blood-Horse*. pp. 1350, 1352.

613. Stakes and Horses. Secretariat. April 16, 1973. *The Blood-Horse*. p. 1352.

614. Stakes and Horses. Angle Light. *The Blood-Horse*. April 30, 1973. p. 1526.

615. Stakes and Horses. Bird Boots. *The Blood-Horse*. April 30, 1973. pp. 1527-1528.
616. Stakes and Horses. My Gallant. *The Blood-Horse*. May 7, 1973. pp. 1623-1624.
617. Stakes and Horses. Knightly Dawn. *The Blood-Horse*. January 1, 1973. pp. 52, 54.
618. Stakes and Horses. Knightly Dawn. *The Blood-Horse*. June 11, 1973. p. 2041.
619. Starting Gate Hurt Sham. *New York Post*. Associated Press. May 8, 1973. p. 79.
620. Stephens, Woody and Brough, James. *Guess I'm Lucky: My Life in Horse Racing*. New York: Doubleday & Company, Inc. 1985.
621. Stevenson, Jack. San Felipe Easy for Linda's Chief. *Louisville Courier-Journal*. Associated Press. March 18, 1973.
622. Stevenson, Jack. Sham Turns Tables on Linda's Chief, eyes Secretariat. *Louisville Courier-Journal and Times*. April 1, 1973. pp. C1, C3.
623. Stockwell (GB). Thoroughbred Bloodlines. http://www.bloodlines.net/TB.
624. Stone, Charles H. Late Items. *The Blood-Horse*. September 4, 1972. p. 3155.
625. Stone, Charles H. Late Items. *The Blood-Horse*. January 8, 1973. p. 95.
626. Stone, Charles H. Late Items. *The Blood-Horse*. March 12, 1973.
627. Stone, Charles H. Pedigree of Secretariat. *The Blood-Horse*. May 14, 1973. pp. 1673-1676, 1688.
628. Stone, Charles H. Late Items. *The Blood-Horse*. May 7, 1979. p. 2225.
629. Strine, Gerald. Pancho Flogs a Dead Horse. *The Washington Post*. May 4, 1973. p. D1.
630. Sullivan, Mike. It's a Split Decision: Shecky Greene to Go in Derby. *Louisville Courier-Journal*. May 3, 1973. p. C2.
631. Sullivan, Mike. Sham Ran Perfectly, but 'Just Got Tired'. *Louisville Courier-Journal*. May 6, 1973. p. C3.
632. Syndication of Sham for $2,880,000 Completed. [unknown source from Belmont Park Press Office]. July 27, 1973.
633. Temple, Wick. From Super Horse to Living Legend. *Lexington Herald*. Associated Press. June 11, 1973. p. 10.
634. Temple, Wick. — He'd Probably Be Lost for Words, Too. *Louisville Courier-Journal*. Associated Press. June 11, 1973.
635. Things and People. Hitchcock Dead. *The Blood-Horse*. October 16, 1972. p. 3870.
636. Things and People. Claiborne Management. *The Blood-Horse*. February 5, 1973. p. 582.
637. Things and People. Claiborne to Consign. *The Blood-Horse*. October 9, 1972. p. 3791.
638. Things and People. Hancocks to Operate Claiborne. *The Blood-Horse*. October 23, 1972. p. 3988.

639. Things and People. Jockey's Guild Officers. *The Blood-Horse*. January 15, 1973. p. 318.

640. Things and People. Preakness Prepping. *The Blood-Horse*. May 21, 1973. p. 1786.

641. Things and People. Preakness Review. *The Blood-Horse*. July 2, 1973. p 2323.

642. Things and People. No Preakness Record. *The Blood-Horse*. July 16, 1973. p. 2616.

643. Things and People. Short Notes. *The Blood-Horse*. February 19, 1973.

644. Things and People. Surgery for Sham. *The Blood-Horse*. July 16, 1973. p. 2616.

645. Things and People. Short Notes. *The Blood-Horse*. August 6, 1973. p. 3040.

646. Thomas, Ben. Our Native Keeps Racing and Scores a Big Triumph. *Lexington Leader*. Associated Press. March 5, 1973.

647. Thomas, T.L. Secretariat's Rival Sham Dead at 23. *Daily Racing Form*. April 11, 1993.

648. Triple Crown Entries. *New York Times*. April 1, 1973. Section 5. p. 8.

649. Tower, Whitney. Under No False Pretenses. *Sports Illustrated*. April 9, 1973. p. 92.

650. Tower, Whitney. Putting a New Light on the Derby. *Sports Illustrated*. April 30, 1973. 38(17). pp. 16-19.

651. Tower, Whitney. The Critic's Choice. *Sports Illustrated*. May 7, 1973. p. 80.

652. Tower, Whitney. It Was Murder. *Sports Illustrated*. May 14, 1973. 38(19). pp. 20-23.

653. Tower, Whitney. Flying High and Heading for Fame. *Sports Illustrated*. May 28, 1973. pp. 24-26.

654. Tower, Whitney. Triple Crown Criteria: Secretariat Has the Goods. *Sports Illustrated*. June 11, 1973. 38(23) p. 36.

655. Tower, Whitney. History in the Making. *Sports Illustrated*. June 18, 1973. 38(24) pp. 14-17.

656. Trimble, Joe. Sommer, 62, Dies of Heart Attack at Aqueduct. *Daily News*. May 1, 1979. p. 62.

657. Tunstall, Ed. Leo's Pisces ($109) Wins La. Derby. *Louisville Courier-Journal and Times*. Associated Press. April 1, 1973. p. C3.

658. Turcotte Enjoys an Easy Ride. *Lexington Herald-Leader*. United Press International. May 20, 1973. p. 25.

659. Twice a Prince. [CBS broadcast]. YouTube.com. http://www.youtube.com/watch?v=7qCZPQCQNCg.

660. Two to Spendthrift. *The Blood-Horse*. July 23, 1973. p. 2767.

661. Two-Year-Olds of 1972: Groshawk. *The Thoroughbred Record*. April 14, 1973. pp. 893, 896.

662. Two-Year-Olds of 1972: Knightly Dawn. *The Thoroughbred Record*. April 14,

1973. pp. 893, 902.

663. Velasquez, Jorge. interview with author. Aqueduct, Jamaica, New York. March 29, 2003.
664. Velasquez, Jorge. telephone interview with author. August 25, 2004.
665. Viola Sommer Takes Title… a Few Dollars at a Time. *Daily Racing Form*. March 28, 1983.
666. Visiting Writers Make Sham Pick. *Louisville Courier-Journal*. May 5, 1973. p. C2.
667. Volponi, Paul. Track Talk. *The Blood-Horse*. October 4, 2003. p. 5308.
668. Voltigeur (GB). Thoroughbred Bloodlines. http://www.bloodlines.net/TB.
669. Wall, Maryjean. Redemption, Indeed for Laurin, 'Sec'. *Lexington Herald-Leader*. May 6, 1973. p. 26.
670. War of Nerves Begins for Kentucky Derby. *Albany Times-Union*. Associated Press. May 1, 1973. p. 17.
671. Ward, Gene. *Daily News*. April 22, 1973. p. 121.
672. Ward, Gene. Agonizing Wood Aftermath. *Daily News*. April 23, 1973. pp. 72, 75.
673. Ward, Gene. Backstretch Feud: Round 2. *Daily News*. May 3, 1973.
674. Ward, Gene. Fire Vasquez off Angle Light, Hire LeBlanc. *Daily News*. May 4, 1973. p. 79.
675. Ward, Gene. Derby Poses Hatful of Questions. *Daily News*. May 5, 1973. p. 29.
676. Ward, Gene. Real Secretariat Wins Record Derby. *Daily News*. May 6, 1973. p. 126.
677. Ward, Gene. Secretariat's Nonstop Run. *Daily News*. May 7, 1973, pp. 70, 73.
678. Ward, Gene. Next Stop, Baltimore. *Daily News*. May 8, 1973.
679. Ward, Gene. Only Five Challenge Secretariat in Preakness. *Daily News*. May 18, 1973. p. 87.
680. Ward, Gene. Good Word from Laurin—'Confidence'. *Daily News*. May 19, 1973. p. 29.
681. Ward, Gene. Jet Lag? *Daily News*. May 20, 1973. p. 128.
682. Ward, Gene. A Party for the Babe. *Daily News*. May 20, 1973. p. 142.
683. Ward, Gene. Preakness: A Romp for Secretariat. *Daily News*. May 20, 1973. p. 128.
684. Ward, Gene. Did Secretariat Set Record? *Daily News*. May 21, 1973. p. 67.
685. Ward, Gene. Swan Song of a Thoroughbred. *Daily News*. May 22, 1973. p. 73.
686. Ward, Gene. … But Sham's Still Very Much in Race. *Daily News*. June 2, 1973.
687. Ward, Gene. Laurin Sweating Out Belmont 'Jinxes'. *Daily News*. June 9, 1973. p. 29.
688. Ward, Gene. The Crowd Saw Perfection. *Daily News*. June 10, 1973. p. 134.

689. Ward, Gene. 22 ⅗ Quarter Sank Sham. *Daily News.* June 11, 1973.

690. Waxy (GB). Thoroughbred Bloodlines. http://www.bloodlines.net/TB.

691. West Australian (GB). Thoroughbred Bloodlines. http://www.bloodlines.net/TB.

692. A "Westernized" Virginian Gives Claiborne Stud a World-Wide Reputation. *Lexington Herald–Lender.* December 16, 1939.

693. Whalebone (GB). Thoroughbred Bloodlines. http://www.bloodlines.net/TB.

694. Wheat, Julian "Buck". interview with author. Churchill Downs, Louisville, Kentucky. May 7, 2003.

695. Whitmire, Tim. Stephens Recalled: Loved People, Horses. *Daily Gazette.* Associated Press. August 27, 1998.

696. Wilkin, Tim. Martin Leads Racing Hall of Fame Inductees. *Saratogian.* August 8, 1981.

697. Willett, Peter. *Makers of the Modern Thoroughbred.* Lexington, Kentucky: The University Press of Kentucky. 1986.

698. Wood, Wally. Angle Light's Upset Victory in Wood Earns Derby Berth. *Daily Racing Form.* May 5, 1973. p. D16.

699. Wood, Wally. Whittaker Faces Reality: Still Feels Secretariat's Best. *Daily Racing Form.* May 5, 1973. pp. 9D-10D.

700. Wood, Wally. Whittaker Says Secretariat 'Super': Must be Realistic about Wood Upset. *Daily Racing Form.* May 5, 1973. pp. 6D, 17D.

701. Woodward, Jay. Santa Catalina Won by Sham. *Daily Racing Form.* February 15, 1973. p. 2.

702. Woodward, Jay. Sham Prevails in Santa Anita Derby: Two, Half Lengths atop Linda's Chief. *Daily Racing Form.* April 3, 1973. p. 4.

703. Woolfe Jr., Raymond G. *Secretariat: Updated Edition.* The Derrydale Press: New York. 2001.

704. The Wow Horse Races into History. *Time.* June 11, 1973. 101(24). pp. 85-91.

705. Zamarelli, Don. Something in the Belmont. *The Blood-Horse.* June 4, 1973. pp. 1934-1935.

# Endnotes

Prologue

p. 5      "He has seasoned horsemen comparing him favorably to the best three-year-olds ever campaigned in the West" (Rogerson "Sham in Field of Eight Seeking Santa Catalina" 3).

p. 5      "graced with a beautifully muscled and streamlined conformation… he looked fast when he was just standing still" (Woolfe 79).

p. 6      "He captured the imagination, filling it with conquests of Arthurian immensity" (Clippinger "So Long, Big Red" 1213).

p. 6      "He was a power that transcended racing. You didn't have to know *anything* about racing to appreciate that great mass of power, that beauty" (Woolfe 177).

p. 6      "I don't believe you could find a better looking Thoroughbred—or have one molded any better, mentally, physically, everyway" (Rudy "Reactions" 2086).

p. 6      "*equinus maximus*" (Bowen "Joining the Giants" 2078).

p. 6      "equine Adonis" (Hatton "Secretariat Rates All Superlatives" 4D).

p. 6      "He had it all—looks, style, and charisma" (Capps 151).

p. 6      "There's absolutely no doubt in my mind that he is the finest athlete of any race, color, family, genus or species ever to have lived" (Kirkpatrick "Secretariat: The Ultimate Superlative" 1439).

p. 7      "It is as if God decided to create the perfect horse" (Hatton "Secretariat Rates All Superlatives" 4D).

p. 7      "power, money, and total male beauty: a triple-win sex symbol" (Curtis 102).

p. 8      "He's the greatest horse that has yet developed in this century" (Schwartz).

p. 8      "He takes off like a derailed roller-coaster" (Hatton "Secretariat's Mere Presence Guarantees Drama, Suspense").

p. 8      "His neck and quarters lined in packs of muscle over which his coat seemed drawn too tight—perhaps a half size too small, as if he were outgrowing it" (Nack *Secretariat: The Making of a Champion* 184).

p. 8      "Sham is an eye-filling specimen. … He is everything a horseman would want. His stride is as reaching as a shopper's arm for 39-cents-a-pound sirloin, as forceful when it meets the ground as a high-powered riveter" (Irwin "Western Derbys to New York Runners" 7).

p. 9      "He is made like a good horse… like a classic horse who can run all day" (Cox "Sham Perfect Thoroughbred Says Proud 'Pancho' Martin" 12D).

## Chapter 1: Nearly Decked at the Derby

p. 10     "Until you go to Kentucky and with your own eyes behold a Derby, you ain't been nowhere and you ain't seen nothing" (Cobb).

p. 11     "Millionaire's Row" (http://www.kentuckyderby.com).

p. 13     "The sun shines bright in the old Kentucky home. ..." (http://www.kentuckyderby.com).

p. 14     "First, Twice a Prince got his feet in Navajo's stall, then in my stall. He kicked my horse once, and his hoof made a mark on my saddle" (Schultz C4).

p. 15     "He was bad all right. ... He gave us enough trouble for all of the rest put together" (Schultz C4).

p. 15     "We weren't in the gate yet... so the delay didn't hurt us. But it sure didn't help the horses who had to stand in there all that time" (Woolfe 101-102).

p. 15     "When I went into the gate... I asked the man to help keep Sham's head straight. But for some reason nobody showed up. He was alone in the gate. When we broke, he went sharply to the outside and hit the door-bars hard" (Rogerson "Pincay Believes Sham Can Beat Secretariat" 12).

p. 17     "God Almighty, don't tell me it's gonna be another one of them!" (Kirkpatrick "Doubts Dispelled" 1162).

p. 17     "The only way Shecky can win at the Derby distance... is to open up 10 lengths and hope that the opposition runs through or over the stable gap on the backstretch" (Tower "The Critic's Choice" 80).

p. 18     "You should have seen the whitewash dust fly when he hit" (Beardsley).

p. 18     "I hit the fence so hard when he changed leads, I don't know how I stayed on him. ...I don't know how we both didn't wind up in the infield" (Heller 31).

p. 19     "Secretariat came by us and took a little bit of heart out of him, *and* me. ... I thought I had a good chance. Thought I had a chance until this chestnut freak came on the outside of all of us" (Blum interview).

p. 19     "I felt this big whoosh of air go by and that was all there was to it" (Woolfe 102).

p. 19     "I glanced back and saw him coming and thought, if I get in his way, I'll get killed!" (Woolfe 102).

## Chapter 2: Best of the Lot

p. 22     "He wasn't that good" (Gustines interview March 30, 2003).

p. 22     "I loved it. I always loved it" (Gustines interview March 30, 2003).

p. 22     "When you're young, 15 or 16 years old, grown people are cheering you. It's not so much the money. It's an ego thing. To be a winner. The winning is the whole

| | |
|---|---|
| p. 23 | thing, even if it's a dollar" (Gustines interview June 21, 2005). |
| p. 23 | "Doing things you're not supposed to do" (Gustines interview May 5, 2004). |
| p. 23 | "That's the way it used to be down there. … You gotta do that. You race only two nights a week" (Gustines interview June 21, 2005). |
| p. 23 | "Grand Dame" (Hialeah History). |
| p. 24 | "Big deal… I make that in two minutes" (Gustines interview September 20, 2003). |
| p. 25 | "without no education" (Nagler 3). |
| p. 26 | "the biggest, the most successful, the single most important man in the Thoroughbred industry" ([Hollingsworth?] "A.B. Hancock Jr." 3524). |
| p. 26 | "very sharp" (Gustines interview May 5, 2004). |
| p. 26 | "The only two horses that are any good are Sham and Breakfast Bell" (Gustines interview March 30, 2003). |
| p. 26 | "This horse was the best horse of all of them" (Gustines interview March 30, 2003). |
| p. 26 | "Sometimes you get nasty ones. But he was good" (Gustines interview March 30, 2003). |
| p. 26 | "like a grouchy person" (Gustines interview June 21, 2005). |
| p. 27 | "He was a nice horse to be around" (Gustines interview March 30, 2003). |
| p. 27 | "You can feel a nice horse. … Nice and smooth. … riding a road with potholes" (Gustines interview May 5, 2004). |
| p. 27 | "Queen of Spas" (http://www.saratoga.com/aboutsaratoga/history/). |
| p. 28 | "Horse Haven" (Hotaling 167). |
| p. 28 | "a summer hotel for blooded horses" (Hotaling 167). |

Chapter 3: First Time on the Oval

| | |
|---|---|
| p. 31 | "He wasn't that way" (Gustines interview March 30, 2003). |
| p. 31 | "He was a nice, quiet horse" (Gustines interview March 30, 2003). |
| p. 31 | "I ride a horse once or twice beforehand … I get to know the horse the second it pulls up" (Gustines interview March 30, 2003). |
| p. 34 | "Leave him alone because sometimes if you try to change their style they get all confused" (Gustines interview March 30, 2003). |
| p. 35 | "It's a split of a second. … You don't got all day to think about it. You make a quick decision. It's very important, your timing and reflex. Gotta be sharp" (Gustines interview September 20, 2003). |

| p. 35 | "You can lose your balance very easy. ... Gotta have good balance" (Gustines interview September 20, 2003). |
| p. 35 | "Some of them respond, some don't. ... Some people sing at them" (Gustines interview September 20, 2003). |
| p. 35-36 | "He was back. ... He was fifth, something like that. He came at the end" (Gustines interview March 30, 2003). |
| p. 36 | "He didn't make the turn the right way. ... He was drifting out. ... Five, six wide. ... I don't know what was bugging him. Something was bothering him" (Gustines interview March 30, 2003). |

Chapter 4: Early Days at the Farm

| p. 37 | "My great horse" (Callahan "Not All Great Horses Win the Triple Crown"). |
| p. 39 | "They don't have a *Racing Form* within 100 miles of Southborough Mass" ([Hollingsworth, Kent?] "A.B. Hancock Jr." 3525). |
| p. 39 | "I never wanted to be anything but a horseman. ... I just never thought of anything else" (Nack *Secretariat: The Making of a Champion* 18). |
| p. 41 | "We had gone for 12 years without replacing stock. ... When I took over he [Arthur Sr.] had about 75 mares and I didn't like any of them, except two" (Gallaher). |
| p. 41 | "An old Hereford breeder one time told me that a good bull was half the herd and a bad bull was all of it. ... That has made a lot of sense" ("A.B. Hancock Jr. Dies at 62." 84). |
| p. 41 | "intense student of international bloodlines" ("Arthur Boyd Hancock Jr." 983). |
| p. 41 | "I look around and try to see what male lines are doing well in other countries, that we don't have here" (Robertson 1345). |
| p. 41 | "You very seldom get a good stallion by a bad stallion. ... I take a good, hard look at the female line" (Robertson 1346). |
| p. 41 | "What I look for is a good burst of speed at some part of the race. ... I like a horse which shows a tremendous burst" (Robertson 1346). |
| p. 42 | "Selecting a stallion is at once the most difficult and most important of factors for success in the horse business. ... Bull Hancock was better at it than any man who came before him" ([Hollingsworth, Kent?] "A.B. Hancock Jr." 3525). |
| p. 42 | "It is the infusion of different blood which invigorates the thoroughbred" (Willett 219). |
| p. 42-43 | "When I was young, a long time ago, we used to believe that we had to go to Great Britain and the European mainland from time to time to bolster "plebeian" American blood. You just had to do it. Then Americans, in large |

measure through Hancock's sagacity pretty nearly cornered the winners' market by purchases of bloodstock, not only from Europe but from any quarter of the globe where they raise decent horses.

"America now has the best horses in the world. The world knows it, and now comes to us" ("Arthur Boyd Hancock Jr." 984D).

p. 43     "We just try to do the usual, unusually well" ("Arthur Boyd Hancock Jr." 984D).

p. 45     "When they finished my father said, 'Well, that's all the barns we'll ever need here.' I can remember him saying that" (Gallaher).

p. 45     "We have a competition around here for horses. . . . I pay $10 for every one that's accepted. My wife, our children, the secretaries—everybody can try. . . . . I'm the judge, too" (Gallaher).

p. 48     "Waxy was one of the finest formed, perfect in symmetry, beautiful in colour, admirable in all his paces, and of the finest temper, when in work; but, in the winter, after being weather-bound from frost and snow for some days, on getting out again, it was a case of "Look out, my boys," with a vengeance. Oft has he kicked the lappets of my coat over my head" ("Waxy [GB]").

p. 48     "the modern ace of trumps in the stud book" (Willett 11).

p. 48     "the lowest and longest, and most double jointed horse, with the best legs and worst feet I ever saw in my life" ("Whalebone [GB]").

p. 48     "The Earl of Egremont tried to train him after he bought him… but he never ran after he came into the Earl's possession. When in training his chief occupation was to rear and knock his hoofs together like a pair of castanettes" ("Whalebone [GB]").

p. 49     "He often left his jockey rather more tired than he at the end of a race" ("Isinglass [GB]").

p. 50     "Emperor of Stallions" ("Stockwell [GB]").

p. 50     "fine, sloping shoulders with a good depth of girth, powerful quarters, good knees and hocks with plenty of bone" ("Voltigeur [GB]").

p. 50     "improve and perpetuate" ("Voltigeur [GB]").

p. 50     "full of character… exceedingly fine and free" ("Macaroni [GB]").

p. 51     "a picture of misery" (Byles "Hermit [GB]").

p. 52     "as if the latter had been pulling a plough" (Byles "Hermit [GB]").

p. 53     "A great horse. . . . A truly great horse" (Byles "Hermit [GB]").

p. 53     "Hermit broke my heart, but I did not show it, did I?" (Byles "Hermit [GB]").

p. 53     "When walking in the paddock, he would often stop and look round like a lion, in a way that did not show a kindly temper" (Byles "Tristan [GB]").

| | |
|---|---|
| p. 55 | "It's all right. You can open your eyes now" (Willett 207). |
| p. 57 | "I wanted to buy Princequillo when I was in the Army in 1944… but then racing was stopped and nothing came of the deal" ([Hollingsworth, Kent?] "A.B. Hancock Jr." 3525). |
| p. 60 | "The Pretenses are popular" (Claiborne Farm advertisement November 25, 1972). |
| p. 60 | "He was a lot of nice breeding. … There was a lot of nice horses by that horse, Pretense" (Gustines interview March 30, 2003). |
| p. 60 | "I've known plenty of horses that failed although they were bred from winners and stakes-placed parents. … And there have been plenty of others that succeeded with nothing much in the way of sire or dam" (Stephens and Brough 128). |

Chapter 5: Trainer Tries Again

| | |
|---|---|
| p. 61 | "A man may well bring a horse to the water, But he cannot make him drinke without he will" (Heywood). |
| p. 63 | "He was just drifting out. … I think he got a little tired" (Gustines interview March 30, 2003). |
| p. 63 | "a carload of trouble" (Stephens and Brough 25). |
| p. 63 | "It's a whole lot easier to ruin a good horse than to train him to bring out his best" (Stephens and Brough 40). |
| p. 63 | "I'd never switched from believing that to do any good as a trainer you had to have affection and respect for the animals in your barn" (Stephens and Brough 108). |
| p. 63 | "There's no gain in treating a champion like a champion and a loser like a loser" (Stephens and Brough 40-41). |
| p. 64 | "I found he was washy and awful nervous. … If you tried to take hold of him, he'd fight the bit, throw up his head, and it was over for the day. But I thought he might be a pretty good horse if he was treated right" (Stephens and Brough 69). |
| p. 64 | "skittery streak in his nature" (Stephens and Brough 71). |
| p. 64 | "That's the first real classic I ever won. … That was the beginning of me" (Nack "He's Got the Horse Right Here" 36). |
| p. 65 | "I concluded that I liked horses an awful lot" (Stephens and Brough 20). |
| p. 65 | "My daddy told me I was a born horseman. I'd rather heard that than I was a born field hand" (Jacobson "Stephens Looks Back"). |
| p. 65 | "I'd reached the point where I was eager to ride anything with a mane and a tail" |

|       |                                                                                                                                                                                                                                                                                                           |
| ----- | --------------------------------------------------------------------------------------------------------------------------------------------------------------------------------------------------------------------------------------------------------------------------------------------------------- |
|       | (Stephens and Brough 24).                                                                                                                                                                                                                                                                                 |
| p. 65 | "I started waking up ahead of the roosters… with my heart set on being a jockey" (Stephens and Brough 1).                                                                                                                                                                                                 |
| p. 65 | "The filly carried 100 pounds and I probably didn't weigh 90" (Krulik 358).                                                                                                                                                                                                                              |
| p. 65 | "Directly… was under restraint to the stretch, but her rider was of little help to her at the finish" (Nack "He's Got the Horse Right Here" 29).                                                                                                                                                         |
| p. 66 | "Put him back on the horse. … I want to see if he can ride him that bad again" (Nack "He's Got the Horse Right Here" 29).                                                                                                                                                                                |
| p. 66 | "We eat a hot dog and go home" (Krulik 358).                                                                                                                                                                                                                                                              |
| p. 66 | "When I went with Jule there were some of the fine things I needed to know. …What makes 'em win and what makes 'em lose? He taught me how to claim horses, how to place horses, how to pace horses. He taught me how to stretch out a horse's speed. Jule was the best handicapper around, without question" (Nack "He's Got the Horse Right Here" 32). |
| p. 66 | "Woody had his antennae out all the time, very receptive. … He had a great eye for a horse and a great touch. A physical touch with a horse. He'd kneel next to a horse and touch and feel around and immediately know where the problem was. He knew when to back off and go on" (Nack "He's Got the Horse Right Here" 32). |
| p. 67 | "I've got a policy. … Nobody but me puts his horses in my stable" (Stephens and Brough 104).                                                                                                                                                                                                              |
| p. 67 | "My one mistake in racing was letting Woody get away" (Jacobson "A Venerable Stephens Puts Tale Before Horse" 154).                                                                                                                                                                                       |
| p. 67 | "who played the horses as well as the trumpet" (Stephens and Brough 179).                                                                                                                                                                                                                                 |
| p. 67 | "The track is one of the very few places left where a man without the price of a fresh shirt on his back can get to talk on level terms with a millionaire. It's only the horses that bring them together" (Stephens and Brough 209).                                                                     |
| p. 68 | "Five o'clock sharp, rain or shine, is the time I'm usually getting myself out of bed seven days a week, twelve months of the year, and I don't allow three minutes either side of that. It isn't hard to do when it's as natural as breathing and a habit that comes from working with horses" (Stephens and Brough 1). |
| p. 68 | "When you lose, you go home, and when you win, you go home, and there isn't much more to it than that" (Stephens and Brough 204).                                                                                                                                                                         |
| p. 68 | "I remembered hunching up well forward over the withers of horses long since dead, head down low to cut down resistance, holding still so I didn't disturb the pace, feeling the wind blowing in my face and the ripple of the mount's muscles under my knees, listening to him pull air into his lungs and the drumming of his feet on the track, maybe saying a word or two to |

encourage him. I'll never forget being a jock even though I didn't make it" (Stephens and Brough 116).

Chapter 6: A Change of Order

p. 69     "internal infection" (Stone "Late Items" September 4, 1972 3155).

p. 70     "Braulio Baeza, me and him we won all the races" (Gustines interview June 21, 2005).

p. 72     "All three times he was drifting out. ... That's the only thing [problem] he had, drifting out. I don't know why. Because he was sound. When a horse does that, it's because something is bothering him" (Gustines interview March 30, 2003).

p. 72     "I think I got up to the front too early. ... And he only got beat a head. I probably lost the race, not the horse" (Gustines interview March 30, 2003).

p. 72     "He's like us, you know. ... Some people are just serious at an early age, others, they're 40 years old and still don't get serious. He wasn't serious. He was immature. He was like a little baby" (Gustines interview March 30, 2003).

p. 73     "He looked a lot like Pretense. That's where he got his looks. Pretense was a big colt that was a little slow to come to hand and so was Sham, but both of them were nice horses" (Hancock interview).

p. 73     "We were just really trying to get a race in him to educate him, and he took to everything real well. ... We were very pleased with him. ...a good work horse" (Hancock interview).

p. 73     "You see, Woody was going easy on him. ... Because he wasn't thinking of that year. He was thinking about the next year, the three-year-old. The two-year-old, you give them a chance. They're not mature yet" (Gustines interview March 30, 2003).

p. 73     "That's a Derby horse" (Goldstein "Claiborne Brand Rides with Sham" 10D).

p. 74     "He stepped on my foot when I took him to get weighed one morning" (Goldstein "Claiborne Brand Rides with Sham" 12D).

p. 74     "the lifework of three generations of Hancocks, spanning more than a century of devotion to the thoroughbred" (Easterling "Dispersal of Hancock Racing Stable Set Today at Belmont" 14).

p. 75     "She had a marvelous eye for horse conformation" (Sommer interview).

p. 75     "He liked him. ... I liked him too" (Martin interview).

p. 75     "It's our only chance if we want a good 3-year-old" (Irwin "Western Derbys to New York Runners" 8).

p. 75     "If anyone should get this colt it should be you" (Goldstein "Fasig-Tipton Sale Smashes Records" 7).

| | |
|---|---|
| p. 75-76 | "I desperately wanted Sham. … I tried to persuade a friend to join me and keep on bidding, but he wouldn't—and I didn't have sufficient available cash to carry on alone" (Cochran "He's the Real Thing" 4). |
| p. 76 | "I wanted a filly and this colt. … The filly got away, but I was determined to get the colt" (Hebert "The Santa Anita Derby" 1264). |
| p. 76 | "I'm sure he would have gone higher than the $200,000 if he had to. … He bought a good horse" (Hirsch "Straight Shooter" 32). |
| p. 77 | "Just as my grandfather had sent my father to run our Ellerslie Farm in Virginia when he was 27 years old… my father wanted me to run Stone Farm" (McGuire 2). |
| p. 77 | "It was Woody who taught me about a horse's form, legs and the inner workings of a racing stable" (Guilliams 8). |
| p. 77 | "knew he loved them, and they ran their hearts out for him" (Whitmire). |

Chapter 7: Last Chance for the Two-Year-Old

| | |
|---|---|
| p. 79 | "He had a lot to learn when we bought him. … Woody Stephens was the first to tell me so. He said that Mr. Arthur B. Hancock had been ill and they had left instructions to go easy with the good colts until he was back in good health. … Sham's schooling, in the meantime, had been neglected, which perhaps was a blessing in disguise. Most of our young horses in America are ruined before they have a chance. In most cases their knees are not properly grown together and they are out there breaking watches and running in stakes. This didn't happen to Sham" (Cox "Sham Perfect Thoroughbred Says Proud 'Pancho' Martin" 12D). |
| p. 79 | "kind" (Martin interview). |
| p. 80 | "When Mr. Sommer bought him he was very green and really did not know much about running. But he took to his lessons like a genius" (Cox "Secretariat Encounters Sham in $116,400 Wood Memorial" 48). |
| p. 80 | "He loved to run. When he went to exercise, he didn't do nothing to [show] that he was wild or something. He was a quiet horse. Quiet all the way. In the stall, very easy to [handle]" (Martin interview). |
| p. 80 | "He had a bad habit of getting out" (Rogerson "Mrs. Tippett Casts Covetous Eyes on Sham" 5). |
| p. 80 | "Sham's don't have any holes in the back. … He doesn't care what's going on behind. He's just interested in what's up front." (Hebert "Sham's Targets" 2). |
| p. 81 | "People don't pronounce it right… so I tell them to call me George or Georgie" (Velasquez interview August 25, 2004). |
| p. 82 | "I thought we were going to have a nice party with him. … I would be the main |

|        | guy. But things happen" (Gustines interview March 30, 2003). |
|--------|---|
| p. 83  | "He won… easy" (Martin inverview). |
| p. 84  | "He was straightened out when I rode him" (Velasquez interview August 25, 2004). |

Chapter 8: Sham's New Stable

| p. 85 | "An expert in caring for bad-legged animals, an adroit wheeler-dealer with claiming horses" (Beyer). |
|---|---|
| p. 85 | "school dropout at the age of 14" (Hebert "Sham's Targets: Wood and Derby" p. 22). |
| p. 86 | "I really can't remember when I wasn't a horse player. … I always hoped that some day I could have a few horses of my own. There was work to be done, though… many problems, depressions, highs and lows, and other factors" (Obituary "Sigmund Sommer" 2378). |
| p. 86 | "It took a while because the money had to be made first" (Trimble 62). |
| p. 86 | "All facets of racing were discussed and debated, agreement never being reached on any subject" (Goldstein "Sommer Typified N.Y. Racing"). |
| p. 86 | "Couldn't run a lick" (Trimble 62). |
| p. 86 | "the horse didn't do anything but win. … He either doubled or tripled his claiming value… making a big profit for his owner" (Cox "Sommers Pass the Test of the 'Greatest' Game" 5D). |
| p. 86-87 | "I decided he was my kind of man and my kind of operation" ("Hold Sigmund Sommer Funeral"). |
| p. 87 | "I have the best breeding establishments: Aqueduct, Saratoga and Belmont Park. It's like dealing in a supermarket" (Trimble 62). |
| p. 87 | "The Phippses, Bradys, Mellons—they really make all this possible. … There'd be no racing if it weren't for the big old families. They keep the bloodlines going with glamour horses so that every once in a while a fellow like me can come in with a fluke" (Harvin). |
| p. 87 | "My husband was in it for the fun. … He liked to see them run, that's why we had so many horses. He always said that [horse racing] was not his business" (Sommer interview). |
| p. 87 | "He didn't wanna be in building and horse training. He don't believe in that. … This is one owner he don't interfere. He let you do what you think was right" (Martin interview). |
| p. 88 | "My mother wouldn't let me ride or go around the track" (Lewin 56). |

| | |
|---|---|
| p. 88 | "I jumped over the fence and a Pinkerton would grab me by the ear and throw me out. … A few minutes later, I jump over the fence again" (Lewin 56). |
| p. 88 | "When I was growing up… young fellows looking ahead to the future could do only two things. … They could play baseball or go to work at Oriental Park. I was a lousy ball player so I wound up with the horses" (Hirsch "Another Long-Winded One for Martin"). |
| p. 88 | "getting smart" (Press release "[Add Notes…]"). |
| p. 88 | "I took horses that other trainers didn't want" (Cunningham "Frank Martin Finally Gets Racing Dues" 27). |
| p. 88-89 | "You have to study them, find out what's wrong, and make them over into winners" (Press release "Pancho Martin's 25 Years on Big Apple"). |
| p. 89 | "the best" (Cox "Martin by Himself as Trainer"). |
| p. 89 | "When you live by the sword you've got to be prepared to die by it. You see, basically we have developed our stable through claiming. And when you claim a trainer's horse you can't expect him to be too happy or friendly. Their horses are their bread and butter, and when they lose them, many of their owners won't allow them to claim back or replace them" (Cox "Martin by Himself as Trainer"). |
| p. 89 | "Pancho can be just talking to you, and you think he's shouting. I heard him the other day in the barn, and it sounded like he must be beating up his help, but he was just talking" (Bowen "Resumption of a Legend" 1662). |
| p. 90 | "My philosophy? Mind my own business. This is my first philosophy" (Gaffer "Pancho Martin Has Big Secret"). |
| p. 90 | "If I had to give a reason why some of my horses win… I'd point out two things. I try to give them the best care possible and I make sure not to place them over their heads" (Press Release "[Feb '59]"). |
| p. 90 | "I have feelings for all my horses. … They don't have to be champions" (LaBelle "Pancho Martin Remembers Sham"). |
| p. 90 | "A very fine horseman, who actually identified the horses' ailments. … He felt very close to them. … There were times when he was not satisfied with a vet's diagnosis and would have two or three vets do the same horse. … He was very well informed with horse ailments and physical attributes" (Sommer interview). |
| p. 90 | "I tell the veterinarians what's wrong with my horses" (Press release "Pancho Martin's 25 Years on Big Apple"). |
| p. 90-91 | "We didn't have much in the way of stock" (Cox "Sham Perfect Thoroughbred Says Proud 'Pancho' Martin" 19D). |
| p. 91 | "I've been very lucky in claiming horses that have developed into stakes winners" (Cox "Martin by Himself as Trainer"). |

| | |
|---|---|
| p. 91 | "I have to get a 'feeling' about a horse before I even look at his record" (Press release "Pancho Martin's 25 Years on Big Apple"). |
| p. 91 | "Pancho will scream curses at me in Spanish that I don't understand and tell me he never looked at the horse" (Obituary "Sigmund Sommer" 2378). |
| p. 91 | "Our relationship is as good as anybody can have it" (Gaffer "Pancho Martin Has Big Secret"). |
| p. 91 | "We discuss all matters pertaining to the stable, the claiming and buying of horses, in fine detail" (Cox "Sham Perfect Thoroughbred Says Proud 'Pancho' Martin" 19D). |
| p. 91 | "We are a great combination. … I never criticize him. Pancho took over my stable when all I had was four cripples, and he has made us champions" (Hebert "The Santa Anita Derby" 1264). |
| p. 92 | "the most distressing, accidental death of the fine horse" (Cox "Sommers Accept Fortunes of Racing" 10D). |
| p. 92 | "I doubt that Autobiography has spent a day of being completely sound since he was foaled" (Cox "Pancho: Perfect Man for a Problem Horse" 26). |
| p. 92 | "A compensating factor is that he is all courage and heart. He sometimes gives magnificent performances when he should be in bed" (Cox "Pancho: Perfect Man for a Problem Horse" 26). |
| p. 93 | "The next morning, I picked up the paper and was stunned… Frank was so shaken that he didn't have the heart to call us late that preceding evening" (Goldstein "Sham's Campaign Mapped Out"). |
| p. 93 | "They had entered the breeding end of racing and, I might say, with some reluctance, mainly for the sake of a horse who had won stakes for them, a horse named El Bonito. It was purely a sentimental gesture with no ideas of monetary reward. "Well, [in 1970] El Bonito's first crop… included a colt named Dust the Plate. …The colt had won his first two races and Sig and Viola were elated. It seemed that they were about to become the breeders of a stakes winner, a colt with a future. The colt finished second the next time, but against better company than those he beat in his first two. "Then, in mid-July [of 1972], Dust the Plate, it seemed was about ready to beat the best… and he was on his way to victory in a race when I saw him bobble. His leg snapped and they had to haul him away. Humanely, they put the colt to sleep" (Cox "Sommers Pass the Test of the 'Greatest' Game" 5D). |
| p. 94 | "I guess this game… yes, I will call it a game… is perhaps the greatest testing lab of 'em all" (Cox "Sommers Accept Fortunes of Racing" 10D). |
| p. 94 | "Viola loves her horses with a passion" (Cox "Sommers Pass the Test of the 'Greatest' Game" 5D). |

| | |
|---|---|
| p. 94 | "chance of a lifetime.... million years of skill" (Sommer interview). |
| p. 94 | "[He] took a nap every day after lunch.... He would lie down.... Most horses don't lie down. They sort of snooze standing up. But he used to lie down and snore." (Sommer interview). |
| p. 95 | "Frank Martin never really liked a horse to have a companion unless it was absolutely necessary to keep him quiet.... But he was such a nice, quiet horse he didn't really need any company, I don't think" (Sommer interview). |
| p. 95 | "He rarely misses his siesta after he has eaten and things begin to settle down under the shedrow" (Cox "Sham Perfect Thoroughbred Says Proud 'Pancho' Martin" 12D). |
| p. 95 | "I know he was a nice horse, you know... potential for the Triple Crown races. But let's face it, I didn't know how nice he was gonna be" (Velasquez interview March 29, 2003). |

Chapter 9: Go West, Young Horse

| | |
|---|---|
| p. 96 | "For most men (till by losing rendered sager), Will back their own opinions by a wager" (Byron). |
| p. 98 | "Sham overcame trouble in the early stages of the mile and one-sixteenth to breeze to the front on the far turn and then draw away as if much the best" (Kivel "Hot Stretch Run by Kentuckian" 10). |
| p. 98 | "The son of Pretense... appeared to be worth every cent" (Kivel "Hot Stretch Run by Kentuckian" 10). |
| p. 99 | "The first thing I had to do was not be afraid of horses.... They are wild over there; very difficult" (Schulman 2682). |
| p. 99 | "it was getting very, very dark" (Soffian 56). |
| p. 99 | "It was kind of big for me... but I need a helmet, so I wore it" (*Laffit: All About Winning*). |
| p. 99 | "I was so excited... I didn't sleep the whole night" (Soffian 56). |
| p. 100 | "Sometimes, they just don't have it and it's very disappointing.... You feel like you failed.... Sometimes... you get here and you have so much horse left. You get cocky. You feel so good. You start to play. What a feeling" (Iandoli 38). |
| p. 103 | "Dad set the standards, how the game was to be played.... I hope we can live up to them" (Hollingsworth "What's Going on Here" February 5, 1973 533). |

Chapter 10: A Derby Winner in this Field?

| | |
|---|---|
| p. 105 | "What I do?" (Mochon interview). |

| | |
|---|---|
| p. 105 | "He blew past the other horses on the track like an express train" (Mochon letter). |
| p. 105 | "He went past the wire, the finish line, Laffit's feet just went forward in the stirrups instead of being straight down. He went forward like he was putting on the breaks. And the horse was really starting to gain momentum at that point" (Mochon interview). |
| p. 105 | "When the horse pulled up, Laffit had to really apply all of his energy and strength to slow him down, and this horse was ready to go another mile" (Mochon interview). |
| p. 106 | "Sham was a standout because there was a presence about him. … Some horses command attention. Sham caught everyone's eye when he was on the track" (Mochon letter). |
| p. 106 | "Is the Derby winner in this field?" (Hebert "Looking for a Derby Winner" 607). |
| p. 108 | "There's no sense in whipping a tired horse… because he'll quit on you. More horses are whipped out of the money than into it" (Arcaro). |
| p. 109 | "like a Rolls Royce" (Rogerson "Sham in Field of Eight Seeking Santa Catalina" 3). |
| p. 109 | "Virtually everyone who saw the Fleet Nasrullah had to feel that the eventual winner of the Santa Anita Derby *was*, indeed, in the field, and that his name is Sham" (Hebert "Looking for a Derby Winner" 607). |
| p. 110 | "I've never seen a more perfectly balanced colt, so large and with such a perfect way of going. He could become one of the truly great ones" (Woolfe 52). |
| p. 110 | "I took my horse out. I was afraid he might get in Secretariat's way when he starts that move" (Woolfe 52). |
| p. 111 | "So the bargain-basement price of $190,000 was predicated on letting us race him at three" (Irwin "The Big Red Machine Rolls to Triple Crown" 20). |
| p. 112 | "listening to the stars and speaking to the horse" (Willett 193). |
| p. 112 | "up to his ears in genetic theories" (Isaak 1369). |
| p. 112 | "'blood alchemy'—an intuitive selection of blood lines, which was more witchcraft than science" (Isaak 1369). |
| p. 112 | "A horse gallops on lung, sustains its speed on heart, but wins on character" (Isaak 1370). |
| p. 113 | "good burst of speed" (Robertson 1346). |
| p. 113 | "Timely utilization of speed means control, while absolute speed is never a guarantee of control" (Isaak 1370). |
| p. 113 | "*proportionatissimo*" (Willett 183). |

| | |
|---|---|
| p. 113 | "What I wanted… was a Nearco stallion" ([Hollingsworth?] "A.B. Hancock Jr." 3525). |
| p. 114 | "would send the big bay off as if the devil were on his heels" (Gallaher). |
| p. 115 | "I knew right then he was one of the greatest horses I ever saw" (Capps 103). |

## Chapter 11: Best Ever Three-Year-Old

| | |
|---|---|
| p. 117 | "He can handle any kind of footing" (Rogerson "Mrs. Tippett Casts Covetous Eyes on Sham" 5). |
| p. 117 | "He has the same size as Pretense had as a three-year-old" (Rogerson "Mrs. Tippett Casts Covetous Eyes on Sham" 5). |
| p. 118 | "Bull loved this colt" (Rogerson "Mrs. Tippett Casts Covetous Eyes on Sham" 5). |
| p. 118 | "At the moment, yes. … But let him tie into some race horses before we say too much about him" (Rogerson "Mrs. Tippett Casts Covetous Eyes on Sham" 5). |
| p. 118 | "one of the most exciting three-year-olds to perform here this season" (Rogerson "Sham in Field of Eight Seeking Santa Catalina" 1). |
| p. 118 | "If Sham does not win the Santa Catalina it will be viewed as an upset of major proportions" (Rogerson "Sham in Field of Eight Seeking Santa Catalina" 11). |
| p. 119 | "Sham broke like the world's unluckiest man had bet on him" (Rasmussen "Still a Champion" 491). |
| p. 119 | "I tried to hustle Sham away to avoid chances of being cut down in close quarters" ([Hebert?] "Victory and Death" 801). |
| p. 120 | "upset of major proportions" (Rogerson "Sham in Field of Eight Seeking Santa Catalina" 11). |
| p. 120 | "Around the turn, I had nowhere to go… but felt that if I could find racing room I'd have plenty enough horse to win" ([Hebert?] "Victory and Death" 801). |
| p. 120 | "I hit him five times—two right-handed and three left-handed. …When he got clear he just took off" ("Sham Overcomes Mud, Trouble and 4 Foes in Catalina" B5). |
| p. 120 | "The biggest surprise was not that he won the Santa Catalina (at 1-10), but that he came out with four legs and torso intact" (Cooper 146). |
| p. 120 | "If Sham had been beaten he would have had enough excuses" (Rasmussen "Still a Champion" 491). |
| p. 120 | "all sorts of trouble to win… heart-throbbing contest" (Kivel "Sham Proves He's Classy" 18). |

p. 120 "Sham demonstrated his class and courage" ("Linda's Chief, Sham Top San Felipe 'Cap'" 9).

## Chapter 12: Pincay Chooses

p. 122 "I was the underbidder at $195,000, and I own the stallion and have six Princequillo mares. Yes, you could say I felt he was worth the money Mr. Sommer gave for him" (Rogerson "Mrs. Tippett Casts Covetous Eyes on Sham" 5).

p. 123 "Clark Gable of horses" (Curtis 102).

p. 123 "not merely... the most beautiful horse in the world" (Curtis 102).

p. 123 "trainers of rival horses... are beginning to shun him.... We don't want any part of Sham" (Cochran "Ain't No Sham!" 8).

p. 123 "No, of course I'm not looking forward to running against Secretariat. ... Nobody is" (Grace "Not looking for Secretariat, but We'll Try When the Time Comes'" 919).

p. 125 "He was so strong after the race that I had to yell to the outrider for help in pulling him up" (Hebert "Looking for a Derby Winner" 607).

p. 125 "a gutsy little campaigner" (Mochon interview).

p. 126 "cat-like burst of speed... an extraordinary racing machine" (Irwin "Western Derbys to New York Runners" 7).

p. 126-127 "Up until a week or two ago, horsemen and handicappers were ready to award the mint juleps to Secretariat without even running the race. ... All of a sudden, though, the notion is circulating out west that Secretariat may not have a walkover after all come May" (Jones "Secretariat Is No Cinch in Derby").

p. 127 "It happens that Santa Anita Park is housing three of the swiftest and toughest young colts in memory this winter in the person of Ancient Title, Linda's Chief and Shaw" (Jones "Secretariat Is No Cinch in Derby").

p. 127 "Vince felt Sham would be the better [Kentucky] Derby prospect... and I went along with him." (Rogerson "Sham Being Ridden by 'Agent's Dream'" 13D).

p. 127 "Linda's Chief is super... but the first time we rode Sham we knew he was our Derby horse" (Rogerson "Mrs. Tippett Casts Covetous Eyes on Sham" 5).

p. 129 "When I asked him for his run, he had it" (Stevenson "San Felipe Easy for Linda's Chief").

p. 129 "We had some trouble, but I don't think we were going to beat the winner. ... We might have been a lot closer with a better trip. He dropped farther back on the backside than I thought he would" (Stevenson "San Felipe Easy for Linda's Chief").

p. 129-130 "I think I should have taken a hold of him at the start, let him settle and then go about our business. ... We might have avoided a lot of trouble that way" (Rasmussen "Doubts Dispelled" 729).

Chapter 13: Rival in the East, Challenge in the West

p. 133 "If Sham doesn't beat me in this one he'll be in real trouble in the Derby" (Rasmussen "Doubts Dispelled" 729).

p. 133 "I'll get tired of looking at a horse in my barn pretty quick if it doesn't win" (Furillo "Frankel Doesn't Talk to Horses" C2).

p. 133-134 "I've heard those stories about how the owner comes to the barn with sugar. ... The horse lets out a whoop and the owner is thrilled because the horse recognizes him. I don't carry sugar" (Furillo "Frankel Doesn't Talk to Horses" C2).

p. 134 "Thoroughbreds are trained just to run. They're not that friendly. I don't know if horses recognize people" (Furillo "Frankel Doesn't Talk to Horses" C2).

p. 134 "Thoroughbreds do what they're taught about running. ... You can't teach them to say hello. They don't count, like Trigger" (Furillo "Frankel Doesn't Talk to Horses" C2).

p. 134 "I wouldn't run a horse if I knew it was going to break a leg. I don't run them to kill them. But if it comes down to running a horse that's hurting and you're going to lose him, then I'll run him. That's business" (Furillo "Frankel Doesn't Talk to Horses" C2).

p. 134 "He had bad racing luck the last time out and will do better" ("'Chief' Gets Challenge" 17).

p. 134 "He's a large, long-striding colt... and when he gets into traps it's sometimes difficult to get him out of them. He needs to be in the clear" (Tower "Under No False Pretenses" 92)

p. 134 "Throw it out" (Rogerson "A Shamful Heart" 44).

p. 134 "I'm not afraid of anything in the Derby. ... I'm just hoping for a clean trip" (Rogerson "A Shamful Heart" 44).

p. 134 "If we have a place to run Saturday... this colt will run by Linda's Chief" (Rogerson "A Shamful Heart" 44).

p. 135 "For the student of performance there is no serious way to make Sham beat Linda's Chief Saturday" (Rogerson "A Shamful Heart" 44).

p. 135 "left the Shamer eight lengths up the track and bloodied... the Shamer" (Rogerson "A Shamful Heart" 44).

p. 135 "Sure he's a good guy. ...But his trainer's got too big a mouth. The only way I'm gonna get him to shut it up is to beat him" (Irwin "Western Derbys to New York Runners" 7).

p. 136     "When he came out you could hear all the cameras. ... You had the wire services, newspapers, magazines, and you had other photographers who were not necessarily into racing that would come out and cover this. And when they saw Sham the cameras just went going. Everybody started shooting up a lot of film" (Mochon interview).

p. 136-137     "And they would have a hell of a time with that because people were trying to get as close as they could to see the horse. ... They were literally climbing on top of each other. Dads would put kids on their shoulders and women would squeeze through to the front. And that place was just packed" (Mochon interview).

p. 137     "It was something about Sham that when he came out that, okay, this is his day, it's his track, and you knew it. You called it. There was something there about him. The head was up high, the ears were straight, and it made a great photo. The horse was beautiful to photograph" (Mochon interview).

p. 138     "beautifully bred" (Sommer interview).

p. 138     "He always tries for you. ... And that makes you like him" (Rogerson "Run Derbys at Fair Grounds" 5).

p. 139     "I knew then he'd be tough" (Kivel "Sham Routs Doubt with Derby Triumph" S-4).

p. 139     "Last time I hustled him going to the front turn because I wanted to be close to Linda's Chief when we hit the stretch. But I think it confused him because he's a big, long-striding horse who doesn't want to be rushed" (Kivel "Sham Routs Doubt with Derby Triumph" S-4).

p. 140     "If he hadn't done that, he would have run even faster" (Stevenson "Sham Turns Tables on Linda's Chief, Eyes Secretariat" C1).

p. 140     "I had to dig him a little then" (Becker 8).

p. 141     "The incident at the start probably cost me several lengths and made me ride differently" ("Sham Survives Claim of Foul Against Entrymate" 2).

p. 141     "We wanted to be laying right off Ancient Title... but after that incident at the start we were way back of him" ("Sham and 'Chief' Go Separate Ways" 3).

p. 141     "It was intentional. They hit my horse. ... Milo [Valenzuela] broke and then he reached down and rapped his horse right into me with his right-hand whip. Braulio Baeza said he lost all chance right then when he had to take back" (Jones "Frankel Cries Foul" D1).

p. 141     "I had my glasses on Sham. ... I didn't see what happened to those other horses on the outside but I can tell you there was plenty of contact against my horses at the start of this meet without anything happening" (Jones

| | |
|---|---|
| | "Frankel Cries Foul" D1). |
| p. 141 | "Sham had his best start ever this time" (Stevenson "Sham Turns Tables on Linda's Chief, Eyes Secretariat" C1). |
| p. 142 | "I told Milo to get him to the lead and then ride his own race. ... I thought Baeza would take back with Linda's Chief when he saw my other horse going out after Ancient Title and I told Pincay to go ahead of him with Sham." (Jones "Frankel Cries Foul" D1). |
| p. 142 | "Braulio rode a great race. ... If what happened to my horse had happened to Sham, I think we would have been an easy winner. I don't want to take anything away from Sham—he's a good horse—but I think my horse should have won" ("Sham and 'Chief' Go Separate Ways" 3). |
| p. 142 | "There is the temptation to report that Sham made a shambles of his field in the Santa Anita Derby. The phrase is accurate, descriptive, and has the added virtue of being right to the point" (Herbert "The Santa Anita Derby" 1263). |
| p. 143 | "Sham is a beautiful colt. ... He's just like his daddy" (Herbert "The Santa Anita Derby" 1264). |
| p. 143 | "If they think they can beat us, they can meet us in a match race a week from now at any distance up to a mile and one half. ... We'll go as short as a mile and one eighth again and run for any price they want" (Jones "Frankel Cries Foul" D1). |

Chapter 14: The Field Takes Shape

| | |
|---|---|
| p. 145 | "I bent over at the five-sixteenth pole and I knew damn well he was going to go sailing. ... I hadn't asked him to run yet" (Grace "The Florida Derby" 1262). |
| p. 145 | "ran himself right into the Kentucky Derby" (Grace "The Florida Derby" 1263). |
| p. 145 | "I think I have a chance possibly to finish third" (Grace "Black Type For Leo's Dam" 1347). |
| p. 146 | "Maybe he'd learn something" (Grace "Black Type For Leo's Dam" 1349). |
| p. 146 | "His race in the Louisiana Derby was a disappointment... but the track that day was very sticky. He likes to hear his feet rattle" (Cox "Secretariat Encounters Sham in $116,400 Wood Memorial" 5). |
| p. 147 | "I reached down and tapped him twice" (Casale "He's Fast, Too" 980). |
| p. 148 | "He must have an unusually big stride... for he runs with so little show of effort that he does not seem to be hitting the speed the teletimer registers" (Smith "Secretariat's Gotham Win Puts Him in Fast Company"). |
| p. 148 | "He again proved that nothing around here at this time can beat him" (Casale "He's Fast, Too" 980). |

p. 148     "Sure, it's a nice spot to be in… but I guess it's a little precarious, too. Assuming Sham and Secretariat meet, I just hope both horses have good racing luck and the best one wins" (Bailey "Secretariat, Sham Put Hancock in Enviable Ky. Derby Position" 4).

p. 148     "I'll be there to see it" (Bailey "Secretariat, Sham Put Hancock in Enviable Ky. Derby Position" 4).

p. 149     When you get a good horse like Sham, you don't avoid anybody" (Woolfe 78-79).

p. 149     "I've seen Secretariat go around five or six horses with one enormous move.… He is truly fantastic. I don't know if Sham is in his class" (Tower "Under No False Pretenses" 92).

p. 149     "Samson the horse, strong all the way" (Velasquez interview March 29, 2003).

p. 150     "I don't know how big he is and I don't want to know.… "I'm superstitious" (Rudy "'Champ'").

p. 150     "We want to get a true line on our colt… and the best way to do that is to run against Secretariat" (Bowmar "Clocking the Candidates" 1114).

p. 150     "They are two good horses running.… It's going to be a good race… This is the best horse Sham will meet in his career" (Nack "Real Threat Or a Sham?").

Chapter 15: High Pressure before the Storm

p. 151     "I put that there so that all the people who go by, he don't bite them" (Rudy "'Champ'").

p. 151     "Champ" (Rudy "'Champ'").

p. 151     "You're the champion" (Rudy "'Champ'").

p. 152     "Got the disposition of a baby" (Rudy "'Champ'").

p. 152     "I put an extension blinker on him.… He runs straight now. I don't even have to use it now, he runs in a closed-cup blinker" (Rudy "'Champ'").

p. 152     "I think my horse is a superhorse, too.… If Secretariat can beat Sham, then I give credit to him. Then I give him all the credit he deserves. I think Secretariat is a good horse—that everybody knows—but I know one thing: Secretariat has never run with a horse like Sham. He has not beaten horses the type like Sham. If Sham had to run with horses like Secretariat ran against, Sham would beat them, too" (Nack "Real Threat Or a Sham?").

p. 152     "At this moment, I think Sham is the best horse in the race" (Cox "Secretariat Encounters Sham in $116,400 Wood Memorial 48).

"Secretariat has a big job ahead of him if he expects to beat my colt" (Cox "Secretariat Encounters Sham in $116,400 Wood Memorial 48).

| | |
|---|---|
| p. 152 | "Sham is the most perfect thoroughbred I've ever been around. ... He is a magnificent individual, is perfectly sound, eats all the oats you can put before him, and does everything else well" (Cox "Secretariat Encounters Sham in $116,400 Wood Memorial 48). |
| p. 153 | "Looks like a battle of S's for the Kentucky Derby. ... Sham and Secretariat" (Cooper "Santa Anita* Gets Its Mud Mark" 146). |
| p. 153 | "Actually he was a faster horse than Sham. ... I wouldn't say that he [Angle Light] was a better horse… but he was faster" (Velasquez interview March 29, 2003). |
| p. 153 | "If he runs two… I'll run three. If he runs only Secretariat, I'll run only Sham" (Cox "Secretariat Encounters Sham in $116,400 Wood Memorial" 48). |
| p. 154 | "It is not as if horses have not ganged up on Secretariat before, if it comes to that, and he is the best alley fighter of his species we have ever seen" (Hatton "The Only Way They Can Beat Him Is Steal It: Lucien Laurin" 3). |
| p. 154 | "Some of them having little more to recommend than their registration papers" (Hatton "The Only Way They Can Beat Him Is Steal It: Lucien Laurin" 3). |
| p. 154 | "In our perhaps astigmatic view, if Secretariat is given a shot, he can break from out in row 12 of the parking lot and win this Wood" (Hatton "The Only Way They Can Beat Him Is Steal It: Lucien Laurin" 3). |
| p. 156 | "The only way they can beat him is to steal it" (Hatton "The Only Way They Can Beat Him Is Steal It: Lucien Laurin" 3). |
| p. 156 | "assurance that nobody is going to purloin the race" (Hatton "The Only Way They Can Beat Him Is Steal It: Lucien Laurin" 3). |
| p. 156 | "standing near the head of the stretch, waved to jockey [Oliver] Lewis on the little red horse to go on because Chesapeake, supposedly the better of the McGrath horses, was far back and had no chance" (Aristides). |
| p. 156 | "Establishment barns" (Strine D1). |
| p. 157 | "Spanish Town" (Ward "Backstretch Feud"). |
| p. 157 | "Society Row" (Ward "Backstretch Feud"). |
| p. 157 | "I became infuriated. ... I have never taken advantage of any man's horse during my career in racing" (Press release "A Statement from Frank Martin"). |
| p. 157 | "Let me tell you, my reputation on the race track is a million per cent honest. ... It was very cheap to say that about me" ("Pancho Martin Scratches at Laurin" 68). |
| p. 157 | "I don't like to run against cry babies. ... They were crying before the race" (Rudy "The Hatton Angle" 1479). |
| p. 157 | "I'm tickled to death he took them out. ... Now they can't say they had a bad |

post position" (Smith "He's Only Human").

p. 157  "I think Laurin put him up to it" (Rudy "The Hatton Angle" 1479).

p. 157  "I did not write the story" (Rudy "The Hatton Angle" 1478).

p. 157-158  "I don't want to get involved in all this… other than to say I never accused Martin of attempting to steal the Wood. I never said that to anybody" (Strine D1).

p. 158  "I just didn't want some horse to get to the front unchallenged and sneak home before the others had a chance. I warned Ronnie [Turcotte] about it" ("Pancho Martin Scratches at Laurin" 68).

p. 158  "He is a free-running colt who sometimes opens long leads when the pace is slow. … The jockey has been told that he is on his own, that he is to try to conserve his horse so he will have something left in the stretch" (Cox "Secretariat Encounters Sham in $116,400 Wood Memorial" 5).

p. 158  "I couldn't use one to help the other if it hurt him" (Bolus "Angel Light Stuns Sham, Secretariat in Wood" C3).

p. 159  "punter" (Wood "Whittaker Faces Reality" 10D).

p. 159  "I've enjoyed every minute of racing. … I'm down at the track at 6:30-7:00 o'clock in the morning, and you couldn't find a nicer group of people than on the backstretch" (Wood "Whittaker Faces Reality" 10D).

p. 159-160  "It was a beautiful work… and the best part was that he finished strongly" (Hirsch "Easy 4-Panel Move by Secretariat Is Just What Laurin Had in Mind" 4).

p. 160  "a hell of a race… something to think about" (Hirsch "Easy 4-Panel Move by Secretariat Is Just What Laurin Had in Mind" 4).

p. 160  "There was a loose horse on the track, and a bunch of green horses galloping, and I just didn't want to take any chances of hurting the horse" (Kirkpatrick "Doubts Dispelled" 1159).

p. 160-161  "Secretariat is, indeed, a great colt and, naturally, I have the utmost respect for him. … But at this moment I am not conceding anything. I feel confident that we'll win the Wood with Sham, and I'm not ready to admit Secretariat's superiority until he proves me wrong" (Cox "Sham Impressive in Wood Tune-up" 2).

p. 161  "They say Secretariat is a great one. I think Sham is a great one, too" (Cox "Sham Impressive in Wood Tune-up" 2).

Chapter 16: Rivals Finally Meet

p. 162  "Who's this?" (Tower "Putting a New Light on the Derby" 17).

| | |
|---|---|
| p. 164 | "I was in striking distance of Angle Light all the way" (Velasquez interview March 29, 2003). |
| p. 164 | "Let 'im go!" (Smith "He's Only Human"). |
| p. 164-165 | "Now I was like in between the knife and the wall. ... Angle Light was fast and Secretariat was closing. ... I have to be careful Angle Light don't steal the race and the other one that was the favorite, the big favorite, was coming off the pace. So I was a length and a half off Angle Light" (Velasquez interview March 29, 2003). |
| p. 165 | "I was trying to save him when Secretariat was coming" (Velasquez interview August 25, 2004). |
| p. 165 | "What I wanna do is be in striking distance that I can get Angle Light at the end and hold Secretariat's big move" (Velasquez interview March 29, 2003). |
| p. 165 | "I gotta watch out for Secretariat. If he fire at the end. He's the one to beat. He's the monster" (Velasquez interview March 29, 2003). |
| p. 165 | "I was worried about Angle Light. He's a nice horse. And he was the speed of the race so I couldn't chase him, being head-to-head with him 'cause I know I won't finish anyway" (Velasquez interview March 29, 2003). |
| p. 165 | "I'm gonna kill him [Sham] and it's gonna kill my chances too. ... So that's why I was in striking distance" (Velasquez interview March 29, 2003). |
| p. 165 | "Velasquez! Let 'im go!" (Smith "He's Only Human"). |
| p. 166-167 | "My horse closed real good when I asked him to go and, if the race were a little longer, we would have passed the winner" (Schuyler "Angle Light Stuns Sham, Secretariat In Wood" 29). |
| p. 167 | "My horse would have won in another couple of jumps" (Bolus "Angle Light Stuns Sham, Secretariat in Wood" C3). |
| p. 167 | "He just didn't have his punch today. ... He finished pretty good, but not with his usual kick" (Schuyler "Angle Light Stuns Sham, Secretariat in Wood" 29). |
| p. 167 | "Congratulations for what? Who won? ... You did. ... With the wrong horse!" (Tower "Putting a New Light on the Derby" 17). |
| p. 167 | "We did it, Mr. Laurin, we won. ... Yeah, yeah... good, good" (Bolus "Angle Light Stuns Sham, Secretariat in Wood" C1). |
| p. 168 | "It looked to me... as though we were racing one horse, Sham, and forgetting the rest of the field. ... What's the difference? ... We got beat by Sham, too" (Tower "Putting a New Light on the Derby" 18). |
| p. 168 | "They were walking" (McCulley "Secretariat Winds Up 3rd in Wood" 115). |
| p. 168 | "He just didn't run his race" (Ward April 22, 1973 121). |

p. 168   "If he had run the way he always has, the pace wouldn't have made any difference" (Miller 132).

p. 168   "Just before the half-mile pole... I thought he was lagging so I hit him. Nothing happened. I don't know how many times I hit him, I should have counted on the rerun" (Ward April 22, 1973 121).

p. 169   "When they went the 6 furlongs in 1:12, I said, 'Good night, Secretariat'" (Miller 132).

p. 169   "If they'd gone another 20 yards Sham definitely would have won" (Casale "New Light on the Derby Picture" 1070).

p. 169   "hero in defeat" (Hatton "It Just Wasn't Secretariat's Day" 24).

p. 169   "exemplary sportsmanship" (Hatton "It Just Wasn't Secretariat's Day" 24).

p. 169   "Hesitation Waltz into the stretch, with nobody venturing to make an issue of the pace... Sham had dead aim all the way, and only just missed vindicating the popular trainer" (Hatton "It Just Wasn't Secretariat's Day" 24).

p. 169   "Maybe because he felt that he shoulda win the race.... Maybe he thought that I rode a bad race. I don't know what it was" (Velasquez interview March 29, 2003).

p. 170   "Maybe he thought that the horse run better for Laffit. ... But I don't think I rode a bad race either" (Velasquez interview March 29, 2003).

p. 170   "He never lugged in before... he used to lug out" (Bowen "Resumption of a Legend" 1662).

p. 170   "lugged in" (Bowen "Resumption of a Legend" 1662).

p. 170   "I was trying to press the pace and at the same time watch out for Secretariat who was coming. So I think I did what was right. But it didn't work out because I didn't win. I know one thing, that I did beat Secretariat" (Velasquez interview March 29, 2003).

p. 170   "Against my better judgment, I decided to run only Sham. I didn't want possible victory to be tainted. ... As it turned out, I played right into Lucien Laurin's hands.... Had I run Knightly Dawn or Beautiful Music to assure a real pace... Sham would have won easily" (Casale "New Light on the Derby Picture 1072).

p. 170   "I should have put Knightly Dawn in. ... This slow pace killed us. ... He knows the horse better than anybody" (Smith "He's Only Human").

p. 170-171  "Secretariat's whimsy turned off many fans... Sham came out of the race smelling might lak a rose" (Hatton "It Just Wasn't Secretariat's Day" 24).

p. 171   "Sham is a better horse than Secretariat or any other three-year-old in America" (Casale "New Light on the Derby Picture 1072).

p. 171   "I'm going to beat him every time I run against him. But... if he beats me

Endnotes ♦ 385

three out of four, I'll take my hat off and congratulate him and say, 'You got the best horse'" (Bolus "Martin Raps 'Cheap Talk,' Drops Laurin as a Friend" B3).

p. 171 "transformed a nice, tidy Kentucky Derby picture into something resembling a painting by Salvador Dali" (Ward "Agonizing Wood Aftermath" 72).

p. 171-172 "The feeling is that Laffit Pincay would have brought Sham home a winner in the Wood had he elected to travel to New York instead of remaining in California to ride Susan's Girl. Pinky knows Sham well. He's a tough horse to ride, but a winner when you know how to handle him. That's what should make him tough to best when he goes at Louisville under the guidance of Pincay. In any event, we like him in the Derby over Secretariat and any other entry in the race" (Kivel "OK for Sunday Racing Near" S-4).

p. 172 "Shaw" (Jones "Secretariat Is No Cinch in Derby").

p. 172 "Frank (Punch) Martinez" (McCulley "Secretariat Winds Up 3rd in Wood" 132).

p. 172 "This is my breakfast and last night's dinner, too. I am disgusted. ... I am tired and I am not feeling well" (Rudy "The Hatton Angle" 1478).

p. 173 "cheap stories" (Rudy "The Hatton Angle" 1478).

p. 173 "She really tried hard, it was a tough one to lose" (Kivel "Bird Boots New Racing Heroine" S-1).


Chapter 17: Other Contenders

p. 174 "One swallow doesn't make a summer. ... One race doesn't change reality. ... Secretariat is still the super horse and every horse, like every person, has an off day. I still think he'll win the Derby" (Wood "Angle Light's Upset Victory in Wood Earns Derby Berth" D16).

p. 175 "He is simply a genius. ... I guess there is no better illustration as to his ability than Sham" (Cox "Sommers Pass the Test of the 'Greatest' Game" 5D).

p. 175 "The second factor depends on how easily Secretariat wins in New York. ... If, for any reason, Sham beats Secretariat, we will definitely go to the Derby" ("Linda's Chief Rated Heavy California Derby Favorite" 9).

p. 175 "I think it's too early in the season for *any* horse, at three, to go that distance" (Parker 1072).

p. 175-176 "Some 40-1 shot will win it. ... I was mildly surprised Secretariat couldn't beat Sham and Angle Light in the Wood, but I didn't buy all that superhorse stuff you heard about him. If you cut through all the baloney what you saw was that he beats a horse called Champagne Charlie. Knightly Dawn and Settecento can run with Champagne Charlie and they're no hell, so I didn't come unglued when Secretariat got beat" (Rogerson "Bright, Rich Future" 40).

386 ♦ SHAM: GREAT WAS SECOND BEST

p. 176-177  "The Flamingo might have been by fault. ... At Hialeah, the rail was dynamite, so I told the boy to stay in there. He could not get clear until late" (Bowen "Prologue to the 99th Running" 1592).

p. 177  "I believe he can give you that big run after a mile, or after 1¼ miles" (Bowen "Prologue to the 99th Running" 1594).

p. 177  "Our Native strikes one as an honest competitor that may be short of championship caliber, but no equine with championship hopes had better make a mistake with him around" (Goldman "Busier and Better" 605).

p. 177  "He's just like a cannon. ... When you pull the string, you know he's going to explode" ("War of Nerves Begins for Kentucky Derby" 17).

p. 177  "Some of the writers have criticized me for running him too often… but if I don't run him I have to work him, and he is not a particularly good work horse. If you run him, they say it is too much, if you don't they say he is short" (Bowen "Kentucky Derby Preps" 1396).

p. 177  "You can't win a fight unless you get in the ring" (Thomas "Our Native Keeps Racing and Scores a Big Triumph").

p. 179  "As far as I'm concerned, I would just pass the race with Shecky Greene. ... I don't think he's a 1¼–mile horse" (Bowen "Prologue to the 99th Running" 1594).

p. 179  "Everything out of that mare [Lester's Pride] has been very quick—and very short"

p. 179  "travel a mile-and-a-quarter only in a van" (Ward "Derby Poses Hatful of Questions" 29).

p. 180  "As soon as Shecky hears feet behind him, when he's right, he just takes off. ... It's likely to take our colt too far, too early" (Sullivan "It's a Split Decision" C2).

p. 180  "He kicked me before he won the Hutcheson and he kicked me before he won the Fountain of Youth. ... And, man, he just kicked me again yesterday" ("Secretariat Drill Pleases Laurin" 25).

p. 180  "Why not? ... When that big horse got beat it opened it up like a raffle" (Rogerson "Bright, Rich Future" 40).

p. 180-181  "If I can correct that… I think I'll have a real top colt" (Herbert "Sundays in the Stand" 1394).

p. 181  "This is a good little horse with just one bad habit. He likes to run at horses but when he catches up to them he has a habit of pulling up. He doesn't like to go past them" (Grimsley "Don't Overlook Unlucky Mr. 13 in Derby Field" C5).

p. 181  "He's so placid, he doesn't care about anything. ... I must have taken his temperature 100 times. ... Last year, I bet he would be down 18 or 20 hours a day, and he still lies down a lot. He's so easy-going he'll embarrass you in the paddock before a race" (Bowen "Ten Days Before" 1481).

| p. 182 | "He seemed to be a little smarter than the average horse… which makes a good horse" (Blum interview). |
| p. 182 | "He looked like a dead-head. … But when we got to the gate and I tapped him on his ass a couple of times, let him know, hey, it's time to run, he walked in that gate and he was ready to go. … In the middle of competition he knew what he was doing. He understood when it was time to go with a flick of the whip, and he was on his way" (Blum interview). |
| p. 182 | "He's so big… he has legs like a giraffe" (Beardsley). |
| p. 182 | "I think there are two or three horses in the race who are tough. Sham is going to be tough and Forego is strictly on the improve" (Bolus "If Royal and Regal Wins Derby, Croll Would Be a Little Ahead" C3). |
| p. 183 | "I'm sort of an unofficial manager without portfolio" (Bowen "Prologue to the 99th Running" 1596). |
| p. 183 | "I'm working on a commission basis. I get zero" (Daley "'Peaceful' Derby Eve Gives Way to Race Where Excitement Builds, Funmakers Revel" 26). |
| p. 183 | "They claim Restless Jet has no chance. … But that's what they said about the New York Jets when we played the Baltimore Colts in the Super Bowl. We were 17-point underdogs" (Daley "'Peaceful' Derby Eve Gives Way to Race Where Excitement Builds, Funmakers Revel" 26). |
| p. 183 | "Ol' Navajo don't know he's a Hoosier. … All he thinks about is working and eating" (Flynn A5). |
| p. 184 | "I don't know if he's seasoned enough, but I'm going with him" ("Laurin's Entry Favored in Derby" 26). |

Chapter 18: Prep for the Roses

| p. 185-186 | "Lucien is always looking for excuses. … He doesn't know how to take defeat. He kicks his feet in the air when he wins. When he loses, he sulks—and excuses" (Strine D1). |
| p. 186 | "It's funny, the only day Secretariat didn't want to run was the day he met Sham" ("Pancho Martin Scratches at Laurin" 68). |
| p. 186 | "That's why most time I don't want to talk to a person like that" (Martin interview). |
| p. 186 | "This whole thing is ridiculous, and I don't like it" (Tower "It Was Murder" 22). |
| p. 186 | "I know Lucien for all my life. … A nice guy, you know. He tried to do the same thing I tried to do. Win" (Martin interview). |
| p. 186 | "a damn good horseman, one of the best" ("Pancho Martin Scratches at Laurin" 68). |
| p. 186-187 | "Actually I was not aware of that at all in the Derby. … The press seemed to be pretty confident that Sham would win the Derby, having come off such a nice |

win with the Santa Anita Derby" (Sommer interview).

p. 188     "He finished full of run. That's what I liked so much" (Hirsch "Straight Shooter" 32).

p. 188-189     "He rated beautifully and the boy held him hard at the start" (Hirsch "Forego Reels off 5 Panels in :57" 30).

p. 189     "I can beat him" ("Sham's Trainer Sees Derby Victory").

p. 189     "I don't say I'm the best trainer. Just say 95 per cent of the trainers are worse than me" (Strine D1).

p. 189     "I never had a horse prepare himself for a race as well as he has. ... He wants to run" (Bowen "Resumption of a Legend" 1664).

p. 189     "Secretariat Drill Pleases Laurin" ("Secretariat Drill Pleases Laurin" 25).

## Chapter 19: It's Official

p. 190     "I couldn't want him to come up to the Derby any better than he is now" (Hirsch "Concern over Angle Light's Status Clouds Derby Picture" 3).

p. 190     "I think he has a chance to win, particularly with Bill Hartack as his rider" (Hirsch "Concern over Angle Light's Status Clouds Derby Picture" 3).

p. 191     "I was looking for him to go in about 36 and change, but he wanted to run" ("Angle Light, 'Regal' Ready for Derby" 19).

p. 191     "He handled the Fair Grounds beautifully this winter. ... This track is similar in many respects to the one at the Fair Grounds so he might run well in the Derby" (Hirsch "Concern over Angle Light's Status Clouds Derby Picture" 3).

p. 191     "attention, carrots, photographers, and winning" (Secretariat.com. "Ask Penny" http://secretariat.com).

p. 191     "He communicates with his groom and the exercise boy and he cooperates with me. ... He's gutty and determined" (Cox "Sham Perfect Thoroughbred Says Proud 'Pancho' Martin" 12D).

p. 192     "about fit as he can be" (Cox "Sham Perfect Thoroughbred Says Proud 'Pancho' Martin" 12D).

p. 192     "He doesn't have to carry his own track around with him. He has won twice in the mud and has trained well on all sorts of tracks" (Cox "Sham Is the Real Thing" 5D).

p. 192     "He has many things in his favor. He has the gait of a natural router, along with the speed to escape the type of traffic jams that usually develop in big fields going into that first turn in the Derby. But they have a good run before they hit there and those with enough speed have a chance to get a good position" (Cox "Sham Perfect Thoroughbred Says Proud 'Pancho' Martin" 12D).

| | |
|---|---|
| p. 192 | "Here is the colt they have to beat. ... Can be had" (Gelardi 29). |
| p. 193 | "This is one of the best balanced fields in recent Derby history. ... Sham has a slight edge with me, but it could be close" (Hirsch "Sham Topweight at 126 If Derby Were Handicap" 36). |
| p. 194 | "hectic but exciting" (Bailey "This Sporting Life" 26). |
| p. 194 | "I don't know any horses that can read tote boards and I ain't a bit superstitious. ... My wife was born on the 13th... and I've been living with her for 30-odd years" (Grimsley "Don't Overlook Unlucky Mr. 13 in Derby Field" C5). |
| p. 195 | "He'd call me two or three times a night. ... He didn't want him to go to the Kentucky Derby. He'd say, pardon the expression, 'Don't bring that son-of-a-bitch to the Derby. There's no Bold Ruler that can go that far'" (Carlson "Silver Anniversary" 6). |
| p. 196 | "You know, I couldn't believe what happened in the Wood. ... It hurt. It hurt terribly" (Fenlon C2). |
| p. 196 | "When Angle Light beat Secretariat she came apart, man. I mean she flipped out. And she stayed flipped out. ... When things went wrong with Secretariat or Lucien Laurin and Secretariat, well, shit, she let him know it, man. ... She thought Secretariat was, nobody could beat him. And nobody *should* beat him. And if anybody beat him it was Lucien Laurin's fault or Ronny Turcotte's fault or whatever. ... She was at the table reading him the *riot act*. I mean she was all over top of him. And he was so embarrassed. He was like looking around, and people looking to see what the hell she was hollering at. ... He just wanted to crawl under the table" (Blum interview). |
| p. 198 | "I don't know what's going on. ... I don't know what the hell happened" (Ward "Fire Vasquez off Angle Light, Hire LeBlanc" 79). |
| p. 198 | "I won't be going down for the Derby under any circumstances" (Ward "Fire Vasquez off Angle Light, Hire LeBlanc" 79). |
| p. 199 | "We, of course, have a big interest in this running of the Derby. Secretariat will stand here next season" (Goldstein "Claiborne Brand Rides with Sham" 12D). |
| p. 199 | "Naturally, we are all very happy at his success and we would like it if he would win today and bring honor to the farm" (Goldstein "Claiborne Brand Rides with Sham" 12D). |
| p. 199 | "It would be the ultimate in irony if Sham would win this Derby. ... Dad always wanted to have a Derby winner. It was one of the few aims in his life that he failed to realize. Now there is a colt with a genuine chance to get the job done and we bred, broke, raised him" (Goldstein "Claiborne Brand Rides with Sham" 10D). |

p. 200     "Flying must agree with horses—they win!" (John J. McCabe Agency, Inc. advertisement).

p. 200     "He can do it" (Goldstein "Martin Hoping for Preakness Luck After Derby Misfortune" 5).

### Chapter 20: The Day Arrives

p. 201     "Sham showed me he's really a runner" (Sullivan "Sham Ran Perfectly, but 'Just Got Tired'" C3).

p. 201     "Derby Field is Wide Open" (Phelps "Secretariat, Angle Light Draw Even Odds, but Derby Field Is Wide Open" 13).

p. 202     "perhaps the most contentious finish in recent Derby history" (Hirsch "Coming Up Roses" D24).

p. 202     "Most horses they know because the day they run, they do different things" (Martin interview).

p. 202     "Good horses run no matter what you do to him" (Martin interview).

p. 203     "You have an expensive hot walker" (Hirsch "Derby Day Notes" 3).

p. 203     "By the time we get to the Belmont Stakes… I'll be ready to ride this horse myself." (Hirsch "Derby Day Notes" 3).

p. 203     "He was laying down flat in his stall like he's dead. … Two o'clock in the afternoon, and he's going to run a couple of hours later. … Boss, he does that every day" (Carlson "Silver Anniversary" 6).

p. 203     "The 'rabbit' hopped into Kentucky Derby festivities after all" (Adair "Sham's 'Rabbit' Wins by Two in Twin Spires" C6).

p. 204     "You know the horse. Lay close to the pace. Don't be too far off it. Don't worry about Secretariat. Last time we did we got beat" (Nack *Secretariat: The Making of a Champion* 256).

p. 204     "You know the horse, Ronnie. Just try to keep clear. Don't worry about a thing. Ride the race the way it comes up. … *Use ton propre judgment*" (Nack *Secretariat: The Making of a Champion* 257).

p. 204     "You damn Frenchman, you don't have any sense. When he gets to the quarter pole, he'll leave you. … I don't think he will" (Carlson "Silver Anniversary" 6).

p. 204-205     "This is the greatest race in the world and you really get the chills when you see your horse out there and hear that song" (Fenlon C2).

p. 205     "still had some horse at the finish" (Rogerson "Pincay Believes Sham Can Beat Secretariat" 5).

| | |
|---|---|
| p. 205-206 | "My horse gave him a fight" (Sullivan "Sham Ran Perfectly, but 'Just Got Tired'" C3). |
| p. 206 | "He ran perfectly. ... He just got tired, I guess. I mean he wasn't really that tired, he was trying, but you know the other horse" (Sullivan "Sham Ran Perfectly, but 'Just Got Tired'" C3). |
| p. 208 | "His two teeth were dangling by a thin strip of gum… and he was bleeding so hard it took us three-quarters of an hour to cauterize the wound" ("Starting Gate Hurt Sham" 79). |
| p. 208 | "It was hanging there like this in his head. ... They had to cut him in his gum" (Martin interview). |
| p. 208 | "Secretariat won it fair and square" (Tower "It Was Murder" 22). |
| p. 208 | "monster" (Velasquez interview March 29, 2003). |
| p. 210 | "Remember… Sham ran faster in losing the Derby than any horse had ever done in winning" (Goldstein "Pancho Hoping for the Breaks" 5). |
| p. 210 | "Pincay was riding a good race on Sham too. ... He had a lot of horse under him, and he tried to get away on that last turn and steal it. ... Oops, I shouldn't say that again" (Jones "Record 134, 476 at Downs" C1). |
| p. 210 | "I have too much headache to talk" (Ramsey C1). |
| p. 210 | "You guys ain't lookin' for me" (Beardsley). |
| p. 211 | "He ran up there second and third at the start, but he just couldn't do it" (Beardsley). |
| p. 211 | "He wasn't making up any ground on the first two" (Beardsley). |
| p. 211 | "He hit the inside fence so hard, he almost tore it down. I was moving up on the rail then and was committed to go. I couldn't change my mind. I got by one horse but I was too close to the fence" (Bailey "This Sporting Life" 26). |
| p. 211 | "I'm not saying it would have changed the outcome, but it would have had some bearing. It cost him third place money, there's no doubt about that" (Beardsley). |
| p. 211 | "I don't want to use the word clumsy, but he wasn't Fred Astaire" (Heller 31). |
| p. 212 | "He ran a good race—as far as he ran" (Beardsley). |
| p. 212 | "He did everything the trainer wanted but win" (Mills 26). |
| p. 212 | "Gold Bag buried me. ... The pace kind of backed up into me and I was running into horses' heels around the first turn" (Beardsley). |
| p. 213 | "Bold Rulers won't go a mile and a quarter, eh?" (Daley "Turcotte Relatively Silent, But Pleased" 26). |
| p. 213 | "This will be short and sweet. ... I'm sorry, really sorry… we're clean out of time" (Sullivan "Sham Ran Perfectly, but 'Just Got Tired'" C3). |

p. 213     "Sham… is as good a three-year-old as I've ever sat on" (Rogerson "Pincay Believes Sham Can Beat Secretariat" 12).

Chapter 21: The Derby Dust Settles

p. 214     "The only apology the beaten can offer is that they happened to be contemporaries of a special and thrilling animal" (Tower "It Was Murder" 22).

p. 214     "What a big race he ran in the Derby! We're very proud of him" (Hirsch "Secretariat and Sham Limber Up at Pimlico" 30).

p. 215     "I imagine I'll wake up smiling all night long!" (Wall 26).

p. 215     "He's going after the other horse now" (Fenlon C2).

p. 215     "There were all those rumors about the horse, and they were even going around this morning. … If I hadn't just come from the barn and seen him myself, I would have dropped dead" (Fenlon C2).

p. 216     "I guess they could crack down on me. … But right now, that's the least of my worries" ("Secretariat's Triple Crown Chances 50-50, Says Laurin" C2).

p. 216     "He also grabbed his left quarter but fortunately the wound isn't too deep and he will be all right for the Preakness. … He was a very game horse to run as well as he did" (Hirsch "Secretariat Continues on Triple Crown Path" 5).

p. 216     "It's hard to make up eight or nine lengths" (Mills 26).

p. 217     "The Derby, as it has for all those years, was run most importantly down the Churchill Downs stretch where thousands of dreams have gone up in dust and sweat" ("Secretariat Writes Record" S-2).

p. 217     "When all that trouble started at the gate, the man who was supposed to stay with the horse disappeared and never came back. … Such a big race as that and they don't have enough men to handle every horse. … I would pay the money myself if that's the problem. … When that horse acted up, they made my horse stay in the gate all that time and Secretariat's outside the gate, walking round and round. All that didn't help any" ("Starting Gate Hurt Sham" 79).

p. 218     "If they'd have left him alone, he wouldn't have become upset and would have started without incident" (Hirsch "Secretariat Continues on Triple Crown Path" 5).

p. 218     "Hell, that type doesn't belong in the Derby. … The way he was rearing, kicking and fussing, it was lucky he didn't hurt one of the other horses. … They're supposed to warn us in advance about a bad actor. Nobody said anything" (Ward "Next Stop, Baltimore").

p. 218     "Watergate would have lost the front page spotlight to the Starting Gate

| | |
|---|---|
| p. 218 | Scandal" (Ward "Next Stop, Baltimore"). |
| p. 218 | "You can see that all a guy wants at the race track is an even shake, such as his horse coming out of the starting gate with all his teeth" (Durslag "Sham in Need of New Plan"). |
| p. 218 | "Horses before had lost their riders, and others had lost their stirrups. … But it had been a long time since one had been asked to go a mile and a quarter without all his teeth" (Durslag "Sham in Need of New Plan"). |
| p. 218 | "left Sham looking like a four-legged hockey player" (Tower "Flying High and Heading for Fame" 24). |
| p. 219 | "The gate episode hurt Sham. … He came out shaking his head and stunned. He usually breaks well on his own, but this time Laffit had to use him right away to get position. His whole race plan was affected" (Tower "Flying High and Heading for Fame" 24). |
| p. 219 | "I really don't know how to answer that. … It's difficult to see how he could have run much better than almost 1:59⅖, and yet, logically, hitting his head on the gate and losing the teeth couldn't have helped him" (Rogerson "Pincay Believes Sham Can Beat Secretariat" 12). |
| p. 219 | "I feel we have a chance to beat him at Baltimore. My horse has more speed than Secretariat and probably will have an advantage at the shorter distance. And he's much handier. I can do anything I want with him. … Another point to remember is that Sham is improving with every race. The way the Preakness comes up I should be able to place him second or third to whoever wants the lead. And when you have a situation like that, and a horse with Sham's class, you have to be given a chance to win" (Rogerson "Pincay Believes Sham Can Beat Secretariat" 12). |

Chapter 22: Round Two in Baltimore

| | |
|---|---|
| p. 220 | "The Derby is a race of aristocratic sleekness, for horses of birth to prove their worth to run in the Preakness" ("Preakness Stakes" http://www.preakness.com). |
| p. 220 | "He keeps improving… he's been improving ever since the Santa Anita. I think Sham and Secretariat gonna keep beating each other, you know?" (Sullivan "Sham Ran Perfectly, but 'Just Got Tired'" C3). |
| p. 221 | "He can't pick grass right now… but outside of that he is fine and is regaining his energies" (Hirsch "Secretariat and Sham Limber Up at Pimlico" 30). |
| p. 221 | "If there is any question at all, he is not going to run. … We are not going to hurt this horse just to race against Secretariat. He can beat him later in the Belmont" (Goldstein "Pancho Hoping for the Breaks" 5). |
| p. 221 | "We're going to meet four times. … We won the first round by four lengths in |

New York. He wins the second by two in Kentucky. Let's see about Maryland" (Jones "Record 134, 476 at Downs" C2).

p. 221   "Secretariat is going to have to work for his Triple Crown. He's not about to win it by default, not if Pancho Martin and Sham can help it" (Ward "Secretariat's Nonstop Run" 73).

p. 221   "What is the sense of using a good colt for nothing more than a rabbit? ... I think we showed in the Derby that Sham doesn't need any pacemakers. He was beaten fairly by Secretariat, but he was out there by himself" (Goldstein "Preakness Regarded as 'Match' by Sommer" 1).

p. 222   "Look at him! He just keeps getting bigger. He's so thick that Ron may have to have a special saddle made just to ride him" (Woolfe 104).

p. 223   "wire ... purse" (http://www.preakness.com).

p. 223   "Old Hilltop" (http://www.preakness.com).

p. 224   "Pimlico Race Course ... Home of the Preakness" (Reed "One-Track Mind" B1).

p. 224   "Go Where the Real Money Is—Baltimore, Preakness" (Reed "One-Track Mind" B1).

p. 224   "Next Stop: Preakness, Pimlico" (Reed "One-Track Mind" B1).

p. 225   "Chick's enthusiasm can get downright sickening" (DeFord 60).

p. 225   "I could have used him in a staff position, but he needs a less structured existence. ... He could always see the humor in things" (DeFord 64).

p. 225   "I never dislike more than three people at the same time. ... I just don't have the time. Actually, one of my three passed away, so now I have one slot open" (DeFord 60).

p. 225   "It takes a little of the old show biz. ... Some of the P.T. Barnum to put the proper life into the game" (Phillips "Chick Lang Top Preakness Booster" 4).

p. 227   "No race like the Preakness should be allowed to get off with only two horses in it. ... If an owner or a trainer has a horse with even half the talent of a Secretariat, and he's a real horseman, he shouldn't allow a walkover or a two-horse race" (McCulley "Preakness" 100).

p. 227   "Torsion can run. ... He went his last eighth in 11 seconds and that ain't bad. ... He can't beat any Secretariats or Shams now, but he will improve. ... If he gets any part of it, I'll be happy" (Hirsch "Secretariat, Sham Head Preakness Saturday" 5).

p. 228   "He's run 10 times this year. ... and if he isn't fit now, it's too late to worry about it" (Hirsch "Secretariat, Sham Head Preakness Saturday" 5).

| | |
|---|---|
| p. 228 | "Whether he will improve enough to threaten Secretariat and Sham remains to be seen" (Hirsch "Secretariat, Sham Head Preakness Saturday" 5). |

## Chapter 23: Facing the Phantom of Pimlico

| | |
|---|---|
| p. 229 | "There are interesting days ahead. Racing needs a superstar, and now it may have two" (Kirkpatrick "Secretariat's Stride" 1216B). |
| p. 229 | "We'll just have to hurry up a little sooner" (Jones "Record 134, 476 at Downs" C2). |
| p. 230 | "We could have sold tickets if we'd promoted it" (Phillips "Racing's 'Giant' Has Stride to Match"). |
| p. 230 | "Can you imagine a horse running a mile and a quarter in 1:59⅖, as he did in the Derby, and then coming back a week later with a work like this?" (Hirsch "Secretariat, Sham Impressive in Drills" 3). |
| p. 230-231 | "He didn't have blinkers on for the work. … He'd have gone in :56 with blinkers." (Hirsch "Secretariat, Sham Impressive in Drills" 1). |
| p. 231 | "He was kind of gawking at the crowd through the stretch, and I had a little trouble keeping his mind on his business" (Kirkpatrick "Secretariat's Stride" 1216B). |
| p. 231 | "When he's relaxed and going easy on his own, he stretches out and covers an awful lot of ground. When he digs in and goes all out for speed—that's when he shortens his stride" (Woolfe 114). |
| p. 232 | "Very, very impressive" ("Secretariat, Sham End Major Drills" 15). |
| p. 232 | "He didn't have his usual punch through the stretch of the Derby. … There was a good reason, for he got off to a bad start, was used up a little in getting a position, and was laying closer to the pace than planned" (Hirsch "Secretariat, Sham Impressive in Drills" 3). |
| p. 232 | "That's in the past, though. … Now we are looking forward to the Preakness" (Hirsch "Secretariat, Sham Impressive in Drills" 3). |
| p. 232 | "He's ready. … Anybody that beats him will have [to] do some running" (Pimlico Race Course Press Release). |
| p. 233 | "Women weaken legs!" (*Rocky*). |
| p. 233 | "It's got to be tough for any kind of a horse, but I think we have one big edge. …This big fellow loves the mud" (Jones "Record 134, 476 at Downs" C2). |
| p. 233 | "Sham has won the only two times he started on an off-track" (Pimlico Race Course Press Release). |
| p. 233 | "I think Sham finishes stronger than any horse in the country—any horse" (Hirsch "Seven Enter Preakness, But Only Six to Compete" 32). |

p. 233-234  "A number of horses have been winning on the lead here. The leaders don't seem to get tired, so I expect the Preakness to be run in fast time" (Hirsch "Seven Enter Preakness, But Only Six to Compete" 32).

p. 234  "He has come up to the Preakness perfectly" (Hirsch "Secretariat Heads Preakness" 6).

p. 234  "Frankly, barring bad racing luck, I don't see how they can beat him Saturday" (Hirsch "Secretariat, Sham Head Preakness Saturday" 5).

p. 236  "The two men were besieged by requests, but insisted on finishing" (Hirsch "Secretariat Heads Preakness" 57).

p. 236-237  "This is my fourth time in the race. ... I was third with Amberoid in 1966, was third with Jay Ray in 1969, and fourth last year with Riva Ridge. If I don't do it tomorrow, gentlemen, you've lost a customer for sure" (Hirsch "Secretariat Heads Preakness" 57).

p. 237  "Let no one here! ... No one! ... I want no one bothering this horse. ... He needs all the rest he can get" (Nack "Not an Unguarded Moment for Sham" 143).

p. 237  "He has trained perfectly for the Preakness and has never been better in his life. If he doesn't beat Secretariat tomorrow then he just can't handle the other horse. I think he can beat him" (Hirsch "Secretariat Heads Preakness" 6).

Chapter 24: Daisies on Old Hilltop

p. 238  "Meadow Stable's record-breaking Kentucky Derby winner, Secretariat... Sigmund Sommer's fleet and courageous Sham" (Hirsch "Secretariat Heads Preakness" 1).

p. 239  "Never forget that the Preakness has one thing that the Derby does not have. ... We have the Derby winner" (Deford 64).

p. 239  "turned the grandstand area into one big sardine can" ("Secretariat Changes Style but not Result in Easy Preakness Victory" 25).

p. 240  "The Golden Arm Corral" (Ward "Swan Song of a Thoroughbred" 73).

p. 240  "Thanks for the Memories Johnny" (Ward "Swan Song of a Thoroughbred" 73).

p. 240  "Unitas Pass" (Ward "Swan Song of a Thoroughbred" 73).

p. 241  "How am I going to see anything?" (Hirsch "Preakness Sidelights" 4).

p. 244  "We'll play it by ear and see what happens once the race starts" (Hirsch "Laurin Remembers, And Is Concerned" 2).

p. 244  "He breaks from the gate a lot better than Secretariat" (Hirsch "Secretariat, Sham Impressive in Drills" 3).

p. 244  "I can't stand it. I don't want to see the race. ... You sit right here" (Carlson

Endnotes ♦ 397

"Silver Anniversary [Part 2]" 6).

p. 244    "Lucien's heart was pounding so hard he couldn't hold his glasses" ("Secretariat... Two-Thirds a Triple Crown King" S-1).

p. 245    "He soon let me know that the pace was slow and so we started to roll" ("Secretariat Changes Style but not Result in Easy Preakness Victory" 35).

p. 245    "like a gentleman straightening the cuffs on his dress shirt" (Phillips "A Superlative Performance" 24).

p. 245    "When he came by, it felt like a freight train passing—blew the number right off my sleeve" (Woolfe 116).

p. 245    "I was on the inside, with Our Native next to me and Secretariat on the outside. Next thing I know, I look over—and Secretariat was gone" (Kindred "Pincay Resigned to Secretariat's 'Super' Handle" C3).

p. 246    "At the three-eighths pole my horse was running pretty strong, and I really hadn't asked him to run yet" (Kirkpatrick and Green "The Name of the Game Is Class" 1256).

p. 247    "He wasn't bothered by them at all" ("Secretariat Changes Style but not Result in Easy Preakness Victory" 35).

p. 249    "The hell with it" (Kindred "Pincay Resigned to Secretariat's 'Super' Handle" C3).

p. 249    "a helluva horse" (Kindred "Pincay Resigned to Secretariat's 'Super' Handle" C3).

p. 249    "Not that I can recall" (Kindred "Pincay Resigned to Secretariat's 'Super' Handle" C3).

p. 249    "I knew Secretariat was some kind of good horse" (Kindred "Pincay Resigned to Secretariat's 'Super' Handle" C3).

p. 249    "He's unreal. ... I've never seen anything like the horse, to move so early and still have so much left" (Kindred "Pincay Resigned to Secretariat's 'Super' Handle" C3).

p. 249    "It doesn't seem like it but I don't know" ("Turcotte Enjoys an Easy Ride" 25).

p. 249    "That other horse is just too much. ... He was running so easy and I kept looking for Ron to hit him but he never did. He went by us flying and I tried to keep close" (Ward "Preakness" 128).

p. 249    "Sham ran a very good race. ... Pincay is a hell of a rider. But my horse ran real big" ("Secretariat Waltzes to Preakness Win" C1).

p. 249    "Once this colt is rolling nobody can catch him" ("Secretariat Changes Style but not Result in Easy Preakness Victory" 35).

p. 249    "My horse ran a powerful race" (Kindred "Pincay Resigned to Secretariat's 'Super' Handle" C3).

p. 249      "Sham kept trying" ("Turcotte Enjoys an Easy Ride" 25).

p. 249      "My horse ran a good race. He just ain't good enough—not for those two, anyway" (Kindred "Pincay Resigned to Secretariat's 'Super' Handle" C3).

p. 250      "My horse is the type of horse that he could go any distance. ... My horse, he tries, you know what I mean. He, he, he... I don't know how to put it. ... He's a fine horse. ... That's right. He's really good horse. ... Well we'll see you in the Belmont Stakes. And hopefully another shot for you to try the big horse" ("Secretariat—1973 Preakness Stakes—Laffit Pincay, Jr., Sham's Jockey, Interviewed!" [CBS broadcast]).

Chapter 25: Broken Record and Broken Clock?

p. 251      "I thought he was running faster than the fractions showed on the board. ... I was surprised when his time came up 1:55. I thought he would be close to the record" (Ward "Did Secretariat Set Record?" 67).

p. 252      "If my horse broke the record, he should have the credit. ... You can bet your sweet life we'll ask for a review by the track, the stewards and the Maryland Racing Commission, if necessary" (Ward "Did Secretariat Set Record?" 67).

p. 252      "This race didn't take anything out of him compared to the Derby" (Ward "Did Secretariat Set Record?" 67).

p. 252      "I have no plans for my horse, and that includes the Belmont Stakes" (Ward "Did Secretariat Set Record?" 67).

p. 253      "No way. ... I don't think Ronnie could hold him that slow" (Ward "Did Secretariat Set Record?" 67).

p. 254      "We are not people to close our eyes and stay with the rules just because they are in the book" ("Maryland Commission to Study Preakness Time").

p. 254      "The official time of any race is that which is clocked by the official timer" ("Secretariat Outrun in Record Bid by Maryland Racing Commission").

p. 254      "It was acknowledged by several of the witnesses including those persons representing CBS that to change records established by the official timer because of later electronic analyses of such events would be destructive of the integrity of all sporting events" ("Secretariat Bid for Mark Foiled" 29).

p. 255      "about three lengths" (Beard "Mrs. Tweedy Requests Review of Secretariat's Time in Preakness" 12).

p. 255      "We're having some difficulty trying to pin down a time" ("Secretariat Outrun in Record Bid by Maryland Racing Commission").

p. 255      "I realize your problem. ... You're stuck" ("Secretariat Outrun in Record Bid by Maryland Racing Commission").

| | |
|---|---|
| p. 256 | "The hell with the Belmont. I don't want any more part of my horse looking at that big behind. Maybe we go to the Jersey Derby" (Woolfe 117). |
| p. 256 | "I never said that. … It's no fair to put things in the paper something I don't say. If I say it I don't care. But if I don't say it… Who wanna go to anyplace else? I'm from New York. I'm not from anyplace else. That's why I wanna win in New York" (Martin interview). |
| p. 256 | "Secretariat, New York" (Anderson "Move Over Elvis" B7). |
| p. 257 | "I think you're wonderful, I'd like to put my arms around you. … Dear Secretariat" (Anderson "Move Over Elvis" B7). |
| p. 257 | "I'm just glad I was born in his lifetime" (Hatton "Aqueduct" July 26, 1973). |
| p. 257 | "People tell me how I should train him" (Schuyler "Sham Disappointing? Not to Pancho Martin" 17). |
| p. 257 | "I think the winner is going to be an equally beautiful colt named Sham" (Tower "The Critic's Choice" 80). |
| p. 257 | "June 9 will rout them all. This is the day when, by winning the mile-and-a-half Belmont Stakes, Secretariat will become only the ninth Triple Crown horse ever" (Tower "Flying High and Heading For Fame" 24). |
| p. 257-258 | "They might just as well mail him the crown now. … The only horse that looked like he had a chance of spoiling Secretariat's bid for immortality… was Sham" (Kivel "Secretariat for Real" S-4). |
| p. 258 | "Meadow Stable's Secretariat ranks 2½ lengths above the second best of the 24,137 registered foals of 1970. That horse is Sigmond Sommer's Sham" (Kirkpatrick and Green "The Name Of The Game Is Class" 1256). |
| p. 258 | "Sham, the beautiful dappled bay… in any other year would be far and away the best colt around" (Kirkpatrick and Green "The Name Of The Game Is Class" 1260). |
| p. 258 | "fleet and courageous Sham" (Hirsch "Secretariat Heads Preakness" 1). |
| p. 258 | "courageous but outgunned Sham" (Hirsch "Secretariat Adds Preakness" 1). |
| p. 258 | "Not being such a good sport as my husband. … The sportsman-like thing to do. … certainly didn't want to go to Belmont" (Sommer interview). |
| p. 259 | "It's tough enough to beat a horse like Secretariat without having trouble. … I want to see him in a race like the Belmont with plenty of room. … He came out of the race just fine and his next race will be the Belmont" ("Secretariat Assured of Challenger—Sham" 9). |
| p. 259 | "I love the prestige, the notoriety, the excitement and the money" (Kazickas 29). |
| p. 259 | There are times in crowds like the Derby when you feel like Joe DiMaggio, but the object is to be pleasant and visibly there and not let the horse |

down" (Duffy 39).

p. 259-260     "Sham is by far the best horse I've ever trained. ... His disposition is the best part of him. He has a good disposition. No matter what happens to him he still runs his race, and you can't say that about 90 per cent of the horses" (Schuyler "Sham Disappointing? Not To Pancho Martin" 17).

p. 260     "I never get disappointed. ... I don't get disappointed because I know he didn't get the best of it. In fact, this horse is a very lucky horse after what happened to him. He came back sound" (Schuyler "Sham Disappointing? Not To Pancho Martin" 17).

p. 260     "I'm not using these as excuses but everything has to go right when you run against a horse like Secretariat. ... You can make no mistakes" (Schuyler "Sham Disappointing? Not To Pancho Martin" 17).

Chapter 26: The Test of Champions

p. 261     "If more than three or four horses show up to offer an argument in the Belmont Stakes, the final jewel in the Triple Crown, it will be a surprise" (Kivel "Secretariat for Real" S-4).

p. 261     "begin to crank him up" (Hirsch "Secretariat Vans to New York in Pursuit of Triple Crown" 4).

p. 261     "We've had enough of Secretariat for a while. ... He [Our Native] ran well in the Preakness but he just wasn't good enough to beat Secretariat and Sham" (Hirsch "Secretariat Vans to New York in Pursuit of Triple Crown" 4).

p. 262     "Normally our colt would have been laying much closer to the pace. ... He finished well, but by that time he was out of the race, for all practical purposes. He's not really a top stakes horse, like Secretariat or Sham, but he has been a useful individual who won two stakes this season, and I felt he might have beaten Ecole Etage again. He beat him before" (Hirsch "Secretariat's Brilliant Effort Should Dispel Slightest Doubt" 5).

p. 262     "The Triple Crown may be a *fait accompli* to Secretariat's huge following, but he still has to run around the race track... and finish ahead of Sham in the mile-and-a-half Belmont Stakes" (Ward "... But Sham's Still Very Much in Race").

p. 262     "two legitimate obstacles to Secretariat becoming the ninth Triple Crown Winner" (Kirkpatrick and Green "The Name Of The Game Is Class" 1260).

p. 263     "It will be fun to see what happens when someone opens up five or six lengths" ("Secretariat in 'Speedy' Belmont?" 1C).

p. 263     "It just means another horse for him to get around" ("Secretariat in 'Speedy' Belmont?" 1C).

| p. 264 | "Maybe I should run him in only $100,000 races. ... He runs real good when he runs for big money" (Zamarelli 1934). |
| p. 265 | "A horse coming into the Belmont stretch sees that endless straightaway, and, if he's easily discouraged, he'll chuck it. ... His eye takes in the whole stretch, not just to the finish line. And a horse trying to come from behind can get discouraged the same way" ("In Riding Strategy, What Goes at Big A Might Not Go at Belmont" 7). |
| p. 265 | "test of champions" (Kindred "Secretariat: The Successor to Citation also Surpasses Gallant Man"). |
| p. 265 | "Triple Crown" (Callahan "Tom. Not All Great Horses Win the Triple Crown"). |
| p. 267 | "Sure I think about it... but I'm not superstitious. I'm just a little nervous and I'll be glad when it's over" (Ward "Laurin Sweating Out Belmont 'Jinxes'" 29). |
| p. 267 | "It's not really a jinx. ... If there is a jinx it is the extra quarter of a mile. The horse can be a champion at the Derby distance and yet fail at a mile-and-a-half. ... I tell you this, I think Secretariat can go the mile-and-a-half as easy as he go the mile-and-a-quarter, but so can my horse" (Ward "Laurin Sweating Out Belmont 'Jinxes'" 29). |
| p. 268 | "Super Horse... Secretariat" (*Time* cover June 11, 1973). |
| p. 268 | "*If* he beats me in the Belmont Stakes on Saturday, *then* I'll call him a super horse. ... fair and square" (Nack "Secretariat Hasn't Convinced Martin"). |
| p. 268 | "C'mon... I gonna show you how discourage he is. ... This son of a gun, he impress me" (Cady 55). |
| p. 268 | "I don't do no business transactions till Monday. ... I'm gonna be busy. Call me Monday. ... I gotta look for a hobby... 'cause I don't drink no more, I don't go out" (Cady 55). |
| p. 269 | "the aplomb one looks for in good horses. ... Sham must be what horsemen call 'a good whip horse.' He was subjected to severe punishment through the stretch in the Preakness. But he goes about his daily chores cheerfully and dutifully" (Hatton "Triple Crown Author Expects to Witness Ninth Coronation"). |
| p. 269 | "He's been in three big wars... and he was always trying at the end. ... He was always stridin' out and doin' the best he could. He didn't chuck the bit and pull back. ... If Secretariat has an off day, Sham will swallow him" (Nack "Secretariat Hasn't Convinced Martin"). |
| p. 269 | "He is facing a very grim competitor in Sham. ... He hung on like a bull dog in those other two races and I have a great deal of respect for him. We could have quite a horse race here Saturday" (Hirsch "Secretariat Completes Belmont Preparation with Half in :46 ⅗" 41). |
| p. 269 | "If ever a horse deserved to have a nervous breakdown, it's Sham" (Cady 55). |

p. 269     "Some horses, they don't care.... They just keep going. But some horses, they're very moody. They're all different. Some give up. Some keep trying. They keep trying, trying, trying" (Gustines interview March 30, 2003).

p. 269-270     "I remember Carmen Basilio, the fighter.... He used to get beat up, but he kept on fighting. You beat me up once, I won't go back again" (Gustines interview March 30, 2003).

## Chapter 27: Sham Refuses to Yield the Crown

p. 271     "My horse has enough confidence to beat three Secretariats.... He knows he got two teeth knocked out in the starting gate and he knows he got knocked against the rail in the Preakness. Oh, he knows he didn't get beat fair and square" (Nack "Secretariat Hasn't Convinced Martin").

p. 271     "The boy did tap him lightly a couple of times" (Goldstein "Sham Turns in Sharp Move for June 9 Belmont Stakes" 1)

p. 272     "Went easy and evenly" (McCulley "Sham Works 6-7 Furlongs").

p. 272     "He start very slow... and the clockers miss him because they maybe think he's just galloping" (McCulley "Sham Works 6-7 Furlongs").

p. 272     "Go too fast... I might fall off" (Ward "... But Sham's Still Very Much in Race").

p. 272     "marvelous" ("Secretariat in Belmont Drill" 21).

p. 273     "He came back playing. ... He just loves to run. It is as if he thinks racing is a game we thought up for his amusement" (Hatton "Charles. SRO to Watch Secretariat Train").

p. 273     "Walk Wednesday... gallop Thursday, gallop Friday, walk Saturday—and then run" (Cady 55).

p. 273     "I get up at 5 a.m. every day. ... I don't need an alarm clock. If a man has trouble getting up at 5 o'clock, he has no business being a trainer" (Press release "Pancho Martin's 25 Years on Big Apple").

p. 273     "I'm not sure he is a distance horse. ... There he is now, picking away at this grass as if he is afraid it won't be here tomorrow" (Hirsch "Secretariat Completes Belmont Preparation with Half in :46 ⅗" 41).

p. 273-274     "I don't drink. ... All I want to do is be with Sham" (Nack "Secretariat Hasn't Convinced Martin").

p. 274     "At four and a quarter a jug... you'd go out of business" (Cady 55).

p. 274     "Only 24 hours more" (Kindred "Secretariat: The Successor to Citation also Surpasses Gallant Man").

p. 274     "He's been raising hell, ready to go. ... Let's hope he stays that way until Saturday" (Ayres 43).

Endnotes ♦ 403

p. 274 "legion—and uncounted" (Press release. "Record Press Coverage for Today's Belmont Stakes").

p. 274 "They make such a fuss about this horse, if we got beat I guess I would hide in a hole like a groundhog." (Smith "Countdown" B4).

p. 274-275 "And playful, man, is he playful. He is always grabbing my shirt with his teeth and yanking me to him. And sometimes he hits me with his nose and almost decks me" (Cunningham "Belmont's Barn 5 Guarded Well" 21).

p. 275 "looking grand. … He's quite a ham" ("The Wow Horse Races into History" 90).

p. 275 "Getting to see Secretariat might be more difficult than arranging an audience with the Pope. Or perhaps, a chat with President Nixon. And your credentials—they better be in order. … I took a walk over to Barn 5 Thursday. I was stopped by six Pinkertons and a German shepard" (Cunningham "Belmont's Barn 5 Guarded Well" 21).

p. 275 "I like Ky.-Bred Sham" (Ward "… But Sham's Still Very Much in Race").

p. 275 "I pull up at a stop light… and people in cars around holler 'Show 'em, Sham' and 'You can do it, Sham'" (Ward "… But Sham's Still Very Much in Race").

p. 275 "Like clockwork, every day at noon he lies down and conks off. … The darndest thing… the most relaxed horse I ever had" (Ward "… But Sham's Still Very Much in Race").

p. 275 "the most dangerous challenger any champion ever had" (Ward "… But Sham's Still Very Much in Race").

p. 275-276 "You can't make a mistake against Secretariat. … But they can't afford to make a mistake against us, either, not even a little one" (Ward "… But Sham's Still Very Much in Race").

p. 276 "He was kind of dumb at the outset of the season, but he is beginning to learn what racing is all about and I think he may turn out to be something special" (Hirsch "Secretariat Next" 24).

p. 276-277 "The Jersey Derby was quite a race. … I sat with Pancho [Martin] and it was so close that he congratulated me. Naturally, I would have liked to have won it but Pvt. Smiles' race was so good that it took a lot of the sting out of dropping a cliff-hanger. … He's ready now" (Hirsch "Secretariat Next" 24).

p. 277 "I think we have a chance. … Mr. Whitney is a sportsman and he isn't running a horse in the Belmont just to see his name in the program" ("Secretariat in 'Speedy' Belmont?" 5C).

p. 277 "had a higher rating than Bob Hope. … My hope is that my horse can get a higher rating than Secretariat before the year is out" (Press release "How Pvt. Smiles Got His Name").

p. 277 "I'd like to be the most hated man in America Saturday" (Smith "Countdown" B4).

p. 278     "I feel sorry for my colt. ... He has to run against Secretariat" (Tower "History in the Making" 16).

p. 278     "He was all out to win the Derby. ... Turcotte had to get into him pretty good, and that was only a mile and a quarter. With six horses there'll be an honest pace. Knightly Dawn and Sham will be rattling and I think Secretariat will be along with them. My horse likes to come from off the pace" (Smith "Countdown" B4).

p. 278     "Sorry no wives" (Press release "Information for Visiting Newsmen").

p. 280     "The Derby had to be the toughest because of the large field; you don't know what kind of racing luck you'll get. ... There will be a small field and the turns on this mile-and-a-half track are sweeping, so if you are on the outside you lose little ground. ... I think he'll win the Belmont easier than the other two" (Tower "History in the Making" 16).

p. 280     "If a match race develops, and it could, Secretariat and Sham *might* be awfully tired at the end of a mile and a quarter. And then a late runner like Pvt. Smiles would have a chance of catching them" (Tower "History in the Making" 16).

p. 280     "Anything can happen in this race, and who knows if Secretariat can handle that last quarter of a mile?" (Tower "History in the Making" 16).

p. 280     "I don't think they can beat him. ... He can do it all. If he has to come from behind, he will. If he has to go to the lead, he will. He's sharp as he can be, and I don't have the slightest doubt he will be able to stay the mile and a half" (Hirsch "Confident Laurin Awaits Act Three" 9, 11).

p. 280     "He will stay as far as horses are asked to run in this country" (Hirsch "Secretariat Bids for Lasting Fame in $151,200 Belmont" 6).

p. 281     "The track has been fast here this meeting. ... Ordinary horses are running fast, and Secretariat and Sham are no ordinary horses. If the pace is real, a record may be set" (Hirsch "Secretariat Bids for Lasting Fame in $151,200 Belmont" 6).

p. 282     "Hello. ... Hello" (Hirsch "Secretariat Bids for Lasting Fame in $151,200 Belmont" 6).

## Chapter 28: Battling a Tremendous Machine

p. 283     "And scarcely had he Maggie rallied. ... And left poor Maggie scarce a stump" (Burns).

p. 284     "The only thing he knows is eat, relax and run" (Denlinger).

p. 284     "It worries me, watching something worth that much. ... This is my first big assignment. I've been with Pinkerton three weeks" (Denlinger).

p. 284     "If Sham runs true, he does not need any help, I think. ... If he does not have any trouble in the Belmont, maybe he will beat Secretariat—finally—but alone" (Zamarelli 1934).

p. 285  "We have two turf tracks out there which must be protected and a couple of lakes.... We don't want any soused customers falling into the water" (Grimsley "While World Awaits Secretariat's Belmont, New York Yawns" 22).

p. 285  "I feel like a Roman emperor or something.... The people all are very nice" (Grimsley "Laurin Thought Secretariat Was Going Too Fast" B2).

p. 285  "Breed More Secretariats" (Grimsley "Laurin Thought Secretariat Was Going Too Fast" B2).

p. 287-288  "I've never seen Sham so nervous as before the Belmont.... He was wringing wet, it was a very hot day, and the long walk from his barn to the paddock in all that heat and humidity took a lot out of him. Sure it was hot for Secretariat, too, but different horses react differently to conditions" (Press release "No 'Broken Heart' for Sham—Martin").

p. 288  "Normally when he was being saddled he was just as cool and calm and collected as could be.... When he was being saddled for the Belmont... he was sweating, which was unusual for him" (Sommer interview).

p. 288  "Bravo, Secretariat... Triple Crown, baby" (Anderson "Bravo, Secretariat" 25).

p. 289  "I'm scared to death" (Grimsley "Laurin Thought Secretariat Was Going Too Fast" B2).

p. 289  "Just sit on him... take a long hold, I want him on the lead all the way. And I hope to God he gets to the wire"(Carlson "Silver Anniversary [Part 3]" 5).

p. 289  "behaved like a lamb" (Tower "History in the Making" 17).

p. 290  "Coming up like a dam [sic] lion" (Gaffer "Turcotte: I Pushed Him for Mark" 156).

p. 290  "I'm worried. ... He may be running too fast" (Grimsley "Laurin Thought Secretariat Was Going Too Fast" B2).

p. 291  "The Belmont will be a match race, just Secretariat and Sham.... The rest will be nowhere" (Tower "History in the Making" 16).

p. 291  "Oh, oh! I'm scared" (Tower "History in the Making" 17).

p. 291  "When he [Secretariat] and Sham hooked up around the clubhouse turn, I thought I might have a shot to come on and get them both" (Hirsch "Secretariat Achieves 'Triple'" 4).

p. 291  "Maybe they'll run each other into the ground" (Press release "Jockey Quotes" June 9, 1973).

p. 292  "a bag full of hopes, but not to win—not at that pace" (Cooper "Triple Crown the Greatest Yet for Turcotte" 25).

p. 292     "None of us going to be second now" (Gaffer "Turcotte: I Pushed Him For Mark" 156).

p. 292     "Once he got inside of Sham he wasn't about to give anything away" (Press release "Jockey Quotes" [1973 Belmont Stakes]).

p. 292     "He drew off on his own down the backstretch" (Hirsch "Secretariat Achieves 'Triple'" 4).

p. 292     "I thought we were doing something like 1:11 for the first 6 furlongs. ... As it turned out, he was going in 1:09⅘. His action is so smooth it's hard to tell" (Hirsch "Secretariat Begins Short Vacation" 5).

p. 292     "Secretariat is blazing along! ... Secretariat is widening now. He is moving like a tremendous machine!" (Secretariat's Triple Crown—Part 2—Belmont Stakes).

p. 293     "All of a sudden Sham started to drop back. ... That's when I looked around. I wanted to see what happened. I didn't expect him to drop out of it that soon" (McCulley "Will Secretariat Run Again?").

p. 293     "Shoot, no... I didn't even cock my whip" (Cooper "Triple Crown the Greatest Yet for Turcotte" 25).

p. 293     "We couldn't keep up in a pace like that" (Cooper "Triple Crown the Greatest Yet for Turcotte" 25).

p. 293     "He'll have to fall on his face now to lose" (Grimsley "Laurin Thought Secretariat Was Going Too Fast" B2).

p. 294     "Wow! What a horse!" (Grimsley "Laurin Thought Secretariat Was Going Too Fast" B2).

p. 294     "I was on the roof, and the noise was coming up to me. ... The crowd was so intense. ... I never heard anything like it before or since. ... It was hard to shoot. ... I was in tears" (Jackson interview).

p. 294     "There were these co-eds lining the rail. This sounds hard to believe, but I swear, half of them were weeping as he went by" (Secretariat's Triple Crown—Part 2—Belmont Stakes).

p. 294     "Everybody was speechless. And then, when it set in, people were crying. I actually saw people crying at this event. I mean, it was such an overwhelming thing" (Secretariat's Triple Crown—Part 2—Belmont Stakes).

p. 294     "I knew we had a record made and I didn't want to blow it" (McCulley "Will Secretariat Run Again?").

p. 295     "He had been fast... but he still had more left when I asked him to go get the record" (Ward "The Crowd Saw Perfection" 134).

p. 295     We both must have wanted the record" (Tower "History in the Making" 17).

| | |
|---|---|
| p. 295 | "There was no reason to punish him trying for fourth" (Cooper "Triple Crown the Greatest Yet for Turcotte" 25). |
| p. 295 | "People were crying, others were speechless, others were jumping around like mad hooligans waving both fists in the air, others were hugging and kissing" (Kirkpatrick "Secretariat: The Ultimate Superlative" 1440). |
| p. 295 | "stopped badly" (*Daily Racing Form Chart Book* "Belmont Park, eighth race: Belmont Stakes"). |
| p. 295 | "The game animal gave Secretariat a tussle, and many, including myself, feel the horse ran just one too many times against the Man O' War of the jet age" (Cunningham "Secretariat's Triumph Popular with Fans" C1). |
| p. 295 | "He was not the same horse that ran in the Kentucky Derby and Preakness" (Press release "Jockey Quotes" [1973 Belmont Stakes]). |
| p. 296 | "I don't believe he was quite the same horse in the Belmont that he was in the Derby and Preakness" (Hirsch "Secretariat Begins Short Vacation" 5). |
| p. 296 | "I hope you notice he acted perfectly in the gate. … He is not used to people. He broke out in the paddock Saturday, but once he got on the track and was by himself,  he calmed right down. He'll get over that sort of thing with maturity and seasoning" (Hirsch "Secretariat Begins Short Vacation" 5). |
| p. 296 | "My horse ran a better race than was expected… but Secretariat is a super horse" (Press release "Jockey Quotes" June 9, 1973). |
| p. 296 | "a little like going after an elephant with a BB gun" (Bowen "Joining the Giants" 2078). |
| p. 296 | "The closest I got to him was when I stood beside him." (Press release "Jockey Quotes" [1973 Belmont Stakes]). |
| p. 296 | "When a horse wins by an utterly unbelievable 31 lengths, as Secretariat did, the next finisher should be listed as fourth" (Barry "Secretariat Makes Shambles of Triple Crown" C1). |

Chapter 29: All Over but the Shouting

| | |
|---|---|
| p. 297 | "Let us aspire to the highest excellence, for, by this means, we shall either attain the summit, or at least see many below us" (Quintilian 428). |
| p. 297 | "Whee! Marvelous! Marvelous!" (Grimsley "Laurin Thought Secretariat Was Going Too Fast" B2). |
| p. 297 | "Back up, back up, please" (Denlinger). |
| p. 297 | "I was afraid they'd crush me. … They're all biggern'n me" (Gaffer "Turcotte: I Pushed Him For Mark" 156). |
| p. 298 | "He won… I feel great… lightheaded… no weight pushing me down" (Ward |

"The Crowd Saw Perfection" 134).

p. 298     "This is the greatest moment of my life.... Nobody had any excuses today.... The best horse won" ("Secretariat Romps in Belmont" C13).

p. 298     "It was perfectly marvelous.... I loved the ending" (Kindred "Secretariat: The Successor to Citation also Surpasses Gallant Man").

p. 298     "Hardened writers and fans of any description went batty as mighty Secretariat unleashed his power. Emotion exploded at Belmont this hot day" (Hendrickson "Secretariat... Incredible" S1-S2).

p. 298     "I'm just glad to be here at a time like this—to be part of it" (Temple " — He'd Probably Be Lost for Words, Too").

p. 299     "I never saw anything like that in all my years on the race track. ... I didn't think any horse could run that far that fast" (Ward "22 ⅗ Quarter Sank Sham").

p. 300     "Sham had nothing left to give.... You cannot run with a whirlwind and not get hurt" (Ward "22 ⅗ Quarter Sank Sham").

p. 300     "He might not need a vacation... but I do" (Schuyler "Five Try to Thwart Secretariat's Triple Crown Bid Today" 110).

p. 300     "the greatest performance by a racehorse in this century" (Tower "History in the Making" 16).

p. 300     "a one-horse stampede" (Temple "From Super Horse to Living Legend" 10).

p. 300     "Secretariat pounded across the finish line, more alone than Greta Garbo ever was" (Anderson "Bravo, Secretariat" 25).

p. 300     "and discovered the rest of the field in Queens" (Durslag "Super Horse Should Hide In New York" B1).

p. 300-301     "They gave him a margin of victory as 31 lengths but it was difficult to be certain. He won from here to Watts. ... Secretariat opened up and Sham shouted: 'Use the lariat. Rope the big galoot'" (Furillo "The Price of Horsemeat (Secretariat), $40,533.33 a Pound" B1).

p. 301     "could actually see Sham's heart breaking. They glanced at each other in unjaded astonishment. Sham's legs were splaying apart. He was swimming instead of running. He was crying out in frustration" (Callahan "In '73, Sham Had Heart of a Champ but Lacked Greatness of Secretariat" C6).

p. 301     "I don't know why I did that.... It's because you've spent your entire life searching for absolute perfection... and you finally saw it" (Callahan "In '73, Sham Had Heart of a Champ but Lacked Greatness of Secretariat" C6).

p. 301     "It was just one of those things.... It was not personal to me at all. I just wanted to win, because I thought he was a great horse and I loved him. I loved him, my children loved him" (Sommer interview).

p. 301     "It's hard to tell if a horse is disappointed. ... I suppose that's very possible. Going into the Belmont, he was not his usual composed self. Maybe he wasn't feeling well, or maybe he just didn't want to take another beating" (Boling).

p. 302     "Sham looks and feels fine. ... Horses don't get broken hearts from losing a tough race, even a couple of tough races to the same winner. ... When he's ready to run again, and the right race comes up, Sham will be in it. Sure, even against Secretariat" (Press release "No 'Broken Heart' for Sham—Martin").

p. 302     "Secretariat is a great horse. He's already proved that. ... One horse against another, that's a matter of their condition in a particular race. Secretariat was at his peak in the Belmont and he gave the greatest exhibition most of us have ever seen. Sham wasn't at his best, far from it, the way things came up. Maybe if they meet again in the Travers, Sham will be at his peak, Secretariat below it, that's the way horses are" (Press release "No 'Broken Heart' for Sham—Martin").

p. 302     "Sham finished ahead of Secretariat in the Wood even though Angle Light won the race, and was beaten only two and a half lengths by Secretariat in the Derby and Preakness. And he was in trouble in both races. So his race in the Belmont has to mean he wasn't at his best, the way he stopped. It happens to a lot of horses, even the best. Secretariat threw in a poor race in the Wood, but look how he came back. ... throw out. ... He's much better than that" (Press release "No 'Broken Heart' for Sham—Martin").

p. 302-303     "Some horse ain't he? ... He definitely will race again unless something happens to him—God forbid" ("Secretariat to Race Again: Laurin").

p. 303     "I went home last night and got drunk and cried" (Nack *Secretariat: The Making of a Champion* 337).

Chapter 30: Sham's Biggest Challenge

p. 304-305     "This type of fracture always concerns us because in addition to the visible fracture on X-ray a continuation of the fracture may occur in the form of microfractures which may not be visible on X-ray" (Reed "Sham's Fracture a Classic Case" 26-S).

p. 305     "I've been feeling bad ever since this happened. ... I'm emotionally involved with the horse. In construction you can put something back together again with manpower and machinery, but no amount of manpower or machinery can put a horse back together" (Nack "Sham Undergoes Surgery" 27).

p. 305     "I think the operation went very well" ("Broken Cannon Bone Will Sideline Sham").

p. 305     "I'm almost certain Sham will race again. I've done the same kind of surgery on many horses who returned to racing following such an injury" ("Sham Has Operation").

p. 306     "In any other year he would have been a champion, and I have wanted this horse for a long time. It's just a shame that he had to run against the horse of the century, Secretariat" (Ellis "Sham Syndicated, Race Career Over" 9).

p. 306     "As a patient Sham is ideal. ... He has a marvelous disposition, is extremely intelligent and certainly has all of the gameness in the world. In some ways I regret that he is being syndicated for breeding as I am confident that he would return to his original racing form" (Reed "Sham's Fracture a Classic Case" 26-S).

p. 306     "I am especially pleased with the people comprising this syndicate... and the quality of mares the members own virtually assures that Sham will be an overwhelming success at stud" ("Syndication of Sham for $2,880,000 Completed").

p. 306     "Sham is the second best three-year-old in America" (Ellis "Sham Syndicated, Race Career Over" 9).

p. 306     "I think both colts are a bargain. Sham pushed Secretariat to greatness" (Ellis "Sham Syndicated, Race Career Over" 53).

p. 307     "We spend a fortune on pasture control, but it's one of our cheapest investments" (Kirkpatrick "Grass-Roots Foundation" 1380).

p. 308     "half-brother to Secretariat" ("Knightly Dawn" Hill 'N' Dale Farms advertisement).

p. 308     "Sham attacked early, gave it everything he had for six furlongs, and then faded into history... Sham was all through for practical purposes but he left the scene with dignity and stature" (Hirsch "Sham Wasn't, but Who Remembers?" 5).

p. 309     "It is noted Secretariat's tail has become a bit long and bosky. Perhaps Lucien Laurin is missing a bet if he does not pull it to the modish hock length and go into the souvenir business" (Hatton "Aqueduct" July 16, 1973).

p. 309     "the complete and unequivocal backing of all the American people. ... But this one has a head" (Buchwald).

p. 310     "I'm just sorry it's not Sham" (Nack *Secretariat: The Making of a Champion* 337).

p. 311     "the man who did the most for racing" ("Secretariat Honored at N.Y. Scribes Dinner").

p. 311     "Secretariat was a Superhorse, rather than a transient Horse of the Year. Veteran turfmen, sophisticates of deep experience and broad, informed tastes, pronounced him 'The Horse of the Century.' He is the only thoroughbred ever given this identity on an official program. ... Secretariat is the most capable horse we ever saw, and geriatrics defeat any thought of seeing his like again" (Hatton "Profiles of Best Horses").

p. 311     "For one thing, we shouldn't limit the possibilities to one great horse each year. ... Some of the Triple Crown winners, to be frank with you, didn't have much to beat. ... Count Fleet beat Fairy Manhurst by 25 lengths in the Belmont Stakes, beat him after bowing a tendon in the first turn. ... The best horse Citation beat in the Belmont was Vulcan's Forge and that's not much. ... Lord Boswell was no hell of a horse. That was the second favorite the day Assault got the Crown. Neither Whirlaway nor Omaha had to beat Sham" (Callahan "Not All Great Horses Win the Triple Crown").

p. 312     "The way he's lost, at first I didn't know whether to be glad Bull [Hancock] didn't see it or to wish he had. But I wish he had. Bull would've seen he's a great horse" (Callahan "Not All Great Horses Win the Triple Crown").

p. 312     "It is conceivable that he will not only capture the Triple Crown but shatter still another track record in doing it. In fact, he may find it necessary to break a record just to beat Sham, a colt who might have won a Triple Crown of his own if he had not been unfortunate enough to be born in the same year as Secretariat" (Axthelm "Superhorse—Secretariat" 69).

p. 312     "Few three-year-olds will even dare take the track against him at Belmont but he will again have to face Sham, the horse that ran second in both the Derby and Preakness in efforts good enough to win in most years" ("The Wow Horse Races into History" 88).

p. 312     "Going into the race Sham was a truly superb horse who... would be the best around in any other year. ... a horse of great beauty, speed and heart, who was, far and away, the best of the others of his generation" (Kirkpatrick "Secretariat: The Ultimate Superlative" 1440).

p. 312-313     "Take Secretariat out of the 1973 picture, and Sham would be going into the Belmont on Saturday as a superhorse—an eight-length winner of both the Derby and Preakness and an overwhelming favorite to become the first Triple Crown winner in 25 years" (Cady 55).

p. 313     "In any other year but the year of Secretariat this strapping son of Pretense... would be the one to have dead aim on the Triple Crown" (Ward "... But Sham's Still Very Much in Race").

p. 313     "Sham, it is widely conceded, would be a champion in any other year" (Hirsch "Confident Laurin Awaits Act Three" 11).

p. 313     "It is conceivable that Sham would have carried off the Triple Crown himself (and perhaps easily) had Secretariat not been born in the same generation" (Irwin "The Big Red Machine Rolls to Triple Crown" 16).

Chapter 31: Adding to the Princequillo Legacy

p. 314     "All the stallions have their own paddock. ... Can't put 'em together or they'll fight" (Simpson interview).

| | |
|---|---|
| p. 314 | "He'd nip at you" (Simpson interview). |
| p. 314 | "Bandit" (Simpson interview). |
| p. 315 | "Like they're coming after or racing after another horse, or whatever" (Simpson interview). |
| p. 315 | "He's a special horse. … He chased Secretariat for all those races, and when he come off the racetrack he was just special to everybody, and he was a kind, nice horse to be around" (Simpson interview). |
| p. 315 | "Everybody kinda, they loved the horse" (Simpson interview). |
| p. 317 | "The heart was perfect—there were no defects. It was simply the largest heart I've ever seen. We didn't weigh it, but we visually estimated it between 21 and 22 pounds" (Haun 16). |
| p. 317 | "This was a heart completely out of anybody's league" (Lowitt). |
| p. 318 | "Looking back to what he had done, it was easy to put a connection to it. … It was just this huge engine" (Lowitt). |
| p. 318 | "He is moving like a tremendous machine!" (Secretariat's Triple Crown—Part 2—Belmont Stakes). |
| p. 318 | "I thought it was ironic… Sham was still finishing second to Secretariat" (Haun 16). |
| p. 318 | "I was very sad, felt very bad when I heard about him. … He was a good horse, a special horse, and I had feelings for him" (LaBelle "Pancho Martin Remembers Sham"). |
| p. 318 | "I still got his halter hanging on the wall. … The last halter to come off of him" (Simpson interview). |
| p. 318-319 | "an exceptional racehorse ironically better remembered for the races he lost than for his own successes" ("Sham, 1970-1993" 12). |
| p. 319 | "Sham had heart of a champ. … dark, leggy, elegant bay who rode alongside history instead of into it" (Callahan "In '73, Sham Had Heart of a Champ but Lacked Greatness of Secretariat" C1). |
| p. 319 | "There's no question Sham would have won the Triple Crown if it wasn't for Secretariat" (LaBelle "Pancho Martin Remembers Sham"). |
| p. 319 | "Sham was a nice horse. And he was born in the wrong time, I guess, the wrong year. The year of Secretariat" (Velasquez interview March 29, 2003). |
| p. 319 | "He come with the wrong year. … Secretariat was there. Secretariat was a fantastic animal" (Gustines interview September 20, 2003). |
| p. 319 | "We'll never know because he came along in the wrong year" (Lowitt). |
| p. 319 | "Sham… has always ranked high on our list of unappreciated or |

underappreciated horses. That is easy to understand, because no matter what he did or the magnitude of his accomplishments, he was competing against one of the most popular and successful Thoroughbreds of all time: Secretariat" (Hirsch "Sham Wasn't, but Who Remembers?" 5).

p. 322     "Sham pushed Secretariat to greatness" (Ellis "Sham Syndicated, Race Career Over" 53).

p. 323     "His only point of reference is himself" (Hatton "Writer Agrees with Kenny Noe: Secretariat Horse of Century" 2).

# About the Author

Phil Dandrea can recall seeing his first Kentucky Derby on TV as a boy, when he watched Riva Ridge take the Run for the Roses in 1972. He has since traveled across the country to see the sport at all levels and from various vantage points, from the box seats at Triple Crown events to the mucked stables behind the scenes. He is a member of both the National Thoroughbred Racing Association and the ownership group IEAH Stables, whose colt Big Brown won the Florida Derby, Kentucky Derby, Preakness Stakes, and Haskell Invitational Handicap.

The author resides in Massachusetts with his wife, Michele, and their two cats (whom he numbers 1 and 1A—as is the custom when two entries run from the same stable).